WORK PSYCHOLOGY IN ACTION

WORK PSYCHOLOGY IN ACTION

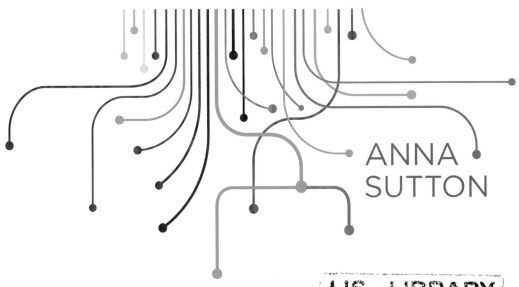

ANNA
SUTTON

palgrave
macmillan

First published 2015 by
PALGRAVE MACMILLAN

Palgrave Macmillan in the UK is an imprint of Macmillan Publishers Limited, registered in England, company number 785998, of Houndmills, Basingstoke, Hampshire RG21 6XS.

Palgrave Macmillan in the US is a division of St Martin's Press LLC, 175 Fifth Avenue, New York, NY 10010.

Palgrave Macmillan is the global academic imprint of the above companies and has companies and representatives throughout the world.

Palgrave® and Macmillan® are registered trademarks in the United States, the United Kingdom, Europe and other countries.

ISBN 978–1–137–30230–4

This book is printed on paper suitable for recycling and made from fully managed and sustained forest sources. Logging, pulping and manufacturing processes are expected to conform to the environmental regulations of the country of origin.

A catalogue record for this book is available from the British Library.

A catalog record for this book is available from the Library of Congress.

Printed in China.

SHORT CONTENTS

LONG CONTENTS

FIGURES AND TABLES

Figures

Tables

ABOUT THE AUTHOR

© Julian Perkins

Anna Sutton is a Senior Lecturer at Manchester Metropolitan University Business School, leading modules in Work Psychology for undergraduate and postgraduate students. Prior to this, she lectured at Leeds Metropolitan University on the BSc (Hons) Psychology programmes, with a specialism in occupational psychology and individual differences.

With experience working in Human Resources, Anna is also a Chartered Psychologist and Associate Fellow of the British Psychological Society. Her consultancy work involves using personality psychology to encourage individuals and teams to develop self-awareness, improve communication and enhance their teamworking.

Anna's research focuses on the role of personality at work and particularly how the development of self-awareness can impact on people's work lives and well-being. In addition, Anna has engaged in research projects which explore teaching-related issues, such as students' understanding of plagiarism and the Research–Teaching link at universities, and is a Fellow of the Higher Education Academy.

ABOUT THIS BOOK

Business studies and psychology are among the most popular subjects to study at university, and no matter what job we have, understanding people will play a critical role in our success. This book bridges the gap between business and psychology: making psychological theories accessible to business students and providing psychology students with an understanding of how key business priorities inform and structure applied psychology.

You will find chapters based around common workplace problems you might want to solve, rather than arranged by theoretical topic. We will explore solutions to business problems from a psychological perspective, building your understanding of both theory and practice. Instead of treating business and psychology as separate topics, we take a truly integrative approach, applying insights from psychology to the practical issues facing managers and workers in today's workplace and demonstrating the real-world importance of research findings.

The recurring theme in this book is that *business is about people* and that a good understanding of psychology can help us to build more fulfilling and successful lives at work. We focus on getting the best out of people at work, including ourselves, by promoting an integration of the business needs and the individual's needs. To help with this, a key feature of this book is the emphasis on practical employability and skills development. You will find activities based on the latest research and best practice to help you apply psychology to your own current and future work life.

Distinctive features

This book is packed with special features to help you learn and apply key psychological knowledge:

Learn (features to enhance your understanding and expand on the contents)

- **Mindmaps:** each chapter starts with a visual image of how the topics link together, giving you an instant framework for your learning.
- **Key Research Studies:** a summary of a seminal research study in the topic, helping you become familiar with well-conducted research and to

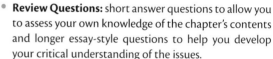

learn how to critically assess and utilise research in work psychology.
- **Review Questions:** short answer questions to allow you to assess your own knowledge of the chapter's contents and longer essay-style questions to help you develop your critical understanding of the issues.
- **Further Reading:** while key references are highlighted in the individual chapter features, each chapter also has suggestions for further guided reading on specific aspects of the content.
- **Glossary:** at the end of the book, you will find a detailed glossary which gives clear definitions of all the terminology you will find in the textbook.

Apply (features to help you apply psychological insights to practical, real-world situations)

- **Activities:** exercises or activities throughout each chapter will help you to work through a practical application of the theories or concepts. Many of these are written so that they can be easily adapted for individual or group work, depending on how you prefer to study.
- **Brief Case Studies:** every chapter contains a few short case studies, based on real events, illustrating how psychological theories can be applied to situations you might face at work.
- **Psychological Toolkit:** this section helps you to use what you have learnt in that chapter to enhance your own employability and work life, demonstrating the immediate applicability of work psychology to your own life.
- **International Perspectives:** in our increasingly global workplace, understanding the influence of national or cultural differences is important. Each chapter has a section which highlights how that topic is viewed in different countries around the world or some of the current debates in cross-cultural applications.
- **Fad or Fact?** A debate section which can be used for class discussion, highlighting a recent management intervention or tool and assessing its evidence base. This will help to develop your ability

to make informed decisions about new trends in popular psychology and management.

- **Extended Case Studies** (one for each of the three parts of the book) with questions to help you explore the chapter topics in more detail.

Throughout the chapters you will also find links to useful websites and further information available online. In addition, the companion website contains.

A note to instructors

As well as all the features outlined above, there is a detailed instructor's manual to help with the delivery of a course based around this textbook. It includes:

- Suggested module timetables
- Lecture outlines
- Recommended seminar/tutorial activities
- Guideline answers for the activities and case studies in each chapter
- PowerPoint slides for every chapter to support your teaching

Organisation of the book

The introductory chapter sets the scene for the rest of the book, looking at how work psychology has developed at the interface between the traditional fields of psychology and management. For business students, this chapter introduces you to the psychological approach to understanding people at work and shows you how psychology is related to the areas of management you may already be familiar with. For psychology students, this chapter provides an overview of how key theoretical areas of psychology are relevant to the world of work and introduces you to important concepts from business studies.

Part 1, Business Is About People, focuses on the day-to-day business of managing relationships and understanding people in the modern workplace. Starting with how to find and develop the right talent for the business needs, it moves on to consider how to motivate people and how to communicate effectively at all levels of the business. The final two chapters in this part give a critical assessment and practical guidelines for teamwork and leadership that will support the business objectives.

Part 2, Surviving and Thriving at Work, considers aspects of work beyond just 'getting the job done': how to use psychological knowledge to survive the challenges of the modern workplace and improve our work lives. After a chapter discussing change management, it considers approaches to psychological health at work, using a broad 'well-being' perspective. It concludes with a discussion of how work can contribute to a greater sense of personal meaning and self-actualisation by drawing on the field of positive psychology.

Part 3, Cutting-Edge Psychology, gives an introduction to exciting new developments in work psychology. The first chapter provides an overview of how psychology is currently being applied to specific areas of business, including consumer and financial psychology. The final chapter helps you to learn how to identify well-conducted research so that you are able to stay up to date with the latest developments in work psychology through the rest of your career.

ACKNOWLEDGEMENTS

Author's Acknowledgements

I am deeply grateful to Julian, Mum and Dad, Mark and Kate and Peter: thank you for your unfailing love and support and for managing to look interested whenever I talked about the latest psychological theories.

My sincere thanks also to Ursula Gavin, Publisher at Palgrave Macmillan Higher Education, for giving me the opportunity to write this book and for your enthusiasm and guidance throughout the process; to Amy Grant, Development Manager at Palgrave Macmillan, for your expert support and creative ideas through the production process; and to Elizabeth Stone for your careful and sympathetic copy-editing.

Special thanks to the BGL Group and particularly Steve Dewar, Senior Manager for Wellbeing, for your involvement in the case study about your evolving well-being programme.

And finally, a big thank you to the anonymous reviewers who gave so generously of their time and expertise.

Publisher's Acknowledgements

The publisher would like to thank the following for permission to reproduce copyright material:

Elsevier Ltd for Table 4.1 'Core job dimensions and their corresponding psychological states', from J. Hackman & G. R. Oldham (1976) Motivation through the design of work: test of a theory. *Organizational Behavior & Human Performance*, 16, 250–79.

Gulf Publishing Company for Figure 7.1 'Blake and Mouton's managerial grid', from R. Blake & J. Mouton (1964) *The Managerial Grid: The Key to Leadership Excellence* Houston, Gulf.

Katy Jones for the illustrative example for the Thematic Apperception Test in Chapter 4.

SAGE Publications for Table 9.1 'Some of the variables included in the Yerkes–Dodson law', from K. H. Teigen (1994) Yerkes–Dodson: a law for all seasons. *Theory & Psychology*, 4, 525–47.

Wiley for Table 2.1 'Comparative predictive validity and popularity of various selection methods', adapted from N. Anderson and N. Cunningham-Snell (2000) Personnel Selection. In Chmiel, N. (ed.) *Introduction to Work and Organizational Psychology: A European Perspective*, Oxford, Blackwell.

Wilmar Schaufeli, Toon Taris and Willem Van Rhenen for Table 9.2 'Comparison of burnout, engagement and workaholism', from (2008) Workaholism, burnout, and work engagement: three of a kind or three different kinds of employee well-being?. *Applied Psychology*, 57, 173–203.

WHAT IS WORK PSYCHOLOGY?

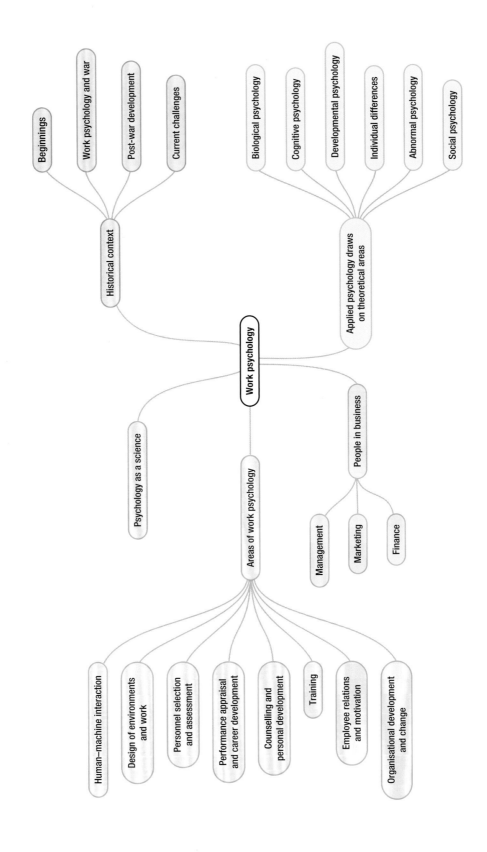

Work psychology

Historical context
- Beginnings
- Work psychology and war
- Post-war development
- Current challenges

Applied psychology draws on theoretical areas
- Biological psychology
- Cognitive psychology
- Developmental psychology
- Individual differences
- Abnormal psychology
- Social psychology

Psychology as a science

Areas of work psychology
- Human–machine interaction
- Design of environments and work
- Personnel selection and assessment
- Performance appraisal and career development
- Counselling and personal development
- Training
- Employee relations and motivation
- Organisational development and change

People in business
- Management
- Marketing
- Finance

Many people are excited by the idea of psychology because they want to find out more about themselves or understand other people better. They are looking for ways to apply psychological theories to their own lives and to use psychological tools and approaches to work out what the people around them are up to, what's really going on in their minds.

This book is designed to help you find the answers to those questions. It will help you develop your appreciation of psychological theories and show you how you can use them to understand yourself and others. It will show you what psychological tools are available to you and how they can enhance your own work life and help you to manage your colleagues, subordinates and even your own manager. It is my hope that, through this book, the curiosity that first drew you to the subject will be rewarded.

Throughout this book, there will be an emphasis on practicality, exploring the implications of psychological theory or insights for normal people at work. We won't just describe theories but will look at how they can be put into action.

In this first chapter we gain an initial introduction to the concept of work psychology. We start by considering the scientific approach to psychology that underpins the rest of this book, looking at what the scientific method is and why it is important to understand it if we are going to try to apply psychology to the workplace. We then move on to consider the different theoretical areas of psychology and look at examples of how they are used to understand behaviour at work. After this, we consider how applied psychology differs from theoretical psychology and the eight different areas of knowledge for occupational psychologists.

Having considered the psychology side, we then turn to look at the business side of work psychology, reviewing three main areas of business studies and how they can inform our understanding of human behaviour. And finally, we have a look at how the subject has developed, outlining some of the key people and theories that have made work psychology what it is today.

This chapter will help you answer the following questions:

1 What does it mean to say psychology is a science?
2 What are the different areas of work psychology?
3 How does work psychology, as an applied discipline, draw on the different theoretical strands of psychology?
4 How can business studies inform and contextualise our understanding of people's behaviour at work?
5 Why is it useful to know about the historical development of work psychology?

You will see work psychology referred to by many different names including occupational, business, organisational or industrial psychology, or sometimes even a combination of these, such as industrial-organisational psychology. In the International Perspectives section later in the chapter we look at where all these different names come from and what differences they are trying to capture.

To simplify things and in line with common usage (e.g. Cassell and Symon, 2011), in this book we will be using the term *work psychology* as shorthand for the whole field and the other terms only when we need to make a specific distinction, for example when referring to qualified and accredited Occupational Psychologists.

PSYCHOLOGY AS A SCIENCE

Although psychology can be defined as the study of the mind (*psyche*), it can be difficult to say what we really mean by 'mind' and even more difficult to say how we can study it. 'Mind' is an abstract concept and yet, as a science, psychology has to take as its subject things we can observe. What can we observe about the mind? You might suggest that we can each observe our own thoughts or feelings, which to a certain extent we can, but how can we observe the thoughts and feelings of other people? How can we make comparisons between them or find out if a particular thought process is common to a lot of people?

If we are going to adopt a scientific approach to understanding people, we need to have something more concrete to observe and test our theories on. So the science of psychology seeks to find explanations for a more observable phenomenon: human behaviour. Our definition of 'behaviour' can be quite broad and include anything that we can observe, including facial expressions, what people say, emotional expression, their tone of voice and so on. If we can find a good explanation for a particular aspect of human behaviour, then we can say we have a good psychological theory; we have explained why people do the things they do.

 Activity Armchair psychologist

An 'armchair psychologist' is someone who does not have any education or training in psychology but likes to come up with their own explanations for human behaviour. It is, of course, a perfectly natural thing for us to do as we try to understand the people around us. This activity is to help you recognise the pitfalls of this approach and to demonstrate how important a scientific approach to psychology is.

Think about the last time you noticed someone arriving late to an event. Maybe you were meeting a friend at a café and they did not arrive on time or were in a lecture and someone walked in late. Did you find yourself coming up with reasons for their lateness? What were they?

If we were going to rely on armchair psychology, we would probably conclude that people are late because they are disorganised, lazy, slow or disrespectful. But is that true? What about if you think about the last time *you* were late? What were your reasons?

Most people will include situational factors such as a bus being late or their car breaking down when they are explaining their own behaviour, which they tend to ignore when trying to explain other people's behaviour. Armchair psychology is not very reliable! We tend to exaggerate the effect of internal factors (such as personality or ability) on other people's behaviour and to downplay any situational causes. This is an example of the *fundamental attribution error.* Clearly, we need a better way to try to explain human behaviour than relying on our own assumptions.

But how do we know whether our explanation for people's behaviour is any good? Just like any other science, psychology uses the scientific method. This is a five-stage process that attempts to find a good explanation for why things are the way they are. It is a way of testing whether the ideas we have about how the world works are actually supported by observable facts. The five stages are:

1 Observe patterns or regularities in the world
2 Develop a possible explanation (theory)
3 From that explanation, develop a specific prediction
4 Test the prediction
5 Evaluate the explanation and refine it if necessary

To illustrate this scientific approach, here is an example based on one of the first studies linking work behaviour with health outcomes: the Type A and B personality distinction. Two cardiologists, Meyer Friedman and Ray Rosenman, used the scientific method to show how personality patterns were related to important health outcomes (Friedman and Rosenman, 1959).

1 Friedman and Rosenman noticed that men with particular behaviour patterns (ambitious, impatient, proactive workaholics) seemed more likely to suffer from coronary heart disease.
2 They suggested that having a particular type of personality (called Type A) increased the chances of developing heart disease.

3 They predicted that people scoring higher on a measure of Type A personality would be more likely to suffer from coronary disease.
4 They compared the cardiovascular outcomes of a group of men who had Type A personality with a second group of men who had the opposite type of personality (Type B: laid-back, relaxed, taking one thing at a time).
5 They found that Type A men were seven times more likely to have coronary artery disease, a finding that supported their initial prediction.

Of course, good science does not end there. It is all very well to develop a good explanation of observable events but we will want to go further and use that theory to try to change or control the event. Finding out that certain personality patterns are associated with worse health outcomes is only the beginning. Psychology is not just about understanding people but trying to help them as well. Just as doctors would not be content with understanding the causes of a disease but would want to develop a way of preventing or controlling it, so many psychologists want to use their knowledge to try to improve people's lives. As we progress through this chapter and the rest of the book, you will find this is a central component of work psychology: how we can use psychology to help people and organisations.

 Activity Applying science

Using the Type A/B personality example above, what would you recommend to try to reduce people's risk of heart disease?

▸ Find out what Friedman and colleagues did by reading this paper: Friedman et al. (1986) Alteration of type A behavior and its effect on cardiac recurrences in post myocardial infarction patients: summary results of the recurrent coronary prevention project. *American Heart Journal*, 112 (4), 653–665.

THE DIFFERENT THEORETICAL AREAS OF PSYCHOLOGY

Several different areas of psychology have emerged which focus on trying to understand the complexities of how and why we do what we do. The British Psychological Society recognises that a grounding in six different areas is important in training new psychologists and only accredits university degree programmes which cover them all.

There are obviously overlaps between these fields – after all, we function as whole people, not as compartmentalised bits – and applied fields of psychology attempt to take relevant findings from all of these different theoretical areas and use them within their own field of expertise. But it is useful for us to understand the aims and approaches of psychologists in these different areas so that we can see how psychology can be applied to work. For each of the theoretical approaches to psychology that are outlined below, we will have a look at some examples of how they have been applied to psychology at work.

Biological psychology

Biological psychology is the study of how our physical makeup explains or affects our minds. It explores how our genes affect our psychology as well as the neural basis of behaviour, or how our brains are linked to our behaviour. While it is unlikely that we will ever describe a simple path from an individual gene to the complexity of work behaviours and interactions, our genetic inheritance is an important contributing factor to how we behave at work.

One system in the brain that has received a lot of attention is the dopamine pathway, which includes areas of the brain that are activated when we feel motivated. It is linked with novelty-seeking behaviour: we are more likely to seek out new experiences if we expect a positive outcome or reward, and dopamine is a neurotransmitter that is associated with our anticipation of rewards. A variation in a gene called DRD4 (which codes for a dopamine receptor) has been found to be particularly closely associated with novelty-seeking behaviour (Ebstein et al., 1996). In a study of salespeople, Bagozzi et al. (2012) distinguished between two types of sales behaviour: Sales Orientation, which tries to persuade and sell to customers, and Customer Orientation, which is more about recognising opportunities by getting the customer talking about their needs so that the salesperson can try to help them find a solution. Bagozzi et al. suggested that this recognition of opportunities is a type of novelty-seeking behaviour, and found that salespeople with the novelty-seeking DRD4 variation were in fact more likely to use a Customer Orientation approach. This is a remarkable finding and is one of a growing number of studies that are finding links between our genes and complex behaviours.

Of course, we cannot assume that the link between biology and psychology is straightforward 'biological determinism'. We need to bear in mind that the brain is very flexible and it changes and adapts even in adulthood. For example, one study found that an area of the brain which stores spatial information and is used in navigation (the posterior hippocampus) was larger in London taxi drivers than non-taxi drivers (Maguire et al., 2000). This area of the brain was also larger in those drivers who had been doing the job longer, which shows us how the brain adapts to what we use it for, rather than simply determining what we do.

Cognitive psychology

Cognitive psychology started out in the 1950s with a focus on how we process information, seeing the brain as similar to a computer and human behaviour as the 'output' of mental processes. Cognitive psychologists try to define these processes as precisely as possible and are interested in areas such as perception, memory, attention and thinking. Research in this area tends to be rigorously experimental, and is sometimes criticised for not relating to the real world, yet some very important advances have been made in understanding our cognitive processes and the impact of these processes on our day-to-day work lives.

One good example of cognitive psychology in the workplace is the work that has been done around selection interviewing. In particular, cognitive psychologists have identified the many biases that influence our decision-making. In selection interviewing, these biases can have a dramatic effect on who gets hired. For example, Kutcher and Bragger (2004) found that people were less likely to hire an overweight applicant than a normal weight one. They also found that a structured interview (which gave interviewers guidelines for scoring the job applicant's suitability) moderated this effect. Structured interviews not only make it easier for interviewers to compare candidates, but they also help to overcome the common biases and errors in judgement that cognitive psychology approaches have identified in human information processing.

Developmental psychology

Although developmental psychology began by trying to understand how children develop, it now covers the whole of the human lifespan, looking at how we change and develop from birth through to old age. It considers such things as how we form our identities, how our personalities develop, how our moral and cognitive reasoning changes as we age, and so on.

This approach to considering how we change across the lifespan is particularly useful when looking at the impact of life stage on careers and work. For example, work–life balance (WLB) is often considered a 'static' component of our work lives and policies tend to focus on the needs of working parents rather than take account of how all employees' career stages might influence their need for WLB initiatives. By identifying four different career stages (early, developing, consolidating and pre-retirement), Darcy et al. (2012) were able to identify that WLB was important to employees at all stages of their career, though for different reasons, and the authors suggest that organisations need to ensure they are providing WLB initiatives to employees in the later stages of their careers as well.

Individual differences

Most areas of psychology look for processes or behaviours that are common to all people, for example, trying to understand how we learn things. The individual differences approach seeks to identify how and why we differ from each other, particularly in terms of personality and intelligence. It helps to answer questions such as why some people are more successful than others, why some people engage in voluntary work and others do not, or why some choose particular careers.

A recent study investigated what impact individual intelligence had on career success. The researchers (Judge et al., 2010) measured people's general mental ability and found that, over a 28-year time period, those with higher intelligence had a higher income and greater occupational prestige than those with lower intelligence. People who were more intelligent seemed to achieve higher levels of education, enter more complex jobs, and gain access to and complete more job training. All three of these factors contributed to the improved career outcomes of these individuals. The authors note that while higher mental ability is obviously advantageous to organisations, there are also some serious questions which need addressing, such as how training initiatives – which are supposed to be addressing a 'skills gap' – actually seem to favour those who already have an advantage in intelligence.

Abnormal psychology/psychopathology

As noted above, most of psychology is about explaining how people in general function. Abnormal psychology studies deviations from this 'norm'. There is intense debate over what exactly constitutes normality and abnormality, and of course just because a pattern of behaviour or thought is different from the norm does not mean it is a pathology. Is the study of abnormal psychology of any use in understanding people at work?

The answer is yes, and for two main reasons. The first is that an estimated one in four people seek help for mental health problems, and this does not include all those who are suffering but are too afraid to ask for help because of the stigma associated with mental illness. So if we are to understand how and why people behave as they do at work, we cannot focus only on explanations founded in 'normal' functioning. The second reason is that certain problems in organisations have been linked to specific abnormal processes, emotions or behaviours. For example, Petit and Bollaert (2012) describe a personality

disorder called the hubris syndrome, defined by a narcissistic attitude and excessive self-belief, and show how hubris in CEOs can be detrimental to the organisation, resulting in negative outcomes such as increased debt and lower shareholder dividends. They suggest that individuals and organisations can guard against hubris by developing authentic leadership, which has a strong moral dimension and where leaders are true to themselves.

Social psychology

Whereas other areas of psychology investigate the individual mind, either by trying to define how it works or seeing how it compares with others, social psychology looks at how we interact with other people and behave in groups. Important issues that social psychology covers include group behaviour, social influence and social cognition. It is probably easy to see how this is relevant to work psychology, as the vast majority of work we do necessitates interaction with other people and it would be a very limited understanding of people at work that did not take account of the social context.

Social psychology defines 'attributions' as the processes we use to make sense of other people's behaviour – in other words, the reason we think they did something. Corporate social responsibility (CSR) is a burgeoning area of research which focuses on how organisations take responsibility for their actions and try to conduct their business in an ethical manner. The attributions that people make about corporate actions determine the extent to which those organisations are seen by the wider society as responsible or not. Recent work (Lange and Washburn, 2012) has found that the extent to which people believe a corporate action was irresponsible rests on three main attributions: how undesirable the effect of the action was, how much the corporation was to blame for the event, and how much the people affected by the action were complicit in it. This shows us how the evaluation of social responsibility is not an objective reality but is subject to change and influence and organisations can use this information to enhance their CSR image.

Having reviewed the theoretical areas of psychology, we now move on to consider how they are applied within work psychology.

APPLIED PSYCHOLOGY

There are several different fields of applied psychology but what they all have in common is the desire to take the theories and models from theoretical psychology and apply them to understanding and solving real-life problems. So, for example, educational psychology would take learning theories from cognitive psychology and an understanding of how group dynamics can improve or reduce learning from social psychology to try to determine the best way to improve student learning. You can think of applied psychology as the context within which we want to study and use psychology.

Applied psychologists tend to evaluate theories and models in terms of how useful they are in solving problems or enhancing our lives. It would be a mistake to conclude from this that theory is not important, however. As Kurt Lewin (1951, p. 169), one of the early social psychologists said, 'There is nothing so practical as a good theory.' A good theory can be applied and used in different contexts and it is of course essential to have a solid understanding of the theoretical areas of psychology so that we can understand some of the underlying assumptions and limitations of each approach.

Work psychology is one of these applied fields – it is not a theoretical approach to understanding how and why humans function, but a specific sub-context within which we want to understand people. Some areas of interest to work psychology are shared with other applied fields. For example, knowing what training methods are effective is useful in work-based learning as well as educational psychology. And some areas are unique to work psychology, such as understanding the impact of having a professional identity on people's work motivation.

The British Psychological Society (BPS) defines eight areas of knowledge for occupational psychologists, and this is a useful framework for us to understand the range of different applications, themes and topics relevant to work psychology.

Human–machine interaction

This area is all about how we can design machines to suit humans, rather than try to make humans adapt to the machines. If people are struggling to work properly with machines, there can be an increase in the errors they make. Human-centred design enhances performance and reduces errors. It is not just about traditional factory or production machines, but increasingly about how we interact with computers – both hardware and software. Developing machines that we can interact with intuitively requires a good understanding of how our minds work.

Design of environments and work: health and safety

Designing the work environment carefully can improve our productivity. This area of work psychology focuses on identifying and understanding the factors that can impact on employee health, job satisfaction and productivity. These factors may include simple physical aspects such as temperature and lighting or more complex issues

such as the impact of shift work on employees' mental and physical health. The aim is to design workplaces and jobs in a way that will protect employees' health and enhance their productivity.

Personnel selection and assessment

Using psychological tools such as validated tests or structured interviews, work psychologists can contribute to better decision-making in employee selection. A good knowledge in this area will ensure that only the best tools are used in making these important decisions and that issues such as developing diversity in the workforce or avoiding adverse impact on minorities are dealt with effectively. Starting with detailed job analysis and using an evidence-based approach to selection, psychologists can help the business to make the right decision first time.

Performance appraisal and career development

There are two sides to this area of knowledge. First is an understanding of the best ways to evaluate employee performance: work psychologists can provide expertise in developing performance appraisal systems that will help an organisation to identify how well their employees are performing and how best to reward or develop them. Second is designing career development initiatives such as fast-track schemes or leadership development pathways that will make the best use of employees' potential.

Counselling and personal development

While occupational psychologists are not qualified to provide therapy in the same way that clinical or counselling psychologists are, they are still able to use their understanding of psychology and work to help clients to manage their careers and work lives. This may include helping employees through difficult or stressful times, such as when the organisation is undergoing significant change, or the individual is being relocated or made redundant. It can also include helping people to develop themselves, perhaps through coaching or support in a new promotion.

Training

In the constantly changing modern workplace, training has become ever more important for organisations to ensure that their employees are able to deal with the varying demands of their jobs. Training needs can vary from the simple (e.g. learning a new computer system) to the more complex (e.g. leadership development). An understanding of how people learn, how to analyse their training needs and how to ensure that training courses meet those needs is essential if organisations are going to make the most of their human resources.

Employee relations and motivation

Maintaining a positive relationship between the organisation as a whole and the people who work for it is key to developing effective performance. And motivation must be one of the hottest topics in organisational psychology: everyone wants to know how to encourage employees to higher levels of productivity. Work psychology can help us understand how rewards work to encourage performance (or even, in some cases, how the wrong rewards can reduce performance!) as well as the impact of employee attitudes on their work behaviour.

Organisational development and change

Organisations change for many reasons and in many different ways. Whether this change is planned or spontaneous, proactive or reactive, an understanding of how people deal with change is essential to success. Changes could include downsizing or restructuring, or introducing new work processes. Work psychologists can help by analysing the need for change and developing implementation plans. They can also provide in-depth knowledge of how change impacts on people and the best ways to support employees through that change.

You may have already noticed that there can often be significant overlap between these different areas. For example, the development of a strategy for organisational change would need to take account of the impact the changes might have on the employment relationship, what new training needs the employees might have, how

they could be best supported or coached and so on. This is why the BPS recognises that occupational psychologists need a broad understanding in all eight of these areas. It should also be obvious that an understanding of psychology at work will be beneficial to more than just Occupational Psychologists. Managers, trainers, HR consultants and many others work in areas where this kind of knowledge is invaluable. Understanding psychology in the workplace can help to ensure that the strategies and plans we develop are as robust as possible.

PEOPLE IN BUSINESS

When we are trying to understand people's behaviour at work, it helps to have a good foundation in the different areas of business to which we can apply psychology. The central premise of this book is that *Business is about People*, and now that we have looked at the theoretical background of the *people* half, we need to turn and look at the *business* half. What are the theoretical areas of business studies? This section provides an overview of three main areas, defining each of them in turn and describing an example of recent research in the area to give you a flavour of the contribution theoretical areas can make to a broad understanding of work psychology.

Management

The study of management is essentially the study of how to get people working together to achieve the goals of an organisation. In its broadest sense it includes how we can best utilise all the resources available to an organisation, including people, technology and finances, as well as raw materials. Management research and theories

Case Study The role of psychology at work

You are a senior manager at a food manufacturing company and your organisation is going through dramatic changes as it tries to remain competitive. One of these changes is that it is simplifying its structure by removing a layer of management. You used to have 15 direct reports but in the new structure, three of the supervisors who report to you are being made redundant and several teams are being reorganised so that you will now be directly responsible for 35 staff.

▸ What do you think are the main issues or problems that you will face during this change?

▸ Where would you turn for help on managing the change (both for yourself and your new team)?

▸ You've been given a budget to help with any training or development costs you think are needed. What expectations would you have of the interventions recommended by the consultants?

© PHOTODISC

attempt to define and explain management activities, such as organisation, coordination, planning, control and the motivation of employees. In doing this, they can add to our understanding of people's behaviour at work and so the management field provides not only an area of application, but also a rich source of psychological theories.

One of the great areas of debate and research in the study of management is decision-making. Everything that is done in order to achieve the goals of an organisation rests on decisions that the employees make. For example, a recent study (Wong et al., 2011) investigated top management teams' decision-making and its impact on corporate social performance – that is, how well the organisation met the needs of its different stakeholders. The researchers measured how intellectually flexible the management team was and the extent to which decisions were decentralised. Their findings show that a management team that looks for a greater range of information and decentralises the decision-making can have a positive impact on the organisation's performance.

Marketing

For those unfamiliar with the area, marketing might be seen simply as a 'sales pitch' or a way to get people to buy more of a product or service. In fact, it is a much wider and more complex arena than that. It is really the process of communicating the value of something to potential consumers and also of managing the longer-term relationship between the producer and the customer. The link between that process and psychology is clear: for marketing to be successful, it needs to be based on a good understanding of how we perceive value, how communication works and what things will influence a decision to purchase.

An intriguing area of research is in how brands can be a part of our identity. A recent study looked at what effect brand loyalty can have during a market disruption, namely the introduction of a radically new brand (Lam et al., 2010). It found that while the strength of consumers' brand identification and their perception of the brand's value both inhibited their switching to the new brand, it was brand identification that maintained loyalty in the longer term. It is clear that research in marketing can contribute to our understanding of how we construct our identities – an area which has traditionally been a focus of social psychology.

Finance

It would be a bit strange if we talked about business and never mentioned money! The study of finance is the study of how money is created and managed and is often divided into three main areas: public, corporate and personal finance. It also includes the study of risks and how people deal with them.

As an example, let us look at a study of how people plan for retirement. There is a great range in the extent to which people plan or save for retirement and how they make decisions to do so. A study by Binswanger and Carman (2012) compared three types of people: those who used a detailed planning approach based on software or expert advice, those who used simple 'rules of thumb' such as setting aside a fixed amount each month, and those who were completely unsystematic. They found that there was no difference in the retirement wealth of the planners and rule-of-thumb savers, but that both had significantly more wealth than the unsystematic group. This means that it is likely to be just as effective to give people simple rule-of-thumb advice as to try to determine a complex and detailed plan.

This has been a very brief review of some of the different theoretical areas of business studies – we will go into more detail on the specific applications and cross-overs in Chapter 11 – but it does highlight how business and psychology can be combined to understand human behaviour.

 Key Research Study

What Works at Work? The Application and Benefits of Occupational Psychology Report of the British Psychological Society

William Scott-Jackson and Alan Bourne (2006)

Background: Most organisations recognise that increasing the value of their human capital is essential if they are to gain and maintain competitive advantage. While research in work psychology is effectively the knowledge base that a lot of HR practices and people management approaches draw on, it seems that managers do not have a clear understanding of what work psychology is and how it can add value.

Aim: This study, carried out by the Division of Occupational Psychology (part of the British Psychology Society), aimed to find out how occupational psychology is applied in UK organisations and what the people in those companies think of it.

Method: A web-based survey gained responses from 36 UK organisations, both public and private, and representing a range of industry sectors. Respondents included HR directors, company owners and in-house practitioners. The survey covered areas such as the spend by organisations on occupational psychology services and the factors influencing their buying choices.

Findings:

▸ An average spend of £231 p.a. on each employee gives a potential market size of £3.03 billion, yet occupational psychologists gain only 13% of that market.

▸ The highest levels of market share in consultancy services for occupational psychologists were 20–25% for executive coaching/mentoring, employee selection and employee attitude surveys. Psychologists were only called in about 1% of the time to help with stress management and work–life balance issues!

▸ About two-thirds of respondents had bought occupational psychology products (such as psychometric tests or development tools) and nearly half had bought training (such as leadership development).

▸ Respondents, while generally positive about occupational psychology, were unclear about what it was and how specifically it added value.

Implications: Essentially, organisations bought specific services or products rather than seeing the discipline of occupational psychology as the basis for quality, practical solutions. This presents a challenge to occupational psychologists to help organisations understand how they can use the knowledge base in psychology to more effectively manage their employees.

WORK PSYCHOLOGY ORIGINS AND DEVELOPMENT

Now that we have seen what work psychology is all about and gained an understanding of the different theoretical areas that contribute to it, we turn to consider how the field has developed since it first began.

The new science of psychology at work

From its beginnings in the late 1800s and for much of its early development, work psychology was dominated by the drive for efficiency that was common to much of the business world. The combination of industrialisation and the emergence of psychology as a scientific discipline led to an attempt by many early work psychologists and management theorists to find the 'best ways' of working, where 'best' meant 'most efficient'. One of the most influential of these approaches is referred to as Scientific Management, developed by management theorist Frederick Taylor. This approach aimed to find the most efficient ways of doing a job in order to improve productivity.

Hugo Münsterberg, one of the first industrial psychologists, was heavily influenced by Taylor's approach and proposed that the best way of working would be to select people for jobs based on their personality and skills. By matching people to jobs, he believed that organisations could increase the motivation and performance of their employees. Today, most people would still agree with this statement and they might be surprised to learn that vocational guidance which tries to help people find a match between potential jobs and their skills and personality was one of Münsterberg's passions.

The first PhD in Industrial Psychology was awarded to a woman who attempted to combine this scientific management with psychology: Lillian Gilbreth. The former did tend to ignore the more human aspects of work and was criticised for treating people merely as parts of a machine that had to be selected properly and strictly controlled in order to function effectively. Before completing her PhD, Gilbreth published a book called *The Psychology of Management* (1914) which tried to address these weaknesses by incorporating a consideration of the human elements, such as communication and individual behaviour. Her focus, however, was still on efficiency: how to measure and manage work to enhance productivity.

Further developing the scientific management approach was another early management theorist, Mary Parker Follett, whose work gave greater centrality to the human relations side of work. Follett was particularly interested in how conflict could be managed within organisations to produce higher-quality, more integrated solutions. She recommended participative power (or what she called 'power-with') as more effective than coercive (or 'power-over') approaches to managing employees (Follett, 1924) and encouraged organisations to try to meet their employees' human needs rather than focusing exclusively on efficiency.

This approach foreshadowed the second major movement in work psychology: the human relations school. This turning point in how psychologists tried to understand and manage behaviour at work was marked by the series of studies carried out by Elton Mayo and colleagues, known as the Hawthorne experiments (1929–32) after the name of the plant where they were carried out. These studies initially started as an attempt to use scientific management techniques to investigate the effects of changes in the workers' physical environment. For example, the investigators made changes to the workers' shift patterns or the illumination of their rooms and measured the impact on their productivity. Instead of uncovering the 'ideal' working pattern or level of illumination, however, the researchers found that social relationships and informal group dynamics were far more important in determining the workers' level of productivity. (You can read about these studies in detail in Chapter 12.) While there has been some criticism of the methods used in these studies and questioning of the reliability of the results, they definitely marked a change: work psychologists no longer viewed people as simply 'parts of a machine' but began to explore the impact of social and psychological factors at work.

Work psychology during the wars

The world wars had an impact on work psychology just as they did on the rest of society. One psychologist who was involved in the First World War was Charles Myers. Having trained as a physician, he later turned to psychology and was appointed as a consultant to the British army. Like many other psychologists he worked on selecting people for specific military jobs. But he was also heavily involved with soldiers suffering from shell shock and worked hard to try to convince the military authorities that this was a treatable psychological condition and not evidence of cowardice (Myers, 1916). After the war, Myers set up the National Institute of Industrial Psychology in the UK to develop and promote efforts in employee selection and worker well-being.

During the wars, work psychologists were primarily involved in trying to find the most effective and efficient way of assigning people to their new, wartime roles. Men were being called up to the armed forces and the forces needed effective methods of identifying those best suited to officer training or to specific military jobs that required special abilities. Women were called to enter the industrial workforce in large numbers to replace the men who had gone to war, and industry needed a way of finding out which jobs each woman would be best suited to when there was no prior industrial experience to draw on. The solution to both of these problems was the same: to develop clear and specific understandings of the abilities an individual needed for specific roles and to construct reliable tests for individual aptitudes that could be matched to those roles.

In fact, one of the most popular personality questionnaires in use in business today has its origins in the work of the mother–daughter team of Katherine Cook Briggs and Isabell Briggs Myers during the Second World War. Initially developed as an application and extension of Carl Jung's personality theories, it was an attempt to help women to identify their own personality preferences in order to find out what kind of jobs they would be most suited to as they entered the workforce. Unfortunately, Briggs and Briggs Myers were met with significant opposition from the academic community when they first publicised their test, as they were not felt to be 'qualified'

enough to produce a reliable inventory (Briggs Myers and Myers, 1995). Undaunted, the duo went on to develop the Myers–Briggs Type Inventory, which was first published in 1962 and is now administered to about 1.5 million people annually with the aim of helping them to understand themselves and others better and create a more harmonious and productive workplace (Consulting Psychologists Press, 2009).

Post-war development of work psychology

In the decades after the Second World War, psychologists were increasingly employed in large organisations such as the armed forces and civil service, where they continued their work on the application of psychology to the demands and requirements of everyday life. While the numbers of psychologists directly employed by organisations fell in the 1980s, there has been an increase in the numbers of work psychology consultancies, demonstrating that interest in the application of psychology to work is alive and well.

The traditional difference in emphasis of US psychologists and European or UK psychologists continues to this day and is rooted in the employment power relations of their respective countries. American psychologists tend to seek ways to get the most out of employees, looking for the most effective ways of working or selecting the right people for jobs. The approach tends to be management-dominated, seeking to measure abilities and behaviour in order to improve productivity. In Europe, psychologists have a greater emphasis on social welfare, being interested in worker stress and well-being and seeking psychological explanations for the positive and negative consequences of work. There is also a strong interest in work teams and organisations as a whole within Europe, as contrasted with the more individualistic focus of the USA.

Work psychology has become a very large field in recent decades and the rest of this book will be considering the major developments, but one way of conceptualising recent progress is by considering some of the current challenges for work psychology.

Current challenges for work psychology

Globalisation and cross-cultural issues

One of the major challenges for modern work psychology is the globalisation of business. All too often, people seem to assume that a common process of industrialisation will overcome any cultural differences, rather than giving careful consideration to how work is done in different places. Modern contingency theories attempt to bring an awareness of the situational context into our understanding of psychology at work and research needs to determine whether the findings established in one context hold true in others. As an example, the personality trait of conscientiousness has been found to be related to increased work performance in many different contexts and countries (Barrick et al., 2001). But the use of individual incentives, while effective in certain types of individual work performance (such as sales), can actually be damaging to performance in other contexts (such as team-based working).

As Erez (1994) pointed out two decades ago, globalisation has already happened, work has crossed cultural borders. We now have a culturally diverse labour force in an international work environment. Organisational change and restructuring has become the norm and instead of a focus on how individual employees do independent parts of the job, we have teamwork as a central component of most jobs. Theories and models that have been developed in the historical strongholds of work psychology in the UK and USA must be tested for their applicability in other cultures and countries.

Profit-focused or people-focused?

A further challenge for work psychologists is in navigating the line between a profit-focused and people-focused view of business. This is certainly not a challenge unique to psychologists. After decades of businesses being allowed and even expected to focus solely on creating profit, there are increasing calls for organisations to behave responsibly, to take account of the impact of their actions on employees, society and the wider natural environment. Work psychology has great potential to contribute to this development, with a tradition reaching back over a century of

 International Perspectives What's in a name?

As you read more in this area, you will come across many different names for 'psychology applied to work'. While there are some differences between these terms, they are all attempting to understand human behaviour at work. For example, there is some distinction between *work* and *organisational* psychology, with the former referring to aspects of psychology concerned more with individuals (such as work attitudes, well-being and career development), while the latter refers to more group-level aspects of psychology (such as team-working and organisational change and development).

On the other hand, some terms have particular historical backgrounds or are simply more or less in vogue in particular countries. For example, the older term *Industrial Psychology* is still used in the USA and New Zealand, with the division of the American Psychological Society concerned with work psychology being called the Society for Industrial and Organizational Psychology (usually abbreviated to I/O psychology). But this term is rarely heard in the UK or Europe, which tend to refer to *Work and Organisational Psychology*, as does Australia.

Registered titles

The term *Occupational Psychology* is popular in the UK but not often used in other countries and *Chartered Occupational Psychologist* is the only protected title in the field of work psychology within Britain. *Business Psychology* has become more widespread in the UK since the Health and Care Professions Council (HCPC) took over the registration of protected psychologist titles in 2009. Before this, the titles had been regulated by the British

Psychological Society. Many people who worked in the work psychology field felt that this new requirement to register with the HCPC did not reflect their work: they did not see themselves as health professionals but more as business consultants.

In the Netherlands, while the title of 'psychologist' is not regulated, titles clearly related to health care, such as psychotherapist or clinical psychologist, are restricted by law. Other countries, such as Australia, New Zealand, Finland and Greece simply protect the title 'psychologist' rather than specific sub-categories. This means that only people who have achieved prescribed levels of education and/or training can call themselves psychologists, no matter what area of psychology they specialise in. In some of these countries, the regulation is also undertaken by a health-care board (for example, Finland) while in others regulation is not related to the health professions.

Discussion point

Is a work psychologist a health-care professional? How do different countries approach this question with their professional registrations?

You may find the following websites of the professional bodies for work psychologists in different countries helpful:

UK http://dop.bps.org.uk/

Netherlands http://www.psynip.nl/
the-dutch-association-of-psychologists.html

New Zealand http://www.industrialpsychology.org.nz/

Australia http://www.groups.psychology.org.au/cop/

USA http://www.siop.org/

considering the human side of work and a deeply rooted ethical framework being seen as essential by psychologists' professional bodies.

One of the issues that consultants using work psychology face on a regular basis is in balancing the expectations of their paying clients with their ethical obligations to the individuals who will be affected by their recommendations and interventions. The British Psychological Society's (2009) ethical code of conduct has four key principles which occupational psychologists are expected to abide by and which can help anyone who wishes to apply psychology to the workplace to develop their ethical awareness.

1 **Respect** for the dignity and worth of all people. This includes being aware of the fact that psychologists may be perceived as authoritative and have influence over their clients as well as having a clear regard for each person's right to make decisions for themselves.
2 **Competence**. It is essential for people working in this area to ensure they are up to date with the latest developments in the field so as to ensure they are not inadvertently harming people by using outdated techniques. Part of this is to be aware of our own limitations and not try to undertake work for which we do not have the requisite skills or knowledge.
3 **Responsibility**. Psychologists are expected to take responsibility for their actions, not only in terms of avoiding harm to their clients or wider society, but also in terms of trying to ensure that their contributions are not misused.
4 **Integrity**. When dealing with clients, we should be honest in our dealings and accurate in the information we give them. This integrity should be evident in professional activities as well as scientific investigations.

Whether or not you go on to become a qualified work psychologist, these ethical guidelines can be useful in helping you think about how you use and apply the psychological information in this book.

Management vs workers perspective

You will probably notice as you learn more about this subject that most research and theories have a bias towards either 'management' or 'workers'. Management-focused approaches tend to be phrased in terms of the most effective ways to control work or workers while worker-focused approaches consider the effect of management systems on employees or how the employees react to those systems. A challenge for work psychology is in striking a balance between these two approaches. To have a rounded and detailed understanding of the psychology of work we need to draw on both perspectives.

Many management theories have the flaw that they do not consider the extent to which employees adopt, adapt or resist the systems. The experience of the employees is key to understanding which management models are most likely to work in any given situation. As employees, we are aiming to achieve our own goals at work and it is a rare situation that the employer's goals completely coincide with our own. Employers' goals can include control of employees, cost-effectiveness of the systems and achieving the maximum output from each employee. Employees' goals on the other hand can include increasing their income, reducing the effort they have to put into work and controlling their own work environment

 Case Study **The ethics of psychology at work**

You work for a business psychology consultancy and have been approached by a medium-sized company which wants to downsize. The manager who contacted you emphasised that the company is facing a tough future and wants to ensure they only keep people who will be willing to work long hours and are dedicated to the company values. They have asked you to develop a process for choosing who should be made redundant.

▸ What ethical issues might you face in this contract? How could you deliver on this manager's expectations while maintaining your ethical and professional standards?

▸ How might your response be different if you were asked to do this in India or the USA? What further information would you need to ensure you could do a good job?

© BRANDX

(Noon et al., 2013). It is also worth remembering that individual managers are also employees, so it is not a simple case of a power struggle between people in management positions and those who are not.

An example of this tension between management theories and workers' experience is given in a case study that investigated the control systems in a call centre and the methods employees used to resist or circumvent that control (Townsend, 2005). Electronic surveillance in a call centre is one method that the organisation can use to try to control employees' work. By recording and monitoring the calls an employee makes, the managers can assess the work on several different measures, such as call length, politeness to the customer, number of dropped calls and so on. If we were to take into account only the management systems in place, we might conclude that there were very tight controls and that employees would have no option but to work exactly as required by management, with no way of controlling their own time or effort at work. However, this case study uncovered several different ways that the employees had found to trick or bypass the system so that they could have extra breaks. For example, if they wanted a quick cigarette break or a cup of tea, they could transfer a caller to the automated pay system but not release the call, so it looks like they are still in contact with the customer. The employee could then go off and have an 'extra' break.

In understanding work psychology, then, we need to make sure we are taking account not only of management requirements but also the employees' needs and expectations.

 Activity Are you on the fiddle?

Examples of 'fiddling' by employees include: exaggerating expense claims, taking a 'duvet day' (a day off sick when you are not actually ill), using the internet or office phones for personal matters and taking work supplies home. Have you ever done any of these things? Get together with a partner and see how long a list of 'fiddles' you can come up with.

▶ To what extent do you think these 'fiddles' are problems for the organisation? What do you think would be the result if managers tried to eliminate them all?

Levels of analysis

While traditionally psychology focused on the individual and sociology focused on the group or wider society in explaining human behaviour, there is a growing recognition that this distinction is unrealistic. One of the key decisions in applying psychology to work is deciding which level of analysis to use: individual, group or organisation. If, for example, we wanted to find ways to improve creativity within an organisation, we could address the issue at three different levels. At the individual level, we would want to know what personality, motivational or cognitive factors are associated with higher creativity so that we could perhaps begin to select more creative individuals for jobs where innovation was key. At the group level, we would need to identify the factors that might encourage that creativity to emerge, such as group size or diversity. And finally, at an organisational level we would want to know what structures, policies or cultures nurture creativity as opposed to restricting it.

Most work psychology models focus on one of these levels at a time, simply because it becomes very complicated very quickly when we try to capture all the different interactions between the levels. To continue our example, what if we had a highly creative person in a supportive, small group but the organisation as a whole had a conservative culture that did not condone any risk-taking with new ideas? Would the creative ideas survive and ultimately change that culture or would the organisation lose that creativity?

While it is certainly a challenge to deal with these questions, multi-level models do exist and help us to build up a clearer understanding of the interactions between findings at each of the three levels. Continuing our creativity example, a recent study looked at how individual-level factors such as growth need strength and creative personality interacted with job complexity and having a supportive context (Shalley et al., 2009). It showed how, instead of taking a one-size-fits-all approach to encouraging creativity, we need different approaches depending on how complex the job is and how supportive the environment. As research continues into these multi-level models, our understanding of the real world of work becomes clearer and the interventions we base on these theories become more effective.

SUMMARY

This chapter began by introducing the concept of psychology as the science of the mind, giving an overview of the different theoretical areas of psychology and how they contribute to a deep understanding of human behaviour. It showed that applied psychology focuses on practical, real-world events but nevertheless follows a rigorously scientific approach.

The second section introduced major areas of business studies, including management, marketing and finance, providing a detailed view of the context of work psychology. The chapter concluded with a history of work psychology, its origins and development, before going on to explore some of the current challenges that work psychology faces.

TEST YOURSELF

Brief Review Questions

1 Outline the steps of the scientific method and illustrate its application to psychology with an example.
2 List the main theoretical areas of psychology. For one of these areas, describe an example of how psychological research or theory can be applied to the world of work.
3 What is the difference between theoretical and applied psychology?
4 Briefly outline the eight areas of knowledge that the BPS expects of occupational psychologists.
5 Describe three main arenas for business studies and briefly outline how they are related to psychology.

Discussion or Essay Questions

1 What does it mean for us to claim that psychology is a 'science'? What are the advantages and limitations of trying to understand people in this way?
2 Work in the different areas of work psychology is not limited to psychologists, so what (if anything) sets work psychologists apart from other HR and management professionals?
3 Is 'business about people'? Why or why not?

FURTHER READING

* For a good introduction to psychology, read *Psychology: European* Edition by Schacter et al. Basingstoke, Palgrave Macmillan, 2011.
* Many of Mary Parker Follett's publications are now available on the internet: http://mpfollett.ning.com/.
* For a worker's perspective on many of the issues dealt with by traditional management science, have a look at M. Noon, P. Blyton and K. Morrell, *The Realities of Work*, 4th edn, Basingstoke: Palgrave Macmillan, 2013.

References

BAGOZZI, R., VERBEKE, W., BERG, W., RIETDIJK, W., DIETVORST, R. & WORM, L. 2012. Genetic and neurological foundations of customer orientation: field and experimental evidence. *Journal of the Academy of Marketing Science*, 40, 639–58.

BARRICK, M. R., MOUNT, M. K. & JUDGE, T. A. 2001. Personality and performance at the beginning of the new millennium: what do we know and where do we go next? *International Journal of Selection and Assessment*, 9, 9–30.

BINSWANGER, J. & CARMAN, K. G. 2012. How real people make long-term decisions: the case of retirement preparation. *Journal of Economic Behavior & Organization*, 81, 39–60.

BRIGGS MYERS, I. & MYERS, P. B. 1995. *Gifts Differing*. Palo Alto, CA, Davies-Black Publishing.

BRITISH PSYCHOLOGICAL SOCIETY. 2009. *Code of Ethics and Conduct*. London, The British Psychological Society.

CASSELL, C. & SYMON, G. 2011. Assessing 'good' qualitative research in the work psychology field: a narrative analysis. *Journal of Occupational and Organizational Psychology*, 84, 633–50.

CONSULTING PSYCHOLOGISTS PRESS. 2009. *History, Reliability and Validity of the Myers-Briggs Type Indicator Instrument*. https://www.cpp.com/products/mbti/mbti_info.aspx (accessed 13 March 2013).

DARCY, C., MCCARTHY, A., HILL, J. & GRADY, G. 2012. Work–life balance: one size fits all? An exploratory analysis of the differential effects of career stage. *European Management Journal*, 30, 111–20.

EBSTEIN, R. P., NOVICK, O., UMANSKY, R., PRIEL, B., OSHER, Y., BLAINE, D., BENNETT, E. R., NEMANOV, L., KATZ, M. & BELMAKER, R. H. 1996. Dopamine D4 receptor (D4DR) exon III polymorphism associated with the human personality trait of novelty seeking. *Nat Genet*, 12, 78–80.

EREZ, M. 1994. Towards a Model of Cross-Cultural I/O Psychology. In Dunnette, M. D., Hough, L. & Triandis, H. (eds.) *Handbook of Industrial and Organizational Psychology*, 2nd edn. Palo Alto, CA, Consulting Psychologists Press.

FOLLETT, M. P. 1924. *Creative Experience*. New York, Longmans, Green and Co.

FRIEDMAN, M. & ROSENMAN, R. H. 1959. Association of specific overt behavior pattern with blood and cardiovascular findings. *Journal of the American Medical Association*, 169, 1286–96.

FRIEDMAN, M., THORESEN, C. E., GILL, J. J., ULMER, D., POWELL, L. H., PRICE, V. A., BROWN, B., THOMPSON, L., RABIN, D. D. & BREALL, W. S. 1986. Alteration of type A behavior and its effect on cardiac recurrences in post myocardial infarction patients: summary results of the recurrent coronary prevention project. *American Heart Journal*, 112, 653–65.

GILBRETH, L. M. 1914. *The Psychology of Management*. New York, The Macmillan Company.

JUDGE, T. A., KLINGER, R. L. & SIMON, L. S. 2010. Time is on my side: time, general mental ability, human capital, and extrinsic career success. *Journal of Applied Psychology*, 95, 92–107.

KUTCHER, E. J. & BRAGGER, J. D. 2004. Selection interviews of overweight job applicants: can structure reduce the bias? *Journal of Applied Social Psychology*, 34, 1993–2022.

LAM, S. K., AHEARNE, M., HU, Y. & SCHILLEWAERT, N. 2010. Resistance to brand switching when a radically new brand is introduced: a social identity theory perspective. *Journal of Marketing*, 74, 128–46.

LANGE, D. & WASHBURN, N. T. 2012. Understanding attributions of corporate social responsibility. *Academy of Management Review*, 37, 300–26.

LEWIN, K. 1951. *Field Theory in Social Science; Selected Theoretical Papers*, ed. D. Cartwright. New York, Harper & Row.

MAGUIRE, E. A., GADIAN, D. G., JOHNSRUDE, I. S., GOOD, C. D., ASHBURNER, J., FRACKOWIAK, R. S. & FRITH, C. D. 2000. Navigation-related structural change in the hippocampi of taxi drivers. *Proceedings of the National Academy of Sciences of the United States of America*, 97, 4398–403.

MYERS, C. S. 1916. Contributions to the study of shell shock, being an account of certain cases treated by hypnosis. *Lancet*, 1, 65–9.

NOON, M., BLYTON, P. & MORRELL, K. 2013. *The Realities of Work*. 4th edn. Basingstoke, Palgrave Macmillan.

PETIT, V. & BOLLAERT, H. 2012. Flying too close to the sun? Hubris among CEOs and how to prevent it. *Journal of Business Ethics*, 108, 265–83.

SCOTT-JACKSON, W. & BOURNE, A. 2006. *What Works at Work? The Application and Benefits of Occupational Psychology*. London, The British Psychological Society.

SHALLEY, C. E., GILSON, L. L. & BLUM, T. C. 2009. Interactive effects of growth need strength, work context, and job complexity on self-reported creative performance. *Academy of Management Journal*, 52, 489–505.

TOWNSEND, K. 2005. Electronic surveillance and cohesive teams: room for resistance in an Australian call centre? *New Technology, Work and Employment*, 20, 47–59.

WONG, E. M., ORMISTON, M. E. & TETLOCK, P. E. 2011. The effects of top management team integrative complexity and decentralized decision making on corporate social performance. *Academy of Management Journal*, 54, 1207–28.

PART 1

BUSINESS IS ABOUT PEOPLE

N THE FIRST PART OF THIS BOOK WE FOCUS ON THE DAY-TO-DAY ISSUES OF managing relationships and understanding people in the modern workplace. We approach these issues from two directions simultaneously. One way to do so is from the point of view of organisations looking to make the best decisions about how they recruit, develop and motivate staff and organise the business. But the second point of view is that of the individuals who are actually working in those organisations, people who can use psychological knowledge and theory to improve their own working lives. This is a recurring theme through this book: work psychology can be used to make organisations more effective but it can also help individuals to lead more fulfilling and rewarding work lives.

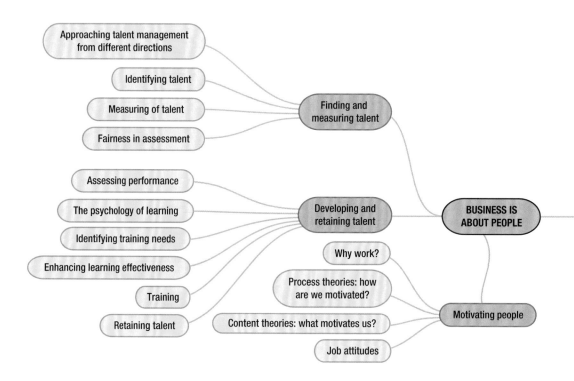

We start this section in Chapter 2 by exploring how psychology can help us to identify our talents and help organisations to find the right people for their business needs. In Chapter 3, we move on to consider how we can measure performance and continually develop our own and others' talent. Closely tied to this is the topic of Chapter 4, which is about the best ways to motivate people at work.

Having established the basics, we then start to consider more complex issues around our interactions with other people at work. In Chapter 5, we consider how we can best communicate and how central good communications are to business success. Chapter 6 critically assesses what psychology can tell us about how to build effective teams and presents some practical guidelines for managers. And finally, we round off this part of the book with Chapter 7, which considers the importance of leadership in supporting the business objectives.

The case study for Part 1 looks at what it is like working for Google, exploring the topics of talent management, motivation and collaboration in one of the most well-known employers in the world.

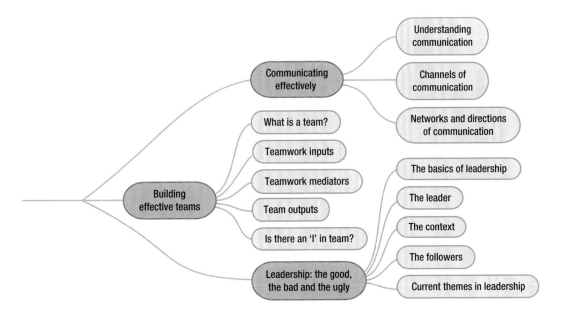

FINDING AND MEASURING TALENT

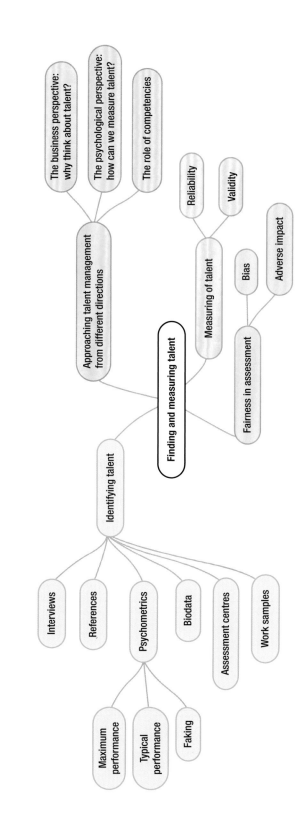

Finding and measuring talent

- Approaching talent management from different directions
  - The business perspective: why think about talent?
  - The psychological perspective: how can we measure talent?
  - The role of competencies
- Measuring of talent
  - Reliability
  - Validity
- Fairness in assessment
  - Bias
  - Adverse impact
- Identifying talent
  - Interviews
  - References
  - Psychometrics
    - Maximum performance
    - Typical performance
    - Faking
  - Biodata
  - Assessment centres
  - Work samples

The starting point for building an effective business is to find and develop the right talent, so in this chapter we begin by examining talent management from both a business and a psychological perspective. Central to this is the concept of competencies, and we will discuss these in detail. We will highlight how effective management of talent rests on accurate measurement of complex phenomena, and take some time to consider the key issues of reliability and validity in psychological measurement.

Having established the ways in which we can compare different measurements of talent, we move on to a detailed review of different selection methods available to organisations. Throughout this section, we will be reminded that these methods can also be used in assessing current employees' performance and training needs, which is the subject of Chapter 3. Finally, we round off the chapter with a consideration of the important issue of fairness and the wider impact of different selection methods.

This chapter will help you answer the following questions:

1   What are the two main approaches to talent management and how can work psychology integrate their concerns?
2   How can work psychology help us to evaluate different methods of identifying employee talent?
3   Why is accurate measurement of employee talent important and how can we ensure this is done well?
4   How can psychology contribute to fairness in assessments?

APPROACHING TALENT MANAGEMENT FROM DIFFERENT DIRECTIONS

Talent management can be approached from two different directions. The first is from a business perspective, where the focus is on having the right people in the right place at the right time, and considers issues such as employee turnover, succession planning and development. The main question we need to answer here is, *Why think about talent?* The second way to approach talent management is from a psychological perspective, where the focus is on scientifically differentiating between people and identifying the things that contribute to success. The main question here is, *How can we identify talent?* Both of these approaches need to be incorporated into a successful talent management strategy.

The business perspective: why think about talent?

The 'War for Talent' was a phrase coined by consultants at McKinsey & Company at the turn of the century and popularised in the book of the same name (Michaels et al., 2001). The phrase was meant to capture what the authors described as a critical shift in the criteria for business success. In this view, success for a business is dependent on the organisation's ability to attract, develop and retain 'talent'. It is about maximising the competitive advantage an organisation can gain from utilising its human capital effectively (Collings and Mellahi, 2009). To achieve this, Collings and Mellahi suggest that a strategic approach to talent management needs to fulfil three key aims:

1   **Identify pivotal positions** which have a differential impact on an organisation's competitive advantage. It is worth noting that these key positions are not limited to higher management but can include posts at any level of the organisation.
2   **Develop a talent pool** of high-performing employees who can fill those positions. This means the organisation will have to think ahead: not just look for people to fill positions when they become vacant, but develop people for those future vacancies. This needs to be done both internally (by developing current employees) and externally (by recruitment) in order to meet the organisation's needs.
3   **Create a differentiated HR architecture** which allows the organisation to invest appropriately in different groups of employees. With the aim of encouraging motivation, commitment and development, the organisation will invest more in those employees who can contribute most to the organisation's strategic objectives.

While many authors have made a convincing case for the centrality of talent management in organisational success, there remains debate over what 'talent' actually is and whether it is inborn or something that can be developed (we explore this further in the activity below). Lewis and Heckman (2006) note that this debate over what talent and talent management is presents a problem for those wishing to make claims about its importance. They recommend that a more strategic approach needs to be based on reliable and valid talent management measures. These measures are essential if we are to answer important questions accurately: *how do we identify high performers? How can we identify untapped potential? Who will respond best to development?* It is here that work psychology can make an invaluable contribution.

 Activity Your talent

What is 'talent'? Write down your own definition and then compare it with others in your group or look it up in a dictionary.

▸ If you had to sum up your own 'talent' in a few words or a short phrase, what would it be?

▸ With a partner, discuss the extent to which you think 'talent' is natural or acquired over the course of your life. What are the implications of this for businesses wishing to manage the talent within their organisations?

The psychological perspective: how can we measure talent?

When we are talking about talent in a business context, what we really mean is how well a person performs a job. But assessing performance is notoriously difficult. Who judges how well someone is performing? Their manager, their co-workers, or their customers and clients? What kinds of measurement do we want? Is it how well people contribute to a team or how well they complete individual tasks? How can we separate individual from team or organisational performance? This problem of measuring talent and performance is even more difficult when it comes to selecting people for jobs because we have such a limited time and experience of the person to make relevant judgements.

Psychological theory and research can make a real contribution to talent assessment. At heart, it is about taking a scientific approach to assessing people. We start by identifying what needs to be measured and then develop reliable and valid measurements that can be used fairly to distinguish between people. The advantage of these methods of assessment is that they can sometimes even identify hidden talents. For example, an employee might have great potential as a team leader but never have had the opportunity to demonstrate it. Using work samples or psychometric testing, the organisation may be able to uncover and utilise this hidden talent.

Once the talent has been identified, the organisation can then build its talent pool by recruiting the right people and developing current employees. Within an overall talent management framework, assessment, selection and development should all be integrated. One way of doing this is to have an organisation-wide competency framework.

The role of competencies

Much of the work psychology research around predicting work performance has focused on finding out what a specific measure can predict, or how good it is at predicting something. Bartram (2005) suggests that instead of this measurement-focused approach, it is more useful to adopt a criterion-focused approach that looks at meaningful workplace behaviours or outcomes (competencies) and tries to identify what will best predict them. This change in focus from job- or task-based management to competency-based management of human resources is seen as an essential part of an organisation's continuous evolution (Soderquist et al., 2010). Competencies are a common feature of many people management policies and practices, and a whole industry has developed around their application in organisations. Matching employee competencies and job requirements is claimed to improve employee and organisational performance, as well as leading to increased satisfaction (Spencer et al., 1992).

There is some discussion over the precise definition of competencies, from a person-centred approach which defines them as characteristics of an individual that underlie effective or superior performance (Boyatzis, 1982) to a more outcome-oriented approach that defines them as 'sets of behaviors that are instrumental in the delivery of desired results or outcomes' (Bartram et al., 2002, p. 7). It is this latter definition that is most useful in identifying and measuring talent within an organisation because it focuses on the aspect that is most important to an organisation: what a person actually does. The usefulness and popularity of competencies in the talent management and general HR literature is primarily due to the way they capture a range of individual characteristics in a performance-focused manner, incorporating not only what a person can do, but what they want to do (Ryan et al., 2009).

Developing a competency model starts with job analysis. The aim of job analysis is to identify the knowledge, skills and behaviours that are associated with job performance. In the USA, the Occupational Information Network (O*NET, http://www.onetcenter.org/) has collected job analysis information for over 974 occupations and combined it with other organisational information to create a database for exploring occupations. It can be a useful resource for people thinking about changing career or wanting to find out what is required for a particular occupation. Job analysis information is then developed into clear descriptions of competencies that are important for good performance.

Competencies need to be based on behavioural indicators – that is, on observable behaviours that indicate certain levels of performance. It is useful for an organisation to specify both positive and negative indicators so that good and bad performance can be identified. This competency framework can then be used at every stage of the talent management process: to select candidates for roles, to assess current employees' performance and to evaluate development needs.

There are, of course, many workplace behaviours that we might be interested in and the different lists of competencies developed by different organisations and researchers may at first seem overwhelming. How can we be sure that any competency framework is sufficient to measure the important factors of work performance while not including any extraneous elements? Tett et al. (2000) constructed a comprehensive and detailed list of management competencies that included 53 different competencies in nine groups. For example, the *Traditional Functions* group included *Problem Awareness* and *Strategic Planning*, while the *Communication* group included *Listening Skills* and *Public Presentation*. The drawback of this approach is that the sheer volume of competencies that it produced made it unwieldy. One suggestion for an integrative and comprehensive model of competencies, based on meta-analyses of many different competency models, is the Great Eight. This model is supported by research evidence showing how different competencies cluster together, and is consistent with practitioners' models (Bartram, 2005). The eight competencies are:

Leading and Deciding	Analysing and Interpreting
Supporting and Cooperating	Organising and Executing
Interacting and Presenting	Adapting and Coping
Creating and Conceptualising	Enterprising and Performing

A generalised model like the Great Eight has the advantage of being more cost-effective, as the organisation does not need to conduct detailed job analysis of every single role in order to identify a unique framework. It does, of course, still need tailoring to individual roles and levels within the organisation. The case study on competency frameworks illustrates how one organisation has tried to do this.

In our discussions of competencies, we have already started addressing one of the major issues in talent management and indeed in work psychology in general: measurement. We will now move to consider this in more detail.

 ### Case Study Competency framework in the Civil Service

The Civil Service Competency Framework (2012–17) is a good illustration of how a generic competency framework can provide a large organisation with strategic direction. Based on the organisation's values of honesty, integrity, impartiality and objectivity, it identifies three clusters of competencies that will lead to high performance within the organisation: Setting Direction, Delivering Results and Engaging People.

© Image Source

Each cluster consists of three or four competencies and each competency is clearly defined with behavioural indicators of both effective and ineffective behaviour. These behaviours are further organised by the level of the person's post, which is essential if the competencies are going to be implemented throughout the organisation.

Go to http://www.civilservice.gov.uk/wp-content/uploads/2011/05/Civil-Service-Competency-Framework-Jan2013.pdf and look through the detailed framework, particularly the descriptions of behavioural indicators.

▶ Why do you think it is important to develop both positive and negative behavioural indicators?
  Compare the competencies in this framework with the Great Eight framework (for detailed descriptions of the Great Eight, go to http://www.shl.com/assets/resources/White-Paper-SHL-Universal-Competency-Framework.pdf).
▶ Can you see any overlaps? To what extent do you think the Civil Service framework is unique?

A NOTE ON MEASUREMENT

A central issue for psychology at work is how we can accurately measure the variables we are interested in. Whether it is in identifying talent or assessing someone's current job performance for promotion or development opportunities, our decisions will only be as good as the measures we rely on. In this section we will review the essential criteria by which we can judge how good those measurements or assessments are, and build a more detailed understanding of how they can be used to inform employee-resourcing decisions.

There are two main ways of judging how accurate a psychological measure is: reliability and validity. A reliable measure is one that gives consistent results. A valid measure is one that is actually measuring what it claims to.

It is easy to understand these concepts when we think about physical measurements. For example, we can use centimetres to measure length or height. If you were to measure your height in centimetres with a tape measure today and do the same tomorrow, you would get the same result: centimetres are a reliable measure of height. Trying to measure your height using millilitres, on the other hand, would be pointless. Millilitres are a valid measure of volume, but not of length.

But assessing the validity and reliability of measures of complex phenomena in the workplace is not so straightforward. We need to have a clear understanding of what psychological measurements can and can't do if we are to use them appropriately to enhance our decision-making.

Reliability

We saw above that a reliable measure is one that gives us consistent results. There are two main types of reliability we might want to know about, depending on the kind of measurement we are looking at. The first is the reliability of the assessors and the second is the reliability of the measure itself.

Reliability of the assessors is assessed using **inter-rater reliability**. Several assessment methods try to achieve an objective measure of a person by ensuring that different assessors use standardised forms and questions. For example, different interviewers may use the same interview schedule or several observers of a role-play activity would use the same form to assess candidates' performance. The objectivity of these measures depends entirely on how much agreement there is between raters scoring the same candidate.

Reliability of measures can be assessed in several ways:

- **Test–retest reliability**: the test must give us consistent results if given to the same people on different occasions.

- *Internal consistency*: this is used to check that different parts of the test are measuring the same thing. For example, if we have a questionnaire that measures cognitive ability, are a person's scores on one half of the questionnaire similar to their scores on the other?
- *Parallel forms*: if we have more than one version of a test, a person's scores must be similar on both versions.

Validity

While reliability is an essential first step in evaluating how good our measures are, in itself it is not enough. We may have a test or a measure that gives very consistent results but is not actually measuring what it claims to. For example, we could have a test purportedly measuring 'general intelligence' that actually measures general knowledge. It is further complicated by the fact that a measure might be valid for one application (e.g. the selection of entry-level graduates) but not valid for another (e.g. identifying potential for leadership development).

There are several types of validity that need to be considered:

- **Face** validity is the easiest type of validity to demonstrate and simply asks whether the measure *appears* to assess what it claims to. Good face validity helps candidates to 'buy in' to the assessment and helps them to believe that the process is fair.
- **Content** validity is more theoretical. While the average person in the street might believe that a measure is valid, it also needs to be based on solid research and up-to-date theory about what the concept includes. To establish content validity, we would need to ask experts in the field the extent to which a measure is representative of the *whole* of the ability or attribute that it claims to measure.
- **Construct** validity asks whether the assessment accurately measures the construct that it claims to. For example, does a particular teamwork role play at an assessment centre really measure a candidate's teamworking ability or is it actually measuring their leadership skills? This is a more difficult type of validity to demonstrate because often the constructs we are trying to measure are quite abstract. However, one way in which this can be done is by establishing that a new measure of a construct correlates with older, established measures in the ways we would theoretically expect.
- **Criterion** validity is perhaps the most important type of validity to consider and refers to how well a measure

predicts something important in the real world of work. The 'criterion' is the outcome that we are trying to predict. For example, we might want to use an intelligence test to select employees who will benefit the most from a training programme. In this case, the intelligence test is the 'predictor' and the benefit from the training programme is the 'criterion' and we are assuming that the more intelligent employees will benefit the most from the training. But if we are to use measurements accurately and responsibly, we can't just assume this kind of link between our measurement and outcome criterion, we need to demonstrate it clearly. This link can be established *concurrently* or *predictively*:

○ Concurrent criterion validity is where the test and criterion measure are taken at the same time – indicating whether the test predicts current employees' performance.
○ Predictive criterion validity is where the criterion is measured some time after the test, indicating whether the test predicts future performance.

Although criterion-related validity is the gold standard of any measure we might use in selecting employees, it is also quite difficult to achieve. Its usefulness depends entirely on how carefully the criterion was chosen and how well it can be assessed. Job performance, for example, is difficult to assess and is subject to many influencing factors that may be completely unrelated to the predictor. However, there are other criteria that could be equally important to an organisation and more easily measured, such as absenteeism or turnover rates. Whatever the difficulties, establishing criterion validity for any measure used to assess candidates is a key part of using these psychological tools well.

Useful rules of thumb for evaluating reliability and validity information

There are two main statistics used for demonstrating the reliability or validity of an assessment method. Both are measures of 'agreement' or similarity between numerical scores.

The first statistic is a correlation and tells you how similar two sets of scores are. These two sets of scores could be from two versions of the same test, two different raters or the same test completed by the same people at different times. Correlations can be positive (an increase in score on one measure is associated with an increase on the second measure) or negative (an increase on one measure is associated with a decrease on the second). They are represented by *r* and can have an absolute value between zero and one. The stronger the relationship between the two sets of scores, the closer *r* is to 1.

The second statistic is the reliability coefficient, also known as the Cronbach alpha and represented by α. It assesses how greatly the different items on a questionnaire agree with each other and also gives a score between zero and one, where one indicates perfect agreement between the different items. A high agreement means that the different items are all assessing the same concept.

Psychometric tests produced by reputable publishers will have this information clearly available in the test manuals, but it is also worth trying to find it for other assessment methods you might use. You can use the following rules of thumb when evaluating whether a measure is reliable and valid:

Reliability

- Internal consistency $\alpha > 0.7$
- Test–retest or inter-rater $r > 0.7$

Construct Validity

- Ability tests $r > 0.7$
- Personality questionnaires $r > 0.6$

Criterion-Related Validity

- Any validity above $r = 0$ is giving you some predictive power. The two important things to bear in mind are a) ensure that the criterion is relevant to your purpose and b) the higher the correlation, the better.

 Activity Assessing validity and reliability

Go online and find a psychometric test manual. (For example, Psytech provides all its technical manuals as free downloads: www.psytech.com/resources-Manuals.php.)

▸ Write a short report (or prepare a brief presentation) which evaluates your chosen test in terms of its reliability and validity, using the rules of thumb outlined in the Measurement section above to understand the statistical results presented in the manual.

IDENTIFYING TALENT

In this section, we will explore the different methods that organisations can use to identify the people they need to fulfil their talent management strategy. While you may be familiar with some of these as selection methods, remember that 'selection' in this case is broader than just choosing the right person to fill a vacant post.

Table 2.1 Comparative predictive validity and popularity of various selection methods

Predictive validity		Popularity	
High (validity >0.5)	Work samples Cognitive ability tests Structured interviews	**High** (used by >80% of organisations)	Interviews References Application forms Ability tests Personality tests
Medium (validity between 0.35 and 0.4)	Unstructured interviews Personality tests Assessment centres Biodata	**Medium** (used by around 60% of organisations)	Assessment centres
Low (validity < 0.3)	References Self-assessment	**Low** (used by <20% of organisations)	Biodata

Source: adapted from Anderson and Cunningham-Snell (2000).

These methods can also be used to decide who should go on a development course or what secondment someone might benefit from. In fact, while this type of internal development decision is often made in quite an informal manner, these decisions are key to the effective internal management of talent and ideally should be made using the most up-to-date, reliable and valid measures that we have.

There are two different approaches we can take in identifying talent: a signs or a samples approach (Wernimont and Campbell, 1968). The first looks for signs that a person will be good at a job they do not yet have. The second assesses their performance on a work sample. We will examine methods that use both of these approaches in the next section, and explore how psychological research has helped to develop reliable and valid ways of measuring both signs and samples.

Anderson and Cunningham-Snell (2000) collated the findings of several meta-analyses of the predictive validity of different selection methods and compared them with the popularity of the same methods. The results, shown in Table 2.1, highlighted how the most popular methods used in organisations were often not the best at predicting performance.

Activity Selection methods

With a partner, talk about your experiences of the selection process for different jobs for which you have applied. Compile a list of all the different selection methods you have experienced and heard about.

When your list is complete,

▸ go through it and note which are 'signs' methods and which are 'samples'. What do you notice about the relative use of each method? Why do you think that is?
▸ Which method do *you personally* think is 'best'. What does 'best' mean to you? Is it the fairest, the easiest, the one you feel you do well in? How similar are your views to your partner's?

Interviews

As we saw in the table above, interviews are the most popular method in employee selection. They are also regularly used in performance appraisals, job analysis and training needs identification. While there has been significant criticism of interviews because of their potential for bias and subjectivity, the good news is that by drawing on decades of psychological research and recommendations we can ensure that interviews have one of the top validity ratings of any selection method.

In interviews we are relying on the interviewer's judgement about a candidate, which is unfortunately subject to several biases and distortions. These distortions are the result of shortcuts that our brains make: they are not in themselves 'bad' or 'wrong' but are ways of helping us make sense of the complicated world we live in without using up too much time or effort. While they can be useful in everyday life, they can cause problems when we are trying to make accurate assessments of others in an interview situation. There are several different cognitive shortcuts that have been identified as sources of bias in interviews:

Table 2.2 Sources of bias in interviews

Bias	Example
Halo/horns Making a general evaluation of a person based on only a limited piece of information about them. (*Halo* refers to a positive general evaluation and *horns* to a negative one.)	A friend mentions to you that Ms Smith, who is coming for an interview tomorrow, is very popular and well respected in her current job. You enter the interview feeling generally positive about her and tend to notice information that confirms your preconception while ignoring information that contradicts it.
Primacy/recency We tend to remember information better when it is at the beginning or the end of a sequence.	In the week just before your performance appraisal, you have been consistently late to work. Despite having been punctual for the whole year before this week, your manager is likely to base an assessment on this most recent behaviour instead of a balanced judgement of the whole year.
Stereotypes Our brains automatically try to categorise people and things based on their similarity and then assume that all members of that category will share all the same characteristics.	You are interviewing for a post in the marketing department which will be using social media to promote the organisation's products. There are two outstanding candidates, one in her 20s and the other in his 50s. It is likely you will assume that the younger applicant will be more up to date with social media.
Attribution bias This bias occurs when we 'attribute' someone's behaviour to the wrong cause. Fundamental attribution error is when we believe someone's behaviour is due to personal characteristics rather than situational causes.	A candidate arrives late for an interview. Despite any excuses that might be given about late trains or transport problems, you believe it is a sign that the candidate is disorganised or habitually late.
'Like me' effect We tend to be attracted to people who are similar to us.	You find out that one of the applicants went to the same university as you. You will tend to have a much more positive impression of this person and believe he or she will be a better choice for the post.

Although these biases are natural ways that our brains function, organisations can take steps to ensure that they are reduced and that interviews are conducted in a standardised, fair and consistent manner.

First, we need to create standardised and structured interviews. This will ensure that all the interviewees are asked the same questions and their answers are assessed or graded in the same way. It should be noted that creating structure is not a simple process. A review by Campion and Palmer (1997) identified 15 different components that contributed to improving the reliability and validity of interviews. While an organisation might not be able to use all the components, the review points out that interviews could easily be improved simply by paying attention to some of them.

The second way to reduce bias in interviews is to make the assessment criteria clear and ensure that they do not include items that are not directly related to the post. Only information that is directly related to a person's ability to perform effectively in the role should be taken into account. This means that a thorough job analysis needs to be conducted in order to identify performance criteria that can be assessed in an interview.

Third, it is important that interviewers record and justify their decisions. Making notes and written justification for decisions helps people to process information carefully and appropriately rather than relying on stereotypes. Once someone is made aware of his or her own stereotypes, s/he is often able to overcome that bias in decision-making (Greenwald and Banaji, 1995). A written record also ensures the organisation has evidence of fairness in the selection process.

Finally, and related to all these points, is the centrality of interviewer training. Only by training interviewers properly can the organisation ensure that all its efforts at creating standardised, structured and valid interviews actually come to fruition.

When conducted well, interviews can provide high levels of validity. But their popularity may well be due to other factors as well. One of these is that the interview provides an essential 'human element' to the assessment process. While we certainly want to aim for consistency

Case Study Interview bias

As a new manager, Sue is involved in the selection process for a Data Input Clerk. This position needs someone who is IT literate, organised, detail-oriented and dependable. After short-listing from CVs, Sue interviews two applicants:

> Joe is 22 and a recent graduate from the same university as Sue. On his CV, he lists hockey as one of his hobbies, which is a game Sue has played since secondary school. He arrives early for the interview and is neatly dressed in a suit and tie.

> Jeremy is 24 and used to work with one of Sue's friends, who has told Sue he was a bit of a joker at work. He arrives only just on time for the interview and apologises for his slightly dishevelled appearance, saying that his car broke down this morning and he had to rush around looking for a taxi.

© PHOTODISC

After the interviews are completed, Sue recommends that Joe is offered the position.

▸ How many biases might Sue have been subject to in making this decision?

▸ What recommendations would you make to an organisation to try and ensure that these biases were reduced in future interviews?

Psychological Toolkit Structured interviews

Being invited to an interview is a key step in gaining your next job, and many universities now offer guidance on interview techniques. Knowing what the interviewer is looking for can help you formulate your answers to make his or her job easier, present yourself in the best possible way and hopefully get that job!

Studies have consistently shown that using a structure improves the validity of interviews (Robertson and Smith, 2001) and most organisations now use structured interviews as the norm in their selection processes. There are two different types of structured interviews that you may come across: the behavioural and the situational interview. Both use behaviourally anchored rating scales (BARS) to grade your responses so that you can be compared more fairly with other candidates. BARS have a numerical scale with clear descriptions of possible responses and allow the interviewer to be consistent in assessing how well different candidates meet the criteria.

The **behavioural** interview is based on the theory that the best way to predict someone's future behaviour is to know their *past behaviour*. It will contain questions designed to elicit information about whether you have demonstrated particular behaviour in past situations that is relevant to

performance on the job for which you have applied. A particularly popular form of behavioural interview uses competency-based questions, which still ask candidates to describe their behaviour but are more focused on a specific competency.

The **situational** interview is based on the idea that it is our *intentions* that predict our behaviour (Latham et al., 1980) and aims to assess how a candidate might behave in a hypothetical situation. The pioneers of this technique have conducted studies which illustrate that situational interviews may be more valid than behavioural ones (e.g. Latham and Saari, 1984), and later reviews seem to confirm this (Robertson and Smith, 2001).

This exercise will work best if you role-play the interview, but it can also be useful if you simply write down your answers. Take it in turns to play the interviewer and interviewee and work through these three questions (they are all assessing the same thing: your organisational ability):

▸ **Behavioural:** Can you give me an example of when you have had to be organised in order to meet a deadline? What did you do to make sure you met the deadline?

▸ **Competency-based** (more specific, focused on *prioritising*): Can you give me an example of a time when you had to prioritise conflicting demands? What did you do?

> ▶ **Situational:** Imagine that you are working on two different projects and the deadlines for both are within a week of each other. How would you ensure that you could complete the tasks within the time frame?
>
> For the next job you apply for, go through the information provided and identify the competencies or qualities the organisation is looking for. Then try writing questions for yourself based on either a behavioural or situational interview, and practise answering them. In doing this, you are using your knowledge of work psychology to enhance your career prospects!

and objectivity in assessing people's suitability for a job (or their performance in a current post), one of the advantages of interviews is that they involve normal (if formal) human interactions rather than the almost machine-like approaches of other methods. Interviews are also more two way than many other assessment methods, giving the interviewee the opportunity to meet and engage with the people in the organisation. Finally, and just as importantly for the organisation's image and ability to attract potential applicants, face-to-face interviews are rated positively by the interviewees themselves (Anderson, 2003).

References

References are the second most popular method used in selection, yet have one of the lowest validities. Why is this? The popularity of references may be simply due to their long history of use in selection. For centuries, domestic servants needed a reference from their previous employer if they were to find another post (Delap, 2011). Their low validity is likely due to the lack of standardisation in the kind of information collected, who provides it and how it is used.

Nowadays, there are two main types of reference. The first is an attempt to verify claims that the applicant has made, such as job titles, reasons for leaving employment or educational attainments. This type of 'factual' reference needs to be supported by relevant evidence or the organisation providing the reference may leave itself open to legal action. The second type is a 'testimonial', which provides personal opinion on a candidate's suitability for a role. These are less useful to a potential employer as they are unlikely to provide a basis for discriminating between applicants. The best use for references is the former, and it may be even more useful for the employing organisation if they inform candidates at the outset that references will be used to check details of employment or education.

Psychometrics

Psychometric means 'measure of the mind' and psychometric tests are widely used in psychology. In their broadest sense, it could be argued that they are the basis of psychological science. Without a way to measure psychological phenomena, psychology as a science would simply not be possible. Within the field of selection or assessment, psychometric tests refer to either measures of *ability* or *personality* and Smith and Smith (2005, p. 187) define them as follows:

> Carefully chosen, systematic, standardised procedures for evoking a sample of responses from a candidate, which are evaluated in a quantifiable, fair and consistent way.

Psychometric tests do not measure a person's performance on the job, but rather the psychological characteristics that can contribute towards performance. This means that they are more flexible than other methods, such as work samples. Tests are also ideally suited to large-scale selection processes because they are cost-effective and many of them can now also be completed online. In the UK, a substantial number of organisations use psychometric tests, with recent figures ranging from about 20% using general mental ability tests to about 40% using literacy/numeracy tests (CIPD, 2011). There has been a significant increase in the number of organisations using these tests over the last couple of decades and they are particularly popular in the selection of graduate, managerial and professional candidates.

It is important, as with all other selection methods, that whatever psychological criterion we are assessing with a test has a clear and demonstrable link with job performance. If this link is not present, the test simply becomes an invalid measure. Reputable test publishers will have information on the types of people or jobs for which each of their tests is suitable.

It is worth noting that in most countries, people conducting psychometric tests need to have specific qualifications to demonstrate their competence and understanding. In the UK, these qualifications are overseen by the British Psychological Society and there is a register of qualified Test Users that organisations or individuals can consult (http://www.psychtesting.org.uk/). Three levels of qualification in psychometric test use are recognised by the European Federation of Psychological Associations (Assistant Test User, Test User and Specialist, depending on competence and knowledge). This effort has been led by UK psychologists and so far only the UK has moved to the new system, though other countries may follow soon.

Tests can be classified according to whether they seek to measure maximum performance or typical performance/behaviour. Tests of maximum performance are also known as ability or aptitude tests, while tests of typical performance include personality assessments. We will now look at each of these in more detail.

Maximum performance

Tests of maximum performance include cognitive ability tests as well as physical or sensory-motor tests. They aim to measure how well a person can do something, whether physical or mental. The tests can measure broad concepts, such as general intelligence, or specific skills, such as finger dexterity.

General Mental Ability (GMA) is a psychometric term for intelligence. Although there is a lot of discussion among theorists over precise definitions of what intelligence actually is, and it is often confused with general knowledge by laypeople, there is good agreement that intelligence is not *what* you know, but what you can *do* with it. It is a measure of how accurately and quickly you can process complex information. It is easy to see why it would be important in job performance, particularly for complex jobs or those which require the ability to learn quickly. GMA is an excellent predictor of both job performance and training success in many countries across the world (Salgado et al., 2003).

More specific tests can be used when we are seeking detailed, job-related abilities and can be measures of mental or physical ability. Common mental abilities that are tested in organisations include numerical, verbal, spatial and mechanical. For example, when recruiting graduates to a managerial position, an organisation might want to use a numerical reasoning test as part of its selection procedure rather than an minimum educational requirement. This would ensure that it did not overlook potentially promising applicants who did not complete a numeracy-focused degree. Physical tests can include sensory-motor and sensory acuity. For example, in recruiting people for assembly jobs, an organisation will want to identify those candidates who have good manual dexterity skills, and there are psychometric tests that will enable this.

Interestingly, GMA seems to be a better predictor of job performance than more specific tests (Salgado et al., 2003), but candidates tend to view tests with more concrete items as more relevant to the application process than those that are more abstract (Smither et al., 1993). This may be an important consideration for an organisation wishing to make itself more attractive to potential candidates.

The rest of this section considers each of these main selection methods in turn, in order of their popularity.

 Key Research Study

The Validity and Utility of Selection Methods in Personnel Psychology: Practical and Theoretical Implications of 85 Years of Research Findings

Frank Schmidt and John Hunter (1998)

Background: The most important characteristic of any employee selection method is its predictive validity – namely, how well it can predict a person's future work performance. Validity determines the practical value of a method: the better a method is at predicting high performance, the greater the payoff for the organisation. Previous meta-analyses have shown that the validity of a measure can be generalised across different situations and jobs, so new validity studies do not need to be conducted for every single job.

Aim: This study evaluates 85 years of psychological research into the use of different assessment methods for selection, training and development, in an effort to identify which methods have the highest validity.

Method: The validities for 19 different selection methods (such as General Mental Ability, Work Samples, Job Experience and even Graphology) were collected from the most recent meta-analyses. The validities reported in this study are therefore based on thousands of studies involving millions of employees.

Findings:

▸ GMA is recommended as the 'primary personnel measure for hiring decisions, and one can consider the remaining 18 personnel measures as supplements to GMA measures' (p. 266)
▸ GMA is also the best predictor of success in job training
▸ While work samples and structured interviews have a similar validity for job performance, they are much more costly to the organisation
▸ Job experience had a low validity for predicting performance (remember, this is only the number of years in a similar job, it does not include any information about how well that job was performed), while age was completely unrelated.

Implications: The most important determinants of job performance are: GMA, practice (as measured by work sample tests rather than experience) and conscientiousness. Two combinations of methods are recommended to organisations that can be used for applicants with or without experience: a GMA test combined with an integrity test (validity of 0.65) or a GMA test combined with a structured interview (validity of 0.63). Both of these combinations also have high validity for job training. For applicants with an understanding of the job, GMA combined with work sample is also recommended (validity 0.63).

Typical performance

These types of test include measures of personality, interests and values. Many people make judgements about these things when they are conducting an interview but, of course, there is no way of knowing how accurate that judgement might be (look back at the list of subjective biases). Using rigorously constructed psychometric tests gives us a way of assessing these criteria in a more reliable and valid way. These types of tests can be used in selection, just like ability tests, when there is a clear link with performance or trainability.

There are many different personality tests on the market. Tests used in selection tend to be based on a 'trait' model of personality. Traits are consistent and enduring patterns of behaviour that these tests can measure on a scale. Some personality tests measure very broad conceptualisations of traits while others focus on more specific ones.

The most well-supported model of personality, and one which has considerable support in occupational settings (e.g. Barrick and Mount, 1991), is the Big Five model. It identifies five broad personality traits:

- Extraversion – outgoing and confident vs reserved and quiet
- Agreeableness – friendly and considerate vs forthright and argumentative
- Emotional stability – calm and unemotional vs sensitive and easily upset
- Conscientiousness – organised and dependable vs flexible and disorganised
- Openness to experience – creative and imaginative vs down to earth and conventional.

Several meta-analyses have demonstrated how these traits are related to job performance and trainability. For example, Barrick, Mount and Judge (2001) found that Conscientiousness and Emotional stability are good predictors of overall work performance. The relationship of the other three factors to performance are also good, but less consistent as they depend more on the type of job.

Most broad-spectrum personality tests on the market will, however, measure a longer list of traits and be able to produce a Big Five score using subsequent calculations. Examples of these are the 16PF (16 Personality Factor, published by OPP) and the OPQ-32 (Occupational Personality Questionnaire with 32 scales, published by SHL). Other personality tests have been developed to measure narrower personality traits, such as integrity or resiliency. Narrower trait measures often have the advantage that they are shorter to complete than the broader measures, but it does mean that an organisation might have to buy lots of different tests rather than one broad one.

Other types of typical performance tests include values and interests. These are not often used in selection but are very good tools for finding out how to motivate and engage staff. They may also be used for assessing person–organisation fit, that is, how well an individual's values fit with those of the organisation. Evidence indicates that people whose values match the organisation's more closely are more committed to that organisation (Kristof-Brown et al., 2005). Interests inventories can also be very useful in careers counselling and development.

A note on 'faking' in psychometrics

A lot of people wonder whether psychometric tests can be faked. Given that they are commonly used in selection (whether for a job or a development opportunity), the motivation to increase one's chances of success will certainly be high. Ability tests cannot be faked as long as there is sufficient control to ensure that it is actually the candidate who is taking the test. However, recent work has shown that about 30–50% of job applicants fake personality questionnaires, and to an extent that would affect hiring decisions (Griffith et al., 2007). There are now special analyses for most personality questionnaires to indicate how 'socially desirable' someone's responses are. This helps the person analysing the scores to interpret them in relation to how other people have answered.

However, an interesting question revolves around the extent to which this 'faking' might actually continue into workplace behaviour. You might try to live up to the personality description you gave because you believe the job requires it. There is also recent research that confirms a large proportion of people report having different personalities at home and work. Many report that they behave very differently in the two roles but that both are still part of who they are. While maintaining different 'role' personalities can cause some people significant amounts of stress, what is more important is how *authentic* a person feels. People who have very different role personalities, but nonetheless feel they are being authentically themselves, will not experience the stress of those who feel they are putting on an act at work (Sutton, 2013).

Biodata

Biodata is a collection of information about a person's life and work experience, such as qualifications or job history, that is used to predict how well they will perform in a specific job. Biodata questions ask about a person's concrete experience, rather than hypothetical or abstract scenarios (Gunter et al., 1993). Results from these questions are then weighted according to how much they contribute to the desired outcome (e.g. high performance or low absenteeism) and collated much as they would be in a test, to give an overall score. You will probably be familiar with the way this kind of data is used because insurance companies use it when calculating risks, and therefore what premiums they will charge.

For example, a biodata question might ask for someone's reasons for leaving a job or when they left school and then use the scores for these questions to predict future performance. When the biodata predictors are correctly developed (by establishing validity as described above), they show a reasonable level of predictive validity, on a par with assessment centres and personality tests. Yet as we have seen, biodata is not a popular method of selection. Partly, this is likely to be due to the costs involved in developing validity data for each job; but it is also because these biodata items can have low face validity for applicants (Anderson et al., 2008).

Biodata is best used at the initial screening stage of selection and is not appropriate for later performance measurement. It can be particularly useful for organisations which receive hundreds of applications, as the scoring and calculations, once set up, can be computerised and help to sift through the many applicants. For a more detailed outline of how to develop and implement a biodata questionnaire, see Smith and Smith (2005).

Assessment centre

Although assessment centres are usually listed as a separate type of selection method, they are in fact simply a combination of other methods. They are based on the idea that the best way to accurately assess competencies is to use several different measures. So for a particular job (say an entry-level managerial role), a list of competencies is drawn up and a series of work sample exercises, psychometric tests and interviews are developed which will allow those competencies to be thoroughly assessed. As with interviews, it is essential that the assessors are properly trained (Lievens, 2001).

While a multi-measurement approach seems like a good idea and there is certainly some evidence showing that assessment centre ratings are related to supervisory performance ratings (Hermelin et al., 2007), research also indicates that there may be problems around the measurement of the competencies across different exercises. Sackett and Dreher (1982) found that ratings across all competencies *within* an exercise were consistent, but that ratings for each competency *across* the different exercises were not. This indicates that the ratings that were given

do not actually represent the competencies very well and may explain why assessment centres, despite including several very valid methods of assessment, do not perform as well overall.

Work sample

Work samples consistently show high validity in predicting job performance, as well as having high face validity for candidates. Instead of looking for 'signs' that a person will be good at a job, work samples can provide evidence of how the person performs in a situation as close to the real job as possible. This has the additional advantage of giving the candidate a realistic preview of what the job will be like, allowing a level of self-selection as well. They are, however, reasonably costly to develop as they need to be specific to a particular job.

Work samples can range from a description of a situation, to which a candidate then has to provide a written response, to a role-play scenario, which may include trained actors. A simple example might be asking candidates for a position involving data input to undertake a data input task and then assess them for accuracy and speed. However, different types of tasks are needed for jobs where the key performance criteria are more complex:

- Group exercises – candidates take part in a group discussion or task while being observed by assessors. These assessors must, of course, be using a consistent scoring scheme for this approach to be valid. Tasks can include discussions over business strategy, budgets, expansion into new markets etc.
- In-tray exercises – these work sample exercises typically take the form of a collection of documents, memos, emails etc., which the candidate has to read through, prioritise and develop an action plan for. They assess how well people can deal with a key part of many managerial and administrative roles.
- Role plays – these can include scenarios such as giving performance feedback to a subordinate or conducting a disciplinary meeting. The candidates are assessed on how well they take account of the preparatory information as well as their interpersonal skills.
- Presentations – this is a key skill for many jobs and commonly used as part of a selection procedure. The candidate can either be asked to prepare a presentation before attending the selection event or be given a limited amount of time to prepare within the event.

One of the drawbacks of work samples from a theoretical perspective is that it is not always clear what is being assessed. For example, in a group exercise several different factors may affect performance. While some of these may be a candidate's own interpersonal skills or verbal persuasiveness, his or her performance can also be affected by the behaviour of the rest of the group. That means that standardisation is more difficult in these kinds of exercises.

Activity Selecting an administrative assistant

You work in HR and your manager has tasked you with developing a selection process for a new administrative assistant to work in the department.

▶ First, identify the key skills and knowledge that you would want to assess in potential applicants.

▶ Second, develop an outline of how you would assess these things. Include details. For example, if you are going to hold interviews, what kind of questions would you ask?

FAIRNESS IN ASSESSMENT

So far, our discussions of measurements and selection methods have focused on the need to choose reliable and valid methods to underpin talent management decisions. But there is another important issue to consider, and that is how these methods are perceived and experienced by the people who take part in them. Fairness in selection and assessment is one of the most important determinants of how people perceive these methods. Perceptions of fairness are influenced by (Arvey and Renz, 1992):

- The components and processes of the selection procedure (e.g. how objective the procedure is or how consistently it is applied across the applicants)
- The nature of the information used to make decisions (e.g. job-related items are perceived as fairer than variables that seem unrelated, information collected in a way that seems to invade a candidate's privacy is seen as unfair)
- The results or outcomes of the selection procedure (e.g. do there seem to be the 'right' number of people from disadvantaged groups?).

Fairness is a complicated concept in selection, because selection is necessarily based on discriminating between people. This discrimination is fair if it is able to distinguish between people who (will) perform well and those who (will) perform less well – that is, when the measurement is related to work performance. The discrimination is unfair if it is based on measurements or characteristics that are unrelated to a person's work performance.

Unfair discrimination can occur in two ways, referred to as 'sameness' and 'difference' (Liff and Wajcman, 1996). Discrimination can be based on treating people differently when they are actually the same; for example, hiring a younger person rather than an equally well-qualified older person. Or it can be based on treating people the same when account should be taken of their differences. For example, the British police force used to have a height requirement of 5ft 10in. This was changed to 5ft 8in for men and 5ft 4in for women and then ultimately removed, as it was recognised that a height requirement was not essential to job performance and it unfairly discriminated against women and people from certain ethnic backgrounds. The French police force removed its minimum height requirement in 2010, also recognising that it was not a justifiable measure of how well someone could do the job.

Equality laws are an attempt to ensure that employers are not able to discriminate unfairly against applicants

Case Study Discrimination and fairness

Joe is the CEO of a large insurance company. When he first took over the position two years ago, there was a lot of upheaval in the top management and he appointed a new Finance Director and HR Director, both of whom were women. He was pleased with their performance and received good feedback from their departments. However, within the last six months, both new directors have gone on maternity leave and one has given notice that she will not be returning to work. Joe is now involved in the selection process for a new Finance Director.

▶ If you were in Joe's position, how would you feel?

▶ Do you think it would be fair of Joe to ask potential female candidates for the post if they intended to have a baby in the next few years?

▶ What do you think the impact of this experience will be on the selection efforts of this organisation?

© GETTY

based on their race, ethnicity, gender, religion, disability and so on. The advantage of using more reliable and scientific approaches to assess people's suitability for jobs or work performance is that this kind of discrimination can be reduced. However, it is unfortunately not true that these methods will guarantee equality of treatment: there are the problems of *bias* and *adverse impact*.

Bias

Bias occurs when a measure (whether a psychometric test or scores on a structured interview or any other measure) systematically over- or underestimates the performance of people from different groups. Imagine we are evaluating a sales team and compare supervisor ratings of performance with actual sales figures. We might find that the supervisor ratings are consistently lower for women than men, but this does not correspond to a difference in their respective sales volumes. In this case, the measure (supervisor rating) is either overestimating the men's performance or underestimating the women's. This can also occur with psychometric tests. To continue our example, imagine that all the salespeople complete a test designed to measure their persuasiveness and interpersonal skills. We find that women score higher on this test than men, but it is again not reflected in a difference in sales figures, showing that this test would provide a biased assessment of the salespeople's performance.

Adverse impact

Adverse impact occurs when a difference between groups on a particular measure results in a lower success rate for one group. This could be success rates in hiring decisions or in the likelihood of being selected for development opportunities. Yet many methods of assessing people which are commonly used in selection show sub-group differences in scores. In a comprehensive review of mainly US evidence, Hough et al. (2001) summarised the differences between groups (age, gender and ethnic groups) on three main groups of criteria commonly used in employee selection (cognitive abilities, personality and physical abilities). They concluded that many methods could result in adverse impact on different groups and made detailed suggestions for how organisations could combat this, for example in providing test coaching for candidates who are not familiar with psychometric tests. Many psychometric test publishers also provide example questions and items on their websites to allow test-takers the opportunity to become familiar with the way questions are phrased and how they should respond to them.

In assessing adverse impact, a good rule of thumb is the four-fifths rule, which originated in the USA. It states that selection is biased, or shows adverse impact, if the selection rate for one group of people is less than four-fifths (or 80%) the rate of another group. This is only a rule of thumb rather than a definite indication of bias, and should be seen as a warning flag that further investigations might be needed.

The best way to avoid bias and adverse impact, as well as increase the perceived fairness of an assessment measure, is of course to ensure that the measure is closely related to actual job performance. As we have seen throughout the chapter, this relies on an accurate job analysis that identifies competencies associated with high performance and an informed choice of method that will reliably and validly measure those competencies.

 International Perspectives Variation in selection practices

Most job applications begin with a CV or application form. In some countries you are nearly always required to attach a photo (e.g. Germany or Austria). In others (e.g. UK or USA) this never happens. There are relatively few studies comparing what type of selection methods are most popular in different countries and those that do exist tend to focus on comparing countries within a particular region (e.g. Europe). However, several differences have been noted; for example, assessment centres are more popular in the UK and Germany than other Western European countries (Shackleton and Newell, 1994).

An interesting question is why these differences might exist. Is it tradition or differences in available resources? Or could it be due to different cultural perceptions of how appropriate each of these methods is?

Ryan et al. (1999) addressed this question in a survey of nearly 1,000 organisations in 20 different countries from all continents except South America. They looked at the relationship between the country's culture (as measured by Hofstede's cultural dimensions) and the type and number of selection methods used. They found clear differences in the selection procedures used in different countries, the most notable of which was a difference in the use of structured interviews, with about 60% of organisations in Australia and New Zealand reporting they used fixed interview questions compared with just over 10% in Italy and Sweden. Graphology was used very rarely in every country except France. They also found that countries high in uncertainty avoidance (i.e. they feel uncomfortable with uncertainty and ambiguity) prefer to have more objective data to base their decisions on, which was evident in their higher use of selection tests. Educational qualifications are a popular contributor to hiring decisions worldwide.

While cultural differences are certainly related to the types of selection methods used, several authors have suggested that cultural dimensions alone are not enough to explain the variation in selection practices. Steiner and Gilliland, for example, note that there is a certain level of consistency in people's perceptions of the fairness of different selection methods across several countries (Steiner and Gilliland, 2001). In fact, it seems that the differences between countries are not that large and the main determinant of how fair a method is perceived to be is job-relatedness, no matter what country the applicant is from.

Discussion point

Do you think attaching a photo to your CV is a good idea or not? Why? To what extent do you think your view on this is affected by your culture and the perceived fairness of this approach?

SUMMARY

We started this chapter by considering talent management from both a business and a psychological perspective. While the former focuses on why talent management is beneficial to the organisation, the latter considers questions around how we can accurately measure talent. We reviewed the central role of competencies here, a topic we will return to in the next chapter.

The second section introduced the concepts of reliability and validity in measuring talent, as a basis for considering the different methods of identifying talent in the selection process. After looking at each of these methods in detail, we then moved on to evaluate selection processes for bias and adverse impact, making recommendation for managers and organisations wishing to avoid these pitfalls.

TEST YOURSELF

Brief Review Questions

1   What is a competency framework?
2   Define reliability and explain why it is important in selection.
3   List and describe the different types of validity.
4   What is the difference between behavioural and situational interviews?
5   How would you define adverse impact?

Discussion or Essay Questions

1   What is talent management and how can it be informed by psychology?

2   To what extent is 'faking' in the job application process a problem for organisations?
3   Evaluate the different methods of selection and make a recommendation as to which is the 'best'.
4   How important is fairness in employee assessment? Do you think there are ever any circumstances when it is justifiable to use an assessment procedure that does not seem to be fair?

FURTHER READING

- For more detail on the use of psychometrics in employee assessment, read M. Smith and P. Smith, *Testing People at Work*. Oxford: Blackwell, 2005.
- For an interesting comparison of CVs in different countries, see http://www.jobsite.co.uk/career/advice/tailoring_foreign_cvs.html.
- For current research in selection and assessment, the *International Journal of Selection and Assessment* is a useful resource.

References

ANDERSON, N. 2003. Applicant and recruiter reactions to new technology in selection: a critical review and agenda for future research. *International Journal of Selection and Assessment*, 11, 121–36.

ANDERSON, N. & CUNNINGHAM-SNELL, N. 2000. Personnel Selection. In Chmiel, N. (ed.) *Introduction to Work and Organizational Psychology: A European Perspective*. Oxford, Blackwell.

ANDERSON, N., SALGADO, J., SCHINKEL, S. & CUNNINGHAM-SNELL, N. 2008. Staffing the Organization: An Introduction to Personnel Selection and Assessment. In Chmiel, N. (ed.) *An Introduction to Work and Organizational Psychology: A European Perspective*, 2nd edn, Oxford, Blackwell.

ARVEY, R. & RENZ, G. 1992. Fairness in the selection of employees. *Journal of Business Ethics*, 11, 331–40.

BARRICK, M. R. & MOUNT, M. K. 1991. The big five personality dimensions and job performance: a meta-analysis. *Personnel Psychology*, 44, 1–26.

BARRICK, M. R., MOUNT, M. K. & JUDGE, T. A. 2001. Personality and performance at the beginning of the new millennium: what do we know and where do we go next? *International Journal of Selection and Assessment*, 9, 9–30.

BARTRAM, D. 2005. The Great Eight competencies: a criterion-centric approach to validation. *Journal of Applied Psychology*, 90, 1185–203.

BARTRAM, D., ROBERTSON, I. T. & CALLINAN, M. 2002. Introduction: A Framework for Examining

Organizational Effectiveness. In Robertson, I. T., Callinan, M. & Bartram, D. (eds.) *Organizational Effectiveness: The Role of Psychology*. Chichester, John Wiley & Sons Ltd.

BOYATZIS, R. E. 1982. *The Competent Manager: A Model for Effective Performance – Richard E. Boyatzis*. Google Books, New York, Wiley.

CAMPION, M. A. & PALMER, D. K. 1997. A review of structure in the selection interview. *Personnel Psychology*, 50, 655–702.

CIPD (CHARTERED INSTITUTE OF PERSONNEL DEVELOPMENT). 2011. *Resourcing and Talent Planning Annual Survey*. London, CIPD.

COLLINGS, D. G. & MELLAHI, K. 2009. Strategic talent management: a review and research agenda. *Human Resource Management Review*, 19, 304–13.

DELAP, L. 2011. *Knowing Their Place: Domestic Servants in Twentieth Century Britain*. Oxford, Oxford University Press.

GREENWALD, A. G. & BANAJI, M. R. 1995. Implicit social cognition: attitudes, self-esteem, and stereotypes. *Psychological Review*, 102, 4–27.

GRIFFITH, R. L., CHMIELOWSKI, T. & YOSHITA, Y. 2007. Do applicants fake? An examination of the frequency of applicant faking behavior. *Personnel Review*, 36, 341–55.

GUNTER, B., FURNHAM, A. & DRAKELY, R. 1993. *Biodata: Biographical Indicators of Business Performance*. London, Routledge.

HERMELIN, E., LIEVENS, F. & ROBERTSON, I. T. 2007. The validity of assessment centres for the prediction of supervisory performance ratings: a meta-analysis. *International Journal of Selection and Assessment*, 15, 405–11.

HOUGH, L. M., OSWALD, F. L. & PLOYHART, R. E. 2001. Determinants, detection and amelioration of adverse impact in personnel selection procedures: issues, evidence and lessons learned. *International Journal of Selection and Assessment*, 9, 152–94.

KRISTOF-BROWN, A. L., ZIMMERMAN, R. D. & JOHNSON, E. C. 2005. Consequences of individuals' fit at work: a meta-analysis of person–job, person–organization, person–group, and person–supervisor fit. *Personnel Psychology*, 58, 281–342.

LATHAM, G. P. & SAARI, L. M. 1984. Do people do what they say? Further studies on the situational interview. *Journal of Applied Psychology*, 69, 569–73.

LATHAM, G. P., SAARI, L. M., PURSELL, E. D. & CAMPION, M. A. 1980. The situational interview. *Journal of Applied Psychology*, 65, 422–7.

LEWIS, R. E. & HECKMAN, R. J. 2006. Talent management: a critical review. *Human Resource Management Review*, 16, 139–54.

LIEVENS, F. 2001. Assessor training strategies and their effects on accuracy, inter rater reliability, and discriminant validity. *Journal of Applied Psychology*, 86, 255–64.

LIFF, S. & WAJCMAN, J. 1996. 'Sameness' and 'difference' revisited: which way forward for equal opportunity initiatives? *Journal of Management Studies*, 33, 79–94.

MICHAELS, E., HANDFIELD-JONES, H. & AXELROD, B. 2001. *The War for Talent*. Boston, Harvard Business School Publishing.

ROBERTSON, I. T. & SMITH, M. 2001. Personnel selection. *Journal of Occupational and Organizational Psychology*, 74, 441–72.

RYAN, A. M., MCFARLAND, L. & SHL, H. B. 1999. An international look at selection practices: nation and culture as explanations for variability in practice. *Personnel Psychology*, 52, 359–92.

RYAN, G., EMMERLING, R. J. & SPENCER, L. M. 2009. Distinguishing high-performing European executives: the role of emotional, social and cognitive competencies. *Journal of Management Development*, 28(9), 859–75.

SACKETT, P. R. & DREHER, G. F. 1982. Constructs and assessment center dimensions: some troubling empirical findings. *Journal of Applied Psychology*, 67, 401–10.

SALGADO, J. F., ANDERSON, N., MOSCOSO, S., BERTUA, C. & DE FRUYT, F. 2003. International validity generalization of GMA and cognitive abilities: a European community meta-analysis. *Personnel Psychology*, 56, 573–605.

SCHMIDT, F. L. & HUNTER, J. E. 1998. The validity and utility of selection methods in personnel psychology: practical and theoretical implications of 85 years of research findings. *Psychological Bulletin*, 124, 262–74.

SHACKLETON, V. & NEWELL, S. 1994. European management selection methods: a comparison of five countries. *International Journal of Selection and Assessment*, 2, 91–102.

SMITH, M. & SMITH, P. 2005. *Testing People at Work: Competencies in Psychometric Testing*. Oxford, Blackwell.

SMITHER, J. W., REILLY, R. R., MILLSAP, R. E., AT, T. K. P. & STOFFEY, R. W. 1993. Applicant reactions to selection procedures. *Personnel Psychology*, 46, 49–76.

SODERQUIST, K. E., PAPALEXANDRIS, A., IOANNOU, G. & PRASTACOS, G. 2010. From task-based to competency-based: a typology and process supporting a critical HRM transition. *Personnel Review*, 39, 325–46.

SPENCER, L. M., MCCLELLAND, D. C. & SPENCER, S. M. 1992. *Competency Assessment Methods: History and State of the Art*. London, Hay/McBer Research Press.

STEINER, D. D. & GILLILAND, S. W. 2001. Procedural justice in personnel selection: international and cross-cultural perspectives. *International Journal of Selection and Assessment*, 9, 124–37.

SUTTON, A. 2013. *Work and Home Personality: Differentiation or Integration? European Association of Work and Organizational Psychology*. Munster, Germany.

TETT, R. P., GUTERMAN, H. A., BLEIER, A. & MURPHY, P. J. 2000. Development and content validation of a 'hyperdimensional' taxonomy of managerial competence. *Human Performance*, 13–205.

WERNIMONT, P. F. & CAMPBELL, J. P. 1968. Signs, samples, and criteria. *Journal of Applied Psychology*, 52, 372–6.

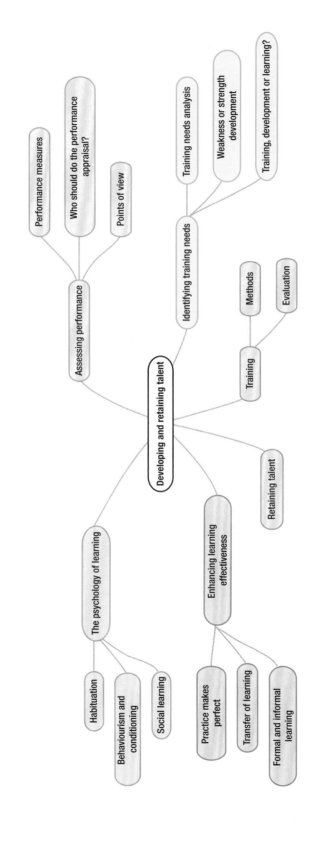

In Chapter 2 we saw that effective management of an organisation's talent is about having the right people in the right place at the right time. We focused in that chapter on how we can make the best recruitment decisions – that is, how we can bring the right people into the organisation. Once people are in place, the next step in talent management is to develop employees. No organisation will survive if it relies exclusively on outside recruitment to provide its needed talent. So, in this chapter, we will discuss how managers can use psychological insights to develop and retain the talent that they already have in the organisation.

We will start by considering how we can assess job-holders' performance, remembering that many of the issues around performance assessment for job incumbents are similar to those we discussed around assessing job candidates. This assessment will provide the basis for an examination of training needs and lead into a consideration of the role of psychology in training and development, particularly the psychology of learning. The concluding section of the chapter will describe and evaluate various training methods, including the recent rise in coaching as an area of psychological expertise. Finally, we will round off by looking at how organisations can retain talent, drawing the chapter together by discussing the increasingly popular concept of employer branding.

This chapter will help you answer the following questions:

1   How can we assess employee performance?
2   How can an individual's training needs be identified?
3   What kind of training methods are there and how can their effectiveness be evaluated?
4   How do people learn?
5   What can we do to build more effective training programmes?

ASSESSING PERFORMANCE

The major issue facing those who are trying to decide on the 'best person for the job' at the selection stage is how to accurately judge future performance. You might think that this problem becomes much easier to solve once a person is in a job: at that stage it is no longer about prediction but simply about judging current performance. Unfortunately, it is rarely this easy. All the biases that we looked at in Chapter 2 influence our judgements in the performance appraisal (PA) as well.

In addition, politics can be an issue in performance appraisal: the rewards and sanctions associated with performance judgements can be substantial and the individuals involved, whether appraiser or appraisee, may well be aiming for outcomes that are different from those of the organisation. This section starts by outlining the

ways performance is measured, before considering issues around who should carry out appraisals and what impact their personal aims will have on the process.

Performance measures

As with selection, our performance appraisal system is only as good as the measures we use. If we are not measuring the right things, we will not be able to build up an accurate picture of an employee's performance. Judgements about performance should be based on an analysis of specific tasks that the employee is expected to do, and the more focused these tasks the better. Output performance criteria have the clearest relation to performance and can include quantity (for example, sales volume) or quality (for example, number of errors made) and, in order to measure employees' performance in regard to the overall aims of the organisation, should ideally be related to organisational goals. These kinds of output criteria are helpful in that they provide an objective basis for performance judgements, but there can be problems in specifying them for jobs where the outputs are not clear. There is also the problem that they do not take into account situational effects, such as whether the employee had the needed resources to achieve the output.

Although clear output criteria are ideal, many appraisals are based on judgements about a person rather than their performance. Employees may be rated, for example, on their 'initiative' or 'creativity' or how approachable they are. While these may be perceived as important qualities in the job or for the organisation, a difficulty arises in how they are judged. Behavioural criteria are more useful since the behaviour of the employee can be directly observed and coded in terms of its effectiveness or desirability.

We saw in the previous chapter how competency assessment is used in selection. Many organisations now recognise the utility of competencies for HR-wide applications, from selection to performance appraisal, training and development. Using this kind of *competency framework* enables the organisation to integrate HR practices through the whole employee life-cycle, as illustrated in the Case Study 'A competency framework at PubGrub'.

As well as there being a range of performance criteria that can be assessed, there is also a range of methods used to assess them. Measures can be standardised across many employees or be individual to each employee. We will now look at these types of measure in more detail.

Standardised measures

To be able to distinguish between employees' performances we will need a standardised measurement. This usually involves some kind of rating scale for each behaviour or competency of interest that can be used

Case Study A competency framework at PubGrub

PubGrub is a leading operator of managed pubs and pub restaurants in the UK with several different brands under its umbrella. For a few years now it has been using a single competency framework to underpin selection and performance appraisal and wants to conduct some research to find out how effective the framework is. There were seven competencies identified as important to performance and success at PubGrub, including *Understanding the Business*, *Focusing on the Guest* and *Living the Values*.

As part of a selection process that included ability tests, candidates for management positions took

part in a structured interview with questions designed to assess the competencies. Performance appraisals were conducted with the line manager 6 to 12 months after selection and performance was assessed on the same 7 competencies as in the interview.

Three main findings emerged when employees' ratings at interview and performance appraisal were compared:

1 Employees' average rating at interview was higher than at their performance appraisal.
2 Employees' ratings on individual competencies at interview were mostly unrelated to their ratings in their appraisal. The only exception to this was the *Understands the Business* competency. Ratings on this competency were also related to performance ratings on three other competencies.
3 Finally, employees who had left the business were compared with those who had stayed. Leavers were found to have had lower ratings at selection on three of the competencies: *Understands the Business*, *Building Capability* and *Making it Happen*.

Adapted from Sutton and Watson (2013)

▸ Why do you think the competency *Understands the Business* is so important to success in this organisation? Do you think it would be similarly important in other organisations?

▸ If you wanted to apply to be a manager at PubGrub, what could you do to enhance your chances of success?

▸ If you were the consultant who carried out this assessment of the competency framework, what recommendations would you make to PubGrub?

---

for all employees. These can be graphical, where the rater marks performance on a line:

Attribute	Poor		Excellent
Punctuality			

Alternatively, rating scales can assign a letter to offer a simple assessment of how well an employee has met expectations, as follows:

E = Exceeds expectations
M = Meets expectations
B = Below expectations

The more clearly a scale is labelled, the higher its reliability will be because it is not subject to individual idiosyncrasies in interpretation. In our example above, one rater might think that arriving on time for work nearly every day was 'excellent' punctuality, while another might think that being late a couple of times was 'poor'. Recognition of the importance of individual interpretation of scales led to the development of the Behaviourally Anchored Rating Scales (BARS), which we looked at briefly in Chapter 2. BARS are based on a job analysis which identifies specific behaviours that are more or less effective for job performance and then uses them to anchor a numerical scale to rate an employee's behaviour. The downside of BARS is that developing them is a long, complicated process when compared with the simple scales above. An example BARS for punctuality might be:

1	Late to start work and causes others delays.
2	
3	Slow to start work but does not hold up or delay others.
4	
5	Starts work on time and meets deadlines for others.

An alternative to BARS is the Behaviour Observation Scale (BOS), which the appraiser uses to rate the frequency of specific job-related behaviours. There is some indication that appraisees are more satisfied with their appraisal when this type of scale is used (Tziner et al., 2000). Obviously, BOS can only be used when the rater has ample opportunity to observe the individual at work.

Attribute	Never				Always
Punctual					

Individualised measures

While standardised measures can be used to compare different employees with each other, perhaps to determine who best deserves a bonus, more individualised measures can be useful too. These are particularly helpful where it can be difficult to find a clear outcome measure of performance or when there are many different ways to effectively do the job. The main approach we are going to consider here is Management by Objectives (MBO), or goal-setting performance appraisal, which is both widely used and has very solid research support.

Goal-setting is used as a basis for performance appraisal in MBO. This approach is very good at improving performance and has the advantage that the measures of performance (goals) can be developed jointly by supervisor and supervisee and be linked to organisational strategy. Because the goals need to be specific, they provide clear performance measures. However, there are some drawbacks, not least of which is that goal-setting has less effect on performance with more complex tasks. This may be due to the difficulty of clearly specifying the goals. The other drawback is that the more tailored to the individual the performance measures are, the less we can compare them. (We will return to MBO when we consider motivation in Chapter 4.)

A review by Locke and Latham, the originators of goal-setting theory, summarised the findings of years of research and recommended goal-setting as an effective tool for performance management (Locke and Latham, 2002). They found that setting specific goals resulted in higher performance than simply telling people to 'do their best' and that challenging but obtainable goals promote higher performance than easy goals. An important moderator of the goal–performance relationship is our commitment to the goals: the more we are involved in setting the goals, the more committed we are to them and the higher our performance.

Comparison

Because one of the reasons organisations conduct performance appraisals is that they need to make decisions based on discriminating between employees' performance, we will look at different ways these comparisons can be made. The first step is, of course, to identify an appropriate measure, as we have observed above. Once that is done, the appraiser needs to rank all the employees. This can be done in three ways:

1 Simple ranking – the appraiser ranks people in first, second, third place and so on. They may be allowed to give some people 'tie' places if they cannot distinguish between them. The difficulty with this approach is that, while the top and bottom performers might be easy to identify, it becomes difficult to rank those in the middle.

2 Paired ranking – in this approach, the appraiser lists every pair of employees and decides which person in each pair is the better performer. By working through every possible pairing, the end result is a ranked list with no ties. It is, however, a time-consuming process and can force a ranking when there is in fact no difference in performance.

3 Forced distribution – the appraiser is only allowed to identify a certain percentage of employees as above or below average. For example, only the top 10–15% can be assigned to the 'outstanding' category and put forward for promotion. Or the bottom 10–15% are actively managed out of the organisation. This is the approach recommended by the authors of *The War for Talent* (Michaels et al., 2001), as a way of enabling the organisation to focus its resources on those who contribute the most to its success. However, this can lead to problems if more than the specified number are genuinely excellent or poor performers.

These rankings can then be used to make decisions about promotion, training opportunities or pay.

Rating reliability

An important consideration in assessing performance measurements is the reliability of the ratings that are being made. Viswesvaran et al. (1996) compared the reliability of peer and supervisor ratings and found that while intra-rater reliability was high, inter-rater reliability was much lower. That means that individual raters showed good consistency in how they rated several different appraisees, but an appraisee was likely to be rated quite differently by different raters. Interestingly, ratings by supervisors were more reliable than those of peers. Subsequent research (Viswesvaran et al., 2005) found that this difference was probably due to supervisors being less subject to the halo effect than peers were. When this kind of error was controlled for, the authors found that a single factor still underlay the performance ratings. They suggested that this underlying factor was likely to have been a combination of the appraisee's organisational citizenship behaviours and his or her mental ability and conscientiousness. In essence, the research indicates that you will be assessed as having higher performance if you voluntarily go beyond the basic requirements of your job and generally appear to be hard-working and intelligent, rather than being good at specific aspects of your work.

Who should carry out the performance appraisal?

Although performance appraisals have traditionally been carried out by supervisors, there is an increasing movement towards including other raters. We saw above how one study had identified that supervisors may be more reliable in their ratings than peers, but many organisations now use *360°* or *multi-source feedback* as a way of helping employees find out how their performance is viewed by supervisors, direct reports, peers and even external clients. A typical 360° appraisal is illustrated in the following case study.

 Case Study 360° appraisal

Mike's company has recently introduced 360° appraisals for its management-level staff. Questionnaires are sent out to Mike's senior manager, other managers who Mike works closely with at the same level and to his direct reports. All these people are asked to rate Mike's performance on several criteria: his ability to build relationships, to plan and organise, use analytical thinking and to develop others.

The results are collated into an overall report. This is theoretically anonymous in that the respondents are not named but, instead, average marks from the three groups are collated. The following diagram is shown in Mike's feedback report and illustrates the findings:

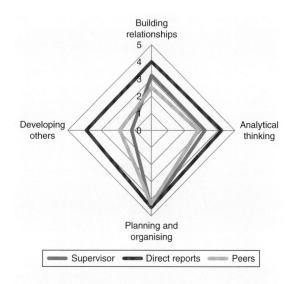

▸ Based on this feedback, what are Mike's main strengths and weaknesses?

▸ Which criteria show the greatest agreement and which show the greatest difference between the ratings he gets from different groups? What do you think might be the cause of these differences?

▸ Why do you think Mike's direct reports give him the highest ratings overall? What does this mean for the reliability of these results?

Appraisal based on several raters can be particularly useful in identifying development opportunities, but differences between raters can be a problem if reward decisions are going to be based on them. While some people have suggested that a lack of agreement between raters is a serious problem for multi-source ratings, Bozeman (1997) points out that we should not expect the raters to agree completely. Each rater will have experienced different performance criteria, and all these experiences are valid. It is not just a supervisor's assessment of an individual's performance that is important, but also the external client's or colleague's. So far from expecting agreement, Bozeman suggests that we should focus on gaining a rounder picture of the person's performance. This more rounded picture is particularly helpful for development.

One of the difficulties with multi-source ratings is the complexity of the information produced. Instead of a simple rating from one person, the organisation has to find a way to deal with multiple ratings for each employee. In implementing a 360° feedback system, several questions need to be dealt with, for example, how should different ratings be weighted or how anonymous should the ratings be? Many 360° feedback systems are abandoned after only a couple of years, probably because of problems dealing with these issues (Fletcher, 2001). Yet there are some steps that we can follow to maximise the chances of success in multi-source appraisals (DeNisi and Kluger, 2000):

- Use them for development only, not for decision-making. Or, if the organisation insists on using them for decision-making, make sure that the outcomes are clear to the appraisees and that they include a goal-setting component.
- Be careful not to overwhelm appraisees with information and ensure feedback is given effectively. This is best done in a one-to-one interview, giving the appraisee the opportunity to discuss the ratings and the appropriate support to deal with potentially upsetting feedback.
- Use the system regularly so that employees can see they are improving.
- Perhaps most importantly, evaluate the system for its effectiveness.

Points of view in performance appraisal

Organisations introduce performance appraisals in order to recognise and improve performance. This can be done in several ways, and research reviews consistently indicate that information gathered in PAs is used for several different purposes concurrently, with the main applications being salary decisions, feedback on performance to employees and identification of strengths and weaknesses (Cleveland et al., 1989). Unfortunately, these aims are potentially incompatible with each other since they involve concurrent within- and between-person comparisons. We can gain an insight into the impact these conflicting aims will have on the PA by considering the appraisal from the points of view of the organisation, the appraiser and the appraisee.

The organisation's point of view

An appraisal can be a means of improving performance in several ways. First, it can provide the employee with feedback on his or her performance, highlighting what has been done well and what needs to be improved. Secondly, distinguishing between employees ensures that bonuses or performance-based rewards can be distributed to those who have earned them. Thirdly, there is a widespread belief that appraisals can be motivating for staff, with managers providing recognition and appreciation of a job well done. And finally, appraisals can also be used to provide clarity in cases where performance is poor by recording unsatisfactory performance.

An alternative use for appraisals is as a basis for development and training. This is often the rhetoric that surrounds performance appraisals in many organisations. The performance appraisal is seen as an opportunity for managers and subordinates to have an open conversation about the subordinate's strengths and weaknesses, to identify areas where the worker may benefit from further training, to identify potential and to discuss opportunities for career development.

The appraisee's point of view

The way the individuals involved in the process view an appraisal, however, can be very different. If employees view the appraisal as a means of gaining positive rewards (whether bonuses or desired development opportunities) and avoiding negative outcomes (such as negative feedback or even dismissal), they will want to present themselves in as positive a light as possible. This is incompatible with a frank and honest discussion about their weaknesses; so, instead of giving an honest assessment of where they are experiencing difficulties, appraisees may exaggerate their own performance or try to improve their appraiser's opinion of them.

The appraiser's point of view

But it is not just the appraisees who will want to use the performance appraisal for their own ends. The managers who conduct the appraisal often have motives that are in conflict with what the organisation is trying to achieve and there is a risk that they may change the performance ratings they give as a result of political factors (Fletcher, 2008). Sims et al. (1987) conducted interviews with 60 executives who had experience of conducting performance appraisals and found that many of them openly admitted manipulating appraisals. The executives' main aim was not necessarily an accurate rating of appraisees' current performance, but a rating that would maintain or improve the appraisees' performance. They often did this by inflating the ratings. The aim was to avoid demotivating their staff by giving negative ratings or to avoid the discomfort or conflict that arises when giving negative feedback. They were also aware of personal circumstances that had impacted on an individual's performance, or wished to reward effort rather than final results. They sometimes even used the appraisal system as a way of promoting difficult employees 'out of the way'. Several also felt that it would reflect badly on their own managerial skills if the department seemed to have low performance ratings. Less commonly, appraisers gave overly negative ratings of performance out of a desire to scare people into working harder, to punish them for something or even to push them out of the organisation.

It is not just the individual point of view that is important in performance appraisals. In the International Perspectives section below we explore how the effect of national culture on performance appraisal effectiveness is important too.

International Perspectives Cultural effect on performance appraisals

Performance appraisal is an essential part of managing talent within the organisation. But many of the studies of appraisal effectiveness have focused on US or Western European organisations, with little consideration of how national culture might affect outcomes. As more and more organisations become multinational and global, they need to consider how to adapt their practices to new cultures. In a study of nearly 6,000 organisations from 21 different countries, Peretz and Fried (2012) investigated how national cultural values affected performance appraisal practices and the effect of those appraisals on organisational outcomes.

They found that national culture certainly did influence performance appraisal practices. For example, in countries with a low power distance (where people relate to each other more as equals, rather than with large power differentials) there was an increased use of 360° appraisals. In countries with high uncertainty avoidance (where people prefer to have set procedures to deal with any eventuality rather than dealing with events in an ad hoc manner), performance appraisals used more formal systems. And in countries that were more collectivist, there was an increased use of organisation-development appraisals rather than individual ones. The study also showed that where there was greater fit between the culture and the PA practices used by the organisation, outcomes such as absenteeism, innovation and quality were improved.

This study highlights how important it is for PA systems to fit with the cultural values of the country they are used in. The authors make four important observations that can guide the use of performance appraisals in different cultures:

1 360° appraisal (which is an expensive and complex system) will be effective only in countries with low power distance.
2 Organisations are likely to benefit from PA only if they are in a future-oriented society as opposed to a past- or present-oriented society.
3 Individual-based PA will work only in individualist societies. In collectivist cultures, organisation-development PA will be better.
4 Formal PA systems benefit organisations in countries that are high on uncertainty avoidance, but do not make much difference in low uncertainty avoidance cultures.

Discussion point

What kind of performance appraisal would you personally want? Why? Can you relate your preference to the values of the culture you grew up in? How would you feel if you were given a performance appraisal based on different cultural values?

Having considered the different ways performance appraisal can be carried out and how the results are used, we now turn to one of the primary applications of appraisals: identifying training and development needs.

IDENTIFYING TRAINING NEEDS

Training needs analysis

A thorough training needs analysis (TNA) requires an analysis of three different levels: the organisation, the person and the specific task. We need to know what the organisation's goals are to ensure that the training feeds into the overall strategy and also what resources the organisation has available to provide the training. There is also the issue of analysing the support for learning in the organisation. As we will see when we look at learning in more detail, one of the key factors influencing training effectiveness is the support of senior managers and a positive training climate.

Secondly, we need to identify the knowledge, skills and abilities required to effectively perform the job or task.

As for the procedure for conducting a job analysis as a precursor to any selection procedure, we first outline the tasks and then identify what individual characteristics or knowledge would be needed to fulfil those tasks.

And finally, we identify the individuals who (a) need to be trained and (b) have the motivation and prerequisite skills to undertake the training. Performance assessment is part of this procedure, but it must be an assessment of performance on the specific tasks we are interested in rather than a global assessment of how well a person is doing the job. Many of the techniques we covered in the previous chapter on selection can be useful here, although it is particularly important that a thorough analysis does not simply rely on a single rating from a supervisor, as is often the case in performance appraisals. If you need a reminder as to why this is, review the section in Chapter 2 about Bias and Fairness.

Weakness vs strength development

Training needs analysis often tends to take a deficit view of performance: we look for the aspects of the task or job that a person cannot yet do and train them to be able to do it. A growing alternative to this approach is to focus training and development on people's strengths rather than their weaknesses. The proponents of this approach suggest that deficit-focused development will only ever result in average or mediocre performance and that it is only by using and building on our strengths that we can achieve excellence. We will return to this concept in Chapter 10, 'Positive Psychology at Work'.

Training, development or learning?

Learning is core to effective work performance and is one of the foundation concepts in psychology. At work, learning can be thought of as underpinning two main activities: training and development. Training focuses on learning the knowledge, skills and abilities that we need for our current job, or perhaps a job we will take on in the near future. Development, on the other hand, is more about growth in our personal and professional lives that will prepare us for our future career (Sonnentag et al., 2008). So as to understand how we can best train and develop people at work, we need a solid understanding of the psychology of learning. An indication of the problems that can arise when we do not have this understanding is illustrated in the following Fad or Fact section.

 Fad or Fact? Learning styles

If you have had any experience of study skills training or gone on any 'how to learn' workshops, it is highly likely you will have come across the idea of learning styles. This concept suggests that different people learn things in different ways, that each of us has a 'style' that suits us best and that we should try to find learning opportunities that match our style. It is used by students who try to improve their learning and by educators to improve their teaching.

There are countless models that try to describe what these different learning styles are: Coffield et al. (2004) conducted a review and found over 70 models, which they grouped into five categories:

1 Dispositional models – these hold that people are born with a particular learning style and that this cannot be changed.
2 Cognitive – these approaches state that people have generalised habits of thought which influence how they will learn most effectively.
3 Stable personality type – models in this group see learning style as part of personality and as being reasonably stable over time.
4 Flexibly stable learning preferences – this set of learning styles is based on Kolb's four-stage model of how we learn and holds that each

person has a preference for one part of the learning process.
5 Learning approaches and strategies – models in this group do not claim we have a fixed style but rather that we choose different strategies to suit different learning situations.

Stop and think: have you ever completed a learning styles questionnaire? (If not, you might like to try the very popular Honey and Mumford questionnaire, which you can easily find online.)

▸ What did you think of the results? Did they help you? If so, how?
▸ Did you find you experienced any drawbacks as a result of identifying your learning style?

Learning styles are a very popular concept and often seem to have intuitive appeal for teachers and students alike. You may think, for example, that lectures 'don't work' for you and you learn much better when you discuss a case study with a group of other students. Or perhaps you really dislike discussing things with others and would much rather take notes in a lecture and think about the theories. But is there any evidence to back up the idea that we do actually learn in different ways?

A recent, and very thorough, review of learning styles (Pashler, 2009) concluded unequivocally that there was *no evidence* to support the use of learning styles in education. The authors do note that both children and adults express preferences for how information is presented to them. They also emphasised that people clearly have different abilities in thinking and dealing with specific types of information. But, for the learning styles concept to be supported, research needs to demonstrate that students will learn better when receiving instruction tailored to their learning style than when trying to learn in a way that is not their style. This extensive review of the learning styles research showed that there was *no interaction* between learning style and optimal learning.

The author concluded (p. 117) that 'The contrast between the enormous popularity of the learning-styles approach within education and the lack of credible evidence for its utility is, in our opinion, striking and disturbing.'

▸ Given the lack of evidence to support learning styles, why do you think it continues to be such a popular concept?

THE PSYCHOLOGY OF LEARNING

Learning has been a central subject for psychologists for decades, so there is a lot of solid psychological theory and research we can draw on in designing training and understanding the best ways to help people learn.

Habituation

A very simple form of learning is habituation, where we become accustomed to a stimulus and learn to ignore it. For example, Banbury and Berry (1997) conducted experiments to find out how office workers adapted to the noise around them in open-plan offices. They found that people could adapt to both background speech and other noises enough to complete tasks well. However, it took about 20 minutes for the participants to habituate to background speech and five minutes of quiet was enough for the disruptive effect of the background noise to recur.

Knowing about habituation and how we learn to adapt to our environment can be useful to managers because not all development is about learning new skills; some of it may well be finding ways to help employees deal with change. Banbury and Berry (2005) followed up on their previous research to make several suggestions for organisations moving to an open-plan office. Based on an understanding of habituation learning, these suggestions include being aware of the fact that it is a *change* in noise that is particularly distracting since change works against the habituation process.

Behaviourism and the 'conditioning' approach to learning

Behaviourism is a branch of psychology that tries to identify how things in our environment influence or *condition* our behaviour – that is, how we learn to adapt our behaviour according to the events we experience. The work in this area led to the development of two theories of learning: classical and operant conditioning.

Classical conditioning

You have probably heard of Pavlov's dogs and how they salivated when a bell was rung. Ivan Pavlov was actually a physiologist, yet his work became one of the foundations of learning theory. He was conducting experiments on digestion in dogs, trying to find out why the dogs salivated before food was presented to them. He found that the dogs learned to associate other stimuli (such as a bell ringing or a whistle) with food and that after a while they would begin to salivate when they heard the bell or whistle even if there was no food present. This association of a stimulus with a response has become known as classical conditioning and shows us how we learn simple associations between things in our environment and responses or behaviours. Work through the following activity to see

some examples of this type of learning at work and identify how different stimuli and responses are associated (or *conditioned*).

It is worth noting that the conditioned response does not have to be physical. A *conditioned emotional response* is one where the response is emotional rather than behavioural. A psychologist called Watson demonstrated this with a nine-month-old boy called Albert. Initially Albert was not afraid of rats, but he cried if there was a loud bang. After Watson had repeatedly shown Albert a rat and at the same time made a loud, frightening bang, Albert became afraid of the rat and started crying when he saw the rat. (It probably goes without saying, but psychologists nowadays would never get ethical approval to induce phobias in young children!)

 Activity Classical conditioning at work

There are four main elements to understand in classical conditioning:

▸ US – unconditioned stimulus. This is the stimulus or aspect of the environment that we already associate with the response. For example, it could be food.
▸ UR – unconditioned response. The response that we naturally have to the US. For example, when we see food, we start to feel hungry.
▸ CS – conditioned stimulus. This is the stimulus we start to associate with the response. For example, we start to associate going into the kitchen with food.
▸ CR – conditioned response. This is the response we now have to the CS. For example, we feel hungry when we go into the kitchen.

For the following examples, see if you can identify the US, UR, CS and CR in each case.

▸ Your computer makes a 'ping' noise every time a new email arrives. You are talking to a colleague but turn and glance at the screen when you hear a ping.
▸ An advert shows a celebrity wearing a particular brand of watch.
▸ Your manager has told you several times over the last few weeks that you are not working hard enough. Now you get nervous every time you see him.

Operant conditioning

While classical conditioning is about a simple association of a new stimulus with a response, operant conditioning explains how the *consequences* of a response or action influence our learning. It is useful for understanding how we can strengthen or weaken a response. B. F. Skinner was a psychologist who investigated how animals learn. He is famous for his experiments with rats, through which he learned that pressing a lever in their cage would result in a certain outcome. Where this outcome was positive – for example, when pressing the lever gave them food – they were more likely to engage in the behaviour. This is known as positive reinforcement. The outcome can also be the removal of a negative result. For example, rats can quickly learn to press a lever to stop a small electrical shock. This is known as negative reinforcement.

Punishment is not the same as negative reinforcement. Reinforcers, whether positive or negative, *increase* the likelihood of a behaviour, whereas punishment *decreases* it. An example of punishment is when a rat presses a lever and receives an electric shock: the rat soon learns not to press the lever. Work through the activity below to see some workplace examples of the difference between reinforcers and punishment.

Activity Operant conditioning at work

Are these examples of reinforcement or punishment? Identify the reinforcer (whether positive or negative) or the punishment. What behaviour does it affect?

▸ Every time you touch the light switch in your office, you get a static electric shock. Now you hesitate whenever you have to switch the lights on or off.
▸ A supervisor watches workers on a packing line, timing them on a stopwatch and making notes on a clipboard. She then reprimands individual employees if they are not working fast enough. Now, when the workers see her appear with a clipboard, they speed up their packing.
▸ You are working in a call centre which records and reviews your calls with customers. Your manager identifies you as 'employee of the month' for the way you have dealt with some particularly difficult customers and gives you a bonus.

Reinforcement schedules

So far, we have been looking at what happens when there is a clear link between a behaviour and an outcome. But at work, behaviours are not necessarily reinforced or punished every time. Instead, we experience different *reinforcement schedules*. These schedules can be based on a ratio, with reinforcement given after a certain number of required behaviours are exhibited, or based on an interval, with reinforcement given after a certain length of time. In addition, ratios and intervals can be fixed or variable. Let's have a look at workplace examples of each of these types of schedules and the effect they have on learning and performance.

Fixed ratio schedules: the reinforcement occurs after a set number of the required behaviours are exhibited. An example of this is piece rate pay, where an employee is paid for the number of products they complete. This type of schedule produces a very high rate of work, but if the reinforcement is stopped, the behaviour is reduced (*extinction occurs*) very quickly as well.

Variable ratio: the number of times a behaviour has to be exhibited in order to gain a reward varies. This type of schedule is usually based on an average. So, for example, a slot machine might deliver a reward after an average of 50 plays on the machine, although the exact number can vary substantially. An example of this type of schedule at work could be a bonus pay for a production team given after a variable number of products had been produced. Although this schedule is also excellent at encouraging fast rates of work and is quite resistant to extinction, because we never know when our efforts will result in a reward, it is also difficult to implement in many organisations.

Fixed interval: the reinforcement is given after a set length of time, for example, pay checks at the end of the week or month. This type of schedule tends to result in variable effort, with people increasing their efforts just before the reinforcement is due and decreasing their effort just after they receive it.

Variable interval: the reinforcement occurs at variable times. An example of this might be if a manager wanders around people's offices at unpredictable times to check how they are doing. Because the subordinates cannot predict when the manager will pop into the office, they tend to maintain a constant, though low, level of effort.

There is some overlap between the use of these behaviourist approaches to understanding learning and their use as motivational tools, so we will return to this idea in Chapter 4. In the meantime, you can see how to use this theory for yourself by completing the Psychological Toolkit activity below.

Psychological Toolkit Reinforcement

You can use what you have learnt about schedules of reinforcement to improve your own work. Let's take the example of revising for an exam. First, think of something you could use as a positive reinforcer. It could be your favourite TV programme, a chocolate bar, going out for a drink with friends or anything that you would value. Come up with a way of implementing each of the four reinforcement schedules to encourage your revision efforts and complete the following table to explore their effect further:

Schedule	Reinforcement given after …	What effect would this have on your revision effort?
Fixed interval		
Variable interval		
Fixed ratio		
Variable ratio		

▸ Which of these schedules would work best for you?

As a manager, you can use these schedules to help your employees learn and exhibit the behaviours that are required of them at work. Imagine you are the manager of a small customer service team. One of the important facets of performance for employees in this team is having a friendly, helpful attitude towards the customers. In a small group, develop a selection of reinforcers (both positive and negative) and outline the reinforcement schedule you would use to improve performance for the team.

Conditioning theories are good explanations for simple learning and it is worth remembering that this associative process underlies much of our learning. But behaviourist approaches do tend to view the individual as quite passive in the learning process, with behaviour simply 'determined' by the associations of stimuli and responses. So while these learning theories are helpful for understanding the basic links our brains make when learning, they cannot help us understand more active learning.

Social learning

The psychologist Albert Bandura expanded on the behaviourist approach to learning by developing the *social learning theory* (Bandura, 1977). He noted that an important aspect of human learning is that we learn by watching others – that is, we not only learn things through direct experience (as the behaviourist theories would have it), but also through observing other people's behaviour and the effects of our own. Bandura's approach emphasises the exceptional human ability to develop hypotheses about what behaviours will be most successful, to gather feedback and to reflect on that feedback to refine behaviour. This means that we can think about what we are doing, rather than simply respond to rewards and punishments. Bandura points out that learning solely through reward and punishment would be extremely laborious, not to mention distinctly dangerous in some situations. Imagine trying to learn to drive a forklift truck simply by trial and error!

Social learning theory suggests that we learn complex behaviours, and even attitudes and language, by copying others. These people we copy are called 'models' and modelling is a type of learning where we reproduce attitudes or behaviours displayed by another person. This modelling is most obvious when we learn how to do a new task by copying someone who is already able to do it. For example, imagine you have just started work as receptionist. On your first day, you are shown how to operate the switchboard. Someone demonstrates which buttons to press to answer a call, transfer it to another line, divert to an answering machine and so on. You learn what to do by copying them. But now imagine that it is your first day of work and no one in the building knows how the telephone system works. Instead, you are given an instruction manual. In this case, you would read the instructions and do what the manual said until you got the hang of it. Instead of imitating a real-life model, you can imitate *verbal* modelling.

Behaviour modelling training

A type of training that is based on this social learning theory is called Behaviour Modelling Training (BMT). A BMT programme involves five essential 'ingredients':

1 Clearly define the set of behaviours or skills to be learned and explain them to the trainees.
2 Provide a 'model' of those behaviours. This can be done through a video or demonstrated directly to the trainees. Including 'negative' models – people modelling the undesirable behaviours – seems to enhance the effects of the training on job behaviours but reduces the effectiveness of training on attitudes or knowledge (Taylor et al., 2005). This is probably because including negative models helps trainees to transfer their knowledge from the training course to their job, but confuses them when they are trying to learn specific skills.
3 Give trainees the opportunity to practise the new skills and behaviours.
4 Provide feedback and reinforcement based on the practice sessions.
5 Maximise the transfer of the new skills to the job. This can be done by using practice scenarios generated by the trainees themselves, training managers as well, and introducing rewards for the new behaviours into the trainee's job.

A recent meta-analysis (Taylor et al., 2005) assessed the impact of BMT on several different training outcomes: procedural knowledge (this is knowledge of how to do things/skills), declarative knowledge (knowledge that you can express, for example in a written test), attitudes, job behaviour, work-group productivity and work-group climate. BMT improved both procedural and declarative knowledge substantially, had a modest effect on employee attitudes, showed a small improvement in job behaviour and had very little influence on work-group outcomes. The effect of the training on declarative knowledge tended to fade after some time but remained stable and sometimes increased for employees' procedural knowledge, probably because they were practising the skills in their jobs.

Having looked at how we learn, we now turn to consider ways we can improve learning or training effectiveness in the workplace.

ENHANCING LEARNING EFFECTIVENESS

Activity Effective learning

Think about the last time you felt you really learnt something well. It could be a new skill, a topic in your degree course or even something you learned about yourself. Take some time to write down the things that you think helped you to learn it. Was it a process? Did you gradually get better at something or gradually understand it better? Or was it a lightbulb moment? How have you used the new skill or knowledge since then?

Refer to these questions as you read through the rest of this section and see if you can see any parallels or any ideas for further enhancing your own learning.

Practice makes perfect

Learning is best seen as a process rather than a one-off event. We all know that the more we practise something, the better we get at it, and no training programme will work unless the participants get the chance to practise what they are learning. But how should that practice be structured? Should people have an intense practice session or breaks between the sessions?

Massed practice is where trainees have to continuously practise something, with no rest between the practice sessions, whereas *spaced* practice is where trainees are given rest periods between the practice sessions. Donovan and Radosevich (1999) found that overall, spaced practice led to better learning than massed practice, but that this relationship was modified by the type of task. Spaced practice was more important for simpler tasks but it did not make as much difference for the learning of complex tasks whether the practice was massed or spaced. The authors also found that longer rest periods between practice sessions were important for complex tasks and shorter rest periods were better for simple tasks.

Transfer of learning

One of the key difficulties in learning at work is around the transfer of learning. What we learn in one situation is not automatically transferred to another situation, as illustrated in the following case study.

Case Study Transfer of learning

Gill was finding it difficult to deal with Tom, a very pushy co-worker who was constantly getting her to agree to do things that were really his job. Every time she tried to object, she felt she just could not get through to him. When she received an email offering assertiveness training to any employees who felt they needed it, she took the opportunity and signed up.

On the training programme, she watched videos of people being assertive and listened to the trainer describe the importance of assertiveness and illustrate some techniques for developing it. She then had the opportunity to practise these techniques in role plays with other participants and received positive feedback from them and the trainer on her ability to use the assertiveness techniques.

© ImageSource

Back in the office the next day, Gill was ready to use all the techniques she had learnt. But when Tom came into her office and started making his usual brash demands, she suddenly felt unable to use the skills she had practised the day before and moments later found herself landed with another pile of Tom's work.

▸ Why do you think Gill could not transfer her learning from the role plays to the 'real' situation of a conversation with Tom?

▸ What should she do to try to improve the learning transfer?

▸ If you were the trainer, what would you do to help your trainees to have an effective learning transfer?

A model for understanding training transfer was developed by Barnett and Ceci (2002), separating the *content* of learning from the *context* of learning. Content looks at *what* is transferred and needs to consider:

- what type of skill is being learned (for example, a specific procedure or a principle to be applied),
- what kind of performance is being changed (is it speed, accuracy or a change in approach?)
- and what kind of memory demands are being made (for example, recall or recognise).

Secondly, we need to consider the context of transfer. This is described as near or far, depending on when and where the learning is transferred to. The closer in time, or the more similar the context, the more easily learning can be transferred. The more different the contexts, the more difficult transfer becomes and the more reliant it is on individual characteristics of the trainees, such as intelligence.

Besides the individual characteristics of the trainees, there are further factors that influence transfer effectiveness. A recent meta-analysis explored the effect of several of these factors (Blume et al., 2010) and identified the following contributors to training transfer:

- *Personal characteristics*: trainees with higher cognitive ability, conscientiousness and self-efficacy had better learning transfer. In addition, those who were more motivated and took part in the training voluntarily also showed a moderate increase in training transfer effectiveness.
- *Environmental factors*: if the organisation has a good transfer climate (availability of equipment and opportunity to practise as well as positive and negative reinforcement), trainees are able to transfer their learning much more effectively. Support from peers and management is also important in encouraging transfer.
- *Learning outcomes of the training*: where training results in higher self-efficacy and knowledge for the participants, they are more likely to be able to transfer the learning to their job situation.

Formal or informal learning?

So far, we have considered learning from a very formal viewpoint: training that is developed and applied in response to a particular need. But a substantial amount of what we learn at work happens informally, with estimates varying from 20% to 90% (Conlon, 2004). We learn how the people around us expect us to do our job, we 'pick things up' as we go along or a colleague informally shows us how to do something. Informal learning can be defined

as learning that happens at work and is directly relevant to job performance but is not organised by the employer in any way (Dale and Bell, 1999).

Before the advent of scientific approaches to management, this type of informal learning was how everyone learnt to do their job, and the specific skills they learnt were embedded within a general socialisation process (Marsick, 2009). There is even some suggestion that, given how expensive formal training courses are and how their success can be difficult to evaluate, organisations should move towards promoting more informal learning. However, because it is informal, there is less scope for the organisation to ensure that it is effective and it can lead to employees feeling lost and helpless (Conlon, 2004).

Informal learning activities include (Cunningham and Hillier, 2013):

- Learning relationships, such as mentoring and peer feedback.
- Opportunities around job enlargement or design, including activities such as temporary job changes, cross-training and stretch assignments.
- Opportunities around job enrichment, such as acting management, temporary assignments or briefer opportunities like webinars, workshops and discussion forums.

There are several things organisations can do to enhance the effectiveness of informal learning, including having clear planning processes, encouraging and developing active learning, promoting positive relationship dynamics and having an orientation towards the application of learning to the job.

Dale and Bell's (1999) report highlighted some of the main advantages and disadvantages of informal learning. The main benefits are around flexibility and adaptability because the learning process and content can be tailored to the individual. However, for learning to be effective, it does still need support from managers. It is also obviously more difficult to accredit and recognise informal learning, to the extent where even employees might not realise how much they have learnt. In their review, Dale and Bell recommend that informal and formal learning are integrated into the organisation.

Svensson et al. (2004) suggest that e-learning could become a way of providing this integration of formal and informal learning. They recommend that experiential, workplace learning be combined with e-learning modules so that trainees can access the formal learning at times convenient to them and in whatever order suits them best.

TRAINING

Training methods

The following table outlines some of the main benefits and drawbacks of different formal training methods. In evaluating these methods, remember that an important issue in effective training is the trainer him or herself. It is no good choosing the 'best' method and expecting it to work no matter who is leading the training course. Similarly, no training will work if the trainee does not engage in the learning process. As you probably know from your own experience, you do not learn simply by having a textbook next to you or sitting in a lecture theatre. At the end of this section we will return to consider ways of making training more effective.

In choosing the appropriate method(s), it is also important to take account of what you hope the training will achieve. For example, if you wish to train people to use a new computer program, a general group discussion is unlikely to be very effective whereas a demonstration or simulation will give the trainees the opportunity to see the program in action.

In discussions of training, people often mention development centres. These are not a 'method' as such, in much the same way as assessment centres are not a unique method of selection. Instead, they combine many of the approaches listed above to provide employees with detailed reports, and highlight their current strengths and opportunities for further development.

Table 3.1 The benefits and drawbacks of different training methods

Method	Benefits	Drawbacks
Case study – an outline of a scenario that helps to illustrate the learning topic, it can be hypothetical or a summary of a real situation.	Trainees have the time and space to think deeply and analyse a situation in order to develop solutions and learn from it.	The case study may not reflect the reality of situations that trainees are faced with, making transfer of learning more difficult.
Coaching and mentoring – is based on a one-to-one relationship between the learner and a more experienced or expert person who can give tailored guidance and direction. Mentoring tends to be more informal and intra-organisational, while coaching often uses external professional coaches.	Instruction and guidance can be tailored to the individual's current situation and needs. Guidance is usually holistic rather than focusing on an isolated skill.	It can be resource-intensive and is very dependent on a good relationship between the coach/mentor and the protégé.
Demonstration – the trainer explains to trainees how to do something and shows them the process.	Trainees can immediately see what needs to be done. It is particularly effective for simple tasks.	Less effective for more complex tasks and only shows trainees one, standardised way of doing things.
Group discussion – trainees can discuss aspects of the training or specific problems or share best practice.	The discussion helps trainees see other people's points of view, discover new ways of doing things, and share and reflect on their own learning.	It can be time-consuming and there is no guarantee that the group discussion will produce helpful or desirable outcomes.
Job rotation or placements – trainees take on temporary assignments within the organisation or with clients/competitors.	Trainees can become multi-skilled and gain a new perspective on their old job or on the organisation as a whole.	Costs can be high because the employee has to be trained and supported in each new placement/rotation.
Lecture – presents information to trainees, usually in verbal form.	An effective way to communicate information to a large number of trainees.	Little opportunity for interaction and it is difficult to tailor to individual levels or needs.
Role play – trainees take on roles and act out how they would handle specific situations.	Can give trainees the opportunity to practise skills, especially interpersonal ones, in a non-threatening environment and help them to transfer learning more easily.	The usefulness of role plays is highly dependent on the type of feedback the trainee receives. In addition, many people feel uncomfortable 'acting', especially in front of a group.
Simulation – these can be equipment simulators or more abstract, for example an in-tray exercise.	An excellent way of allowing trainees to practise skills that would normally have high costs associated with failure (for example, flight simulators).	Can be expensive to set up and are only useful to the extent they accurately portray the real tasks and environment the trainee will be faced with.

Many of the training methods listed above can also be delivered using e-learning. For example, lectures or demonstrations can be podcasted, group discussions can take place on forums and case studies can be read online. There is even a growing interest in virtual coaching and e-mentoring, where the participants communicate via the internet. A recent study outlined how e-mentoring could be enhanced, highlighting the frequency of interaction between the protégé and mentor (DiRenzo et al., 2010). E-learning has the advantage of being more cost-effective to deliver, though the initial development of high-quality materials is a significant factor to consider. E-learning also allows employees access to learning at times convenient to them.

We discuss coaching psychology in more detail in Chapter 11.

Training evaluation

Training budgets are often among the first to be cut when an organisation is trying to save money. Yet continuous learning is also recognised as essential to organisational success. So why is there a mismatch? One reason is that many managers feel it is difficult to demonstrate the effectiveness of training programmes, or they simply don't know how to go about it. One of the most widely used models for evaluating training was developed by Kirkpatrick and outlines four levels at which training can be evaluated (Kirkpatrick and Kirkpatrick, 2006):

1   Reaction – how the trainees reacted to the training, how they felt about it. This is often assessed by feedback sheets at the end of the training programme asking the participants what they enjoyed or how satisfied they are with the programme.
2   Learning – how much the trainees learnt on the programme. This can be assessed using tests or interviews.
3   Behaviour – to what extent the trainees actually change their work behaviour as a result of the training. This is more difficult to assess and can involve further interviews and observations.
4   Results – this is the extent to which the training impacts on organisational-level outcomes and is the most difficult level at which to assess training, primarily because organisational measures have so many contributing factors.

This model can be used to evaluate individual training programmes but was also used as the basis for an extensive review of training evaluation by Arthur et al. (2003), which demonstrated that training had a substantial impact on effectiveness at all four levels. For more detailed information about their findings, look at the Key Research Study.

 Key Research Study Training effectiveness

Effectiveness of Training in Organizations: A Meta-Analysis of Design and Evaluation Features

Winfred Arthur Jr, Winston Bennett Jr, Pamela S. Edens and Suzanne T. Bell (2003).

Background: Organisations invest huge resources into formal training programmes in an attempt to improve employee performance. But there was, until this article was published, no overall assessment of how effective different training techniques are or whether training needs analysis contributed significantly to outcomes.

Aim: The authors had three main aims:

1   To compare the effectiveness of different training techniques.
2   To explore the relationship between training needs assessment and training effectiveness.
3   To find out which techniques worked best for different types of skills/tasks:
    a.   Psychomotor – physical or manual tasks
    b.   Interpersonal – skills for interacting with others, like leadership or communication
    c.   Cognitive – understanding, problem-solving and knowledge.

Method: This was a meta-analysis which drew together the findings from 162 research studies reporting on 397 evaluations of organisational training programmes. The authors noted how the training was evaluated (using Kirkpatrick's four evaluation criteria), how needs assessment was conducted, how the training was delivered (e.g. lectures or simulation) and whether the skills were psychomotor, cognitive or interpersonal.

Findings:

▸ Overall, training was found to have a medium to large effect on all four of the evaluation criteria.
▸ There was no clear relationship between training needs analysis and training effectiveness. However, this finding was based on a small sample as most studies did not report whether they had conducted TNA or not.
▸ Training in psychomotor skills was most effective when equipment simulators, audiovisual and discussion techniques were used.
▸ Interpersonal training was most effective when it used lectures, audiovisual and programmed instruction.
▸ Cognitive training was most effective when delivered using lectures, audiovisual and self-instruction (i.e. from books or other materials)

Implications: The money that organisations spend on training is a good investment. Training has demonstrably positive impacts at all four levels of evaluation: trainee reactions, learning, behaviour and organisational results. To enhance training effectiveness even further, trainers should choose the training technique best suited to the type of skill they are focusing on. Interestingly, lectures come out as one of the top techniques!

RETAINING TALENT

We are now coming to the end of our discussion of talent management. In Chapter 2 we looked at how organisations can select the best candidates and in this chapter we have considered how they can develop and train job holders. The final step is to consider how an organisation can hold on to these talented, developed individuals. For this, we are going to look at the concept of employer branding.

Employer branding has grown out of the idea of applying product or service marketing principles to human resources management. The brand is essentially the organisation's reputation as an employer: what do people think about the way the organisation treats its employees? A successful employer brand, just like a product brand, is one that 'creates a unique and particular employment experience' (Edwards, 2010, p. 6). Its main benefits are that it creates brand association (the meaning a person associates with the brand, such as its quality) and brand loyalty (Love and Singh, 2011).

The psychological contract between the employees and employer plays a key role in employer branding (Edwards, 2010). The brand gives rise to employees' expectations of what the organisation will do for them as well as their understanding of what they are expected to do in exchange. The extent to which these expectations are met will determine the employees' attitudes towards the brand.

A widespread measure of employer branding can be found in the annual reviews of the 'Top 100 Companies to work for' which are published in many different countries. Love and Singh (2011) identify eight main themes that contribute to being rated as a 'top' employer:

1 Inspired leadership
2 A strategic plan that focused on achieving 'top employer' status
3 Open and consistent communication with employees
4 Effective performance management
5 Training and development are given a high priority
6 Employee benefits are based on best practice (for example, are individualised, flexible and encourage work–life balance)

7 Appealing and ergonomically designed physical workplace
8 Have a real focus on corporate citizenship.

The following activity helps you to explore the idea of employer branding in an organisation you are familiar with.

Activity Employer brand

At the time of writing, no UK universities were in the *Sunday Times* 100 Best Companies/Not For Profit Companies. Why do you think this is?

Imagine that your university wants to get on this list and be recognised as a good place to work. Take some time to think about the following questions:

▸ How would you describe your university as an employer? How does it seem to treat its employees?
▸ What do you think the university stands for? What do you think of its reputation overall?
▸ Write down some keywords that sum up the university's 'employer brand'.

Now imagine you are a consultant, brought in to help because the university has realised it is losing its top-performing employees to the competition. What suggestions would you make to improve their employer brand?

Coming full circle, an effective employer brand also helps the organisation to attract people to it in the first place, meaning that it has a greater pool of potential applicants from which to select the best.

SUMMARY

This chapter started with a consideration of how organisations measure performance, making a comparison between standardised and individualised measures. We then looked at who should do the appraisal and how individuals involved in the process can try to influence outcomes in a way that runs contrary to what the organisation is trying to achieve.

One of the reasons for appraising performance is to identify training needs, and we considered how this could best be done as a basis for designing training. The importance of learning theories in effective training was reviewed in depth and several suggestions for enhancing learning effectiveness were considered, including practice, transfer and informal learning.

Finally, we looked at the practical details of how training can be delivered and how its effectiveness can be evaluated, particularly using Kirkpatrick's four-stage model. The chapter concluded with a discussion of employer branding as a way of drawing together all the efforts that employers put into performance management, reward and development.

TEST YOURSELF

Brief Review Questions

1 List the different types of standardised performance measures that can be used in organisations and give an example of each.
2 What is 360° appraisal and what is it best used for?
3 Distinguish between training, development and learning.
4 What is the difference between behaviourism and social learning?
5 When is it best to use massed and spaced practice?
6 List three training methods and their associated advantages and disadvantages.

Discussion or Essay Questions

1 Outline the problems an organisation might face in gaining accurate assessments of its employees' performance and describe what steps could be taken to overcome these problems.
2 Describe how best to evaluate a training programme.
3 As a trainer, what could you do to enhance your trainees' learning? Draw on the theories in this chapter to develop practical suggestions.
4 To what extent do you think employer branding is a good idea? Can you think of examples of organisations where it might be particularly beneficial or not work at all?

FURTHER READING

- An introductory psychology textbook will give further details on learning theories, for example, *Psychology: European Edition* by Schacter et al., Basingstoke, Palgrave Macmillan, 2011.
- The Kirkpatrick Partners' website has details of the Kirkpatrick model for training evaluation and some useful resources: www.kirkpatrickpartners.com.
- Best Companies (www.bestcompanies.co.uk) is the UK organisation that conducts the surveys to determine who are the best companies to work for. Their lists are published by the *Sunday Times*.
  - Equivalent surveys for other European countries, Australia, the USA and the rest of the world can be found at: www.greatplacetowork.com.

References

ARTHUR JR, W., BENNETT JR, W., EDENS, P. S. & BELL, S. T. 2003. Effectiveness of training in organizations: a meta-analysis of design and evaluation features. *Journal of Applied Psychology*, 88, 234–45.

BANBURY, S. & BERRY, D. C. 1997. Habituation and dishabituation to speech and office noise. *Journal of Experimental Psychology: Applied*, 3, 181–95.

BANBURY, S. & BERRY, D. C. 2005. Office noise and employee concentration: identifying causes of disruption and potential improvements. *Ergonomics*, 48, 25–37.

BANDURA, A. 1977. *Social Learning Theory*. Englewood Cliffs, NJ, Prentice Hall.

BARNETT, S. M. & CECI, S. J. 2002. When and where do we apply what we learn? a taxonomy for far transfer. *Psychological Bulletin*, 128, 612–37.

BLUME, B. D., FORD, J. K., BALDWIN, T. T. & HUANG, J. L. 2010. Transfer of training: a meta-analytic review. *Journal of Management*, 36, 1065–105.

BOZEMAN, D. P. 1997. Interrater agreement in multi-source performance appraisal: a commentary. *Journal of Organizational Behavior*, 18, 313–16.

CLEVELAND, J. N., MURPHY, K. R. & WILLIAMS, R. E. 1989. Multiple uses of performance appraisal: prevalence and correlates. *Journal of Applied Psychology*, 74, 130–5.

COFFIELD, F., MOSELEY, D., HALL, E. & ECCLESTONE, K. 2004. *Learning Styles and Pedagogy in Post-16 Learning: A Systematic and Critical Review*. London, Learning and Skills Research Centre.

CONLON, T. J. 2004. A review of informal learning literature, theory and implications for practice in developing global professional competence. *Journal of European Industrial Training*, 28, 283–95.

CUNNINGHAM, J. & HILLIER, E. 2013. Informal learning in the workplace: key activities and processes. *Education + Training*, 55, 37–51.

DALE, M. & BELL, J. 1999. Informal Learning in the Workplace, DfEE Research Report No. 134. London, Department for Education and Employment.

DENISI, A. S. & KLUGER, A. N. 2000. Feedback effectiveness: can 360-degree appraisals be improved? *Academy of Management Executive*, 14, 129–39.

DIRENZO, M. S., LINNEHAN, F., SHAO, P. & ROSENBERG, W. L. 2010. A moderated mediation model of e-mentoring. *Journal of Vocational Behavior*, 76, 292–305.

DONOVAN, J. J. & RADOSEVICH, D. J. 1999. A meta-analytic review of the distribution of practice effect: now you see it, now you don't. *Journal of Applied Psychology*, 84, 795–805.

EDWARDS, M. R. 2010. An integrative review of employer branding and OB theory. *Personnel Review*, 39, 5–23.

FLETCHER, C. 2001. Performance appraisal and management: the developing research agenda. *Journal of Occupational and Organizational Psychology*, 74, 473–87.

FLETCHER, C. 2008. Performance Appraisal. In Chmiel, N. (ed.) *An Introduction to Work and Organizational Psychology: A European Perspective*, 2nd edn. Oxford, Blackwell.

KIRKPATRICK, D. & KIRKPATRICK, J. 2006. *Evaluating Training Programs: The Four Levels*. San Francisco, Berrett-Koehler.

LOCKE, E. A. & LATHAM, G. P. 2002. Building a practically useful theory of goal setting and task motivation. *American Psychologist*, 57, 705–17.

LOVE, L. F. & SINGH, P. 2011. Workplace branding: leveraging human resources management practices for competitive advantage through 'best employer' surveys. *Journal of Business and Psychology*, 26, 175–81.

MARSICK, V. J. 2009. Toward a unifying framework to support informal learning theory, research and practice. *Journal of Workplace Learning*, 21, 265–75.

MICHAELS, E., HANDFIELD-JONES, H. & AXELROD, B. 2001. *The War for Talent*. Boston, Harvard Business School Publishing.

PASHLER, H. 2009. Learning styles: concepts and evidence. *Psychological Science in the Public Interest*, 9, 105.

PERETZ, H. & FRIED, Y. 2012. National cultures, performance appraisal practices, and organizational absenteeism and turnover: a study across 21 countries. *Journal of Applied Psychology*, 97, 448–59.

SIMS, J. H. P., GIOIA, D. A. & LONGENECKER, C. O. 1987. Behind the mask: the politics of employee appraisal. *Academy of Management Executive*, 1, 183–93.

SONNENTAG, S., NIESSEN, C. & OHLY, S. 2008. Learning and Training at Work. In Chmiel, N. (ed.) *An Introduction to Work and Organizational Psychology: A European Perspective*. Oxford, Blackwell.

SUTTON, A. & WATSON, S. 2013. Can competencies at selection predict performance and development needs? *Journal of Management Development*, 32, 1023–35.

SVENSSON, L., ELLSTRÖM, P.-E. & ÅBERG, C. 2004. Integrating formal and informal learning at work. *Journal of Workplace Learning*, 16, 479–91.

TAYLOR, P. J., RUSS-EFT, D. F. & CHAN, D. W. L. 2005. A meta-analytic review of behavior modeling training. *Journal of Applied Psychology*, 90, 692–709.

TZINER, A., JOANIS, C. & MURPHY, K. R. 2000. A comparison of three methods of performance appraisal with regard to goal properties, goal perception, and ratee satisfaction. *Group & Organization Management*, 25, 175–90.

VISWESVARAN, C., ONES, D. S. & SCHMIDT, F. L. 1996. Comparative analysis of the reliability of job performance ratings. *Journal of Applied Psychology*, 81, 557–74.

VISWESVARAN, C., SCHMIDT, F. L. & ONES, D. S. 2005. Is there a general factor in ratings of job performance? A meta-analytic framework for disentangling substantive and error influences. *Journal of Applied Psychology*, 90, 108–31.

MOTIVATING PEOPLE

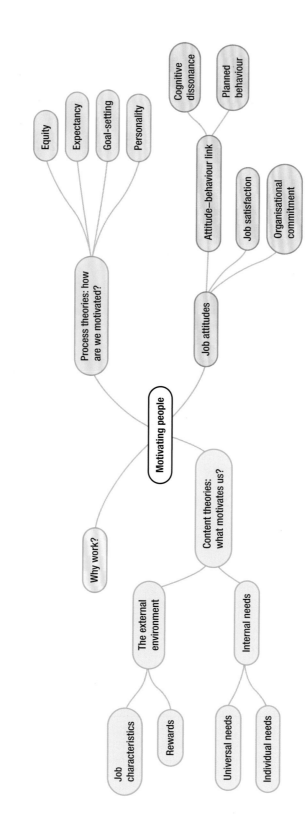

Motivating people

Why work?

Process theories: how are we motivated?
- Equity
- Expectancy
- Goal-setting
- Personality

Job attitudes
- Attitude–behaviour link
  - Cognitive dissonance
  - Planned behaviour
- Job satisfaction
- Organisational commitment

Content theories: what motivates us?
- The external environment
  - Job characteristics
  - Rewards
- Internal needs
  - Universal needs
  - Individual needs

So far, we have looked at how psychology can help organisations to find and develop the best employees. Alongside that, we have considered how individuals (like you) can use their knowledge of psychology to enhance their careers. We now turn to consider a closely related concept: motivation. In an environment where organisations are attempting to get higher productivity out of fewer people, this chapter will discuss the best ways to motivate people at work. We will start by considering the general question of why people work, and use that as a springboard into an exploration of psychological theories of motivation. These theories are grouped into two broad categories: content theories, which outline what motivates us, and process theories, which describe how the way we think about work affects our motivation.

The chapter explores the important role of job attitudes and why they are considered to be of such importance in the study of employee motivation. We will look at the link between attitudes and behaviour or performance at work before going into detail on the two most well-researched attitudes: job satisfaction and organisational commitment. Throughout, the emphasis will be on defining the evidence base for the theories, to enable you to draw your own conclusions about the effectiveness of different approaches.

Finally, the chapter concludes with a brief checklist of practical things that managers can do to help motivate employees.

This chapter will help you answer the following questions:

1   Why do we work?
2   What kinds of things can motivate us in our jobs?
3   Why is the way we think about work important for understanding motivation?
4   How do our attitudes towards work influence our performance and motivation?

WHY WORK?

Throughout this book we are exploring how psychology and business interact and inform each other. We saw in Chapter 2 that we can approach talent management from different directions depending on whether we have a psychological or business orientation. The same is true for motivation. From a psychological perspective, we want to answer the question 'Why are people motivated to do things?' Note that this is broader than just describing why people do things at work, so we will need to assess these theories for their applicability to the workplace. From a business perspective, we are more interested in finding out 'What can we do to motivate people to work harder?' In this chapter we will see how we can use the

psychological theories of motivation to develop effective interventions to encourage people to work to the best of their ability.

Activity Why work?

Think about your work on your university degree. Why are you studying for this degree? Share your answers with other people in the group and see if you have any similarities or differences.

Now think about times during your degree when you have worked really hard and times when you just could not seem to get going on your work. Make two lists: one of what motivates you to study and one of what seems to stop you working hard.

As you go through the rest of this chapter, see whether your lists fit in with the theories we discuss.

Let's start at the beginning. Why do people work in the first place? Instinctively, most people will respond to that question by saying they work to earn money, with the assumption that money is needed for survival. However, it is not as straightforward as that. The majority of developed societies have welfare systems that can provide the basic means of survival and many people work in jobs where they earn far more than what is needed for 'survival'. So there must be more going on. One way we can explore this idea is by asking people whether they would continue working if they suddenly won the lottery.

The lottery question is simple: *If you won the lottery and had enough money to live comfortably the rest of your life, would you continue to work?* A comparative survey of workers in eight different countries (MOW International Research Team, 1987) found that less than a third of workers would stop work completely, ranging from 31% of British down to only 4% of Yugoslavian workers. However, the majority of workers in all countries would continue working, either in their current job or under different conditions.

Investigation of the concept of *non-financial employment commitment* has continued and some interesting developments have been noted. For example, a survey in Israel (Harpaz, 2002) showed that while the percentage of people who said they would remain in work if they had no financial needs remained approximately the same across a 12-year time span (88–90%), the reasons people gave for staying in work changed. Occupational satisfaction was a more important determinant of continuing to work in the later study, while organisational obligation was more important in the earlier study. At both times, those with a more instrumental approach to work (i.e. those working to get a specific benefit or reward rather than for the

Case Study Lottery winner who keeps working

Tyrone Curry won nearly $3.5 million in the Washington State Lottery in 2006 but carried on working as a school janitor for five years, after which he had to step down in order to take up his seat as the school board president in 2011. He has said, 'You need to be doing stuff: That's my philosophy,' and 'If you're not busy you get old, and I never want to feel that way.'

▸ What would you do if you won the lottery? Would you continue working? Why or why not?

© Thinkstock

enjoyment of the work itself) were more likely to leave their jobs.

An American study looking at answers to the lottery question from 1980 to 2006 found evidence that the 'work ethic', or working because it is the 'right' thing to do, was declining (Highhouse et al., 2010). This finding has been expanded in a study of real lottery winners, which showed that some winners, particularly those with good working conditions, stayed in work (Hedenus, 2012). Clearly, there is more to work motivation than simple financial incentive.

Theories of motivation

Psychological explanations of work motivation are concerned with explaining three aspects of the effort we put into work:

1 Intensity – how much effort do we put into the task? How effective this effort is depends on how well we are directing it.
2 Direction – what do we channel our efforts towards? It is important from an organisational point of view to ensure that the individual's goals coincide with the organisational aims, otherwise the individual's efforts will be wasted.
3 Persistence – how long do we keep going? High intensity and the right direction for our efforts are not enough. We also need to keep persisting in a task in order to reach the goal.

Before we continue, a word of warning. There may well be more theories of motivation than you will find in any other area of work psychology, and it can sometimes feel overwhelming or leave you with the impression that they are all conflicting. One of the problems in this area is that everyone is looking for a single, all-encompassing theory that can be used as a basis for motivating everyone. Yet we know that each of us is motivated in different ways at different times. So when reading through these

theories, remember that we are not looking for the 'single best theory' that will enable us to motivate everyone, but instead we will be trying to build a good understanding of the range of motivational tools available to us. This solid knowledge base will then help us to know how best to motivate ourselves and others at different times.

Motivation theories attempt to explain these aspects of motivation in different ways and can be grouped into two types: content and process. Content theories focus on identifying *what* motivates us and process theories explain *how* we are motivated. We will look at theories in these two categories next.

CONTENT THEORIES: *WHAT MOTIVATES US?*

The behaviourist approach that we looked at in the last chapter would claim we engage in particular behaviours in order to gain a reward or to avoid a negative result. But these rewards and negative outcomes are very complex when it comes to work behaviour. We have already seen that the simple reward of 'money' is not enough to explain why people work. So what kinds of things *do* motivate us?

There are two approaches to identifying these motivators. The first is to focus on aspects of the external environment that will motivate us, either by identifying the external rewards we will try to gain or the characteristics of the job that people find motivating and then adjusting the jobs as far as possible to contain more motivators. The second approach focuses on our internal environment and identifies the internal rewards we try to gain. Theories in this approach tend to conceptualise these 'rewards' as internal needs that we are motivated to fulfil. Much as we experience hunger and this motivates us to eat, these internal needs urge us to find and gain satisfaction. Some theorists say that there are 'universal' needs which we all have but differ only in terms of which one is active at any time, just as we all get hungry and thirsty but at any time of the day one of these may be dominant. Others say that there are a number of human needs but each of us differs in terms of their inherent strength.

The external environment

Job characteristics

One of the earliest ways of trying to motivate people at work was by changing aspects of the job. Hackman and Oldham (1976) brought together much of this work in a model that tried to capture how changes in job characteristics would lead to increased motivation. Their model can be summarised in a simple diagram:

Core Job Dimensions → Critical Psychological States → Personal and Work Outcomes

The personal and work outcomes include high internal motivation, high-quality work, high satisfaction and low absenteeism and turnover. Hackman and Oldham suggested that three critical psychological states determined these outcomes, which were in turn influenced by five core job dimensions:

Table 4.1 Core job dimensions and their corresponding psychological states

Core job dimensions	Critical psychological states
1 **Skill variety** – how many different skills do I use in order to complete my job? 2 **Task identity** – to what extent do I complete a 'whole' piece of work? 3 **Task significance** – how much impact does my work have on other people?	Experienced **meaningfulness** of the work – do I think my work is genuinely meaningful, valuable and worthwhile?
4 **Autonomy** – how much freedom and discretion do I have to decide how and when I will do my work?	Experienced **responsibility** for the outcomes – do I think I am personally responsible and accountable for the results of my work?
5 **Feedback** – to what extent do I receive clear and direct information on my effectiveness?	**Knowledge** of the actual results of the work – do I know how well I am performing my job?

So when we feel that our work is meaningful, that we are personally responsible for the results and we gain feedback on what those results are, we will have better personal and work outcomes. Essentially, Hackman and Oldham present this model as a way of explaining positive reinforcement at work: we feel good about our work so we do more.

Activity Motivating potential score

Hackman and Oldham's model of motivation has an added benefit: you can use it to calculate how 'motivating' a particular job will be. They used the Job Diagnostic Survey to evaluate 62 different jobs for their motivating potential, and you can use a simple version to evaluate how motivating you find two different jobs.

First, decide which two jobs you are going to compare. Here are some suggestions:

▸ A current part- or full-time job
▸ The 'job' of being a student
▸ A previous job
▸ A possible future job (in this case, you will have to guess to rate the different job characteristics, but it could still provide you with an interesting comparison).

Now rate each of the jobs on the five characteristics of Skill Variety, Task Identity, Task Significance, Autonomy and Feedback. You could use a five-point scale where one is 'none at all' and five is 'a lot' – just make sure you keep the scale consistent across the two jobs.

Now work out the Motivating Potential Score (MPS) of the two jobs as follows:

$$MPS = \frac{(Skill\ Variety + Task\ Identity + Task\ Significance)}{3} \times Autonomy \times Feedback$$

▸ Which job is 'most motivating' according to this calculation? Does that surprise you? Does it seem right? Why or why not?

A recent meta-analysis has updated Hackman and Oldham's model of job characteristics by evaluating 250 studies on work design (Humphrey et al., 2007). This demonstrated that a total of nine work characteristics explain a substantial amount of work performance and satisfaction. In addition to the five dimensions in Table 4.1, these nine characteristics include:

6 **Task variety** – how many different tasks do I complete in my work?

7 **Interdependence** – how much is my job dependent on others and theirs on mine?

8 **Feedback from others** – how much feedback do I get on my performance from other people?

9 **Social support** – to what extent can I get advice and assistance from colleagues or supervisors?

Humphrey et al. separate these characteristics into two groups: job-related (characteristics 1–6) and social (7–9). Social characteristics are related to turnover intentions, whereas job-related characteristics are related to job involvement and internal work motivation. They are both important in explaining other outcomes such as performance ratings, organisational commitment and stress. The authors also discovered that social characteristics have become increasingly important over the years, an important reminder that motivational theories need to be constantly updated to reflect the realities of current working practices.

Rewards

The behaviourist tradition made it clear that the way to get more of the behaviour we want is to use rewards. But a strong counter to this came in the form of the concept of *intrinsic* reward, the suggestion that some activities are inherently rewarding (Deci, 1972). Initially, it was assumed that intrinsic and extrinsic rewards would simply combine to make someone even more motivated. But the research showed something very different and more challenging for work motivation theories: it seemed that extrinsic rewards for a task actually *undermined* intrinsic motivation. People who are given or expect an extrinsic reward for a task are less likely to freely choose to do it and report feeling less interested in the task. To illustrate this, imagine you are inherently interested in reading about work psychology, so

you pick up books on the subject in bookshops and read articles on the internet that are related to the topic. Then you have to write an essay on the subject in order to get a grade for your degree. Suddenly you find yourself less interested in work psychology and have to force yourself to read the relevant articles.

Tangible rewards (e.g. pay) have a negative effect on both self-reported interest and free-choice behaviour. On the other hand, positive feedback (e.g. verbal praise) has a positive effect on intrinsic motivation. What the rewards are given for also affects motivation, as the following table shows (Deci, 1999):

Table 4.2 The effects of different types of rewards

Type of reward	Effect on free choice of the activity	Effect on self-reported interest in the activity
Verbal (e.g. acknowledgement or approval)	Positive	Positive
Tangible (e.g. pay or credits) • For engagement in the activity • For completion of the activity • For performing at a certain level	Negative • Negative • Negative • Negative	Negative • Negative • Negative • None

Why should being given an external reward make us less intrinsically motivated? Cognitive evaluation theory (CET) (Deci and Ryan, 1980) explains this apparently paradoxical finding by suggesting that it is not the reward itself, but our interpretation of what it means that matters. This theory proposes that we have an underlying need for

Case Study Intrinsic rewards

Sarah works for a large multinational energy company. She worked hard to get this job, completing a postgraduate degree in engineering and going through a tough selection process to be one of only five newly qualified engineers to be appointed when she graduated. After two years in the job, however, she is finding that she really dislikes it. In her spare time, she volunteers at a local animal rescue centre and she is now thinking about going to work for them full time, even though it would mean a large cut in pay.

▶ If you were Sarah's friend, using what you know about implicit and explicit rewards, what advice would you give her?

▶ If you were Sarah's manager and became aware that she was thinking about leaving, what would you do?

© John Foxx Images

autonomy and competence in what we do and that we interpret rewards in relation to these feelings. We can see rewards either as indicators of our competence (in which case they will promote satisfaction and improve our motivation) or as signs of control over our behaviour (in which case the rewards are preventing our feelings of autonomy and decreasing our motivation). We are more likely to see rewards as indicators of competence when they are informational and give us feedback on how well we are doing.

The implications of these findings for motivation at work are substantial, but they do need to be combined with other research to give an overall picture. For example, we could not conclude from all this that there is no point paying anyone to do a job! We have already seen that tangible rewards such as pay are useful for controlling behaviour, such as increasing the rate of work using piece-rate pay, and these findings do not contradict that. Instead, CET helps us to identify the difference between external control of behaviour and self-determination of behaviour, or between controlled and autonomous motivation (Marylène and Edward, 2005). Many external aspects of the work environment, such as deadlines and surveillance, tend to decrease workers' sense of autonomy, and can be grouped with tangible rewards as methods of control rather than ways of enhancing self-motivation. CET shows us that it is important to take account of how rewards are perceived when understanding their effects. Essentially, it recommends that when we are aiming to increase self-regulation and self-motivation, we should make rewards more informational than controlling, thereby increasing the sense of competence and autonomy and boosting intrinsic motivation (Deci, 1999).

A consideration of the difference between intrinsic and extrinsic rewards leads us into a discussion of needs theories.

Internal needs

Universal needs theories

If you have studied motivation before, you are very likely to have come across Maslow's 'Hierarchy of Needs' (Maslow, 1954). This model suggests that we have five different needs (physiological, safety, social, self-esteem and self-actualisation), which are arranged in a hierarchy. At the first level, we are motivated by physiological needs such as food, water and shelter. Once we have fulfilled those needs, we move up a level and are motivated by the need for safety, and so on up the hierarchy. However, we will not be reviewing this model in detail here because, despite its popularity in management textbooks, there is very little evidence to support it. In fact, reviews of studies based on Maslow's theory have shown no or very limited support for the hierarchy (Wahba and Bridwell, 1976). What has emerged from the research is some support for the idea that there are different types of needs: survival and personal growth. The popularity of this model, despite the lack of evidence, can probably be explained by its simplicity (Watson, 1996): it gives people an easy way of conceptualising their intuitive understanding that there are differences in what motivates different people. Maslow's theory certainly was an influential starting point for many that followed.

Alderfer expanded on Maslow's idea of needs being the basis of motivation to develop the ERG theory (Alderfer, 1969). He suggested there are three main needs: existence, relatedness and growth. Contrary to Maslow, Alderfer did not claim that 'lower order' needs have to be satisfied before we engage in fulfilling 'higher order' needs. Instead, we can be motivated by any or all needs at any one time. Existence needs are those that are to do with our survival or physical well-being, while relatedness needs concern our motivation for interpersonal relationships and growth needs motivate us towards personal development.

Another of the influential early theories of motivation is Herzberg's two-factor theory. Herzberg and colleagues explored what made people most satisfied with their work (Herzberg et al., 1959). They discovered that some factors (which they named hygiene factors) influenced people only in a negative direction – that is, when things such as good pay or working environment were not present, employees were dissatisfied. Other factors, such as recognition or level of responsibility of work (named motivators), were needed in order for workers to feel satisfaction in their jobs. The figure below illustrates this.

A criticism of this theory is that it equates satisfaction with motivation. While there is good evidence to support

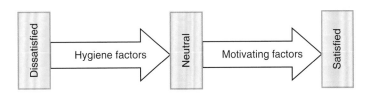

Figure 4.1 Herzberg's two-factor theory of motivation

the differential effects of these job characteristics on satisfaction, it does not necessarily follow that satisfaction automatically leads to motivation.

Individual or trait needs

McClelland's theory of motivation (McClelland, 1987) is quite different from Alderfer and Maslow's theories. It does not suggest that we all have the same needs and simply vary in terms of which ones are active, but instead that we each have differing levels or strengths of three main needs: achievement (nAch), affiliation (nAff) and power (nPow).

- nAch is a drive to do well, to succeed and to do things better. People with a high nAch will want to succeed for their own personal satisfaction rather than for external rewards. Perhaps not surprisingly, this motive is the most studied in work psychology, and it has been found that people with high nAch like to take responsibility for solving problems and set moderately challenging goals, enough to be a challenge but not so high that their success would be due to chance. They also like to have constant feedback to help them judge how well they are doing.
- nAff is the desire to build friendly, cooperative relationships, and people with a strong nAff will be motivated to do teamwork, where they can work in an interdependent way with others.
- Lastly, people high on nPow want to have influence over others and will be motivated by the opportunity to gain prestige and control.

McClelland emphasised that these motives have both a conscious and an unconscious (or *implicit*) component. That is, if you completed a self-report questionnaire about your motives, your scores could well be very different from a measure that assessed the strength of your implicit motives. There is a lot of debate over the extent to which these unconscious motives can be measured, with some psychologists claiming that if the person cannot even report on it, it cannot be measured accurately. But many psychologists believe we can measure unconscious parts of the mind and one way of doing this is to use *projective* tests.

You may be familiar with the Rorschach or ink blot tests, where a person is shown an abstract ink blot and asked to say what they see in it. The idea behind these tests is that when there are ambiguities in how something can be perceived, we *project* our own internal thoughts and feelings onto the picture. The psychologist can then interpret these projections as indications of our unconscious mind. A projective test that is used to measure implicit motives is the Thematic Apperception Test (TAT). In the

TAT, the person is shown an ambiguous picture (that is, a picture which can be interpreted in different ways) and writes a brief story in response to it. The psychologist then analyses the story to identify the unconscious needs or motives that it demonstrates (McClelland et al., 1953). Work through the activity below to see how this works.

Activity Measuring implicit motives

Implicit motives are often assessed using the TAT, where respondents are asked to write a story based on a picture. This activity gives you a chance to experience this yourself. Look at the following picture and write as dramatic a story as you can, including the following:

▸ what has led up to the event shown
▸ what is happening at the moment
▸ what the characters are feeling and thinking
▸ what the outcome of the story was.

© Jones, K. (2013), used with permission

Write your story before reading further!

When you have finished, read through the story again and try to identify the kind of themes that came out. Was it power issues? Is one person the boss watching the other? Or perhaps affiliation themes: did you write about the relationship between these two people? Or was it achievement? Is someone in the story focused on doing a good job or worried about failure? It's quite possible that you wrote about more than one of these themes. This can give you an insight into how strong these three implicit motives are for you.

Once you have an idea about your implicit motives, you can also look back over your life and see if you can see how your unconscious needs for power, affiliation and achievement might have guided your behaviour. Remember that implicit motives tend to be seen most clearly over the long term and in situations with less conscious restrictions. For example, we would expect implicit motives to guide a choice of profession if a person had the ability and resources needed to follow that career path, but not if she or he was desperate for money and there was only one job available.

There is debate over how accurate TAT measures are, although more recent work by McClelland and colleagues has helped to create a more reliable and valid test than some of the original versions (Winter, 1999). Using these more reliable measures, there is good evidence that conscious and unconscious motives affect behavioural outcomes differently (McClelland et al., 1989). Implicit motives predict our spontaneous behavioural trends over time, while self-reported motives predict more specific behavioural choices. For example, self-reported motives would predict what kind of task someone with a high nAch would be better at. In addition, conscious or implicit motives respond to task incentives in different ways. Someone with a high implicit nAch will do better on a challenging task than someone with a low nAch. However, someone with a high self-reported nAch will only do better on the task if they are explicitly told that it will show they are better than others.

An advantage of McClelland's theory is that the strengths of these needs have been related directly to work performance. For example, a longitudinal study of managers found that those with a moderate to high nPow and low nAff were more successful at gaining promotion eight and 16 years later (McClelland and Boyatzis, 1982). nAch was only important at the lower levels of management where an individual's contributions were important: at the higher levels, the ability to influence others was more important.

If you think back to our definition of motivation, you can see how this theory of implicit needs helps us to understand the different elements. An individual's needs determine what things they will be motivated to do (*direction*), and the relative strength of each of those needs determines their *intensity* and *persistence*.

PROCESS THEORIES: *HOW* ARE WE MOTIVATED?

A different way of thinking about motivation is to try and understand the processes that happen in our minds when we are motivated to do something. Instead of identifying the needs that people are motivated to fulfil, this approach describes how we are motivated by the way we think about work.

We will look at three influential theories in this section. Equity theory outlines how we are motivated by a sense of fairness: a fair day's pay for a fair day's work. Expectancy theory describes how we are motivated by our expectations of the result of our work. Goal-setting theory outlines how we are motivated by goals. All of these theories extend the basic reward motivation of behaviourist approaches to understanding the complexities of human thought processes.

Equity theory

Equity theory basically says that we want fairness and that we are motivated by how equitable we think our efforts and rewards are in comparison with other people's (Adams, 1965). It is a *social comparison* theory: we want our work to be rewarded at the same level as other people doing similar work. We compare our inputs (that is, the amount of work we do) with how much other people do, and then see how our outcomes compare. For example, if you spend a whole week on an essay and someone else in your group spends only an hour on it but gets the same grade, you'll feel it is very unfair and you'll be motivated to correct the inequity.

How do we try to correct inequities?

- If we perceive that we are being under-rewarded, we will reduce the work we put into the task.
- If we perceive that we are being over-rewarded, we will work harder in an attempt to 'earn' the reward.

There is good evidence for the first of these propositions, though less for the second. It seems we are less motivated to correct inequity if we are benefiting from it. In addition, the effects have been found to be somewhat short-lived

My inputs to job / My outcomes or rewards   Others' inputs to their job / Others' outcomes

△

Figure 4.2 Equity theory

(Carrell and Dittrich, 1978). That is, if we feel we are being overpaid for a job, we will initially work harder to try and create equity, but after a while we will start to believe that our work is actually worth that much and performance levels will drop again.

Expectancy theory

Initially proposed by Vroom (1964), expectancy theory claims that our level of motivation is based on our answers to three basic questions about the outcome or end result of our efforts.

1 How much do I want this outcome?
   - This is known as *valence*, or how desirable the outcome is. Valence can be positive (for an outcome we value) or negative (for an outcome that we do not wish to attain).
2 Will good performance lead to this outcome?
   - This is called *instrumentality*, the probability that good performance will result in the outcome I want.
3 How likely is it that my hard work will result in a good level of performance?
   - This is *expectancy*, the key to the whole model. It is our understanding of how much our efforts will actually lead to the level of performance we need in order to access the valued outcome.

Our level of motivation, or the amount of effort we will put into a task, is represented by a simple combination of these three variables:

$$F = V \times I \times E$$
Force or Effort $=$ Valence $\times$ Instrumentality $\times$ Expectancy

This VIE model is a concise and simple way of understanding how motivated we are for any task. We will be more motivated if we expect that our hard work will lead to a level of performance that will get us that coveted outcome. It is also a good basis for understanding the differences between individual motivation levels. We can differ in terms of how much we value the outcome, the extent to which we think we can work to the required level and the extent to which we believe performance at that level will enable us to attain the outcome. But is this intuitively appealing model supported by research evidence?

One of the problems with testing the model is how we actually measure 'force' or effort. A meta-analysis by Van Eerde and Thierry (1996) looked at how the model was related to both behavioural outcomes (such as performance or choice of occupation) and attitudinal outcomes (such as intentions to apply for a job or preferences about different jobs). They found that while the individual elements of the model (valence, instrumentality

and expectancy) were related to attitudinal outcomes, they were not strongly related to behavioural outcomes. In addition, combining the elements as Vroom suggested did not show any improvement in predicting the outcomes. So while the individual elements might be useful in understanding our attitudes towards tasks, the model is not very helpful in predicting behaviour.

Goal-setting theory

Locke and Latham have conducted research over several decades exploring the idea that conscious goals can affect performance. In 1990, they reviewed the evidence that had accumulated in their own and others' research and outlined two core findings (Locke and Latham, 1990):

1 The more difficult the goal, the higher the level of effort and performance the person produces
2 Specific, difficult goals lead to a higher level of performance than simply being told to 'do your best'.

So how do goals affect our performance? Locke and Latham (2002) propose four main mechanisms. First, goals give direction to our efforts, ensuring that we focus on tasks that are related to the goal rather than putting effort into unrelated things. Second, they are energising, with higher goals leading to greater effort than lower goals. Third, they improve persistence. And finally, goals have an indirect effect on performance by activating our goal-related knowledge and skills, or encouraging us to develop them if we do not yet have what is required.

There are also several variables that moderate the effectiveness of goal-setting (Locke and Latham, 2002):

- **Commitment**. The more committed a person is to a goal, the more effort s/he will put into achieving that goal. Commitment can be affected by the *perceived importance* of the goal and a person's *self-efficacy* (belief in their ability to meet the goal). You may be thinking that this is remarkably similar to Vroom's VIE model, and it is. Remember that research has shown that the individual components of Vroom's model are related to effort, and it seems that goal-setting theory combines these components in a meaningful way.
- **Feedback.** We need to know how we are doing in relation to the goal so that we can adjust our efforts accordingly.
- **Complexity.** The more complex a task is, the less effect goal-setting will have on performance. This is because, as a task becomes more complex, other variables such as knowledge, ability or skill levels will affect performance.

A final element of goal-setting theory is the role of satisfaction in the process. We will discuss job attitudes like this in more detail in the next section, but within goal-setting theory, satisfaction is an important part of the performance cycle. Achieving goals brings us satisfaction, and Latham and Locke argue that this is essential in determining our willingness to commit to further challenges (Locke and Latham, 2002). So while difficult goals produce greater effort and performance, when managing motivation we need to be aware that setting unattainable goals will lead to a drop in satisfaction and a lack of commitment to future goals.

But satisfaction is more complicated than this. An interesting study by Mento et al. (1992) looked at satisfaction and goal-setting within an academic environment. They found that achieving and exceeding goals increased people's satisfaction, while failing to achieve goals made people more dissatisfied. This would imply that people would be more satisfied more of the time if they only ever set themselves easy goals. Indeed, their research showed exactly that: people with higher goals were less satisfied with their performance. People with high standards need to achieve more in order to feel satisfied. The authors ask the question: why, then, doesn't everyone opt for low standards? They suggest two possibilities:

1 It is an important part of some people's self-image to have high standards, so it would be *less* satisfying for them to drop their standards than to keep trying to achieve difficult goals.
2 Meeting high standards leads to greater practical outcomes than meeting low standards. For example, achieving good marks at school gives you greater choice of university degrees, achieving a good degree gives you a better chance of the job you want, and so on.

 Psychological Toolkit Goal-setting theory and your career

Goal-setting theory tells us that we perform best when we have set difficult and specific goals. This activity will help to guide you through how you can use goal-setting theory to turn your career dreams into specific goals.

First, write down your career dream. (Don't worry about specifics at this point, or about how realistic or otherwise it might appear.)

```
My career dream:



```

The next step is where you start turning that dream into specific goals. Think of about three or four goals that will help you achieve your dream. Remember these should be difficult but not completely impossible. For example, if your dream is to have a career which involves travelling to other countries and working with people from different cultures, one goal could be to learn a new language. If your dream is to earn a certain amount of money, one goal might be to gain the qualifications or experience that will help you get that promotion. At this stage, your goals may well be quite broad – we will consider how to break them down in the next step.

```
My specific goals:

1.

2.

3.

4.
```

Remember the moderators of the goal → performance relationship? You can use these to consider what you can do to enhance the effectiveness of your goals. Ask yourself these questions:

▶ **How complex are these goals?**
   An important consideration here is how the complexity of the goal matches your own abilities. If the goal looks too complex to you, break it down into smaller goals. Some of these goals might be to learn a new skill or develop your ability in order to achieve the bigger goal.
▶ **How committed am I to each of these goals?**
   If you find that your commitment to the goal is low, think about why that might be. Is it because it does not feel very important or perhaps that you feel you will not be able to do it? You could either replace it with a goal you are more committed to, or find a way of increasing your belief in your own ability. You can do this by setting yourself shorter-term objectives – the theory tells us that as you achieve these smaller goals, it will increase your satisfaction and your willingness to commit to new challenges. For example, if you had set yourself the goal of 'learning a new language' but felt this was far beyond you, you could break it down into smaller goals: 'complete a beginner's course in

Spanish' and 'use my Spanish skills next time I go on holiday'.

▸ **What kind of feedback can I get to help me assess my progress towards these goals?**
Continuous monitoring of our progress is the best way to ensure we achieve our goals. Without feedback, you won't know how well you are progressing or whether you need to change your approach. So try to identify ways you can get this feedback. For example, can you do online quizzes to assess your language learning progress? Do you have any friends or colleagues who know the language you are studying and could give you an outside opinion on your progress?

Overall, the key with using goal-setting theory to your advantage is to recognise the importance of progressive achievements: each time you perform well, you will increase your satisfaction and increase your willingness to commit to new challenges, thereby increasing your motivation for the new goals.

One last thing to remember is that your career dream may well change over time. So it is worth revisiting your goals every now and then to check they are still things you are committed to.

These different elements of goal-setting theory can be combined in the high performance cycle (Locke and Latham, 2002), an adapted version of which is shown below:

Goal-setting can be just as effective for teams as it is for individuals, with goals leading to higher performance than a simple 'do your best' instruction (Wegge and Haslam, 2005). However, when considering team motivation we need to be aware of the issue of incompatible goals. It is only if an individual's goals are in harmony with the team's goals that performance is increased (Latham and Locke, 2007).

One of the attractions of goal-setting theory is the way it highlights how we can consciously control and direct work behaviour. This fits in very well with a scientific approach to management and allows managers to feel they have a clear, reliable method to improve workers' motivation. However, as we saw in our discussion of needs theories, some motivation is unconscious, and there is good evidence that our unconscious goals are as important as our conscious goals in determining behaviour (Latham et al., 2010). Research on how unconscious goals interact with conscious ones in workplace behaviour is one of the current areas of study in this evolving theory (Latham and Locke, 2007).

The role of personality

All of the theories we have looked at so far have a place for individual differences in motivation. These differences are variously described as differing levels or strengths of needs, differing perceptions of reward attractiveness, different goals and so on. It may leave you wondering if perhaps some part of motivation is down to an individual's personality. Are some people just inherently 'more motivated' than others?

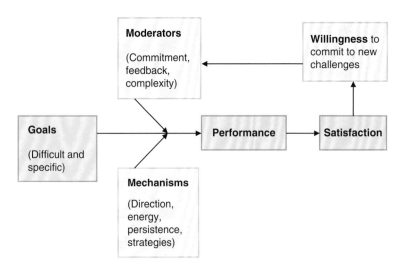

Figure 4.3 The high performance cycle

Source: E. A. Locke and G. P. Latham (2002) Building a practically useful theory of goal setting and task motivation. *American Psychologist*, 57 (9), 705–17. American Psychological Association; adapted with permission.

International Perspectives Work motivation and culture

Work motivation research is strongly culturally based, and a theory which works well in one culture will not necessarily translate well to another. Both personal and situational factors have different effects on motivation in different cultures (Gelfand et al., 2007). For example, while motives such as a need for achievement are present across cultures, their meaning varies somewhat. A comparison of achievement goals showed that Australians placed a higher value on individualistic goals such as personal health and happiness, while Sri Lankans valued collectivist goals such as family and social responsibility more highly (Niles, 1998).

However, the individualistic/collectivist distinction should not be used in a simplistic manner to make assumptions about what will work for different cultures. Based on an understanding of collectivism, we might assume that the best kind of feedback for people in a collectivist culture would be group feedback. In fact, while personal feedback does work best for those in an individualistic culture, the picture is more complex for collectivists. It seems that collectivists use both group and personal feedback in building their sense of how successful they are. In addition, only personal feedback had an impact on collectivists' feelings of satisfaction with their performance (Earley et al., 1999).

One of the tenets of goal-setting theory is that goals should be difficult and that managers should avoid imposing goals on their employees and instead get them involved in jointly creating goals. But when we consider the impact of power distance, we find a more complex picture emerges. People tend to be more committed to and perform at a higher level for assigned goals in high-power distance cultures than in low-power distance, and those who are also in collectivist cultures actually perform better when set moderate rather than difficult goals (Gelfand et al., 2007).

Taken together, these findings sound a note of caution when it comes to applying motivational theories in different cultures. While the general principles might hold across cultures, we need to be sure to take account of indigenous perspectives in understanding their application to a specific culture.

Discussion points

The individualist/collectivist distinction is probably the most well-known cultural difference and often applied in a very simplistic manner. Why do you think this is?

What other aspects of culture do you think are relevant for our understanding of work motivation?

If culture can have such a big effect on motivational theories, is there any point in trying to develop such theories?

One of the advantages of the Big Five model of personality that we reviewed in Chapter 2 is the fact that it can be used as a basis for meta-analyses to answer questions like this. Judge and Ilies (2002) reviewed 65 studies which explored the link between personality and motivation. They found that higher Emotional Stability and Conscientiousness scores predicted higher performance motivation. This is a useful finding for organisations, as it implies that more motivated individuals can be selected on the basis of personality testing. Given that there is good evidence for a heritable component of personality, this finding also implies that a certain level of motivation is outside management control. You can read more about this in the Key Research Study below.

Key Research Study Personality and motivation

Relationship of Personality to Performance Motivation: A Meta-Analytic Review

T. A. Judge and R. Ilies (2002)

Background: Although most researchers recognise that there are individual differences in motivation, there is a lack of clarity about what those differences are and how they affect work motivation. This is probably because there are so many different models of personality and motivation that it is difficult to gain an overview of the many research studies.

Aim: To find out the extent to which individual personality affects work motivation, using the Big Five model of personality and three models of motivation: goal-setting, expectancy and self-efficacy.

Method: Meta-analysis is a very useful tool in making sense of the vast array of research studies in a particular area. It statistically combines the findings of hundreds of studies and present the reader with an overview of the current state of the science. The steps taken were:

1 Identify all relevant studies and exclude those which did not measure traits or motivation as

specified above, did not report primary data or did not use direct measures of task motivation.

2   Classify data into the relevant models.

3   Conduct statistical analysis. For meta-analysis, this involves making a statistical estimation of the population correlation from the results reported in the individual studies, as well as reporting the variability in the studies' correlations (e.g. confidence intervals).

Findings:

▸ Overall, the Big Five traits had a strong relationship with motivation

▸ Emotional Stability and Conscientiousness were positively related to motivation in all three models

▸ The other three traits were more inconsistent, with relationships depending on which model of motivation was used.

Implications: Individual personality has a substantial impact on work motivation, and this finding holds true regardless of which model of motivation is used. The two traits with the strongest relationship to motivation are also the two traits which are most strongly related to job performance. It is suggested that Emotional Stability influences performance mostly through motivation, while Conscientiousness also has more direct effects on performance.

Limitations: Because meta-analyses combine the results of so many studies, they miss out on the important situational variables that are captured in the originals. So while they are invaluable aids in understanding general principles, they should not be relied on for the details of application to specific situations.

Having reviewed theories of motivation, we will now explore job attitudes. In work psychology, attitudes are closely related to motivation because they are another way of explaining why people work.

JOB ATTITUDES

On Facebook, the most basic interaction you can have with something someone has posted is to click 'like'. This is expressing an attitude towards it (though strangely Facebook does not allow you to express a 'dislike'). An attitude is an evaluative judgement of an object on a good–bad scale, and we form attitudes without even consciously thinking about it (Ajzen, 2001). Or, as Eagly and Chaiken (1993, p. 1) put it, an attitude is

a psychological tendency that is expressed by evaluating a particular entity with some degree of favour or disfavour.

The 'object' of an attitude can be anything: a boss, a colleague, our job, the place we work or where we live. Judge and Kammeyer-Mueller (2012, p. 344) define job attitudes as 'evaluations of one's job that express one's feelings towards, beliefs about, and attachment to one's job', highlighting the three components of attitudes: affective, cognitive and behavioural (Breckler, 1984):

1   The cognitive component is a statement of evaluation or a belief about an object; for example, 'My colleagues are unfriendly'

2   The affective component is how we feel about that person or thing; for example, 'I don't like my job'

3   The behavioural component is how we act based on that attitude; for example, if we don't like our job, we might start looking for another one or complain about it to our friends.

It is important to note, however, that these three components are just a useful way of thinking about attitudes (a heuristic), not clear and distinct parts of an attitude (Judge and Kammeyer-Mueller, 2012). The cognitive and affective components are often difficult to separate out and may even be in conflict with one another. In addition, people may well express an attitude which they never act on.

It is the behavioural component that is important for psychology at work and attitudes are substantial predictors of our future behaviour, with the correlation between attitudes and behaviour at around 0.5 (Glasman and Albarracin, 2006). But the link between our behaviour and our thoughts or feelings about an object is not straightforward, and we will now look at ways in which this link has been theorised.

The attitude–behaviour link

To what extent do you think your behaviour is influenced by your attitudes? Or have you ever considered whether behaving in a particular way may actually change your attitude? These questions have occupied psychologists for years, and two important concepts have emerged that help to clarify how our attitudes and behaviours affect each other: cognitive dissonance and planned behaviour.

Cognitive dissonance theory

The cognitive dissonance theory (Festinger and Carlsmith, 1959) holds that a mismatch between our privately held attitudes and publicly displayed behaviour (or between two different attitudes) is uncomfortable to us. This means that if we do or say something that does not match our internal attitude, we will want to change our behaviour to match.

There are several factors that moderate the extent to which our attitudes affect behaviour (Kraus, 1995, Ajzen, 2001, Glasman and Albarracin, 2006):

1 Certainty – how certain you are of your attitude. The more certain you are, the greater the effect of your attitude on your behaviour.
2 Experience – the more experience you have of something, the more likely your attitude will affect your behaviour. This links well with the point above: the more experience you have of a job, for example, the more certain you will be of your attitude towards it.
3 Specificity – an attitude that is more specific to the particular behaviour we are interested in will have a greater effect on behaviour. For example, asking people about their general attitudes towards working will be less useful in predicting whether they will accept a job offer than asking them about their specific attitude towards that organisation or the job itself.
4 Accessibility – attitudes that you talk about more and are more easily remembered are more likely to affect your behaviour. So, for example, if you talk to everyone you know about how much you dislike your job, you are more likely to act on that attitude and leave the job than if you just don't think about it.

Self-perception theory (Bem, 1973) adds to our understanding of cognitive dissonance by showing us how behaviour influences attitudes. This theory says that when we are asked about our attitudes, we review our behaviour in relation to that topic and create plausible reasons for why we behaved like that. We don't want to feel that we are behaving in a way that contradicts our attitudes, so we 'create' attitudes to match our behaviour. So if we are asked how committed we are to our organisation, we review the past few months, realise we have not applied for any other jobs and decide we must be quite committed. The evidence indicates that this inferring of our attitudes from behaviour is particularly true when our attitudes are ambiguous or we have not really thought about the object of the attitude before.

Planned behaviour

Ajzen (1991) proposed the theory of planned behaviour as an explanation for how our attitudes, subjective norms and perceptions of control over our own behaviour interact to influence our intent to behave in a particular way. Based on this theory, Eagly and Chaiken (1993) developed a composite model that shows how our attitudes are related to our behaviour. It highlights three important influences on our behaviour:

1 First, and of central importance in this model, is the role of attitudes in shaping our intentions. Eagly and Chaiken, in common with many other attitude researchers, propose the basic link as: attitude → intention to behave → actual behaviour.

Let's illustrate this using the example of leaving a job. If our attitude towards leaving is positive we will have a greater intention to leave, and this is more likely to result in actually looking for a new job and leaving the old one.

2 The second important point that this model highlights is that there are two types of attitudes that are important in determining our intention:
   • our attitudes towards the *object* (whether we like the job itself, or our boss or colleagues).
   • our assessment of the possible *outcomes* of our behaviour. These possible outcomes can be utilitarian (e.g. we might consider what the effect of leaving will be on our income), normative (perhaps our feelings of guilt for leaving our colleagues) or related to our self-identity (what will it mean to us to no longer have that occupational identity?).

3 The third and final contributor to the attitude–behaviour link is simply habit. Our habits influence our attitudes towards both the behaviour and its outcomes, as well as having a direct effect on what behaviour we actually display. For example, our habit of going to work every day makes it more likely we will simply continue to do so. The habit can also have a positive effect on our attitudes towards work, as well as our attitudes towards the outcomes of work (it feels 'normal' and positive).

This model is very useful in highlighting the complexities of the attitude–behaviour link. Most notably, it shows us that job attitudes (e.g. job satisfaction or organisational commitment) are only part of an interactive process, not a direct causation of behaviour.

 Activity Your attitudes

Use the attitude–behaviour model to explore your own attitude towards continuing or leaving your course. Work through each of the steps in the model, identifying how positive or negative your attitudes are (towards continuing with the course and towards aspects of the course such as your interest in it, your fellow students, your lecturers and so on), and also what outcomes you think there might be if you left or continued. See if you can identify some habits that might affect your attitudes and behaviour as well.

When you have finished, consider the following questions:

▸ Is it useful to analyse attitudes in this way? Do you think it provides a useful understanding of how our attitudes affect behaviour? Why or why not?

Bearing in mind that the relationship between attitudes and behaviour is complex, let's look at some of the most important attitudes at work.

Job satisfaction

If there is one work attitude that has received more attention than any other, it is job satisfaction. Job satisfaction is an evaluation of how happy we are with our jobs. From a management point of view, people have wanted to know if more satisfied workers are more productive, and if they are, how we can ensure satisfaction. A meta-analysis at the beginning of the twenty-first century summarised what had been found in over 300 studies of the satisfaction–performance relationship and concluded that yes, job satisfaction did indeed have a moderately strong relationship (correlation of 0.3) with job performance (Judge et al., 2001). But what it did not tell us is what direction this relationship is in. Does satisfaction with our jobs improve job performance, or do we feel more satisfied with our jobs when we are working well? The answer is probably both.

Judge et al. (2001) identified 17 different potential moderators of the satisfaction–performance relationship, including moral obligations and job characteristics, and noted that much of the research in this area is ongoing. Here are a couple of the more well-supported moderators:

- Job complexity: the satisfaction–performance relationship is stronger for people in more complex jobs, who have greater discretion over how they perform and the extent to which they can allow their attitudes to affect their performance.
- Personality: the relationship is stronger for people who are less conscientious (Barrick et al., 2001). People higher in conscientiousness will tend to work hard and complete tasks regardless of their attitudes towards them.

Job satisfaction is not only an important part of understanding individual performance, it also has a big impact on organisational performance. A meta-analysis of nearly 8,000 business units showed that employee satisfaction at the level of the whole business unit was substantially related to improved customer satisfaction, productivity and profit, as well as reduced employee turnover and accidents (Harter et al., 2002). Job satisfaction is also related to organisational citizenship behaviours (Ilies et al., 2009) – extra or discretionary work that the employee is not obliged to do.

Given that employee satisfaction can have so many benefits, managers will want to know what they can do to ensure the satisfaction of their team (or indeed their own satisfaction). One approach to understanding overall job satisfaction examines different 'facets' for how much they contribute to overall satisfaction. For example, the Job Descriptive Index (Smith et al., 1969) conceptualises satisfaction in terms of pay, co-workers, the work itself, opportunities for promotion, and supervision. Which of these do you think is most related to overall satisfaction?

Your first thought might be 'pay'. If you get paid more, surely you'll be more satisfied with your job? The answer is a bit complicated. First, employees' satisfaction with both their pay and their job overall is mostly unrelated to their actual level of earnings (Judge et al., 2010). Instead, the main determinant of how satisfied we are with our pay seems to rest on our judgements of how we are paid *in comparison* with other people, either within our organisation or outside it (Williams et al., 2006). To be satisfied with our pay, we want to feel we are being rewarded fairly compared with others – as we saw when we looked at equity theory. In fact, the facet most closely related to overall job satisfaction is the work itself (Judge and Kammeyer-Mueller, 2012) rather than the pay or social context.

 Case Study Overpaid CEOs?

In 2011, CEOs in the UK were paid 185 times more than the average worker (High Pay Centre, 2013). Thinking about both job satisfaction research and the equity theory of motivation, explain what effect it might have on an employee who is paid £26,000 to find out that their boss's salary is £4.8 million.

▸ If you were a middle manager at this organisation, what might you be able to do to ensure that your team remained motivated even though they have become aware of this inequity?

▸ Do you personally think CEOs' pay is equitable – that is, do you think that the work they do is worth 185 times more than what the average worker does? Why or why not?

© PhotoDisc/Getty Images

As we saw earlier in this chapter, the job characteristics model (Hackman and Oldham, 1976) outlines which aspects of work can contribute to job satisfaction. More recent research has found that 'high-quality work' is the aspect of a job that is most strongly related to overall satisfaction (Barling et al., 2003); that is, work which involves extensive training, variety and autonomy makes people more satisfied.

Finally, it is worth noting that about a third to a half of our job satisfaction seems to be simply down to who we are and not necessarily related to the job we are doing (Judge and Kammeyer-Mueller, 2012). Some people – those higher on extraversion and emotional stability – will simply be more satisfied with whatever job they are doing than others (Judge et al., 2002). This is an important consideration for the many employee satisfaction surveys that organisations conduct (and indeed customer or student satisfaction surveys), as it shows that a substantial proportion of a person's attitudes may well be out of the organisation's control.

Organisational commitment

The second job attitude we are going to consider is organisational commitment. This is a person's psychological bond to an organisation: how attached do they feel to the organisation and how much effort will they put into supporting it (Judge and Kammeyer-Mueller, 2012)? Organisational commitment is based on the extent to which we identify with the values and goals of our employer. It was originally conceptualised as having three elements (Allen and Meyer, 1990):

- Affective commitment – how much a person values the organisation, how attached and included they feel
- Normative commitment – how much the employee feels obliged to stay, or sees leaving as negative behaviour
- Continuance commitment – the extent to which a person feels there are costs associated with leaving.

But as you can see from these definitions, two of the elements (normative and continuance) are attitudes towards behaviours (quitting and staying) and only one (affective) is an attitude towards the organisation. In fact, affective commitment has the strongest relationship with workplace behaviours such as attendance, levels of performance and organisational citizenship behaviour (Meyer et al., 2002). Work in clarifying the concept of organisational commitment is ongoing, and a recent book by Klein et al. (2009) reconceptualised the original model to suggest that it was capturing commitment as a 'bond' between an individual and a target rather than an attitude.

Certainly, the research around organisational commitment has not supported this three-component model and instead recommends using the generalised attitude–behaviour model developed by Eagly and Chaiken that we looked at above (Solinger et al., 2008) and the affective/cognitive/behavioural approach to understanding specific attitudes.

We saw above that job satisfaction has a positive relationship with job performance, and we know that the reason work psychologists are interested in attitudes is because of their relationship to work behaviours. So what outcomes have been identified for organisational commitment?

Organisational commitment is strongly related to absenteeism: those who are more committed are less likely to be absent from work. Absenteeism is further reduced when employees are satisfied with their jobs as well (Hausknecht et al., 2008). In contrast, the effect of organisational commitment on job performance is generally positive but not particularly strong (Judge and Kammeyer-Mueller, 2012). Interestingly, the relationship between commitment and performance decreases the longer someone remains in the job (Wright and Bonett, 2002). Note that this is not saying people do not perform as well when they have been in the job longer, but that their performance is less related to their levels of organisational commitment.

SUMMARY

We have covered a lot of ground in this chapter, looking at what boosts or inhibits work performance from several different angles. There are many things that affect motivation and performance and it would be oversimplistic (and simply wrong) to try to reduce them to one easy-to-use formula. But what we can do is draw out reliable findings from all these different approaches to create a practical checklist of things that managers can do to improve motivation at work.

1 Provide rewards that are:
   a. Directly and obviously linked to performance.
   b. Equitable: employees need to know that the efforts they put in are rewarded at a similar level to others'.
   c. Be aware that if you are trying to increase *intrinsic* motivation, the best rewards are verbal and informational.
2 Enhance job-related and social characteristics to increase employees' experienced meaningfulness and responsibility.
3 Set difficult and specific goals. If possible, this should be done participatively.

4 Feedback is essential. This comes out in several different theories: people want to know how they are doing so they can adjust their performance as necessary. Feedback helps both intrinsic and extrinsic motivation.

5 Provide opportunities for training and development. This helps with job satisfaction and organisational commitment as well as providing goals and meeting needs for achievement.

6 And finally, get to know individual employees. If there is one take-home message from this chapter, it is that there is not a single way of motivating everyone. The better you know the people you are trying to motivate, the better you will be at choosing the right approach.

TEST YOURSELF

Brief Review Questions

1 What is non-financial employment commitment and why is it important in understanding motivation?
2 How would you define motivation?
3 Briefly summarise Hackman and Oldham's five core job characteristics. How has this model been extended?
4 Name and define McClelland's three implicit needs.
5 What is the high performance cycle?
6 Define job satisfaction and explain why it is important in the study of motivation.

Discussion or Essay Questions

1 Does money motivate people at work?
2 Is there any evidence that social factors are important in work motivation? Why do you think this is?
3 Compare and contrast the equity and expectancy theories of motivation. How useful are they in explaining motivation at work?
4 To what extent do you think managers can actually increase employees' motivation?
5 How are job attitudes related to behaviour at work?

FURTHER READING

- Locke and Latham's summary of goal-setting theory is available online at http://faculty.washington.edu/janegf/goalsetting.html, and gives a thorough, accessible overview of research and findings.
- Judge and Kammeyer-Mueller's recent review paper of job attitudes provides a good overview of the current state of knowledge. T. A. Judge and J. D. Kammeyer-Mueller, Job attitudes. *Annual Review of Psychology*, 63 (2012), 341–67.

References

ADAMS, J. S. 1965. Inequity in social exchanges. *Advances in Experimental Social Psychology*, 2, 267–300.

AJZEN, I. 1991. The theory of planned behavior. *Organizational Behavior and Human Decision Processes*, 50, 179–211.

AJZEN, I. 2001. Nature and operation of attitudes. *Annual Review of Psychology*, 52, 27–58.

ALDERFER, C. P. 1969. An empirical test of a new theory of human needs. *Organizational Behavior & Human Performance*, 4, 142–75.

ALLEN, N. J. & MEYER, J. P. 1990. The measurement and antecedents of affective, continuance and normative commitment to the organization. *Journal of Occupational Psychology*, 63, 1–18.

BARLING, J., KELLOWAY, E. & IVERSON, R. D. 2003. High-quality work, job satisfaction, and occupational injuries. *Journal of Applied Psychology*, 88, 276–83.

BARRICK, M. R., MOUNT, M. K. & JUDGE, T. A. 2001. Personality and performance at the beginning of the new millennium: what do we know and where do we go next? *International Journal of Selection and Assessment*, 9, 9–30.

BEM, D. J. 1973. Self-perception theory. *Advances in Experimental Social Psychology*, 6, 1–62.

BRECKLER, S. J. 1984. Empirical validation of affect, behavior, and cognition as distinct components of attitude. *Journal of Personality and Social Psychology*, 47, 1191–205.

CARRELL, M. & DITTRICH, J. 1978. Equity theory: the recent literature, methodological considerations, and new directions. *Academy of Management Review*, 3, 202–10.

DECI, E. L. 1972. The effects of contingent and noncontingent rewards and controls on intrinsic motivation. *Organizational Behavior and Human Performance*, 8, 217–29.

DECI, E. L. 1999. A meta-analytic review of experiments examining the effects of extrinsic rewards on intrinsic motivation. *Psychological Bulletin*, 125, 627.

DECI, E. L. & RYAN, R. M. 1980. Self-determination theory: when mind mediates behavior. *Journal of Mind and Behavior*, 1, 33–43.

EAGLY, A. H. & CHAIKEN, S. 1993. *The Psychology of Attitudes*. Orlando, FL, Harcourt Brace Jovanovich College Publishers.

EARLEY, P., GIBSON, C. B. & CHEN, C. C. 1999. 'How did I do?' versus 'how did we do?' Cultural contrasts of performance feedback use and self-efficacy. *Journal of Cross-Cultural Psychology*, 30, 594–619.

FESTINGER, L. & CARLSMITH, J. M. 1959. Cognitive consequences of forced compliance. *Journal of Abnormal and Social Psychology*, 58, 203–10.

GELFAND, M. J., EREZ, M. & AYCAN, Z. 2007. Cross-cultural organizational behavior. *Annual Review of Psychology*, 58, 479–514.

GLASMAN, L. R. & ALBARRACIN, D. 2006. Forming attitudes that predict future behavior: a meta-analysis of the attitude–behavior relation. *Psychological Bulletin*, 132, 778–822.

HACKMAN, J. & OLDHAM, G. R. 1976. Motivation through the design of work: test of a theory. *Organizational Behavior & Human Performance*, 16, 250–79.

HARPAZ, I. 2002. Expressing a wish to continue or stop working as related to the meaning of work. *European Journal of Work and Organizational Psychology*, 11, 177–98.

HARTER, J. K., SCHMIDT, F. L. & HAYES, T. L. 2002. Business-unit-level relationship between employee satisfaction, employee engagement, and business outcomes: a meta-analysis. *Journal of Applied Psychology*, 87, 268–79.

HAUSKNECHT, J. P., HILLER, N. J. & VANCE, R. J. 2008. Work-unit absenteeism: effects of satisfaction, commitment, labor market conditions, and time. *Academy of Management Journal*, 51, 1223–45.

HEDENUS, A. 2012. Who wants to work less? Significance of socio-economic status and work conditions for work commitment among Swedish lottery winners. *Acta Sociologica*, 55, 335–50.

HERZBERG, F., MAUSNER, B. & SNYDERMAN, B. 1959. *The Motivation to Work*. New York, Wiley.

HIGH PAY CENTRE. 2013. *Key Facts You Should Know About Executive Pay*. http://highpaycentre.org/bigpay/key-facts-you-should-know-about-executive-pay (accessed 19 June 2013).

HIGHHOUSE, S., ZICKAR, M. J. & YANKELEVICH, M. 2010. Would you work if you won the lottery? Tracking changes in the American work ethic. *Journal of Applied Psychology*, 95, 349–57.

HUMPHREY, S. E., NAHRGANG, J. D. & MORGESON, F. P. 2007. Integrating motivational, social, and contextual work design features: a meta-analytic summary and theoretical extension of the work design literature. *Journal of Applied Psychology*, 92, 1332–56.

ILIES, R., FULMER, I. S., SPITZMULLER, M. & JOHNSON, M. D. 2009. Personality and citizenship behavior: the mediating role of job satisfaction. *Journal of Applied Psychology*, 94, 945–59.

JUDGE, T. A. & ILIES, R. 2002. Relationship of personality to performance motivation: a meta-analytic review. *Journal of Applied Psychology*, 87, 797–807.

JUDGE, T. A. & KAMMEYER-MUELLER, J. D. 2012. Job attitudes. *Annual Review of Psychology*, 63, 341–67.

JUDGE, T. A., HELLER, D. & MOUNT, M. K. 2002. Five-factor model of personality and job satisfaction: a meta-analysis. *Journal of Applied Psychology*, 87, 530–41.

JUDGE, T. A., THORESON, C. J., BONO, J. E. & PATTON, G. K. 2001. The job satisfaction–job performance relationship: a qualitative and quantitative review. *Psychological Bulletin*, 127, 376–407.

JUDGE, T. A., PICCOLO, R. F., PODSAKOFF, N. P., SHAW, J. C. & RICH, B. L. 2010. The relationship between pay and job satisfaction: a meta-analysis of the literature. *Journal of Vocational Behavior*, 77, 157–67.

KLEIN, H. J., BECKER, T. E. & MEYER, J. P. 2009. *Commitment in Organizations: Accumulated Wisdom and New Directions*. Hove, Routledge.

KRAUS, S. J. 1995. Attitudes and the prediction of behavior: a meta-analysis of the empirical literature. *Personality and Social Psychology Bulletin*, 21, 58–75.

LATHAM, G. P. & LOCKE, E. A. 2007. New developments in and directions for goal-setting research. *European Psychologist*, 12, 290–300.

LATHAM, G. P., STAJKOVIC, A. D. & LOCKE, E. A. 2010. The relevance and viability of subconscious goals in the workplace. *Journal of Management*, 36, 234–55.

LOCKE, E. A. & LATHAM, G. P. 1990. *A Theory of Goal Setting & Task Performance*, Englewood Cliffs, NJ, Prentice-Hall, Inc.

LOCKE, E. A. & LATHAM, G. P. 2002. Building a practically useful theory of goal setting and task motivation. *American Psychologist*, 57, 705–17.

MCCLELLAND, D. 1987. *Human Motivation*. Cambridge, Cambridge University Press.

MCCLELLAND, D. C. & BOYATZIS, R. E. 1982. Leadership motive pattern and long-term success in management. *Journal of Applied Psychology*, 67, 737–43.

MCCLELLAND, D. C., KOESTNER, R. & WEINBERGER, J. 1989. How do self-attributed and implicit motives differ? *Psychological Review*, 96, 690–702.

MCCLELLAND, D. C., ATKINSON, J. W., CLARK, R. A. & LOWELL, E. L. 1953. *The Achievement Motive*. East Norwalk, CT, Appleton-Century-Crofts.

MARYLÈNE, G. & EDWARD, L. D. 2005. Self-determination theory and work motivation. *Journal of Organizational Behavior*, 26, 331–62.

MASLOW, A. H. 1954. *Motivation and Personality*. New York, Harper & Row.

MENTO, A. J., LOCKE, E. A. & KLEIN, H. J. 1992. Relationship of goal level to valence and instrumentality. *Journal of Applied Psychology*, 77, 395–405.

MEYER, J. P., STANLEY, D. J., HERSCOVITCH, L. & TOPOLNYTSKY, L. 2002. Affective, continuance, and normative commitment to the organization: a meta-analysis of antecedents, correlates, and consequences. *Journal of Vocational Behavior*, 61, 20–52.

MOW INTERNATIONAL RESEARCH TEAM. 1987. *The Meaning of Working*. London, Academic Press.

NILES, S. 1998. Achievement goals and means: a cultural comparison. *Journal of Cross-Cultural Psychology*, 29, 656–67.

SMITH, P. C., KENDALL, L. & HULIN, C. L. 1969. *The Measurement of Satisfaction in Work and Retirement: A Strategy for the Study of Attitudes*. Chicago, Rand McNally.

SOLINGER, O. N., VAN OLFFEN, W. & ROE, R. A. 2008. Beyond the three-component model of organizational commitment. *Journal of Applied Psychology*, 93, 70–83.

VAN EERDE, W. & THIERRY, H. 1996. Vroom's expectancy models and work-related criteria: a meta-analysis. *Journal of Applied Psychology*, 81, 575–86.

VROOM, V. 1964. *Work and Motivation*. New York, John Wiley.

WAHBA, M. A. & BRIDWELL, L. G. 1976. Maslow reconsidered: a review of research on the need hierarchy theory. *Organizational Behavior & Human Performance*, 15, 212–40.

WATSON, T. J. 1996. Motivation: that's Maslow, isn't it? *Management Learning*, 27, 447–64.

WEGGE, J. & HASLAM, S. 2005. Improving work motivation and performance in brainstorming groups: the effects of three group goal-setting strategies. *European Journal of Work and Organizational Psychology*, 14, 400–30.

WILLIAMS, M. L., MCDANIEL, M. A. & NGUYEN, N. T. 2006. A meta-analysis of the antecedents and consequences of pay level satisfaction. *Journal of Applied Psychology*, 91, 392–413.

WINTER, D. G. 1999. Linking Personality and 'Scientific' Psychology: The Development of Empirically Derived Thematic Apperception Test Measures. In *Evocative Images: The Thematic Apperception Test and the Art of Projection*. Washington, DC, American Psychological Association.

WRIGHT, T. A. & BONETT, D. G. 2002. The moderating effects of employee tenure on the relation between organizational commitment and job performance: a meta-analysis. *Journal of Applied Psychology*, 87, 1183–90.

COMMUNICATING EFFECTIVELY

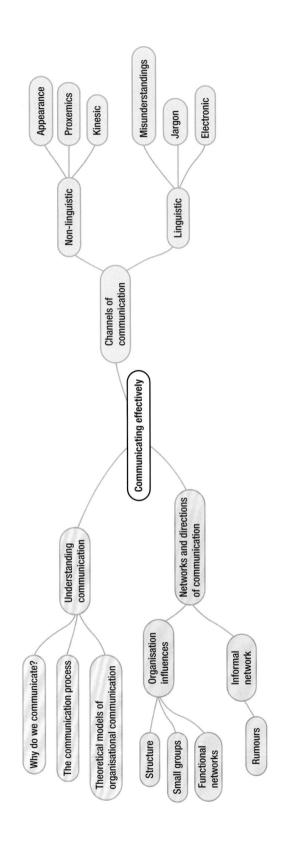

Every job requires communication with other people, but how can we make our communication more effective? We start this chapter with an overview of the theoretical context for studying communication, highlighting how our inherent views of what communication is all about influence our interpretation of events at work. By extending our understanding of communication, we can start to develop a clearer picture of how and why communication breaks down and what we can do to improve it.

It's a well-known saying that we can't *not* communicate. Even if we do not intend to communicate anything, our silence, lack of actions or even our appearance can be interpreted by someone else as a communication. So in this chapter we look closely at non-verbal communication and all the ways we send messages without using words, before turning to spoken and written language in more detail. Throughout, we will be emphasising the importance of context in understanding communication accurately and illustrating ways that miscommunication can happen – and be avoided.

We move on to consider the organisational context for communication. We review the different ways in which organisations can influence communication and then consider the more informal side of communication at work, including a detailed discussion of the role of rumours.

This chapter will help you answer the following questions:

1   What issues are important when trying to understand communication in the workplace?
2   What different options do we have available to us when trying to communicate?
3   How does communication happen within organisations?

UNDERSTANDING COMMUNICATION

Why do we communicate?

Activity Why communicate?

Think about all the communication you have taken part in within the last 24 hours: face to face, online, by phone and so on. Remember that communication can also be one way, such as reading a newspaper or a book. See if you can write a list of the main reasons people communicate with each other.

There are several different ways of conceptualising the reasons that we communicate at work, and Scott and Mitchell (1976) categorised them into four broad groups:

1   Control – this can include formal and informal communication. For example, your job contract communicates important information about what the organisation expects from you and details such as notice periods and holiday allowances. But control can also be communicated informally; for example, frowns from co-workers if you leave the office early.
2   Motivation – we saw in the last chapter how important it was to clarify goals and provide feedback to help motivate employees. Clear communication is essential to any motivational efforts that managers engage in.
3   Emotional expression – communication is a way of sharing your feelings with other people. Work is a major source of social interaction for most people and communication of emotions helps us to create and maintain social bonds.
4   Providing information – communicating information is important to organisational decision-making. When this is the focus of communication, people can often forget that the way a message is delivered can be just as important, and sometimes more so, than the 'factual' information it contains.

While this model is helpful in outlining some of the reasons for communication, it is not exhaustive and several of these functions can overlap. For example, emotional expression by leaders can be motivational: it increases their perceived effectiveness and results in extra effort by their followers (Ilies et al., 2013). Also, the informational component of communication is difficult to separate from the other functions: information can be provided in an attempt to control behaviour or to motivate individuals, and the argument could be made that emotions themselves are information.

The communication process

A simple definition of communication would be that it is the sending and receiving of a message. In this chapter, we will be unpacking that seemingly simple process to see what happens at each of those stages, what can go wrong and how we can work towards more effective communication. Having a straightforward model of communication like the one below to help us with this analysis will be useful.

The first stage is where a sender encodes the message. This is effectively 'translating' the message we want to get

Figure 5.1 A simple model of the communication process

across to someone, whether an idea or a thought or a feeling, into some kind of symbol that we can transmit. The thought or feeling itself is not transmitted, but we use commonly understood symbols to try to express our meaning, and the symbols that humans use in communication are very varied. We can use words to symbolise ideas, expressions or body language to symbolise feelings and so on.

Once we have encoded our message, we need to choose a channel to transmit it through. This could be linguistic (using written or verbal language) and/or non-linguistic (using expressions or gestures). The receiver then has to decode our message in order to understand what we were trying to express.

There are a few important points that this simple model can help us to appreciate about communication. First, communication can be disrupted in many ways. We could encode our message incorrectly or use the wrong channel to transmit it, or the receiver could decode our message in a way we did not mean. All of these problems would lead to a different message being received from the one we tried to transmit.

Second, communication is an active process. The sender has to actively encode the message and the receiver has to decode it. Although this all happens quite naturally for us, we are not passive participants in the process. And that means we can adjust how we encode or decode messages in order to improve our communication.

Third, communication is a symbolic process. Every time we convert an internal thought or idea or feeling into words or gestures or expressions, we are using symbols. For example, the word 'happy' stands in for, or symbolises, the positive feeling we experience internally. When we encode a message, we need to be sure we are using a symbol that our receiver will understand in the same way we do.

Activity Encoding

Imagine that you are feeling happy about starting a new project at work. How would other people know that you were happy about it? Think of all the different ways you could symbolise (or encode) happiness.

▸ Which encodings do you think would be most easily understood by other people? In what situations might they be misunderstood?

Finally, this model is a brief snapshot of communication. Communication is rarely a one-way process. Usually, the receiver will respond to your message in some way. That response can be immediate and externalised; for example, a puzzled expression can indicate the receiver did not understand your message. Or the response can be delayed;

for example, if you looked puzzled when reading something Freud wrote in the last century, it would be years after the message was first transmitted. These are both examples of externalised responses, but the response can also be internal. You may feel you do not quite understand something but not express it in any way.

As we go through the rest of this chapter, it will be useful to keep this model in mind and see how the various issues we discuss link up with the three basic steps.

Theoretical models of organisational communication

Communication in organisations has been studied from many different angles and with different purposes, which Dalmar Fisher (1993) summarised into five different theoretical approaches. The theoretical approach that we have towards communication influences how we will interpret what happens at work (Jensen, 2003), and as we go through each of these five approaches, we will consider the impact of this understanding on communication at work.

The *mechanistic* approach views communication as merely the transmission of information. It focuses on defining the channels that communication travels through and assumes that the message a person receives is primarily determined by the source of the message. In early organisational studies such as Taylor's scientific management and Weber's bureaucracy, the emphasis was on formal, top-down communication or communication within a logical and ordered bureaucracy. For example, if you have a mechanistic approach and there is a communication breakdown, you will focus on what has gone wrong with the receiver of the information. If you find that a colleague has not sent you some information you asked for, you might say 'I was quite clear that I needed this, he just never listens to me'. The problem is that the message, which you transmitted via the appropriate channel, was ignored.

In the *psychological* perspective, the focus is on the people involved in the communication. People are seen as active interpreters of communication rather than passive recipients of a message. There is also a strong belief that we suffer from 'information overload' and therefore need to pick and choose which information we attend to, which influences how we decode the message. A more psychological approach would recognise that individuals interpret communication in different ways and try to find the most effective way of matching communication to the individual's needs or values. To continue our example above, if you had a psychological approach to understanding communication, you might interpret your colleague's lack of response as an indication that something else was going on. You could perhaps recognise that your colleague was under a lot of pressure and adapt your communication to try to convince him that prioritising your request would ease some of that strain.

The *systems interaction* approach looks at communication patterns in organisations and sees the communication process as greater than the sum of its parts. It focuses on the external behaviours, patterns and routines of the people involved, rather than internal processing as the psychological approach does. In this view, communication is not sending or receiving messages but an act of participation, and by identifying the recurring patterns of communication we can predict how likely a certain pattern is to recur. This approach is less frequently encountered within organisations, but if you had this perspective on our example, you might consider how often requests for information are ignored in your organisation and whether there is a different pattern of behaviour that is more likely to result in you getting the information you need.

Taking a rather more abstract view than either the mechanistic or the psychological, the *interpretative-symbolic* approach sees communication as the way in which people construct their social reality. The focus here is on understanding the shared meanings that people create. Again, it is unusual to find managers or other workers who have this perspective on communication in the workplace as it is so much more complex than the first two. However, if you had an interpretative-symbolic approach you would look at how you and your colleagues are interpreting the events at work and how you could influence the construction of meaning. For example, you might realise that requests for help in your organisation are seen as a sign of weakness in a very competitive culture and are therefore ignored. Effective communication, in this approach, would necessitate an understanding of how communication is given meaning beyond the mere content of the message.

Finally, the *contemporary* approach takes an even larger view, looking at the role of communication in how an organisation defines itself. It sees communication patterns and styles as essential parts of what makes an organisation what it is. In this chapter, we will mostly be concentrating on the first two approaches, laying the foundations for an understanding of communication at work. If you would like to explore the other perspectives in more detail, and particularly the contemporary approach, you will find a Further Reading section at the end of the chapter.

CHANNELS OF COMMUNICATION

The model of communication we looked at earlier highlights the critical role of *how* the message is transmitted in influencing the transfer of meaning from sender to receiver. To fully understand this, we need to bear in mind that we often communicate meaning to others in ways other than language and also to consider the different channels of communication. To structure this discussion,

 Case Study Fired for Facebook?

In August 2011, after 13 years working for the same company, David Rowat was fired. The reason? According to newspaper reports it was because he had posted a couple of comments on Facebook about his work: *'Had a great day back at work after my hols who am I kidding!!'* and *'Back to the shambles that is work.'* His employer, Argos, stated that Mr Rowat had been dismissed for gross misconduct and that his comments were seen as bringing the organisation into disrepute (Blunden, 2011).

© BRANDX

In the UK, 'professional' behaviour is generally understood to mean being free of negative emotion, balanced and objective. What David Rowat saw as 'a little moan' was interpreted by his organisation as unprofessional. Do you think this was an appropriate reaction by the employer?

▸ Have you ever posted about your work on Facebook? What do you think your employer would have done if they had found out?

▸ Mr Rowat obviously did not intend that his communication would result in him being fired. Why did this communication go so disastrously wrong? Analyse this case from a mechanistic and a psychological perspective in turn to see how the two perspectives can result in quite different answers to that question.

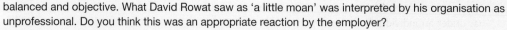

we can divide these channels into two groups: linguistic and non-linguistic.

Non-linguistic channels

Everything we do can be seen as a communication: for example, our body movements, the intonations or emphasis we give to words, facial expressions and the differing physical distance we maintain between each other. These non-verbals give a fuller meaning to our message, and are particularly used to communicate how much we like someone, how interested we are in what they are saying or even to signal status.

Appearance

Appearance is a powerful communication channel, although subject to great misunderstanding and abuse. It is common for people to make assumptions about a person's ability from judgements about their physical appearance. There are three aspects of our appearance that are used in communication (either by ourselves in sending a message or by others in interpreting one):

- Physical characteristics that a person has no control over, such as skin colour or height
- Characteristics that may have both a biological and a behavioural contribution, such as body size or hairstyle
- Voluntary characteristics, such as the style of clothes or tattoos.

A person may be judged on any of these characteristics, on the assumption that this aspect of appearance is transmitting a message – that is, it is a channel of communication.

For example, there is good evidence that aspects of appearance over which we have no control can have a significant impact on our success: height is positively associated with leadership emergence, performance and earnings (Judge and Cable, 2004). This effect varies by occupation, with height having a greater effect on earnings in jobs based around social interaction, such as sales and management, than in professional or technical occupations. Judge and Cable suggest that these effects are due to taller people having greater social and self-esteem, which contribute to both their objective performance and subjective judgements about their performance, and therefore subsequent career success. Appearance factors that are judged to be at least somewhat under an individual's control are also subject to these kinds of assumption, with people who are overweight stereotyped as lazy, unintelligent and lacking in self-discipline (Puhl & DePierre, 2012).

Most people are aware of how appearance can be used as a method of communication and try to adjust these factors to suit the message they are trying to convey. When you go to a job interview, for example, you will, in all likelihood, wear a suit in an effort to portray the impression that you are professional and would be an asset to the organisation. Hairstyles can also be a way of transmitting a message. A recent study indicated that men were perceived as stronger and more dominant when they had shaved heads than when they had their normal haircut (Mannes, 2013).

It is worth noting that many of the judgements we make that are based on someone's appearance rely on stereotypes, and even the performance differences that have been found could well be due to the longitudinal effect of being subjected to these stereotypes. Understanding this channel of communication will enable us to both avoid the pitfalls of these stereotypical judgements ourselves as well as to ensure that we are utilising this channel as effectively as possible in transmitting the message we want.

Proxemics

We often use spatial relations to express information about relationships. For example, you might say you feel 'close' to someone or that you prefer to 'keep them at arm's length'. Proxemics is the study of the role of interpersonal space and touch in communication and the messages that they transmit (Hall, 1959). Edward Hall, an anthropologist who studied how distance was used and understood in different cultures, developed a categorisation of interpersonal distances illustrated in the following figure (Hall, 1966):

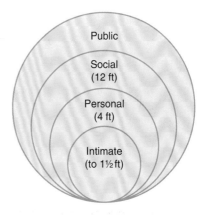

Figure 5.2 Interpersonal distances

When people are within each other's intimate distance sphere, physical contact is uppermost in their minds and they can become very uncomfortable if others come into that space inappropriately. We generally only allow close family members or lovers into this space. Personal space is a bit further out, from about an arm's length to where we are still close enough to touch if we both reach out, and we use this spacing when chatting to friends or close acquaintances. Social distance is where most of our work communication takes place, with the further reaches for more formal communication. Finally, public distance is well outside our 'circle of involvement', and communication in this circle loses the finer facial expressions and intonation.

Hall pointed out that the measurements associated with this categorisation were very culture-specific and represented the norm for Western, or more specifically, mostly white, middle-class American, interpersonal spacing. Interpersonal distances and their meaning vary dramatically across cultures. A distance that a Briton would find comfortable for work conversations may signal aloofness or a lack of interest to someone from an Arab culture, while in return the Arab's attempts to 'close the gap' and maintain what is viewed as the appropriate conversational distance might be experienced as uncomfortable and overly familiar to the British person. An accurate understanding of the 'message' conveyed by distance is only possible if we are aware of the culture of the people involved. Try the activity below to explore how these distances differ across cultures.

Activity Personal distances

This is an activity you can do with a friend or acquaintance from another culture. One of you should stand still and the other stand at a distance that feels comfortable for a normal friendly conversation. Then try it the other way round. It is very likely you will find a difference in what distance feels 'right'. Discuss why this might be. What does the other person's distance signal to you? What does yours signal to them?

You may find it interesting to visit www.culturecrossing.net, a user-built guide to understanding different cultures. It has a section for 'personal distance' for each country.

It is not just cultural context that determines how we interpret the message conveyed by proxemic communication, but also immediate context. We can see this in how we understand touch, where many factors contribute to the message that touching conveys, or is interpreted as conveying. These factors include who does the touching, which part of the body is touched and for how long, whether anyone else is present and what movement there is after contact is made (Heslin and Alper, 1983). For example, a rugby player slapping a teammate on the back after he scored a try would be understood to have a very different meaning to the same man touching a female colleague lingeringly on the arm when no one else is in the office.

We can see that the messages touching conveys are many and varied. Touch can be an expression of power or intimacy and it can enhance the intensity of an emotional expression (Hertenstein et al., 2006). It can also be ritualistic (e.g. a handshake greeting) or instrumental (e.g. when you show someone how to carry out a specific task). While there is a lot of attention given to negative or inappropriate touch in our society, for example in sexual harassment cases, there are good reasons to explore the positive side of touch, as Fuller et al. (2011) explain:

1 Touch is a basic human need
2 Touch has many psychological and physiological benefits, such as reduced anxiety and improved mood
3 Touch is associated with increased prosocial behaviour
4 Touch can effectively communicate many emotions.

Managers can use touch to build positive relationships with their subordinates. In their study of touch in the workplace, Fuller et al. identified that supervisors who used touch to communicate positive feelings were rated as more likeable, supportive, sincere and interpersonally effective by their subordinates. These findings were, however, affected by how strong the subordinate's need for touch was, which sounds a note of caution for supervisors in being careful to adapt their tactile communication to the individual. In addition, some sex differences in the use of touch were reported, with women more likely to report using touch at work, feeling more confident of their ability to use it well and less anxious about doing so. Given issues of harassment in terms of how touch is interpreted, it is, of course, possible that men are being more cautious in using touch at work for very good reason.

Not only is touch useful in building long-term relationships at work, it can even increase the tips that servers in a restaurant receive. Servers who briefly touched the restaurant patron's shoulder when returning their change received a greater tip than those who did not (Hubbard et al., 2003). In addition, in a bar-style restaurant, servers who used touch and were the opposite sex to the patrons received an even larger tip.

We can see that touch can communicate something positive, and several studies have shown how important touch is in persuasion. In one study, shoppers were greeted as they entered a shop. For half of the shoppers, the greeting included a light touch on the arm. Those who received this touch browsed for longer in the shop, reported a more positive impression of it and did more shopping (Hornik, 1991). However, the context or type of touch is very important in determining the message people receive. When shoppers experience someone briefly brushing past them, again a light, non-threatening touch but this time not in the context of a greeting, they report negative brand evaluations, are less willing to pay and spend less time in the shop (Martin, 2012). The importance of context and the interaction of different communication channels in determining the message that someone understands cannot be overemphasised.

Kinesic

Having looked at how we use distance and touch, we now consider the movements we make when we communicate, such as gesturing with our hands, nodding our heads or making eye contact. These are all part of the kinesic channel. Instead of looking at the different movements in terms of which part of the body is involved (face or hands), a more useful approach is to define these movements in terms of their functions. For this, we will use a classification developed by Paul Ekman and colleagues over several decades of research into emotional expression and communication. This model describes emblems, illustrators, manipulators, regulators and emotional expressions (Ekman, 2004).

When we talk about 'body language', only one of these categories really counts. *Emblems* are the only gestures or signals that we make that are socially learned and understood by the members of a particular culture, like spoken language. We are generally aware of the emblems we are using and they can either emphasise or replace words, or provide a separate comment on what we are saying. As an example, if a friend asks you how an exam went, you may simply shrug in response or you might say 'Don't really know' and emphasise it with a shrug. We can also use emblems to give a paradoxical message to our words. For example, if you are asked whether you like your boss, with your boss standing behind you, you might say 'Yes, he's really approachable and knows what he's doing' while at the same time rolling your eyes to the person you're speaking to.

While an emblem has a direct verbal translation, *illustrators* are movements we use to illustrate our speech. We may point to an object or person under discussion, mime out a particular activity we are describing, or draw a picture in the air to try and illustrate a concept. Illustrators are also used to 'beat time' or match the rhythm of our words. You can often observe this with people giving speeches, such as politicians, who hit the podium in time with their words. Our use of illustrators increases with our involvement or interest in a subject and is generally

unconscious. A useful part of learning presentation skills is to watch a video of yourself and see what your hands are doing while you speak. You may be surprised at how much they wave about.

The third type of kinesic activity was originally called 'adapters', but Ekman changed this to *manipulators* in later writing because it more clearly captures what the movements do. Manipulators are movements where one part of the body manipulates another; for example, licking your lips or scratching your nose. It is believed that these actions are partly just habit, but they often increase when we are either very nervous or completely relaxed with friends and not worrying about what we're doing. Although we are usually quite unaware of manipulators, when our attention is drawn to them we tend to interpret them as signs of nervousness.

Regulators are movements which help to direct the flow of conversation. We can use movements to encourage someone to continue or to tell them to hurry up. Try it now. Which movements would you use to do both of those things? There are many of these movements and they include things like shifting posture – leaning forward can indicate that you want a turn to speak – or slight nods of the head to indicate agreement and 'please continue'.

Finally, we also use the kinesic channel to *express emotion*. There is good evidence that our facial expressions for some emotions (anger, fear, disgust, contempt, surprise, enjoyment) are universally similar around the world. Facial expressions also indicate the intensity of our emotions. For example, we can tell the difference between slightly annoyed and completely furious.

While the expressions associated with each of these 'basic' emotions are inborn, not learned, we do learn how to manage our expressions so that we can use facial movements to express emotion – either felt or faked – as another tool in communication. Ekman distinguishes between false expressions, where we try to express an emotion we do not feel, and referential expressions, where we refer to an emotion we felt earlier or might feel in the future (Ekman, 1997). The former expressions are intended to look just like the real emotion, though they can be detected by some skilled people, while the latter are not meant to be confused with the real emotion. For example, a hotel receptionist who is feeling upset might give a false expression of happiness to a customer, intending that the customer should believe it is real. But when talking to a friend about how she pretended to find her boss's joke funny, she might hold a fixed grin on her face for a long time. The friend would then rightly interpret this as 'referring' to her emotional expression from earlier, rather than as an attempt to look amused now.

Psychological Toolkit Improving your presentation skills

For a lot of people, making a presentation is a nerve-racking experience. Yet it is a very important skill to learn for your future career. Delivering a good presentation is really all about developing specific communication skills, and you can use what you learn in this chapter to help you do that.

A study on students delivering oral assessments analysed their use of gestural behaviour, and found that the students who scored higher were using gestures that integrated well with their speech (Gan and Davison, 2011). For example, one mimed giving a gift to someone while discussing what the appropriate gift would be (an illustrator), and another looked at a group member and opened his hand to him to indicate it was his turn to speak (a regulator).

You can find out how well you use the different communication channels by completing this exercise. You will first need to spend some time preparing a short presentation or speech on a subject of your choice – it only needs to be about five minutes long. Next, you are going to record yourself doing the presentation (using a phone or webcam). It would be even better if you could do this exercise in a group, so that your peers can act as your audience and help with the analysis.

The aim of the analysis is to identify the emblems, illustrators, manipulators, regulators and emotional expressions you use and see how they might be interpreted by your audience. Use the following table as a basis for your analysis and complete it as you watch yourself on the video (and ask your audience to complete it as well).

	Examples that you used	What do they communicate to the audience?
Emblems		
Illustrators		
Manipulators		
Regulators		
Emotional expressions		

▸ Overall, were you surprised at how many movements you made? Do you think you should reduce or increase them to help get your message across more clearly?

▸ Work through the table, drawing on your audience's interpretations as well if you have them, and evaluate how well you think you use kinesic communication. To what extent do you think your kinesic communication is integrated with what you are actually saying?

From this, you can draw up an action plan for improving your presentation skills. For example, if you find that you are making a lot of movements that might indicate nervousness, you could consciously try to reduce them. Or if you find that you seem very wooden, you could draw up a list of ways in which you can use gestures to emphasise or enhance your presentation. You can repeat this exercise as often as you want.

Linguistic channels

So far, we have looked at all the different things we do to communicate that do not involve words. Yet it is the linguistic channel that is our most highly developed channel of communication (Ellis and Beattie, 1993). The major part of this channel is language, the spoken or written words we use. But in spoken language, there are also intonation, rhythm and so-called 'paralanguage' – that is, the other noises we make, such as sighing, um-ing and ah-ing, and silence. We will consider these contextual factors first before moving on to consider language in more detail.

Any noises we make that are not speech itself are *paralinguistic* elements and also serve to communicate a message. For example, a sigh can communicate boredom or a feeling of futility or even indicate relief. As with other communication channels, it is the overall context which helps us to interpret what a specific 'piece' of communication means. Our tone of voice, the speed at which we speak and how we use silence are also important elements of paralanguage.

Activity Paralanguage

To see what effect paralanguage can have on the meaning we convey with our words, try saying the following sentence out loud, emphasising the word in bold each time. How does the meaning change in each sentence?

I really like my new job.

I **really** like my new job.

I really **like** my new job.

I really like **my** new job.

I really like my **new** job.

I really like my new **job**.

Now try saying the sentence again, this time sighing just before you start. Then say it again with a yawn in the middle. Does this change how you say the sentence? What meaning do you think it conveys to the listener?

The use of language can be written or oral. Written communications have the advantage that they can be stored and referred to if necessary at a later date; they provide a record of the communication. They also tend to be more thought through than oral communication, meaning they have the potential to be clearer and better reasoned. However, there is the downside that they are more time-consuming, and feedback is harder to come by. This means it can be more difficult to find out if the person you sent the message to has actually received or understood it.

Oral communication is much faster and feedback is easier to receive. If someone is not understanding you, you can try to make your message clearer as you go along. These advantages are offset by the problem that a verbal message is more subject to distortion as it is passed on than a written communication.

Electronic communication such as email, instant messaging or social media is an interesting mix of oral and written communication. The record is at least semi-permanent, like written communication, but feedback can be instant and easy to receive, much like oral communication. And although much electronic communication is written, people often express themselves with as little thought as they would verbally, and sometimes even less.

Linguistic misunderstandings

In our discussion of non-linguistic communication, we emphasised the importance of context in determining the meaning of a communication. This is just as important when we consider language. Although for any language to function effectively there needs to be a shared understanding of what the words mean, there is a surprising amount of ambiguity in language as well. Unfortunately, many people do not realise this. You will probably be able to think of an example of a time when you thought you had been crystal clear in a communication with someone, only to find out that what you thought you were saying had been completely misinterpreted.

Sometimes misunderstandings can arise if people are using a language that is not their mother tongue, but often ambiguity can be seen even when it seems people are speaking the same language. For example, if an American were to say 'I'm really mad', a British person might think it was time to call a psychiatrist rather than thinking that the American was feeling angry. Another example is the phrase 'with respect' when disagreeing with someone. Americans use this sincerely, to indicate that they respect the person while disagreeing with them. A British person, however, would use the phrase sarcastically, to indicate that they thought the other person was an idiot. You can see how this might lead to some serious misunderstandings. Have a look at Table 5.1 for some more examples of how British English can be misunderstood by others:

Table 5.1 What the British say and what they mean

What the British say	What the British mean	What others understand
I hear what you say	I disagree and do not want to discuss it any further	He accepts my point of view
This is in no sense a rebuke	I am furious with you and letting you know it	I am not cross with you
Correct me if I'm wrong	I know I'm right – please don't contradict me	Tell me what you think
That's not bad	That's good or very good	That's poor or mediocre

Source: adapted from L. E. Johnson (2011) Euphemistically speaking: this may interest you. *The Economist*, 27 May 2011. http://www.economist.com/blogs/johnson/2011/05/euphemistically_speaking (accessed 4 July 2013).

Jargon

Another important aspect of language in organisations is the use of jargon: vocabulary or terminology used in a particular organisation or group that is unfamiliar to people outside that group. It often arises as a kind of 'shorthand' or abbreviation for work elements that are common within the group. For example, employees in the National Health Service may talk about ALBs or Arm's Length Bodies, meaning national bodies that are sponsored by the Department of Health to carry out specific functions but are stand-alone. While jargon can be a useful aid to speed up communication within an organisation, it makes it much harder for newcomers or outsiders to understand what is going on.

Electronic communication

We have already mentioned how electronic communication carries a mix of the advantages and disadvantages of verbal and written communication. Computer-aided communication is an essential part of the modern organisation. A recent report indicated that dealing with email takes up about 28% of interaction workers' time (Chui et al., 2012). (An interaction worker is someone whose work necessitates complex interactions with other people and making independent judgements, such as managers, salespeople, professionals and other knowledge workers.) In 2011, corporate email users received an average of 72 emails a day and sent 33. There are signs that although the number of emails a day is still increasing, the growth rate is at least slowing (Radicati and Levenstein, 2013). However, this does not indicate that the amount of electronic communication is reaching a plateau, but is instead in all likelihood due to a rapid rise in other forms of computer-mediated communication, such as instant messaging and social media.

International Perspectives Communication preferences

How do you like to communicate with people? Take a moment to do a quick survey of your friends or the other people on your course and find out what your preferred option is.

While there are individual differences in whether we prefer to speak to people on the phone or face to face, text them or email them, it appears there are also differences across countries. A study of the use of information communication technologies (ICT) in four countries (UK, USA, Australia, China) looked both at people's preferences and at the impact that communication technologies had on them (Mieczakowski et al., 2011).

The most popular option in all four countries was face-to-face communication, ranging from a low of 46% of people in China to 65% in the UK preferring to speak to people directly. In contrast, only 6% of British people preferred to use the phone, compared with 11% of Americans and Australians and 16% of Chinese.

The Chinese were also highest in their preferences for instant messaging: 21% of them preferred this option, compared with only 2% in other countries.

While 60% of British people felt they spent too much time using communications technology, less than 30% of Chinese felt the same. Despite this, it was not the amount of ICT that was used that affected well-being but the *way* it was used, with people reporting that they felt constantly distracted, and one in three people in all countries reporting that they felt 'overwhelmed to the point of needing to escape from communications technology'.

Discussion points

▸ Why do you think there are differences in preference for types of ICT across the different countries?
▸ How can you explain the fact that, despite these differences, the most popular form of communication is still face to face?
▸ What are the implications of this study for international organisations?

Case Study Jargon in higher education

In November 2012, the *Times Higher Education* ran a competition to find the worst examples of jargon use in higher education. The winner was this extract from a university pro vice-chancellor for staff and organisational effectiveness, attempting to explain what organisational effectiveness was:

We can reframe the way we define it, so that it's not viewed as simply foregrounding cost savings, but instead a much more complex interplay of influences and drivers that facilitate opportunities for enhancing the ways in which we manage movement.

▸ Try 'translating' this quote into plain English. What do you think the pro vice-chancellor is actually saying?
▸ Why do you think people use jargon like this instead of language that is easy to understand?

© DIGITALVISION

There are, of course, advantages and disadvantages to using email. Advantages include the fact that emails can be distributed to many people very easily and quickly, they provide a written record of the communication and they can be sent and read at the individual's convenience. The downsides centre mainly on how little emotional tone people usually manage to express in emails. This is, of course, a problem for all written communication. We have looked at a vast range of different communication channels and seen how important the emotional content of a message is, yet written language has to be very well constructed to express emotions. Most people do not take the time needed to do this, or perhaps simply do not have the skills to do so. This can result in emails that express emotion inappropriately or even appear devoid of emotional content – which we then tend to interpret as cold and negative. And finally, many people are concerned about the privacy of emails. They can be very easily forwarded to people you did not expect to receive them, or even hacked into.

The growth in computer-aided communication may seem like a great opportunity to increase flexibility in work, increasing the possibility that a lot of work can be done wherever and whenever suits the worker. But success in telecommuting or virtual working needs more than just the presence of these communication tools. A key factor of success in organisations is trust, and trust is built through frequent and high-quality communication (Jensen, 2003). Virtual workers seem to need more frequent communication with their managers than non-remote workers in order to build trust (Staples, 2001). But there is evidence that effective implementation of a move to virtual working, using excellent technology, supportive incentive systems and a restructuring of the workflow, can actually increase job satisfaction for virtual workers (Akkirman and Harris, 2005).

 Key Research Study Detecting lies

Lie Detection and Language Comprehension
Nancy Etcoff, Paul Ekman, John Magee and Mark Frank (2000)

Background: Most people are not very good at detecting when someone is lying, even when there are clues from facial expression and tone of voice. This may be because they are focusing on the meaning of the words to the exclusion of other information.

Aim: To demonstrate that people who had difficulty understanding sentences because of brain damage (known as aphasics) were better able to detect lying than people who could still understand words.

Method: Four groups of participants were recruited: ten aphasics, ten people with brain damage unrelated to their language-processing abilities, ten healthy controls and 48 undergraduate students.

Participants watched videos of ten people, once where the person was trying to conceal a powerful negative emotion and once where the person was honestly revealing a positive emotion, and asked to decide which one was the lie.

Findings: Aphasics were significantly better than all the other groups at detecting lies and were the only ones to score above chance. Subsequent analysis showed that this was because of their ability to pick up on facial cues rather than vocal ones.

Implications: It is likely that aphasics have developed their ability to pick up meaning from non-verbal cues in order to compensate for the loss of ability in understanding words. This study highlights how the different communication channels can interfere with each other. The prominence we give to one may very well cancel out information that is transmitted in another.

NETWORKS AND DIRECTIONS OF COMMUNICATION

We can approach the study of organisational communication from two different directions: how the organisation influences communication or how communication influences the organisation. In the first approach, we look at how different formal networks or relationships influence what communication takes place and how, while the latter looks at how emergent or informal networks communicate.

The organisation influences communication

Structural dimensions

The way an organisation is structured affects how communication flows and how decisions are made. Some researchers have even suggested that formal structure can substitute for communication in providing coordination. There are four main structural dimensions that influence communication in the formal organisation (Jensen, 2003), which we will consider in turn.

1 Configuration – the 'shape' of an organisation. This covers aspects such as span of control (how many people each manager is responsible for), size and hierarchical level. The fewer people a manager has to supervise, the greater the potential for communication, but this is offset by the fact that many organisations with narrow spans of control also have many more hierarchical levels. More hierarchical levels means greater upward and downward communication, but it does not mean that subordinates feel communication is more open.

2 Complexity – the number of parts or divisions within an organisation. The frequency of communication seems to increase with the number of occupational specialities in an organisation, but to decrease with the number of departments.

3 Formalisation – the extent to which job behaviours are codified into policies. The greater the formalisation in an organisation, the lower the levels of communication, presumably because it simply becomes too difficult for people to share information outside the specified channels.

4 Centralisation – the degree to which authority is concentrated in higher management. The greater the decentralisation, the greater the frequency and flow of communication, as more employees are involved in decision-making and problem-solving.

Small group networks

In the 1950s, some work was done on evaluating the effectiveness of different configurations of small groups.

Mostly laboratory-based, the studies typically put a small number of people into cubicles and got them to communicate with each other via notes through interconnecting slots that could be opened or closed according to what network pattern the experimenter wished to study (Bavelas, 1950). The members of the groups needed to share information with each other in order to complete the task. Three different networks were studied (illustrated below) and their effects on task completion recorded.

Researchers using this approach found that centralised networks (such as the wheel) were faster but had higher error rates and lower member satisfaction. The networks which allowed freer communication (such as the all-channel network) were better for tasks requiring innovative thinking.

Circle	Wheel	All-channel

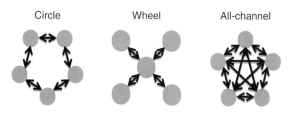

Figure 5.3 Communication networks in small groups

Functional networks

At the beginning of this chapter, we outlined the different theoretical approaches to communication. One of these, the systems interaction approach, defines communication as a system and tries to identify the elements that interact to produce it. Greenbaum (1974) did this by identifying four types of networks in organisations, based on their function in contributing towards achieving their organisation's goals (see Table 5.2):

Informal networks

There are, of course, informal networks of communication which are less structured than these formal networks and emerge spontaneously at work (Langan-Fox, 2002). Informal networks are not haphazard but actually have patterns and predictability of their own. They tend to have shorter communication chains than formal networks and to change frequently as the people involved have more or less contact with each other. They are also quite different from formal networks in that they can transcend or ignore status differences. In fact, there is good evidence that much of the important communication at work takes place within these informal networks (Jensen, 2003). For example, a worker who comes up with a new way of solving a problem will, in all likelihood, discuss it first with colleagues she feels will support her or help her work through it, before using a formal suggestion system.

 Fad or Fact? Men and women communicate differently

Do men and women communicate differently at work? John Gray, in his book *Men are from Mars, Women are from Venus*, claimed that sex differences (including the way we communicate) are so large that we may as well be from different planets. Carol Kinsey Goman, author of several top-selling books on communication, believes these differences are true in the workplace as well. A popular speaker and business coach who teaches on the Stanford MBA programme, Kinsey Goman says that men are seen as better at monologue and straightforward communication and women at dialogue and reading body language (Kinsey Goman, 2009).

But what does the research evidence tell us about this? There is certainly evidence that women are

Table 5.2 Types of organisational network

Type of network	Concerned with	Examples	Organisation goal
Regulative	Controls, orders, direction and task-related feedback	Policy statements, rules, procedures	Conformity
Innovative	Problem-solving, adaptation, strategy, implementation of new ideas	Suggestion systems, participative problem-solving meetings	Adaptiveness
Integrative/maintenance	Feelings about self, colleagues and work	Status symbols, rewards, praise, promotion	Morale
Informative/instructive	Getting and giving information	Bulletin boards, publications, training	All of the above, plus Institutionalisation

slightly better than men at reading non-verbal cues, such as identifying someone's emotions from facial expressions (Kirkland et al., 2013, McClure, 2000). In addition, men with higher levels of testosterone are reported to have lower empathic accuracy by their colleagues (Ronay and Carney, 2013), indicating that this difference might have a biological basis. However, there is little evidence for other differences in communication, and a meta-analysis summarising 50 years of research on the topic concluded that the differences between men and women were 'negligible' and where they did exist they were moderated by other factors (Canary and Hause, 1993).

If the differences are so small, why is there this persistent belief that men and women do communicate differently? Dindia and Canary (2006) point out the pervasive effects of stereotypes. If you asked around your fellow students or people at work whether men and women communicate differently, you would probably find they said similar things. It is highly likely that asking people to contrast the communicative strengths and weaknesses of women or men in general makes them rely on stereotypes in answering. The fact that we then find agreement among our respondents only means that there are agreed-upon stereotypes about how men and women communicate, not that there are real differences.

Instead of taking such a basic, polarised view of our communication skills, it would make more sense to look at detailed factors that influence communication. For example, there is good evidence that people who are more intelligent are more accurate judges of someone's emotional state or personality traits (Murphy and Hall, 2011). It's more useful to find out how our communication skills are related to other psychological facets and what can be done to develop them than to exaggerate the very small differences between men and women.

Rumours

We can't consider informal communication in organisations without giving some attention to the role of rumour. A rumour is a statement containing information that is not verified. Rumour is different from gossip in that, while both contain elements of unsubstantiated information, gossip deals with the social network while rumour is defined as communication that tries to make sense of ambiguity or help employees deal with threats (whether real or imagined) (DiFonzo, 2010). When there is a lack of clarity or formal communication about a situation that concerns employees, rumours are a way of the group trying to make sense of things, a process of group interpretation.

Rumours help people to make sense of uncertainty, and three different motivations can drive how and what kind of rumours get spread (DiFonzo and Bordia, 2007). The first is fact-finding: we want to discover relevant information about an ambiguous situation. For example, if we hear that our department will be downsizing, we will want to know how it will affect our own job. The second is relationship-building: we want to build positive relationships with others. In this case we prefer rumours that will create a good impression with other people in the group, such as the rumour that our immediate work group is considered too valuable to downsize. And finally, there is self-enhancement: when feeling threatened, we tend to prefer information that will make us feel good about ourselves and won't focus so much on how accurate it is. For example, if we hear a rumour that our own job is safe, we will tend to believe and spread that version rather than a version that says we are going to be made redundant.

There are two broad categories of rumours: wish and dread (Rosnow et al., 1988). Wish rumours are optimistic and express something that people are hoping is true. Dread rumours contain information that people hope is false, information that is negative or anxiety-provoking. Of the two, dread rumours are more often transmitted and are associated with higher stress levels (Bordia et al., 2006). Interestingly, a comparison of dread and wish rumours showed that people were less cautious about the wish rumours; that is, they were not so concerned with verifying them (Bordia and Difonzo, 2004). This indicates that we tend to be more concerned with the consequences of spreading negative rumours than positive ones.

In a study of internet forum rumours (Bordia and Difonzo, 2004), it was found that rumours consisted of the following aspects:

- The largest proportion of statements about the rumours (29%) were concerned with trying to verify the information
- A second large proportion (17%) was made up of statements which provided information related to the rumour
- There was also a large proportion of digressive statements (19%), things that were unrelated to the rumour itself
- The remaining statements included people giving opinions about whether they believed the rumour or not, requests for further information and so on.

Because rumours are a form of 'collective problem-solving', management can reduce the impact or spread of rumours by ensuring that clear information is given, especially in situations that involve uncertainty or ambiguity. In addition, because dread rumours are more likely to be spread than wish rumours, it is worthwhile for managers to ensure that their communication includes a fair consideration of negative consequences, rather than skipping over them to focus on the positive.

SUMMARY

With 'effective communicator' appearing as an essential requirement of nearly every job, there is a clear recognition in business that communication is key to good performance at work. In this chapter, we have discovered how psychological theory can help us to understand what happens when we communicate, and can draw out some lessons for improving our communication. We have emphasised throughout the importance of context in understanding communication: from the interpretative-symbolic approach to the situational context of a specific interaction.

Identifying the different channels available for communication, we have also looked at how conflicting messages might be understood from different channels. Communication will be more effective when the messages we send in both linguistic and non-linguistic channels support each other. And finally, our review of networks in organisations shows us how managers can either change the formal structure of groups to facilitate particular tasks or even try to utilise informal networks and rumour to get a message across.

TEST YOURSELF

Brief Review Questions

1   Briefly define the five different theoretical approaches to communication.
2   List the non-verbal communication channels.
3   What structural dimensions influence communication in organisations?
4   What is 'paralanguage' and what role does it play in communication?
5   What is the difference between dread and wish rumours?

Discussion or Essay Questions

1   What are the advantages and disadvantages of using a simple Sender-Message-Receiver model to understand the communication process?
2   'Most of our communication is non-verbal.' To what extent do you agree with this statement?
3   Compare and contrast kinesic and proxemic communication.

4   What advice could you give someone who wanted to be a more effective communicator?
5   Why is it important to know about informal communication networks at work? When might informal communication prove more important than formal?

FURTHER READING

* J. K. Krone, F. M. Jablin & L. L. Putnam (1987) Communication Theory and Organizational Communication: Multiple Perspectives. In F. M. Jablin, L. L. Putnam, K. H. Roberts & L. W. Porter (eds.) *Handbook of Organizational Communication*. Newbury Park: Sage.
* For more on a contemporary view of communication as defining organisations, try Gareth Morgan's *Images of Organization*, London, Sage, 2006.

References

AKKIRMAN, A. D. & HARRIS, D. L. 2005. Organizational communication satisfaction in the virtual workplace. *Journal of Management Development*, 24, 397–409.

BAVELAS, A. 1950. Communication patterns in task-oriented groups. *The Journal of the Acoustical Society of America*, 22, 725–30.

BLUNDEN, M. 2011. Argos sacks cancer sufferer who moaned about job on Facebook. *London Evening Standard*, 9 August.

BORDIA, P. & DIFONZO, N. 2004. Problem solving in social interactions on the internet: rumor as social cognition. *Social Psychology Quarterly*, 67, 33–49.

BORDIA, P., JONES, E., GALLOIS, C., CALLAN, V. J. & DIFONZO, N. 2006. Management are aliens! rumors and stress during organizational change. *Group & Organization Management*, 31, 601–21.

CANARY, D. J. & HAUSE, K. S. 1993. Is there any reason to research sex differences in communication? *Communication Quarterly*, 41, 129–44.

CHUI, M., MANYIKA, J., BUGHIN, J., DOBBS, R., ROXBURGH, C., SARRAZIN, H., SANDS, G. & WESTERGREN, M. 2012. *The Social Economy: Unlocking Value and Productivity Through Social Technologies*. McKinsey Global Institute.

DIFONZO, N. 2010. Ferreting facts or fashioning fallacies? Factors in rumor accuracy. *Social and Personality Psychology Compass*, 4, 1124–37.

DIFONZO, N. & BORDIA, P. 2007. *Rumor Psychology: Social and Organizational Approaches*. Washington DC, American Psychological Association.

DINDIA, K. & CANARY, D. J. 2006. *Sex Differences and Similarities in Communication*, 2nd edn. Mahwah, NJ, Lawrence Erlbaum.

EKMAN, P. 1997. Should we call it expression or communication? *Innovation: The European Journal of Social Science Research*, 10, 333–44.

EKMAN, P. 2004. Emotional and Conversational Nonverbal Signals. In Larrazabel, J. M. & Perez Miranda, L. A. (eds.) *Language, Knowledge and Representation*. Netherlands, Kluwer Academic.

ELLIS, A. W. & BEATTIE, G. 1993. *The Psychology of Language and Communication*. Hove, Lawrence Erlbaum.

ETCOFF, N. L., EKMAN, P., MAGEE, J. J. & FRANK, M. G. 2000. Lie detection and language comprehension. *Nature*, 405, 139.

FISHER, D. 1993. *Communication in Organizations*. Minneapolis, West.

FULLER, B., SIMMERING, M. J., MARLER, L. E., COX, S. S., BENNETT, R. J. & CHERAMIE, R. A. 2011. Exploring touch as a positive workplace behavior. *Human Relations*, 64, 231–56.

GAN, Z. & DAVISON, C. 2011. Gestural behavior in group oral assessment: a case study of higher- and lower-scoring students. *International Journal of Applied Linguistics*, 21, 94–120.

GREENBAUM, H. H. 1974. The audit of organizational communication. *Academy of Management Journal*, 17, 739–54.

HALL, E. T. 1959. *The Silent Language*. New York, Doubleday.

HALL, E. T. 1966. *The Hidden Dimension*, 1st edn. New York, Doubleday & Co.

HERTENSTEIN, M. J., VERKAMP, J. M., KERESTES, A. M. & HOLMES, R. M. 2006. The communicative functions of touch in humans, nonhuman primates, and rats: a review and synthesis of the empirical research. *Genetic, Social, and General Psychology Monographs*, 132, 5–94.

HESLIN, R. & ALPER, T. 1983. Touch: A Bonding Gesture. In Wiemann, J. M. & Harrison, R. P. (eds.) *Nonverbal Interaction*. Beverley Hills, Sage.

HORNIK, J. 1991. Shopping time and purchasing behavior as a result of in-store tactile stimulation. *Perceptual and Motor Skills*, 73, 969–70.

HUBBARD, A. S., TSUJI, A., WILLIAMS, C. & SEATRIZ JR, V. 2003. Effects of touch on gratuities received in same-gender and cross-gender dyads. *Journal of Applied Social Psychology*, 33, 2427–38.

ILIES, R., CURSEU, P. L., DIMOTAKIS, N. & SPITZMULLER, M. 2013. Leaders' emotional expressiveness and their behavioural and relational authenticity: effects on followers. *European Journal of Work and Organizational Psychology*, 22, 4–14.

JENSEN, M. T. 2003. *Organizational Communication – A Review*. Kristiansand, Norway.

JUDGE, T. A. & CABLE, D. M. 2004. The effect of physical height on workplace success and income: preliminary test of a theoretical model. *Journal of Applied Psychology*, 89, 428–41.

KINSEY GOMAN, C. 2009. *Men and Women and Workplace Communication*. Business Analyst Times. http://www.batimes.com/articles/men-and-women-and-work place-communication.html (accessed 8 July 2013).

KIRKLAND, R. A., PETERSON, E., BAKER, C. A., MILLER, S. & PULOS, S. 2013. Meta-analysis reveals adult female superiority in 'reading the mind in the eyes' test. *North American Journal of Psychology*, 15, 121–46.

LANGAN-FOX, J. 2002. Communication in Organizations: Speed, Diversity, Networks, and Influence on Organizational Effectiveness, Human Health, and Relationships. In *Handbook of Industrial, Work and Organizational Psychology*, vol. 2: *Organizational Psychology*. Thousand Oaks, CA, Sage.

MCCLURE, E. B. 2000. A meta-analytic review of sex differences in facial expression processing and their development in infants, children, and adolescents. *Psychological Bulletin*, 126, 424–53.

MANNES, A. E. 2013. Shorn scalps and perceptions of male dominance. *Social Psychological and Personality Science*, 4, 198–205.

MARTIN, B. A. 2012. A stranger's touch: effects of accidental interpersonal touch on consumer evaluations and shopping time. *Journal of Consumer Research*, 39, 174–84.

MIECZAKOWSKI, A., GOLDHABER, T. & CLARKSON, J. 2011. *Culture, Communication and Change: Summary of an Investigation of the Use and Impact of Modern Media and Technology in Our Lives*. Cambridge, Engineering Design Centre.

MURPHY, N. A. & HALL, J. A. 2011. Intelligence and interpersonal sensitivity: a meta-analysis. *Intelligence*, 39, 54–63.

PUHL, R. M. & DEPIERRE, J. A. 2012. Appearance discrimination and the law. In T. F. Cash (ed.), *Encyclopedia of Body Image and Human Appearance*. Oxford, Academic Press.

RADICATI, S. & LEVENSTEIN, D. 2013. *Email Statistics Report 2013–2017*. Palo Alto, CA, Radicati Group.

RONAY, R. & CARNEY, D. R. 2013. Testosterone's negative relationship with empathic accuracy and perceived leadership ability. *Social Psychological and Personality Science*, 4, 92–9.

ROSNOW, R. L., ESPOSITO, J. L. & GIBNEY, L. 1988. Factors influencing rumor spreading: replication and extension. *Language & Communication*, 8, 29–42.

SCOTT, W. G. & MITCHELL, T. R. 1976. *Organization Theory: A Structural and Behavioral Analysis*. Homewood, IL, Irwin.

STAPLES, D. S. 2001. A study of remote workers and their differences from non-remote workers. *Journal of Organizational and End User Computing (JOEUC)*, 13, 3–14.

BUILDING EFFECTIVE TEAMS

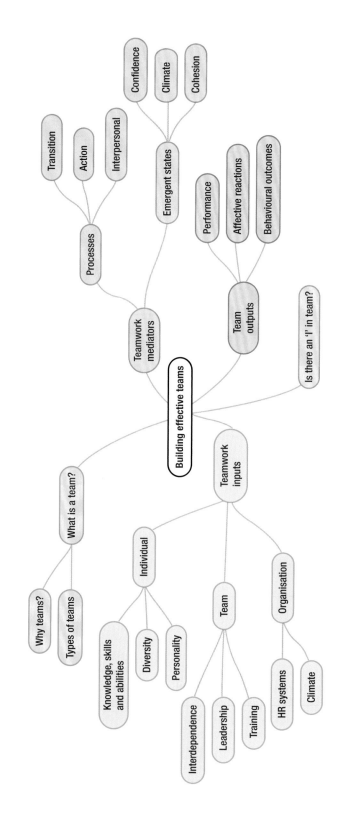

Teamworking skills are highly prized by the majority of employers, and many organisations have restructured their work around teams; yet lots of people remain unsure how they can improve teamwork. In the previous chapter we looked at communication, an essential aspect of teamwork, and here we will explore how we can use psychological insights to ensure that teams work as effectively as possible.

We begin by distinguishing 'real' teams from 'pseudo' teams, and discuss the types of teams that organisations commonly have and the context in which they operate. We use a model of teamwork to structure our exploration of team effectiveness that, although simple, provides a useful way of making sense of the vast array of research evidence about teamwork. As we work through the model of team inputs, mediators and outputs, you will find practical recommendations for managing teams and developing your own teamworking abilities.

This chapter will help you answer the following questions:

1 What is a team and why are teams used at work?
2 How do team inputs, such as individual diversity, team leadership and organisational systems, influence team performance?
3 What kind of processes and states moderate team effectiveness?
4 What team outputs are important?
5 Are some people just not suited to teamwork?

WHAT IS A TEAM?

Activity What is a team?

Part 1: In a small group, come up with your own definition of a team. You can take whatever approach to this you like: you could write a definition, draw a picture or tell a story that illustrates what a team is. Present your definition to the whole class.

Part 2: Do you think your group for this activity qualifies as a 'team'? Why or why not? How does this help you to refine your definition?

Teamwork is a very popular way to organise work, with 68% of private and 88% of public organisations in the UK reporting that they used formally designated teams (Kersley et al., 2005), and the majority also reporting that over half their employees were involved in these teams. Most of the teams had responsibility for specific products or services and had some control over how they did the work, but only a tiny minority (6%) were allowed to choose their own leaders. With such variety in how teams are structured, there is a lot of discussion about how we define teams, not least because it has an impact on how we can evaluate their effectiveness.

In some books, you will find that the authors differentiate between a work 'group' and a work 'team', while others distinguish 'real' teams from 'pseudo' teams. While using teams might be an effective way to get certain tasks done, it is only when teams are structured, supported or supervised in certain ways that good team performance actually emerges. Many different constellations of 'groups of people' can be found at work, but not all of them are teams. If we want to know how to manage teams more effectively, we need to be clear about what a team is, or indeed, how we can ensure we have an effective team rather than an ineffective group of people who are a team in name only.

Some definitions of work teams list the 'requirements' of a team and include such things as a team being defined as a group of two or more people which (Kozlowski and Bell, 2003, West, 2008):

- Exists to perform organisationally relevant tasks and is given responsibility for that task
- Shares common goals
- Has task interdependence (i.e. members are reliant on the other members' work, have to work closely together and be supportive in order to achieve the overall goals).

In addition, the definitions often emphasise that a work team is embedded in an organisational context. That context sets the boundaries and constrains the team, and influences how the team interacts with other parts of the organisation. Overall, most definitions of teams include the key elements of interdependence and the importance of the organisational context that defines and constrains them.

However, a different approach to defining teams is to find ways to distinguish them from pseudo teams, groups that are called teams by managers but do not actually function like teams. West and Lyubovnikova (2012) suggest four dimensions to help us distinguish real from pseudo teams:

1 Interdependence – do the typical tasks require team members to work in a closely coordinated manner towards common goals? Or do the members work towards different goals on their own or perhaps with just one other person?
2 Shared Objectives – to what extent do the team members agree on what their objectives are? Pseudo team members will each have their own ideas of what the team objectives are.
3 Reflexivity – in pseudo teams, members will only meet occasionally to share information, while in real teams

they will review their performance systematically in order to develop or adapt their future efforts.

4 Boundedness – a real team is clear about who is in the team and who is not, but pseudo teams are 'permeable', with no one being sure who is actually in it.

Many of the problems that arise with teamwork are actually due to the team not really being a team. Putting a group of people together and telling them they are a team is not magically going to deliver the results that the organisation wants. If the organisation is serious about wanting effective teamwork, it needs to be serious about setting up and managing the teams as well.

Why teams?

This leads us into considering why an organisation might want to use teams. While it is certainly fashionable to have teams, it is a simple fact that most of the work in organisations simply could not be done by individuals. There are also real practical benefits to teamworking A recent meta-analysis (Richter et al., 2011) showed that teams have a positive effect on organisational performance (e.g. reduced patient mortality or increased productivity). The other advantage of teamworking is that it improves employee attitudes, such as organisational commitment, satisfaction and motivation. These positive benefits are further enhanced if the organisation has supportive HR practices in place.

Besides this general positive effect on performance and employee attitudes, there are also more specific benefits of teamwork (Mohrman et al., 1995). Teams can improve both the development and delivery of products and services, reducing costs and increasing quality. The organisation can manage its knowledge and learning more effectively because team members can learn from each other and integrate their knowledge. Another major advantage of teamwork is that it can promote innovation as people come into contact with new ideas or develop new approaches together.

In a recent review of quantitative studies, Delarue et al. (2008) explored the links between teamworking and four different organisational outcomes. They found that teamwork was associated with a generally positive impact on operational outcomes, such as productivity, quality and efficiency, as well as financial outcomes, such as value added per employee. At the individual level, employees working in teams had more positive attitudes to work, including increased job satisfaction, belongingness and organisational commitment. There were also positive behavioural outcomes, such as reduced absenteeism and turnover.

Teams are able to bring more resources to a task, and use those resources in a more flexible way, than

an individual could. They can overcome the functional and organisational barriers that limit individuals and provide the opportunity for synergy – achieving something together that no one person could achieve alone (Hackman, 1998). That potential, however, is not always attained. In fact, some authors suggest that teams fail more often than they succeed. In his book *Groups that Work (and those that don't)*, Hackman (1990) points out that only a minority of the groups he studied were effective and that his analysis was based mostly on what went wrong in the majority. The problems he identifies relate back to our discussion of the difference between real and pseudo teams. If an organisation is able to set up and support real teams, it will reap the benefits, but if a group is a team in name only, we can't expect it to provide the positive outcomes found in the literature.

Types of team

Now that we have an understanding of what a work team should be and why organisations would choose to have them, what kinds of groups at work fit this definition? There are several different types of teams, which we can classify into five main groups (drawing on Cohen and Bailey, 1997, Mohrman et al., 1995): Work, Parallel, Project, Management and Action teams summarised in Table 6.1.

As you read through the types of team, you may notice some of the ways in which they differ. First is how permanent they are, with some teams staying together for years and others only for a few hours. Second, there is the authority dimension, with some teams only able to make recommendations and others able to carry out whatever decisions they make. Third, there is the extent to which skill development is an important part of the team's functioning. For example, medical teams need to continually update their knowledge and develop their skills. Fourth, teams differ in terms of how routine their tasks are. And finally, teams also differ in how stable or turbulent their environments are.

These dimensions and taxonomies are useful in recognising that different teams will have different requirements. But in themselves they do not give us a very good basis for identifying what effective management of teams would look like. For that, we need to consider a model of the overall teamwork process: how does 'team' translate to 'performance'? And what can we do to ensure the best outcomes? (See Table 6.1).

A model of teamwork

One of the most popular and well-researched models of teamwork today is based on a simple outline put forward by Joseph McGrath (1964) as a framework for analysing group phenomena: seeing them in terms of cycles of

Table 6.1 Types of team

WORK TEAMS	are stable and long-lasting, having responsibility for a particular service or product. People are usually members of these groups full time. Although traditionally directed by a supervisor who makes all the decisions about workflow, process and so on, self-managed work teams have become more popular in recent years. Examples of work teams include assembly teams or maintenance crews.
PARALLEL TEAMS	exist alongside (or parallel to) the existing organisational structure, drawing together people from different departments or jobs to engage in problem-solving or improvement activities. Generally, they make recommendations to the higher management but do not have authority themselves to implement those recommendations. Examples include ad hoc committees to consider specific tasks and quality improvement circles in manufacturing.
PROJECT TEAMS	have a much more limited lifespan. Members are drawn from many different functions so as to bring together the needed specialist knowledge and expertise. After it has achieved its aims, the team disbands and members move on to other things. Examples could include a new product development team or a team put together to manage the transfer of the company to a new location.
MANAGEMENT TEAMS	provide direction to the business units under them, coordinating and integrating their efforts. Unlike several of the other teams we have considered, management teams have a considerable amount of authority, due to the members' formal hierarchical positions. An example might be the top management team of an organisation working to define a five-year strategic plan.
ACTION TEAMS	come together for a specific action and have brief performance cycles which are often repeated. They often require extended training or preparation and members have highly differentiated and specialised skill sets. Examples include surgical teams or teams that form to take part in negotiations between employer and trade unions.

Case Study Types of team

Read through the following examples of work groups and decide:

1 Is this a real team or a pseudo team? Why?
2 If it is a team, what type of team is it?
3 Is this the best way to organise the work in this company?

TopService Ltd has a Customer Support Team to deal with customer queries or complaints. The team consists of 20 customer service representatives supervised by one manager, and deals with an average of about a thousand phone calls a day. A computer system organises their workflow by queuing incoming calls to the first available representative, who is expected to deal with the query within ten minutes.

© CORBIS

A large Japanese car manufacturer has implemented quality circles (QCs) – groups of employees who are given the task of identifying, analysing and solving manufacturing problems. Participation in the QCs is voluntary and employees meet during work time to work on the issues. When the team has developed recommendations for improvement, they present them to management, who then decide how to act on them.

A Better Computer (ABC), a computer manufacturing company, has recently lost a major customer to one of its competitors. A small team of people from the manufacturing, sales, research and development, and marketing departments of ABC is meeting representatives of their old customer to see what they can do to win back the business.

inputs-processes-outputs. Inputs consist of things that affect the groups, such as member characteristics or group structure. Processes are how the group does things, and include aspects such as communication and influence. Outputs are the results of the processes, which in work groups would include task completion. In McGrath's view, these outputs provide the basis for the next cycle's inputs.

It is, of course, an oversimplified model: groups change constantly, and when teams are together for longer periods they will develop and mature, so a snapshot like this of a single cycle cannot provide us with a full picture of the team. However, as a way of identifying and analysing the impacts of different inputs and processes on a team's ultimate performance, it is a useful tool.

This input-process-output model has since been significantly expanded at all three stages (Mathieu et al., 2008). First, many different inputs have been identified, and work has been done to find out how they interact with one another both to enable and to constrain interactions between team members. The inputs can be grouped into:

- Individual characteristics, such as competencies and individual personality traits
- Team factors, such as task structure and leader influence
- Organisational/contextual factors, including environmental complexity and organisational design.

The second stage of the model has been expanded to include 'emergent states', along with processes to describe how inputs combine to produce outputs. Whereas processes are actions that team members take that affect outputs (e.g. how often they communicate), emergent states are thoughts, feelings or motivations that affect the output.

Thirdly, the output stage of the model now includes measures of both performance and affective reactions. Performance results could include quality or quantity of goods or services, while affective reactions include job satisfaction, organisational commitment and so on.

And finally, several researchers have been looking at the longitudinal development of teams or how they use different processes in different cycles of their work, finding ways to explore teamwork beyond the static picture built up by the simpler model. This extended model is illustrated below:

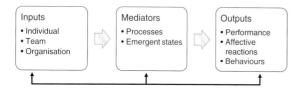

Figure 6.1 The input-mediator-output model of teamworking
Source: adapted from Mathieu et al. (2008) and Ilgen et al. (2005).

We will use this model to explore some of the latest developments in teamworking in more detail in the following sections.

TEAMWORK INPUTS

Team inputs are all those things that contribute towards the team itself: the personality or skills of individuals, how interdependent the team is or how good its leadership is, what kind of organisational systems are in place to support the team, and so on. What we will do here is gain an overview of the most important individual,

team and organisational inputs, rather than making an exhaustive list of everything that can contribute to team effectiveness.

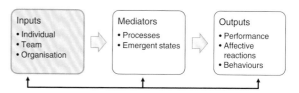

Individual

When we are looking at individual inputs that contribute to effective teamwork, what we are really trying to do is discover whether the team composition makes a difference to how effective the team is. Are particular personality traits associated with better teamwork? Is it better to have a culturally diverse team? Should we choose people with higher IQs to work in our teams?

There are two approaches to answering these types of questions. First, we could look at the average (mean) level of a particular trait or skill across the whole group. For example, we might compare a team with an average IQ of 110 with a team with an average IQ of 98 and see which one performed better; or we could look at the diversity (or variance) within the team. For example, perhaps it doesn't matter what the average IQ of our team is, as long as they are all quite similar. Perhaps we will find that having a team whose members have very different intelligence levels is detrimental to performance. We will consider both of these approaches as we study the following inputs.

Knowledge, skills and abilities

We have already seen that general mental ability (GMA) predicts job performance at an individual level, but does the same hold true for teams? The answer seems to be yes. Teams with higher mean GMA are more effective than teams with lower mean GMA (Barrick et al., 1998). However, the effect is less pronounced in real organisational settings than it is in laboratory studies, meaning that the team task and context is important in determining how much of an impact the team's cognitive abilities will have on its performance (Devine and Philips, 2001). GMA is likely to be more important for teams undertaking ad hoc, complex tasks than those doing routine, standardised activities.

But what about more specific abilities? In Chapter 2, we saw how the assessment of competencies (or combinations of knowledge, skills and abilities, KSAs) can contribute to better selection decisions. This approach has been used in teamwork research as well. Stevens and Campion (1999) identified a list of KSAs needed for effective teamwork and divided them into two broad areas: interpersonal and self-management. Interpersonal KSAs include conflict resolution, collaborative problem-solving and communication, all of which are important for ensuring that the team is able to work together well. The self-management KSAs are important because teams are often given a certain level of managerial control over themselves, and so they need to be capable of setting their own goals and managing performance, as well as planning and coordinating their tasks.

Stevens and Campion developed a Teamwork Test which described several different teamwork situations that people might encounter at work and asked them to say how they would respond, with responses rated as more or less effective. Scores on the five KSAs were clearly related to performance ratings, but there was a problem: team members' scores on this Teamwork Test were very highly correlated with their general mental ability. So while it is possible, and indeed likely, that these interpersonal and self-management KSAs are important in effective teamwork, we probably need to find a better measure of them.

Activity Measuring teamwork competencies

Stevens and Campion's (1999) list of teamwork KSAs includes collaborative problem-solving, which is defined as:

▸ Identifying those situations which require group problem-solving and using the appropriate level of participation
▸ Being able to recognise the obstacles that group problem-solving encounters and implementing strategies to overcome them.

Review the section on competencies in Chapter 2 and then outline how you might assess collaborative problem-solving competencies if you wanted to select people for a team project.

Diversity

With the increased diversity of the modern workplace, many people are interested in knowing how people's backgrounds, education, culture or other demographics might affect teamwork. Work in this area has produced two conflicting theories. The first sees diversity as a source of improved team performance, because team members with a variety of backgrounds will be more likely to provide a richer source of information and perspectives. The alternative view sees diversity as reducing team performance, because heterogeneous teams will have lower cohesion and poorer communication and coordination.

In exploring this issue further, we need to define what we mean by diversity. There are three different ways of conceptualising it (Harrison and Klein, 2007):

Separation: This is how much the team members differ from each other or are similar on a single continuous variable. In this way of conceptualising diversity, it doesn't matter where on the scale the group is, but how much separation there is between the members. For example, a very homogenous team might consist of a group of people who all have university-level education, whereas a team with high 'separation' diversity would have half its members with only secondary school education and half with a higher degree.

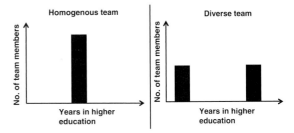

Variety: This is how much team members differ based on a categorical variable. For example, we could have a diverse team whose members all come from different departments or a very homogenous team where all members except one are from the same department.

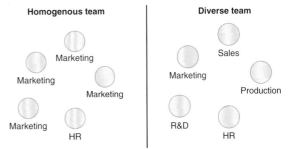

Disparity: This is a measure of the equality within the team. A team with high disparity might have one or two members at a very high organisational level, with access to more resources and with greater authority than all the other members.

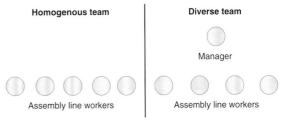

You can see how the different types of diversity might have very different effects on performance. A high level of disparity is likely to make for a more conforming team: most of the team members will not feel able to contradict what the high-status person says. On the other hand, a team with high variety in the occupations of its members will likely be able to address an issue from many different angles and have access to an increased amount of relevant information.

Indeed, research shows that having a team composed of people from several different functional backgrounds (i.e. different occupational specialisations, such as finance, marketing or production) consistently leads to higher team performance (Bell et al., 2011). It is especially important when the team's task includes innovation or design. In addition, variety in educational backgrounds (e.g. people's degree subjects) is also related to creativity and, in top management teams, to general team performance. Interestingly, the mean level of education was not related to these performance measures. This supports the notion that if we are looking for creative and innovative solutions, we need team members with diverse experiences and backgrounds, and mere level of education is not a substitute for this.

 ### International Perspectives Cultural diversity in teams

People from the same culture share norms, values and basic assumptions about life. It can be a shock when we are exposed to a culture different from our own because we suddenly realise that 'they' have a very different way of doing things to 'us'. This is a particular challenge in the multicultural teams that are becoming an ever more normal part of working life. However, there are potential benefits to having a culturally diverse team: that very difference in assumptions and values can become a source of creativity and innovation. Stahl et al. (2009) capture these potential benefits and losses by exploring how culture diversity affects *convergent* and *divergent* team processes.

▸ Convergence. When team members are all from the same or similar cultures, they are more likely to have effective communication, be satisfied with how the work is being done and be more socially integrated. However, the downside is that the team is more likely to be subject to groupthink – coming to a decision too quickly because everyone seems to agree on it.
▸ Divergence. When team members are from different cultures, they may experience more conflict. There can be disagreements about how the work should be done or what the best way forward is. However, there is a potential advantage in that different perspectives can improve the team's creativity.

In an effort to explore these potential losses and gains, Stahl et al. conducted a meta-analysis and found that cultural diversity was clearly associated with divergence, but did not have the expected impact on convergence. The results are summarised in the following table:

Cultural diversity		
Increases	*No effect on*	*Decreases*
Conflict Creativity Satisfaction	Communication effectiveness	Social integration

They also looked at several moderating variables and found that multicultural teams that were geographically dispersed had less conflict than those located in the same place.

Overall, culturally diverse teams bring both gains and losses to the teamwork process, but this study helps us to identify what those gains and losses might be so that they can be more effectively managed. One major contributor to effective diversity management is the creation of an inclusive work environment, where differences are integrated rather than ignored or minimised (Guillaume et al., 2013). Groggins and Ryan (2013) suggest that this can be achieved by making diversity central to the organisation's identity, respecting difference and being accommodating towards individual needs, encouraging continuous learning and embedding structural inclusiveness in the organisation. These approaches create a positive diversity climate, improving attitudes and competencies, and enhancing the organisation's success.

Discussion points

Have you experienced working with people from another culture? Contrast that experience with when you have worked with people from your own culture. Can you relate your experiences to the idea of convergence and divergence proposed above?

If you were assigned to a multicultural team for a new project, what practical steps would you take to try to ensure your team reaps the benefits and avoids the pitfalls?

Results for diversity in other demographic variables have been very inconsistent, with some studies showing that age diversity has a positive impact on performance and others showing the opposite (Mathieu et al., 2008). This is probably because so much is dependent on the team's task and context, and it highlights a major drawback of this approach to understanding team inputs: it is not really measuring the inputs directly. We are using demographic details as a proxy for the underlying variable which is really impacting on team performance. For example, while there could be a relationship between years of education and team performance, it is likely to be specific skills or abilities that determine the team's performance rather than education level per se.

In support of this, it has been shown that task-related diversity (e.g. expertise or organisational tenure) is related to team performance, while bio-demographic diversity (age or gender) is not (Horwitz and Horwitz, 2007). A more accurate method of improving performance would be to identify these other variables instead, much as a good selection process will measure the factors that directly contribute to job performance rather than substitutes, such as 'years in the job'. So let's turn to look at some of those variables.

Personality

You may have come across Belbin's Team Roles already. Meredith Belbin developed his ideas through observing how people behaved in team-based business games and proposed that a successful team needs to have the right 'mix' of people in it. That is, it needs to have people who can fulfil nine different roles – although people can fulfil more than one role at a time. For example, a team needs to have someone who can be a Plant, coming up with new ideas and ways to solve difficult problems, as well as a Completer Finisher, who keeps an eye on the details and ensures the team delivers a quality result on time. (You can read about all the different roles at http://www.belbin.com/.)

Belbin does not see these roles as 'personality types' but instead as collections of behaviours that need to be fulfilled for the team to function correctly. However, as the inventory used to measure the team roles asks respondents to describe their typical behaviour – which is what personality measures do – this distinction is difficult to justify. Although still widely used in business, Furnham et al. (1993) have shown that the questionnaires to measure Belbin types have poor psychometric properties.

Yet the idea that a good 'mix' of personalities is a positive thing for teamwork seems to be quite deeply embedded in our intuitive understandings of teams. Perhaps it is because we know one of the advantages of teams is

that people can bring their different knowledge and skills together, so that the group is capable of more than an individual, that we assume the same should be true for personality. Let's have a look at what the evidence suggests. You may want to refresh your memory of the Big Five model of personality (covered in Chapter 2) to ensure you understand the following discussion.

In a large-scale study of 51 work teams, teams that had higher mean levels of agreeableness, emotional stability and conscientiousness were rated as performing better by their supervisors (Barrick et al., 1998). In addition, teams which did not have any members who scored particularly low on extraversion or agreeableness also performed better.

We saw in the introduction to this section that we can measure team traits in different ways, and when we look at the variance in personality traits among team members, we find that having high variance in conscientiousness scores (i.e. a combination of highly conscientious members in a team with low-scoring members) actually results in lower performance (Barrick et al., 1998). This may be because the conscientious members have to redo the other members' work or because a feeling of inequity negatively impacts on the effort they put into the work. A more recent meta-analysis (Bell, 2007) found that there also needs to be a certain minimum level of agreeableness across the team, presumably so that the team does not become sidetracked with disagreements and conflict.

The findings relating personality to team performance are certainly not straightforward, and the context and task of the team have a large influence on this relationship. So while we can probably identify aspects of personality that would have a negative influence on performance (such as very low agreeableness), it seems that a lot of different people can contribute effectively to the team's performance in different ways. It is important, therefore, that personality traits alone are not used to select people for teams, as we do not yet know the details of how individual personalities interact with each other in team situations (LePine et al., 2011).

Team

Earlier in this chapter we discussed how to distinguish real from pseudo teams, looking at issues such as how interdependent the members are or how bounded the team is. Here we expand on that by considering how team features like this impact on the team's effectiveness.

Interdependence

While interdependence is one of the ways in which we can identify a team, the degree of interdependence has

Case Study Devil's advocate

Although research evidence tells us that agreeableness is an important contributor to team effectiveness, the role of 'devil's advocate' is increasingly being promoted as an essential part of good decision-making in groups. Read this short case study and think about the questions below to see why.

Gerry is the logistics manager at a medium-sized manufacturing business. The company is expanding and the management team is trying to decide where to open their new plant. They have reports on three potential sites and so far the discussion seems to be

going very well, with everyone agreeing that one site is a clear winner: skilled labour is available in the area, the financial incentives offered by the local council are excellent and the buildings the company would be taking over are in a good state.

However, Gerry points out that the site has very poor transport links, and says that in her opinion this will lead to serious problems with the supply of raw materials and the delivery of their products to customers. The rest of the team seem annoyed at this spanner in the works and try to gloss over the problem. 'Of course no site will be perfect,' the MD says. 'But this site is obviously the best. We'll find ways round the logistics issue.' The rest of the team nod in agreement and Gerry, who much prefers to get on with people than to disagree, goes along with their final decision.

▸ Do you think the team have made a good decision?

▸ If someone in the team was officially designated as the devil's advocate, how might it have changed the decision?

▸ When do you think it's necessary to have an official devil's advocate?

an effect on the team outcomes. Interestingly, its impact varies according to the type of task the team is working on (Stewart and Barrick, 2000). If the task is conceptual, for example planning or negotiating, teams perform best when interdependence is either very low or very high – at medium levels of interdependence, performance is not as good. The opposite is true of tasks which are more manual: teams perform best when interdependence is at medium levels and their performance drops off as interdependence increases or decreases. These relationships are summarised in the figure below:

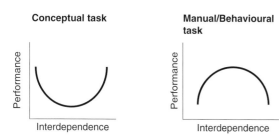

Figure 6.2 The effect of interdependence on team performance for different tasks

Leadership

The importance of the type of task the team engages in is further emphasised when we turn to consider how a team is led. Teams carrying out conceptual tasks perform better when they are given responsibility and authority for their own work, deciding for themselves when and how the work should be carried out. This is called self-leadership, and although it is beneficial to conceptual teams, it has a negative impact on teams engaged in manual tasks. For this type of team, it is better to have external supervisors who make the decisions about how the work should be organised and carried out (Stewart and Barrick, 2000).

Irrespective of the type of task, external team leaders can act as a valuable point of connection between the team and the rest of the organisation and provide the vision to help guide the team's efforts (Mathieu et al., 2008). We will discuss leadership in its own right in a later chapter, so will not go into too much detail here, but leadership behaviours are generally focused on the *people* or the *task*. Examples of both types of behaviours (e.g. showing consideration towards team members and initiating structure for their tasks) have been related to the team's effectiveness and productivity

(Burke et al., 2006). People-related behaviours, particularly empowerment, also improve the team's learning.

Before we move on to consider the organisational level inputs, it is worth mentioning that not everyone in a team will experience the team-level inputs in the same way, nor will they have the same effects (Mathieu et al., 2008). For some members a high level of interdependence may well be needed, while others may need a certain level of independence, and these needs are likely to vary across the lifetime of the task. This is also true for the organisational inputs we will look at in a moment.

Training

We saw above that individual team members' KSAs are critical to the team's success. An important consideration for organisations implementing team-based work is whether these KSAs and other important team processes can be developed through training. A meta-analysis of training interventions with teams has shown that training does indeed have a positive impact. It improves both affective and cognitive outcomes for the team members, as well as team processes and ultimately the team's performance (Salas et al., 2008).

While there are many different types of team training, they can be grouped into three main categories (Salas et al., 2007):

1 Cross-training – team members rotate around all the jobs in the team so that they can understand what is involved in each other's tasks
2 Coordination and adaptation – team members are trained in specific teamworking skills, including how to use appropriate coordination strategies and how to become more efficient in their communication
3 Guided self-correction – team members are trained to identify problems and develop effective solutions to them, thereby improving performance.

Of these three types, cross-training does not make much contribution to team performance, but the others do, with coordination and adaptation training being most effective.

 Psychological Toolkit Virtual teamworking

With the rise in IT as a means to link employees who may not work in the same place, there has been an increase in the use of virtual teams. Virtual teams face particular challenges in carrying out their tasks, not least because of the limitations on face-to-face communication. But they do bring advantages to organisations, such as being able to bring people together who would not normally be able to collaborate. In this exercise, you will be able to assess your own virtual teamworking skills and draw

up a plan for their development to ensure you are well prepared to contribute to any future virtual teams you may join.

Hertel et al. (2006) identified three groups of competencies that are important in virtual teamworking. The first two, taskwork and teamwork, you will recognise from our discussion of 'regular' teamwork KSAs. Added to these is a *telecooperation* group, which assesses how well you can respond to the challenges of virtual teamwork. We will focus on these competencies here. First, take some time to read through the following descriptions of each competency and honestly evaluate yourself in terms of how good you think you are at each of them.

Self-management skills Virtual teams have less social and managerial control than other teams, so the ability to manage your own work becomes more important	**Independence** – Planning and organising your own work without external support **Persistence** – Keeping going with your work despite disruptions Learning motivation – Being interested in new things and willing to learn about them **Creativity** – Developing new and unusual solutions to problems
Interpersonal trust Trust is essential in virtual teams, contributing to a positive team climate	Trusting your team members to do their work and to support you in yours
Intercultural skills Virtual teams tend to be more culturally diverse than regular teams and require intercultural cooperation	Being sensitive to cultural differences and able to work well with people from different backgrounds

Now identify two or three telecooperation competencies you think you need to improve on and draw up a development plan. For example, if you think you need to practise your intercultural skills, think about where you could meet people from different backgrounds. If you need to develop trust, the next time you are involved in a team task see if you can find reasons to trust your team members rather than find reasons not to.

Make sure you have a clear way of measuring your progress, so that after a couple of months you will be able to look back and see how your skills have developed. This kind of reflection will also be very useful to you when you are asked about your teamwork competencies in job interviews, because you will have examples on hand you can talk about.

Organisation

It is not just the individual team members or characteristics of the team as a whole that contribute to the team's effectiveness. The wider organisational context is also an important influence. Here we will consider aspects of the organisation itself, and also how the wider cultural context can contribute to the team's performance.

HR systems

We already know that rewards are most effective when they are clearly related to performance around the specific tasks that the organisation wants to encourage. The same is true for teamwork: to encourage teams to perform well, the rewards need to be related to the team's task. HR systems that facilitate team empowerment are particularly effective in improving team performance (Mathieu et al., 2008). Team performance measures should be broad rather than narrow in order to be effective: not simply focusing on a single task outcome, but also including measures of how the team carried out its work. For example, while it is important to include team goal-setting and have clear measurement of progress towards these goals, it is also important to consider how the team interacts with other parts of the organisation. In addition, measures of performance could also include individual development and learning. Having systems which support these different outcomes sends a clear signal to employees that teamwork is valued by the organisation.

As with other performance management systems, it is important to ensure that team members perceive the distribution of rewards as fair and equitable. One of the drawbacks of a group-based task is that it is often not possible to identify individual contributions, and this can mean that lazy or ineffective team members simply coast by on the efforts of others.

Climate

For teams to flourish, the organisation needs a climate of openness (Mathieu et al., 2008). Organisations which encourage employee involvement and provide both social and political support for teamwork have more participative teams and subsequently better performance. An individualistic or competitive organisational climate will not foster teamwork, as each employee already knows that it is only their individual contribution which will be recognised by higher management.

Where the organisation is using teams to improve innovation, it needs to create a supportive *and* challenging environment (West, 2008). New ideas can only survive if they are given the space to grow. An organisation which wants innovation but does not allow any risk-taking will find that its teams simply do not seem to implement any new solutions; instead they will tend to develop ideas that are very similar to the processes already in place.

Related to organisational climate is the wider environment within which the organisation operates, which is also an important input for the teamwork process. We explore this more in the International Perspectives section, but at this point it is worth noting that teams seem to be more effective when they are embedded in a more cooperative, collaborative culture than an individualistic one (Mathieu et al., 2008).

TEAMWORK MEDIATORS

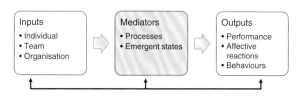

We have looked at a wide range of different team inputs, ranging from personal attributes of team members to the organisational context that the team is in. But if we are trying to build effective teams, it is not enough to simply choose the right people, the right combination of skills or to provide the right training. We also need an understanding of how those inputs are converted into outputs. For that, we need to know about the *processes* and *emergent states* of the team itself. How do team actions, thoughts and feelings impact on their productivity?

Processes

Much as leadership behaviours have traditionally been divided into task- or people-focused efforts, team processes have been divided into actions focused on what needs to be done to accomplish the task and actions focused on the interaction of the team members. However, more recently, these processes have been classified into a transition group, an action group and an interpersonal group (Marks et al., 2001), recognising that different processes occur during different phases of the team's work. This approach sees teamwork as dynamic rather than static, and these three dimensions of teamwork processes have been shown to contribute to overall team performance – the better the teams are at engaging in these processes, the better their performance (LePine et al., 2008). We will now consider these three groups of processes in turn.

Transition

The transition phase of teamwork is when the team looks back at its previous work and evaluates progress as well as looking forward to its future work and planning how it will carry it out. To do this, the team engages in three processes:

1 *Mission analysis* involves identifying the overall tasks of the team, the resources it has available in order to accomplish the task and the environmental factors that may impact on performance. The more accurate this analysis is, the better the team is able to guide its future work and cope with changing circumstances.
2 *Goal specification* is based on this mission analysis and involves breaking down the mission into specific goals. We have seen in previous chapters how important it is to have specific, challenging goals to encourage optimum performance.
3 *Strategy formulation* gives the team clear plans for accomplishing the goals, outlining the members' roles and expectations. Good strategy formulation includes contingency planning and helps the team members to know precisely what they need to be doing.

The majority of these team processes are carried out before the team actually gets started on the task. There is good evidence that teams which are more effective at these transition activities, in other words can set the stage properly for future efforts, perform more effectively (Mathieu et al., 2008, LePine et al., 2008).

Action

During the action phase, the team works directly towards achieving the tasks. The processes in this phase that impact on the end result include communication, coordination and monitoring. Monitoring is an important part of this phase because it gives the team feedback on how it is progressing towards the goals and allows team members to adjust their efforts as needed (Marks et al., 2001). For example, if a production team finds that it is running behind its original deadlines, it can either readjust its goals or try to draw on extra resources, such as overtime or extra team members, in order to meet the deadline.

The importance of feedback during the action phase cannot be overemphasised. If a team is unaware of how well it is progressing, the members will not know whether they need to speed up, readjust their efforts or change direction. Feedback therefore needs to be communicated well to all members. The more dynamic the team's environment, the faster this feedback and communication needs to be. For example, a heart surgery team needs constantly updated feedback about the patient's vital signs in order to adjust their efforts accordingly. However, a team in a more stable environment, for example an administration team in a local library, may only need to meet and discuss feedback once a month.

It is not only the team's progress as a whole that needs to be monitored, but also individual members'. One of the advantages of teamwork is that individuals can help each other out. If one member goes off sick or is struggling to complete a task in time, an effective team will be able to adjust its efforts and help.

For these action processes to be effective, communication between team members is essential. The effectiveness of a team's performance is reliant on the extent to which it shares information among its members (Mesmer-Magnus and DeChurch, 2009). Interestingly, it has been found that groups tend to spend more time discussing information that everyone already knows than that known only to one person. Teams tend to share more information when:

- All members already know all the information
- All members could actually make decisions independently
- All members are similar to each other.

Unfortunately, it seems that precisely those teams which could benefit from sharing information (teams whose members have different knowledge, diverse approaches and are highly interdependent) are less likely to do so. So what can we do to encourage these teams to engage in better information sharing? Mesmer-Magnus and DeChurch suggest the following:

1 Structure team discussions – the more formal and structured the discussion is, the more likely it is that unique information will be shared with the whole team
2 Frame team tasks as 'intellective' – that is, frame the task as one for which a correct answer or solution can be found if the team pools its knowledge and skills, telling the team they have what is needed to achieve their goals
3 Promote a cooperative team climate – encourage team members to work together to achieve the task rather than developing a competitive climate.

Key Research Study Groupthink

Groupthink
Irving Janis (1971)

Background: Janis was interested in finding out why people who were intelligent and highly competent still seemed to make very poor group decisions. He focused on high-level governmental decisions: decisions made by people at the highest level of government that had an impact on millions of people.

Aim: To understand the group dynamics underpinning poor decision-making, as well as to develop recommendations for how to combat it.

Method: Case study analyses were used, contrasting five examples of poor group decision-making (e.g. the escalation of the Vietnam War) with two cases of good decision-making (e.g. the Marshall Plan after the Second World War).

Findings: Janis used the word 'groupthink' to describe the tendency some groups have for *concurrence-seeking*, where they avoid looking for alternative courses of action or appraise their current situation realistically. He identified eight symptoms of groupthink, which he believed was an attempt by group members to maintain self-esteem and emotional ease with each other:

1 Invulnerability – the group has an illusion of invulnerability, becoming over-optimistic and ignoring obvious warning signs
2 Rationalisation – the group continually develops rationalisations to support its dismissal of warnings or negative feedback
3 Morality – the group has a strong belief in its own morality and does not consider the moral or ethical implications of its decisions
4 Stereotyping others – people opposed to the group are seen very negatively, for example, weak or evil
5 Pressure – the group applies social pressure to any members who express doubts or criticisms, reinforcing the concurrence-seeking norm
6 Self-censorship – team members keep their doubts to themselves and minimise their importance
7 Unanimity – the group has the illusion that every member is in complete agreement with their course of action. Silence by any member is viewed as agreement
8 Mind-guards – members shield the group from any information which might call its decisions into question.

Implications: Identifying groupthink symptoms enables a set of recommendations to be made for groups who want to make better-quality decisions. These include encouraging a diversity of opinions and the expression of doubts, bringing in outside experts and nominating a devil's advocate.
In essence, any efforts to reduce conformity-seeking will help to reduce groupthink.

Interpersonal

Interpersonal activities focus on managing relationships between team members. Unlike transition and action activities, they are not associated with a specific point in the teamwork cycle but instead are important throughout. There is some overlap between interpersonal activities, such as conflict management, and the emergent states, such as team cohesion, that are often the result of these processes, but we will focus here on the specific actions that teams engage in and consider the states separately.

Marks et al. (2001) identify three dimensions of interpersonal processes: conflict management, motivation and confidence building, and affect management. The first of these, conflict management, has an interesting history, and we explore it in more detail in the Fad or Fact section below.

 Fad or Fact? Conflict is good for teams

For a long time, it was believed that there were two different types of team conflict and that they had differing effects on a team's performance (see, for example, Jehn, 1995). *Task* conflict could include disagreements over the allocation of resources or decisions while *relationship* conflict included differences in values or personal beliefs. Conflict over a team's task was seen as beneficial to performance, because it encouraged the consideration of a wider range of information and helped the team come to better conclusions. In contrast, relationship conflict was believed to be detrimental, because it destroyed team cohesion and made team members focus on each other rather than the task.

However, more recent evidence indicates that, in fact, *both* types of conflict have negative impacts on team performance (De Dreu and Weingart, 2003). Relationship and task conflict both have a strong, negative relationship with team member satisfaction and team performance. This relationship was slightly weaker in teams that were engaged in routine, less complex tasks than it was for teams engaged in complex tasks. It seems that while a *small* amount of task conflict can be useful in helping teams to consider diverse perspectives or information, increased levels of conflict quickly become detrimental to performance.

It is therefore very important that teams manage task conflict well, and they can do this by:

1 Having cooperative, interdependent goals
2 Cultivating an open environment which allows team members to express divergent views without them being interpreted as personal attacks
3 Using collaborative communication styles.

▸ Why do you think conflict is so detrimental to team performance?
▸ Have you ever experienced conflict with someone over work and yet found them easy to work with? If so, what do you think helped to separate this 'task' from 'relationship' conflict? If not, can you think of any circumstances in which it might be possible?

The second dimension of interpersonal processes is motivation and confidence. Members can build each others' confidence in the team and others' motivation to do well by giving feedback on successful performance and encouragement, and maintaining a positive dialogue about the team's abilities and competence. Unfortunately, teams can fall into a negative spiral, which destroys their confidence and impacts negatively on performance (Lindsley et al., 1995). If this happens, the role of an external leader or mentor becomes important in helping the team to break the negative spiral.

The third dimension concerns affect management processes, which aim to increase team cohesiveness, boost morale and provide empathy for team members. Effective teams are able to manage their emotions by, for example, finding ways to diffuse frustration or increase team members' sense of excitement about a project (Marks et al., 2001). It is important here that we are aware of how a specific activity impacts on a particular team, as each activity itself could have positive or negative effects. For example, letting off steam to a colleague about a particularly difficult customer might be beneficial to the team in helping to manage frustration levels or building empathy between team members. But if this becomes a common occurrence, the moaning can serve to undermine morale or increase anxiety levels within the team.

In discussing these interpersonal processes, it has become obvious that another important mediator of team effectiveness is the team's emergent states, that is, members' feelings and thoughts about the team itself. We turn to consider these next.

Emergent states

'Emergent states describe cognitive, motivational, and affective *states* of teams, as opposed to the nature of their member interaction' (Marks et al., 2001, p. 357). There is some discussion over whether these states can also be considered as inputs or even outputs of the team model. However, we certainly need to distinguish them from activities or processes, because they are not actions that the team members take, but instead dynamic states that influence how the team behaves over time.

Confidence

One of the most important factors to consider here is the team's belief in its own ability – that is, its confidence. This can be confidence in the team's capability to perform a specific task (also known as team efficacy) or the team's general sense of its capabilities for any task (also known as team potency). Both of these beliefs are positively related to performance, though the team's general sense of its capability (potency) is mediated by its efficacy beliefs (Stajkovic et al., 2009). As the interdependence of the team increases, these beliefs have an even stronger effect on performance.

Climate

We have mentioned climate already in our discussion of teamwork, particularly its role in encouraging information sharing and mitigating the negative effects of conflict. Climates are the emergent collection of norms and attitudes within the team – that is, what kind of behaviour is expected within the group. Climates that support or encourage the team tasks are, not surprisingly, associated with higher performance. For example, a team climate that is conducive to creativity will (Shalley and Gilson, 2004):

• Encourage risk-taking
• Be comfortable with ambiguity and uncertainty
• Have a high level of participation in decision-making by team members
• Allow open communication, both within the team and outside it.

Cohesion

Team cohesiveness is a measure of how strong the bonds between team members are. It consists of team members' interpersonal attraction (how much they like each other), their shared commitment to the team task and their pride in the group (Beal et al., 2003). All three of these dimensions of cohesion have a positive influence on group performance, and cohesion is particularly important for teams which are focusing on efficiency as their performance criterion (e.g. team output over a period of time).

Activity Team cohesion

Imagine you are part of a new team of eight members, some of whom you know quite well and others whom you have never met before. Given what we know about the three aspects of team cohesion, what could you do to try and increase cohesion within your team? What kind of problems might you have in trying to implement these ideas, and how could you overcome them?

In this section, we have considered a range of mediators for the teamwork model, distinguishing between processes and emergent states. While we can make clear conceptual distinctions between these different activities and states, we face the problem that much of the research has found that they are highly correlated. This means that it is quite possible that normal people in their everyday work in teams do not make these kinds of distinctions but simply have an overall general impression of how well their team functions (Mathieu et al., 2008). This also helps explain why the suggestions for improving different team processes and states show some overlap. Building a high-performing team requires us to look for ways to improve all these processes rather than trying to focus on one to the exclusion of the big picture.

TEAM OUTPUTS

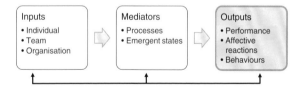

Finally, in our model of teamwork, we come full circle to the outputs, the reason teams are used in the first place. We considered several of these outputs at the beginning of the chapter when we discussed why organisations use teams, and throughout the rest of the chapter we have been finding out how teams can become more effective. But how can we measure that effectiveness and be sure that teamwork is actually worthwhile? Cohen and Bailey (1997) suggest that there are three important aspects of team effectiveness: performance, attitudes and behaviours. Performance measures include the quantity or quality of the team's output, while member attitudes include commitment and satisfaction. Finally, we can also measure behavioural outcomes such as turnover or absenteeism. We will look at each of these in turn as we consider what impact teamwork has on the organisation and the individuals.

Team performance

Performance effectiveness is probably the first measure of a team's success that we think of. We want to know how well a team did its job, and for this, measures of performance can be developed that reflect the specific team task. For example, we might want to know the output levels for a production team, response times for customer service call centres or the number of new product ideas from a research and development team.

In their meta-analysis, LePine et al. (2008) found that teams demonstrating better processes scored higher on performance measures such as supervisor ratings, quantity and quality of the team's output, innovation, and the team members' own ratings of their teams' performance. Other studies have found a positive effect of teamwork on performance ratings by external customers or clients (Mathieu et al., 2006). In health care, effective teams show improvements in patient care and reduction in medical errors (Buljac-Samardzic et al., 2010). The benefits that good teamwork can bring to the whole organisation can best be seen when we consider top management teams, and here, research has demonstrated an improvement in organisational-level financial outcomes (e.g. Srivastava et al., 2006).

There is another aspect of team performance that many people consider important but is not captured in the outcome measures we have looked at so far, and that is 'performance behaviours' (Beal et al., 2003). Performance behaviours are outcomes that are related to better work but are not themselves the actual 'task' of the group. For example, good teams can engage in learning behaviours, improve their own processes or decision-making, or increase their proactivity (Mathieu et al., 2008). While not directly captured in measures of a team's current performance, these outcomes are particularly important when we consider the reality of teams engaging in cycles of work where they can learn from previous experience.

Affective reactions

There is another benefit to teamwork, and that is the impact on the individual team members. Good teamwork is associated with members' increased satisfaction with and commitment to the team and the organisation (Mathieu et al., 2008), particularly when the team is highly participative or self-directed (Cohen and Bailey,

1997). Working in teams also has a positive effect on team members' job motivation (Richter et al., 2011). In fact, some organisations have introduced teamworking with the explicit aim of improving employee motivation and attitudes, rather than solely for performance benefits, recognising that social interaction is an important part of work for many people.

Behavioural outcomes

Given the positive impact of teamwork on employee attitudes such as satisfaction and commitment, it should come as no surprise that teams with better teamwork processes have lower absenteeism levels (Rousseau and Aube, 2013) and lower turnover (Apker et al., 2009).

Overall, the organisational and individual benefits of well-managed, effective teams are manifold and make it obvious why teamwork is such a popular way of organising work today.

IS THERE AN 'I' IN TEAM?

If you were to take a quick survey of the other people on your course, you would find clear preferences among them as to whether they preferred to work with others in a team or on their own. You probably also have personal experience of a team where one person did not seem to fit or could not get on with other members of the group. Perhaps that person was you. Does this mean that some people are just not suited to teamwork?

In our input-mediator-output model of teamwork, we have considered a very wide range of factors that can influence the effectiveness of teams. The complexity of teamwork literature may make some people think it is impossible to build an effective team and wonder whether we are better off with an individualistic organisation. However, this is simply not an option for the vast majority of organisations, as most of their work just cannot be done by individuals in isolation (Richter et al., 2011).

There is certainly clear evidence that some people have the skills and personality traits that are associated with better teamwork (Stevens and Campion, 1999). In building an effective team, our first step would be to select those people who already have the skills and attributes we are looking for (Morgeson et al., 2005). It may well be that some employees would perform better and have higher affective outcomes if allowed to make an individual contribution to the organisation rather than being part of a team. Indeed, psychological researchers have long known that, while a group can outperform the average individual both quantitatively and qualitatively, the 'best' individual often outperforms the group (Hill, 1982).

 Activity When is a team not a good idea?

If a job can be done better by an individual than a group, then it should be obvious that trying to create a team for the task is not a good idea. West (2008) describes several other barriers to effective teamwork:

1 A lack of team tasks
2 A lack of freedom and responsibility
3 Too many members (six to eight is ideal for work teams)
4 Directive rather than facilitative leaders
5 An individual-focused organisation
6 No development of team processes like clear objectives, sharing information, coordination of work
7 Conflict with other teams.

Thinking about your own experience of working in teams, draw up a list of groups that had some of these problems. Do you think the work should have been assigned to individuals rather than a group, or could the team have been managed better?

A caveat to conclude this chapter. We have seen that teams bring great benefits, but when considering how to build an effective team, we need first to ask the basic question: is this task suitable for a team or is it better completed by an individual? All the benefits we have reviewed, whether organisational or individual, performance or affective, are *only* going to happen with effective teams. And no team will be effective if it is given an inappropriate task.

SUMMARY

We have looked at how real teams can be distinguished from groups that are teams in name only, and identified the different ways in which managers can try to improve the effectiveness of their teams. In many cases, this will involve a thorough understanding of the task of the specific team and how best to fulfil it, rather than a general one-size-fits-all approach. For example, we saw that diversity in functional roles can be beneficial to teams looking for novel solutions, but that diversity in status would be detrimental. We have also seen that the wider context of the team, for example the organisational support for teamwork, is an important factor in determining its success.

We used a simple input-mediator-output model to explore teamwork in this chapter. Having reached the end of the discussion, you will no doubt have become aware of some complexities that do not fit into these nice neat divisions. Perhaps the single most important lesson to take away is that building effective teams is not a simple step-by-step process. It is a complex managerial task that requires a good understanding of the individuals involved, the team inputs and the organisational context, as well as the best ways to encourage good teamwork processes and states.

TEST YOURSELF

Brief Review Questions

1 Distinguish a 'real' from a 'pseudo' team.
2 List five types of teams with examples of each.
3 What are two different ways of measuring team composition?
4 Briefly outline two emergent states that affect team performance.
5 What positive impacts does teamwork have on an organisation?

Discussion or Essay Questions

1 To what extent are diverse teams more effective than homogenous ones?
2 Is a model of teamwork such as the input-mediator-output model presented in this chapter of any use to managers? Why or why not?
3 Are teamworking competencies or an individual's personality traits more important in teamwork? Why?
4 How important is it to consider emergent states alongside team processes in developing our understanding of team effectiveness?
5 Are teams always the best way to organise work?

FURTHER READING

- For a broad introduction to teamwork from a managerial point of view, any recent edition of Robbins and Judge's *Organizational Behavior* textbook contains chapters on group dynamics and teamwork. (S. P. Robbins & T. A. Judge *Organizational Behavior*, 15th edn. Harlow, Pearson Education, 2012.)
- Details of the input-mediator-output model of teamwork can be found in: Mathieu et al. Empowerment and team effectiveness: An empirical test of an integrated model. *Journal of Applied Psychology*, 91 (2006), 97–108.

References

APKER, J., PROPP, K. M. & FORD, W. S. 2009. Investigating the effect of nurse-team communication on nurse turnover: relationships among communication processes, identification, and intent to leave. *Health Communication*, 24, 106–14.

BARRICK, M. R., STEWART, G. L., NEUBERT, M. J. & MOUNT, M. K. 1998. Relating member ability and personality to work-team processes and team effectiveness. *Journal of Applied Psychology*, 83, 377–91.

BEAL, D. J., COHEN, R. R., BURKE, M. J. & MCLENDON, C. L. 2003. Cohesion and performance in groups: a meta-analytic clarification of construct relations. *Journal of Applied Psychology*, 88, 989.

BELL, S. T. 2007. Deep-level composition variables as predictors of team performance: a meta-analysis. *Journal of Applied Psychology*, 92, 595–615.

BELL, S. T., VILLADO, A. J., LUKASIK, M. A., BELAU, L. & BRIGGS, A. L. 2011. Getting specific about demographic diversity variable and team performance relationships: a meta-analysis. *Journal of Management*, 37, 709–43.

BULJAC-SAMARDZIC, M., DEKKER-VAN DOORN, C. M., VAN WIJNGAARDEN, J. D. & VAN WIJK, K. P. 2010. Interventions to improve team effectiveness: a systematic review. *Health Policy*, 94, 183–95.

BURKE, C., STAGL, K. C., KLEIN, C., GOODWIN, G. F., SALAS, E. & HALPIN, S. M. 2006. What type of leadership behaviors are functional in teams? A meta-analysis. *The Leadership Quarterly*, 17, 288–307.

COHEN, S. G. & BAILEY, D. E. 1997. What makes teams work: group effectiveness research from the shop floor to the executive suite. *Journal of Management*, 23, 239–90.

DE DREU, C. K. & WEINGART, L. R. 2003. Task versus relationship conflict, team performance, and team member satisfaction: a meta-analysis. *Journal of Applied Psychology*, 88, 741–9.

DELARUE, A., VAN HOOTEGEM, G., PROCTER, S. & BURRIDGE, M. 2008. Teamworking and organizational performance: a review of survey-based research. *International Journal of Management Reviews*, 10, 127–48.

DEVINE, D. J. & PHILIPS, J. L. 2001. Do smarter teams do better: a meta-analysis of cognitive ability and team performance. *Small Group Research*, 32, 507–32.

FURNHAM, A., STEELE, H. & PENDLETON, D. 1993. A psychometric assessment of the Belbin team-role self-perception inventory. *Journal of Occupational and Organizational Psychology*, 66, 245–57.

GROGGINS, A. & RYAN, A. M. 2013. Embracing uniqueness: the underpinnings of a positive climate for diversity. *Journal of Occupational and Organizational Psychology*, 86, 264–82.

GUILLAUME, Y. R., DAWSON, J. F., WOODS, S. A., SACRAMENTO, C. A. & WEST, M. A. 2013. Getting diversity at work to work: what we know and what we still don't know. *Journal of Occupational and Organizational Psychology*, 86, 123–41.

HACKMAN, J. R. 1990. *Groups that Work (and those that don't): Creating Conditions for Effective Teamwork.* San Francisco, Jossey-Bass.

HACKMAN, J. R. 1998. Why teams don't work. *Social Psychological Applications to Social Issues*, 4, 245–67.

HARRISON, D. A. & KLEIN, K. J. 2007. What's the difference? Diversity constructs as separation, variety, or disparity in organizations. *Academy of Management Review*, 32, 1199–228.

HERTEL, G., KONRADT, U. & VOSS, K. 2006. Competencies for virtual teamwork: development and validation of a web-based selection tool for members of distributed teams. *European Journal of Work and Organizational Psychology*, 15, 477–504.

HILL, G. W. 1982. Group versus individual performance: are N+ 1 heads better than one? *Psychological Bulletin*, 91, 517.

HORWITZ, S. K. & HORWITZ, I. B. 2007. The effects of team diversity on team outcomes: a meta-analytic review of team demography. *Journal of Management*, 33, 987–1015.

ILGEN, D. R., HOLLENBECK, J. R., JOHNSON, M. & JUNDT, D. 2005. Teams in organizations: from input-process-output models to IMOI models. *Annual Review of Psychology*, 56, 517–43.

JANIS, I. L. 1971. Groupthink. *Psychology Today*, November, 43–6, 74–6.

JEHN, K. A. 1995. A multimethod examination of the benefits and detriments of intragroup conflict. *Administrative Science Quarterly*, 40, 256–82.

KERSLEY, B., ALPIN, C., FORTH, J., BRYSON, A., BEWLEY, H., DIX, G. & OXENBRIDGE, S. 2005. *Inside the Workplace: First Findings from the 2004 Employment Relations Survey.* London, Department of Trade and Industry.

KOZLOWSKI, S. W. J. & BELL, B. S. 2003. Work Groups and Teams in Organizations. In *Handbook of Psychology: Industrial and Organizational Psychology*, vol. 12 Hoboken, NJ, John Wiley & Sons Inc.

LEPINE, J. A., BUCKMAN, B. R., CRAWFORD, E. R. & METHOT, J. R. 2011. A review of research on personality in teams: accounting for pathways spanning levels of theory and analysis. *Human Resource Management Review*, 21, 311–30.

LEPINE, J. A., PICCOLO, R. F., JACKSON, C. L., MATHIEU, J. E. & SAUL, J. R. 2008. A meta-analysis of teamwork processes: tests of a multidimensional model and relationships with team effectiveness criteria. *Personnel Psychology*, 61, 273–307.

LINDSLEY, D. H., BRASS, D. J. & THOMAS, J. B. 1995. Efficacy-performance spirals: a multilevel perspective. *Academy of Management Review*, 20, 645–78.

MCGRATH, J. E. 1964. *Social Psychology: A Brief Introduction.* New York, Holt, Rinehart and Winston.

MARKS, M. A., MATHIEU, J. E. & ZACCARO, S. J. 2001. A temporally based framework and taxonomy of team processes. *Academy of Management Review*, 26, 356–76.

MATHIEU, J. E., GILSON, L. L. & RUDDY, T. M. 2006. Empowerment and team effectiveness: an empirical test of an integrated model. *Journal of Applied Psychology*, 91, 97–108.

MATHIEU, J. E., MAYNARD, M. T., RAPP, T. & GILSON, L. 2008. Team effectiveness 1997–2007: a review of recent advancements and a glimpse into the future. *Journal of Management*, 34, 410–76.

MESMER-MAGNUS, J. R. & DECHURCH, L. A. 2009. Information sharing and team performance: a meta-analysis. *Journal of Applied Psychology*, 94, 535.

MOHRMAN, S. A., COHEN, S. G. & MORHMAN JR, A. M. 1995. *Designing Team-Based Organizations: New Forms for Knowledge Work.* San Francisco, CA, Jossey-Bass.

MORGESON, F. P., REIDER, M. H. & CAMPION, M. A. 2005. Selecting individuals in team settings: the importance of social skills, personality characteristics, and teamwork knowledge. *Personnel Psychology*, 58, 583–611.

RICHTER, A., DAWSON, J. & WEST, M. 2011. The effectiveness of teams in organizations: a meta-analysis. *International Journal of Human Resource Management*, 22, 2749–69.

ROUSSEAU, V. & AUBE, C. 2013. Collective autonomy and absenteeism within work teams: a team motivation approach. *Journal of Psychology: Interdisciplinary and Applied*, 147, 153–75.

SALAS, E., NICHOLS, D. R. & DRISKELL, J. E. 2007. Testing three team training strategies in intact teams: a meta-analysis. *Small Group Research*, 38, 471–88.

SALAS, E., DIAZGRANADOS, D., KLEIN, C., BURKE, C. S., STAGL, K. C., GOODWIN, G. F. & HALPIN, S. M. 2008. Does team training improve team performance? A meta-analysis. *Human Factors: The Journal of the Human Factors and Ergonomics Society*, 50, 903–33.

SHALLEY, C. E. & GILSON, L. L. 2004. What leaders need to know: a review of social and contextual factors that can foster or hinder creativity. *The Leadership Quarterly*, 15, 33–53.

SRIVASTAVA, A., BARTOL, K. M. & LOCKE, E. A. 2006. Empowering leadership in management teams: effects on knowledge sharing, efficacy, and performance. *Academy of Management Journal*, 49, 1239–51.

STAHL, G. K., MAZNEVSKI, M. L., VOIGT, A. & JONSEN, K. 2009. Unraveling the effects of cultural diversity in teams: a meta-analysis of research on multicultural work groups. *Journal of International Business Studies*, 41, 690–709.

STAJKOVIC, A. D., LEE, D. & NYBERG, A. J. 2009. Collective efficacy, group potency, and group performance: meta-analyses of their relationships, and test of a mediation model. *Journal of Applied Psychology*, 94, 814–28.

STEVENS, M. J. & CAMPION, M. A. 1999. Staffing work teams: development and validation of a selection test for teamwork settings. *Journal of Management*, 25, 207–28.

STEWART, G. L. & BARRICK, M. R. 2000. Team structure and performance: assessing the mediating role of intrateam process and the moderating role of task type. *Academy of Management Journal*, 43, 135–48.

WEST, M. A. 2008. Effective Teams in Organizations. In Chmiel, N. (ed.) *An Introduction to Work and Organizational Psychology: A European Perspective*, 2nd edn. Malden, Blackwell Publishing.

WEST, M. A. & LYUBOVNIKOVA, J. 2012. Real teams or pseudo teams? The changing landscape needs a better map. *Industrial and Organizational Psychology: Perspectives on Science and Practice*, 5, 25–55.

LEADERSHIP: THE GOOD, THE BAD AND THE UGLY

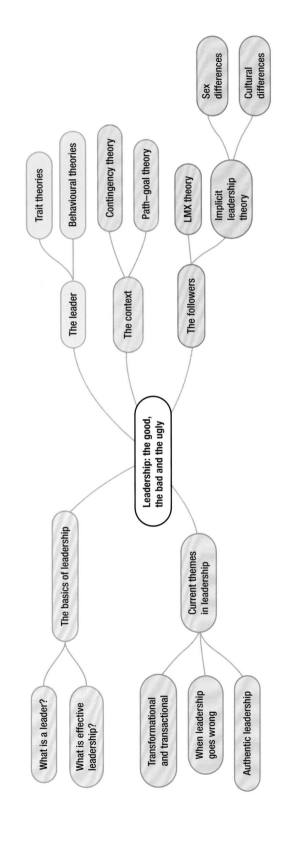

This chapter is entitled 'the good, the bad and the ugly' for a reason. As you will see as we explore the various approaches to understanding leadership, the majority of theories focus on what makes 'good' or effective leadership. We discuss ways of determining effectiveness in some detail in the introductory section. We then move on to consider these theories in greater depth. Leadership is a popular topic with a great many competing theories and models. We will make sense of these by looking at how they help us to understand the three key aspects of leadership: the leader, the leadership situation and the followers. We will bring our discussion together by reviewing some of the current themes in leadership research.

But we are not only going to focus on good leadership, we are also going to look at the bad (how leadership goes wrong) and the ugly (prejudice in leadership). In the wake of serious organisational malfeasance and corruption, as well as the costly derailment of top executives, there has been an increased emphasis on the darker side of leadership, as well as how we can encourage authentic leadership. When it comes to understanding prejudice in leadership, we will focus on how follower perceptions can influence leadership effectiveness and the role of biases in perceptions of 'good' leadership.

This chapter will help you answer the following questions:

1   What do we mean by effective leadership?
2   What personal qualities or skills are important in leaders?
3   How does a leader's context influence his or her effectiveness?
4   What role do followers play in leader performance?
5   Why does leadership remain an important topic in work psychology and what recent advances have been made in understanding it?

THE BASICS OF LEADERSHIP

Activity Leaders

Think about a good leader you have had experience of. It could be, for example, a political leader, the captain of your sports team or a boss at work. Write down what you think made them such a good leader.

▶ When you have your list, compare it with a colleague's. Are there any similarities or differences? Why do you think this is?
▶ As we go through the chapter, see if you can relate items in your list to some of the theories we

cover. For example, if you wrote 'confident', it's an example of the trait approach, whereas 'took time to get to know me' is an example of the behavioural approach.

What is a leader?

As with other areas of psychology, many people have spent a large amount of time trying to define precisely what we mean by a 'leader'. At first glance, you might think this was a lot of wasted effort: surely we can all identify a leader? Certainly, formally designated leaders are easy to spot. We know who the department head is, we know who is captain of the team, we know who the prime minister is, or president of a country. But where it gets more complex is when we think about informal leadership, for example the person in the team who seems to keep everyone's morale up or the person in the department who manages to persuade everyone to agree with their way of thinking, or the way some formal leaders are good at what they do and others are not. If we want to find out what makes a leader effective, we need to look at all of these aspects of leadership, and not simply focus on the person who seems to be the 'boss'.

Definitions of leadership tend to revolve around the idea of influence – a leader being a person who is able to influence others towards the achievement of a goal (Robbins and Judge, 2007). That influence can be from the person's formal authority within an organisation or it may be due to other factors, such as their oratorical skill or apparent expertise in the area.

It seems a popular approach in current thinking about leadership to claim that leadership does not involve coercive power (Rothmann and Cooper, 2008), but this is rather an idealistic view. Certainly, defining leadership in this way will help us to identify inspiring and highly persuasive people, but there is no doubt that plenty of people leading organisations and even countries today rely heavily on coercive power to influence their followers towards a goal. Ignoring this aspect of leadership has tended to make psychological theories a bit bland or unrealistic – unable to help us explain or avoid the 'dark side' of leadership. There are, however, some exceptions to this, and we will consider them in detail later in the chapter.

Another issue to consider in understanding leadership in organisations is how it differs from management. Kotter (2001) points out how important it is to distinguish between leadership and management, with good management being about coping with complexity, while good leadership helps the organisation cope with change. Both have three main tasks but they achieve them in different ways:

Table 7.1 Management and leadership

Task	Management (dealing with complexity)	Leadership (dealing with change)
Decide what needs to be done	Planning and budgeting	Setting a direction (vision and strategy)
Create networks to achieve these aims	Organising and staffing	Aligning people with the vision
Ensure people do the job	Controlling and problem-solving	Motivating and inspiring people

As we continue through this chapter, remember that good leadership, while essential to organisational success, is not enough on its own to ensure that success.

What is effective leadership?

If we want to know what contributes to successful leadership, we need to know how it can be measured. Studies have operationalised success in leadership in three ways (Brodbeck, 2008):

1   How well does the leader influence others?
    A successful leader changes individual employees' behaviour, values and attitudes or a group's climate and norms.
2   How much does the leader affect performance?
    A successful leader will improve the employees' job satisfaction or work performance, improve organisational outcomes such as accident rates or turnover, influence quality and quantity of output, and so on.
3   How well recognised is the leader?
    A successful leader is recognised by others, having greater income and increased symbols of status and esteem, and advancing up the organisational hierarchy.

But there could be some argument about the extent to which these measures of success are the same as measures of effectiveness. We can all think of people who are recognised as leaders and have high-status jobs, high income, flashy cars and so on, yet whom we would not consider 'effective' in their leadership role. In fact, equating success with effectiveness can have disastrous consequences for

Case Study Success vs effectiveness

Fred Goodwin was CEO of the Royal Bank of Scotland from 2000 to 2008. After qualifying as a chartered accountant in 1983, his career rapidly took off and by the age of 40 he was deputy CEO of RBS. Just two years later, he took over as CEO. He received several awards and accolades, including Forbes' Businessman of the Year in 2002, and he was knighted in 2004. Goodwin's leadership of the bank led to increased share prices until, in early 2007, RBS shares had reached an all-time high.

However, in 2008, RBS essentially collapsed, with shares dropping to a fraction of their previous value, and the bank having to be bailed out by the UK government. Goodwin stepped down as CEO, and four years later his knighthood was rescinded.

▶ One of the ways researchers attempt to define effective leadership is by using external measures of success. What are some of the dangers of this approach illustrated by this case study?

▶ What do you think 'successful' leadership during the banking crisis would have looked like? Can you find any examples of this?

© JUPITER GETTY

understanding good leadership, as the 'Success vs effectiveness' case study illustrates.

Measures of leader effectiveness have changed over the years. Since the recent financial crisis, a lot more attention has been given to outcomes that go beyond the short-term maximisation of profits that was a popular measure in the preceding years. Good measures of leader effectiveness need to include a consideration of the impact on employees, the wider environment and longer-term issues of success.

THE LEADER

Trait theories

People have always wanted to know what makes a good leader. In *The Republic*, the Greek philosopher Plato describes his ideal society as being ruled by philosophers who are trained to pursue the good and lists several of their essential qualities, including justice, courage and temperance. In fact, most people, when they are first thinking about leadership, will focus on the personal qualities or traits of successful leaders. This was also the approach taken by the earliest psychologists to study the subject: trying to identify the personality traits that set leaders apart from non-leaders.

Unfortunately, all these early research efforts ended up identifying different 'leadership traits'. Reviews by Stogdill (1948, 1974) identified around 20 different personal qualities associated with leadership, including personality traits and even variables such as height or age. However, he also pointed out that these qualities need to be directly relevant to the situation for the leader to be effective. Similarly, a review by Geier (1967) found that only 5% of supposed leadership traits were common across different studies.

This picture changed as the Big Five model of personality emerged, because researchers could now organise their findings around the five broad traits. Certain personality traits are associated with both the emergence of leaders (i.e. who is most likely to take on a leadership role in a group) and their effectiveness (Judge et al., 2002):

- High extraversion: leaders tend to be confident and outgoing, comfortable with asserting themselves
- High conscientiousness – leaders have self-discipline and stick to their commitments
- High openness to experience – leaders are flexible and look for new ways of doing things
- High emotional stability – leaders tend to be calm and not easily stressed or moody

- High agreeableness is negatively related to leader emergence: people who are happy to go along with others in the group are also less likely to put themselves forward as leaders. Interestingly, however, agreeableness is positively related to leader effectiveness.

The first three of these traits are most strongly related to leadership across different situations, with emotional stability and agreeableness showing more variation. For example, agreeableness is more strongly related to leadership in student groups than in organisational settings.

We now have a good overview of the sorts of people who will become leaders and be effective in that role, but what motivates them to want leadership positions? McClelland and Boyatzis (1982) identified a 'leadership motive pattern' that was associated with managerial success over an extensive period of time. This pattern was: a moderate to high need for Power, low need for Affiliation and, at lower levels of management only, a high need for Achievement. Interestingly, it was only the socialised need for power (wanting to work towards the organisation's aims or enable followers' development) that was important here, rather than the desire to dominate other people.

In building on Stogdill's work, Bass noted the importance of competencies in effective leadership (Bass and Stogdill, 1981). As we have seen in previous chapters, competencies are combinations of behaviours and personality factors that are directly related to getting the job done, so we will now move on to consider behavioural approaches to understanding leadership.

Behavioural theories

Because trait theories, before the emergence of the Big Five model, could not seem to agree on what made a good leader, several researchers decided to try and identify the *behaviours* that leaders exhibited rather than their personal traits. One of the major hopes of this approach was that, if we could find out what successful leaders did, we could train other people to become leaders. This is different from the assumptions of the trait approach, which considered leadership to be more of an inborn quality.

Two universities in the USA were working on this topic at around the same time: Ohio State University and the University of Michigan. They analysed the different behaviours that leaders engaged in and independently developed two main dimensions which appeared to underlie leader effectiveness. Although not exactly the same, as the Michigan dimensions were broader than the Ohio State dimensions, they are remarkably similar, as the following table shows.

Table 7.2 Leader behaviour dimensions

Ohio State	Michigan	Example behaviours
Consideration	Employee orientation	Focus on people: supporting employees, listening to them, helping them solve problems, being friendly
Initiating structure	Production orientation	Focus on task: setting targets and monitoring performance, ensuring resources are available, planning

A leader can be high or low on both these dimensions independently, which led Blake and Mouton (1964) to develop the managerial (or leadership) grid. How low or high a leader scores on each of the dimensions determines what leadership style they show. (You will note that despite our discussion earlier about how management and leadership are different processes, they are remarkably difficult to separate in practice.) Although the grid is useful as a summary of how leaders behave based on the findings of the Ohio and Michigan studies, and can certainly be helpful to managers in identifying what behaviours they exhibit, it does not add to our understanding of leadership beyond the original studies.

Activity People and task focus

Using Blake and Mouton's (1964) managerial grid, we can give names to different leadership styles depending on how low or high they score on the two leader behaviour dimensions:

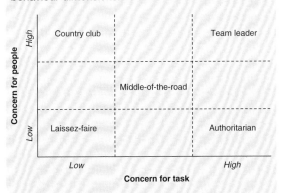

Figure 7.1 Blake and Mouton's managerial grid

Think about leaders you know (either those you have direct experience of or leaders you have heard about in the media). Write the name of an example leader in each of these categories.

▸ How effective do you think each of these leaders were? Do you think there is a 'best' style?
▸ For the leader you think was most effective, can you think of a situation where that style would not work? What does this tell us about the importance of context in understanding leadership?

These two dimensions of leader behaviour fell somewhat out of favour until a recent meta-analysis showed that there was good evidence of their relationship to leader effectiveness across different situations, measures and time (Judge et al., 2004). Six different outcomes were assessed: leader effectiveness; leader job performance; organisation or group performance; followers' motivation; followers' job satisfaction and finally, followers' satisfaction with their leaders. People-oriented behaviours had the strongest relationships overall, and were particularly important for followers' satisfaction with their leaders.

THE CONTEXT

The trait and behavioural approaches both focus entirely on the leader and tend to ignore the influence of situational factors in determining leader effectiveness. This is despite very early recognition in work psychology that studying the leader in isolation can never explain how leadership works (Stogdill, 1948). Other approaches have attempted to take account of the context within which people lead, and say that there is not a single 'best way' to lead, but that it depends on situational factors. We will look at two here: contingency theory and path–goal theory.

Contingency theory

Contingency theory was developed by Fred Fiedler (1967) and states that leaders are more effective when their leadership style matches the situation. He measures leadership style as either task- or relationship-orientated with similar definitions to the leader behaviour dimensions we reviewed above, and believes that a person's leadership style is fixed, in much the same way as personality traits are viewed as reasonably stable. Leader style is measured in a unique way, so let's take a closer look at it.

Least preferred co-worker (LPC) scale

The LPC scale is a questionnaire which asks people to think of the person they work least well with (not necessarily the person they *like* the least), and then rate that person on 16 pairs of adjectives.

These descriptions include efficient–inefficient, hostile–supportive, friendly–unfriendly and so on.

People who describe their LPC in relatively positive terms, despite not working well with them, are said to have a relationship orientation; that is, they are motivated to maintain good relationships. Those who describe their LPC in relatively negative terms are said to have a task orientation: they are focused on productivity rather than relationships.

Once we know a leader's style, we then need to know more about the situation in which we are expecting them to lead. Here, the important issue is how much control the leader has over the followers, and there are three contributing variables:

1 Leader–member relations – how confident the followers are in their leader, how much they trust and respect the leader
2 Task structure – how procedural or structured the task is
3 Position power – how much influence a leader has over rewards and punishments, such as hiring, firing, salary and disciplinaries.

Contexts can be summarised as favourable (good leader–member relations, high task structure and strong position power) or unfavourable (low on all three variables). Where this model really adds to our understanding of leadership is in the way it explains effective and ineffective leadership. Effective leadership happens when the leader style matches the situation. Task-oriented leaders are more effective at the extremes, very favourable or very unfavourable situations, whereas relationship-oriented leaders are more effective in intermediate situations.

The research evidence to support this model is strong (Strube and Garcia, 1981), but there are a few criticisms. First, and perhaps most importantly, the relationship of the LPC scores to a person's actual leadership style is not clear and it seems that the LPC score can change over time, which runs contrary to Fiedler's claim that leader style is fixed (Schriesheim et al., 1979). Second, it can be difficult to measure the situational variables (Kabanoff, 1981). Despite these criticisms, the contingency approach represents an excellent first step in trying to take account of the complexities of the leadership context.

Path–goal theory

In the early 1970s, Robert House proposed the path–goal theory as a way of making sense of the research findings that showed certain leader behaviours were effective in one context but ineffective in another. The theory combines the findings of the Ohio State research studies with the expectancy theory of motivation. It sees leadership as essentially *motivational*; that is, an effective leader will clarify the path employees need to take in order to achieve goals, thereby increasing their motivation (House, 1996).

Path–goal theory is a development of contingency theory in that it shows how an effective leader will adapt his or her style to suit the situation. The original theory specified four different kinds of leader behaviours as well as the environmental and personal variables that would influence how effective they were. Environmental factors include task structure, formal authority and work group autonomy, while personal factors include the employee's locus of control, experience and ability. The following table summarises each leader behaviour and gives an example of when it is most effective:

Table 7.3 Leader behaviours in path–goal theory

Leader behaviour	Aim	Best suited to (examples)
Directive (Scheduling work, giving specific guidance, clarifying policies)	Reduce role ambiguity, clarify perceptions of how effort will result in performance and how performance is linked to rewards	Situations where task roles are ambiguous or employees highly experienced/capable
Supportive (Displaying concern for welfare, creating supportive work environment, being friendly)	Satisfy followers' needs and preferences, decrease stress	Situations with structured tasks, especially where tasks are emotionally or physically distressing
Participative (Consulting with subordinates, involving them in setting goals)	Encourage followers to contribute to decision-making, facilitate communication	Employees with an internal locus of control undertaking tasks with a high level of interdependence
Achievement-oriented (Setting challenging goals, showing confidence in followers' ability, seeking improvement)	Encourage excellent performance and individual pride in work	Employees who have high achievement motivation in tasks requiring personal competence

Case Study Path–goal leadership

George has just started work as manager
of a small team of PR officers in a
large consultancy. While he has over a decade's
experience in the PR industry, he recently
took a year out of work to complete an MBA,
and this is his first management position.
He is eager to apply and test some of the
leadership theories he learned about
at university and thinks that path–goal leadership
is the most relevant for him.

After two weeks in the job, he has
analysed the situation and his new team in terms of
the variables outlined by path–goal theory as follows:

© PhotoDisc/Getty Images

▸ Environment
  ▸ Tasks are reasonably unstructured, requiring his PR officers to work creatively to plan new campaigns and respond to crises immediately.
  ▸ George has formal authority as the manager of his team of PR officers, but he knows from his own past experience that micro-managing simply does not work in a PR context.
  ▸ His team are expected to work autonomously, using their initiative and imagination to develop new campaigns and respond to clients' needs.
▸ Personal factors of the team
  ▸ George is reasonably sure that nine out of ten of his team have an internal locus of control; that is, they believe they are responsible for their own achievements and failures. He is not so sure about the last member of the team, who seems to have a more external locus of control.
  ▸ His team is relatively inexperienced. Five of the PR officers have been in post for less than a year and the other five for between two and four years.
  ▸ He is very confident of the ability of his team. Although their PR experience might not be very extensive, they have all been very successful in previous, related work and are enthusiastic about their current jobs.

Questions

▸ According to path–goal theory, what leader behaviour(s) should George adopt to be most effective in his new role?
▸ Can you foresee any problems with this chosen approach? How might they be resolved by using a different model of leadership?

A later development of this theory (House, 1996) broke the leader behaviours down slightly differently and added some more to take account of more recent research. For example, directive behaviours were broken into path–goal clarifying (clarifying goals and means of achieving them) and work facilitation (planning, scheduling, organising) behaviours, while participative behaviours including facilitating interaction and using group-oriented decision processes. The basic proposition, however, remained the same: an effective leader uses behaviours which *complement* the environmental factors and personal characteristics of the employees.

Although the central proposition of this theory is relatively simple and straightforward, testing all its predictions is quite complex. This means that while there is some good evidence that this theory is reasonably accurate, much more work still needs to be done on the specifics (Schriesheim and Neider, 1996).

THE FOLLOWERS

So far, we have considered the leaders, what they are like, what they do and so on, as well as how the situation they are in influences effective leadership. But leaders can't exist without followers, and to gain an in-depth understanding of how leadership works we need to explore the relationships that leaders have with their followers.

Leader–member exchange theory

One well-supported model for these relationships is the leader–member exchange theory (LMX), which points out that leaders do not treat all their followers the same, but have different relationships with different followers.

LMX theory proposes that leaders have an 'in-group' and an 'out-group' of followers (Dansereau et al., 1975). Followers in the in-group have a high quality of exchange with their leaders (high LMX), investing more effort and loyalty into the relationship with their leader, while those with low LMX do not go beyond the formal work expectations. The leader trusts members of the in-group more, spending more time with them and giving them special privileges and extra support. In contrast, leaders have a much more formal relationship with followers who are in the 'out-group', giving them less attention and fewer rewards. High LMX is associated with better work outcomes, including job performance, satisfaction, commitment, role clarity and turnover intentions (Gerstner and Day, 1997).

Members of the in-group also have the advantage that the fundamental attribution bias we looked at in Chapter 1 works in their favour: their successes are seen as evidence of their hard work and ability, while failures are seen as due to environmental factors. The out-group members unfortunately suffer under the reverse: their successes are seen as due to situational effects, and their failures are seen as due to their laziness or lack of ability.

The relationship between the leader and the follower develops over time and, as it does so, it has implications for the followers' power and influence over the leader. There is good evidence that followers with high LMX are in a more egalitarian relationship with their leaders. They feel empowered and are able to exert some influence over their leader, while the leader does not need to control these subordinates as much and delegates to them (Schriesheim et al., 2001).

Given the positive outcomes of high LMX, what determines whether a follower is in the in- or out-group for a particular leader? While some research indicates that similarity between leader and follower personality or attitudes may be an important determinant (Gerstner and Day, 1997), recent work indicates that dissimilarity in personality traits is actually beneficial (Oren et al., 2012), and that high LMX might rely more on social exchange or reciprocity. What is certain is that this relationship develops over time: while there is some stability in LMX quality, it is certainly open to amendment based on the followers' behaviour (Gerstner and Day, 1997). This development in the relationship can be summarised as follows (Graen and Uhl-Bien, 1995):

Stranger (low LMX)
• Exchange is contractual and formal
• Reciprocity is immediate

Acquaintance (medium LMX)
• Increased social exchange, sharing of information and resources

Maturity (high LMX)
• Includes emotional exchange (trust, respect)
• Exchange of favours over long time periods

Figure 7.2 Leader–follower relationship development

Of course, not all leaders and followers will develop their relationship to the maturity stage. Some may stay permanently at the 'stranger' stage, unable or unwilling to move beyond a simple transactional relationship. However, the more a leader or follower is able to develop the relationship, the better will be the work outcomes. It is important to note that LMX theory gives equal emphasis to both the leader's and the follower's efforts to build the relationship: leadership is not something a leader can do on his or her own, but requires a mutual relationship with the followers.

Implicit leadership theory

Contingency theories have shown us how important it is for a leader to match his or her style and behaviours to the situational demands in order to be effective. However, it is not just a case of choosing the right behaviours for a structured or unstructured work task or encouraging participative decision-making for particular employees. There is another level of complexity, and that is how the followers interpret those leadership behaviours. Have a look at the following case studies for some examples.

Unfortunately, just as in other areas of life, people's perceptions of a leader's effectiveness are tainted by stereotypes. Lord and Maher (1991) called this the implicit leadership theory. We have an unconscious (implicit) representation of what a leader is like (a leader schema), and when we notice that a person fulfils a few of those attributes, such as chairing meetings, being successful or acting decisively, the leadership schema is activated and we assign other attributes to the person that we have not actually observed. For example, we might assume they work hard, they know lots of influential people and are powerful within the organisation. When a leader matches this implicit schema, we perceive them as being more effective.

Sex differences

The practical problem with these implicit ideas about what a leader is like is that they are essentially stereotypes. For example, one of the basic leadership attributes many people have is that leadership is inherently a masculine role (Eagly and Karau, 2002). That means that a female leader starts from a position of being viewed as

Case Study Implicit leadership

John was a well-liked and effective manager in his old job in the UK, which is why he was chosen for an exciting opportunity to run a similar department in the firm's recently acquired subsidiary in Portugal. However, he has been in his new post for nearly a month now and things are not going well. Even more frustratingly, John just doesn't understand why. For example, he introduced a system with individual performance goals that worked really well in his old department: his subordinates there told him it was really helpful to them to know what each person was aiming for. However, his new team seem to resent it, and he has overheard a couple of conversations which seem to imply that they still don't understand what the team is supposed to be doing. John just doesn't know what he can do to make it clearer.

© PhotoDisc/Getty Images

▸ The GLOBE study of leadership (Brodbeck et al., 2000) identified that leaders are seen as more effective in Portugal when they are less individualistic, whereas in the UK, more individualistic leaders are held to be more effective. How might this knowledge help John to analyse his problem?

▸ Can you suggest how John could overcome this issue?

▸ What could his organisation have done to better prepare him for the culture differences?

Sally has just been promoted to her first managerial post. She has decided to model her leadership style on a previous boss whom she really respected. He was direct, decisive and confident. Sally is naturally a very straight-speaking person anyway, so she thinks this approach will suit her and be effective in her job. At the end of her first week, she is feeling pleased with how things are going, but then she overhears a conversation between two of her subordinates:

Alex: I don't think Sally is coping with her new job at all. She seems to be really stressed out all the time.
Gabi: I know. She's really on edge, keeps shouting at everyone. And she seems so full of herself now, as if she's somehow better than us. Maybe she shouldn't have taken the promotion.
Alex: Yeah, she was great at her old job, but she just doesn't seem to have what it takes for management.

Sally is crushed by this and can't understand what she has done wrong. She doesn't feel at all stressed and is absolutely certain she hasn't been shouting at people. What's going on?

▸ Research shows that female leaders who act in ways that most people associate with a masculine stereotype, such as being assertive, confident and ambitious, tend to be viewed negatively (Eagly and Karau, 2002). Yet these are precisely the traits associated with leaders. What do you think Sally should do?

---

less effective than a male leader. Eagly and Karau point out that prejudice against women in leadership positions stems from two sources:

1 Leadership is viewed as more stereotypical of men than women, so women's potential for leadership is less favourably evaluated.

2 Effective leadership behaviours are themselves seen as more appropriate for men than women, so a woman displaying these behaviours is evaluated less favourably.

Women in leadership are effectively caught in a double bind. They can either conform to the leader role and fail to meet the stereotypical requirements of their gender role, or they can conform to their gender role and fail to meet the stereotypical requirements of their leader role. These stereotypes mean that organisations could be missing out on the potential leadership contributions of half of their workforce.

But are there signs of change? Although attitude surveys still indicate bias against women as leaders, there has been a steadily increasing positive view over the last few decades, and there is an indication that stereotypes of women are changing (Eagly and Karau, 2002). Gallup has collected data on the question 'If you were taking a new job and had your choice of a boss would you prefer to work for a man or a woman?' since 1953 in the USA. There

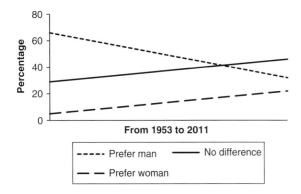

Figure 7.3 Would you prefer a man or a woman as boss?
Source: adapted from Newport (2011).

has been a steady decline in the numbers preferring a male boss and an increase in numbers preferring a female boss or having no preference (Newport, 2011). In fact, over the last ten years, nearly half of respondents have consistently said it makes no difference.

 Activity Overcoming leadership stereotypes

As we become more aware of our stereotypes, we can start to notice their effect on our thinking, decision-making and attitudes. Remember that in Chapter 2 we discussed how stereotypes and biases are cognitive 'short cuts': they are normal methods that our brain uses to make sense of complex information, but they are limiting and lead us into bad decision-making. In this activity, you have the opportunity to identify your own stereotypes about leadership so that you can start to overcome them.

Write the word 'leader' in the middle of a blank page. Now allow yourself ten minutes to write down anything that you associate with that word. This should be free association, so don't try to judge anything you write – if you don't like what you see later, you can always destroy the evidence.

When you have finished, look back over the words and circle any that you think might bias your perceptions of someone as a leader.

▸ Why do you think you have these stereotypes?
▸ Do you have a reasonable basis for these beliefs? (Remember that a reasonable basis needs to be more than your experience of a single person.)
▸ What can you do to stop stereotypes restricting your understanding of good leadership? (One way is to seek out contradictory evidence. If you had a male manager who was dictatorial and aggressive, you could look for evidence that other male managers are not like this.)

In addition, recent work on transformational leadership (which we consider in more detail in the following section) has emphasised different leadership qualities from the traditional control-and-direct style. Transformational leadership includes some qualities traditionally associated with female stereotypes, such as being inclusive, nurturing and participative. Transactional leadership, in contrast, is based on an exchange of rewards and punishments between the leader and follower. In fact, a meta-analysis of comparisons between women's and men's leadership styles showed that women were more likely to engage in these more effective leadership behaviours than men: they were more transformational and used more contingent-reward behaviours (Eagly et al., 2003). In contrast, men were more likely than women to use management-by-exception and laissez-faire behaviours. These findings indicate that, contrary to widespread stereotypes about leaders, women may actually be more effective than men.

How does that last statement make you feel?

It is unlikely that you will have no emotional response at all. Perhaps it makes you feel angry or relieved or upset or even justified in your beliefs. It is important to remember when we are dealing with stereotype issues that they are emotive. We are not talking in abstractions here, but about real people and the impact that stereotypes have on their lives.

In fact, the research reviewed above does show a small difference between men and women, but it also shows an extensive amount of overlap between the two. It would be very difficult, if not impossible, to predict someone's leadership ability just from knowing whether they were male or female. So it is no more useful to have a view of women as better leaders than it is to regard men as better leaders. The sex divide is just too simple a category to have any meaningful impact on our understanding of leadership. We have seen, through all the different theories we have considered so far, that leader effectiveness is an incredibly complex topic. While it is useful to have good, solid evidence of women's leadership effectiveness as a way of counterbalancing the predominant view that male leaders are better, it should be obvious that an understanding of effective leadership requires a much more fine-grained and individualised approach.

Cultural differences

Our implicit schemas of leadership are not only influenced by our male/female stereotypes, but also by the culture we have been brought up in. But as with much of the management and work psychology literature, theories have predominantly been developed in the United States and Western Europe, so it can be difficult to know how applicable the theories are to different countries. It is rare that we come across a truly international research effort, but in the leadership literature there is one: the

GLOBE project (Global Leadership and Organisational Behaviour Effectiveness).

In the GLOBE project, over 17,300 middle managers in 951 organisations completed questionnaires that assessed how their cultural values impacted on their views of leadership (House et al., 2004). They rated leadership attributes on a seven-point scale from *greatly inhibits* to *greatly contributes* to outstanding leadership. One of the project's aims was to find out whether there are leadership attributes that are *universally endorsed* as contributing to effective leadership; that is, are there some things that a leader does which provide effective leadership in all cultures? The research team used a stringent test of whether an attribute was universally positive: it had to be scored as five or more on the scale by 95% of the cultures surveyed and have an overall mean over six. Similarly, attributes which were universally seen as inhibiting leadership had to be scored less than three by 95% of the cultures and have an overall mean of less than three. The table below shows some examples of each of these, as well as some of the culturally contingent attributes. The latter are particularly interesting because in some countries they were viewed as contributing to outstanding leadership and in others as inhibiting it.

Table 7.4 Ratings of leader attributes in the GLOBE study

Universal positives (total number 22)	Universal negatives (total number 8)	Culturally contingent (total number 35)
Dynamic	Non-cooperative	Cunning
Encouraging	Irritable	Sensitive
Dependable	Egocentric	Evasive
Motivational	Dictatorial	Class conscious
Communicative	Asocial	Sincere

The International Perspectives section describes some of the major findings of the project in more detail. The GLOBE studies have clearly demonstrated that culture has an important effect on how we view leadership. Countries with similar cultural values also have similar leadership concepts, so that there is greater compatibility between the leadership concepts of countries in a similar culture cluster (Brodbeck et al., 2000). For example, autonomous leaders are seen as more effective in Germanic countries (such as Austria and Germany) than they are in Latin European countries (such as Portugal and Italy). It can be helpful to organisations and individuals to know what kind of problems or misunderstandings might arise because of these differences, so that they can plan ahead and be proactive in developing effective leaders.

A recent expansion of this project has looked at how cultural and leadership values impact on such things as corporate social responsibility (Waldman et al., 2006). Higher levels of institutional collectivism and lower power distance predicted greater corporate social responsibility (CSR) in decision-making by top managers. In addition, CEOs with vision and integrity influenced managers to believe CSR was more important. These findings can help multinational organisations to plan their CSR approach in different subsidiaries, for example in encouraging leaders with vision and integrity to promote CSR values in countries where low collectivism and high power distance would otherwise demote the importance of these values.

We have now been through all three components of leadership: the leader, the context and the followers. We have seen how there are separate models to deal with the complexities of these elements, and it can sometimes feel as if there is no clear way of identifying effective leadership at work. However, there are current themes in the leadership literature that are attempting to bring these ideas together in a practically relevant form, and we turn to these next.

CURRENT THEMES IN LEADERSHIP

Transformational and transactional leadership

One of the most popular of the current models of leadership distinguishes between two main leadership styles: transformational and transactional (Bass, 1985). Transactional leadership is based on a transaction between the leader and the follower in which good performance is rewarded and poor performance is punished. There are three different ways in which managers engage in transactional leadership:

- Contingent reward: the leader clarifies what is expected of followers and gives recognition for achievements. This approach is constructive, with the leader creating exchanges that will encourage followers to reach the required levels of performance.
- Active management by exception: in this approach, the leader closely monitors subordinates' performance, intervening only when they do not reach the required performance levels and taking corrective action.
- Passive management by exception: leaders using this approach don't clarify what is expected of their subordinates and wait for problems to arise before doing anything. Sometimes they might not take action even when problems appear. In this extreme situation, it is called laissez-faire leadership, and is very ineffective.

All these transactional approaches focus on the task and behavioural exchanges, but only the contingent reward approach has a positive impact on subordinates' commitment, satisfaction and performance (Bass, 1999).

Transformational leadership, in contrast, engages the emotions. Proponents of transformational leadership

International Perspectives The GLOBE project

The Global Leadership and Organisational Behaviour Effectiveness project was founded in the early 1990s by Robert House and surveyed managers in 62 societal cultures. It specifically identified groups of people by shared culture rather than just country (e.g. distinguishing French- from German-speaking Swiss) as a way of more accurately identifying cultural differences. Managers were asked to rate leadership attributes according to how much they contributed to or impeded outstanding leadership. The results allow us to see what differences there are in people's implicit leadership theories. Any mismatch between a leader's behaviours and the followers' expectations is likely to result in performance losses or misunderstandings (House et al., 2004).

Although this research project is vast and whole books have been written based just on the results (e.g. Chhokar et al., 2012, House et al., 2004), we can summarise three of the main findings here:

1 Some 65 leadership attributes emerged from the data. Of these, 22 were universally seen as contributing to effective leadership, 8 were universally seen as impeding leadership and 35 were culturally contingent (i.e. they were positive in some cultures and negative in others).
   ▸ More of the leadership attributes are culturally contingent than are universal.
2 These leadership attributes were statistically reduced to 21 'Primary Leadership Dimensions' and then further to 6 broad dimensions along which leaders could differ:
   ▸ Charismatic/value-based – the ability to inspire, motivate and expect high performance from others, based on firmly held values
   ▸ Team-oriented – effective team building and developing a common purpose among team members
   ▸ Participative – degree to which the leader involves others in decision-making

▸ Humane-oriented – supportive, considerate and compassionate leadership
▸ Self-protective – ensuring the safety and status of the individual or group member (includes such things as face saving, status conscious and conflict inducer)
▸ Autonomous – individualistic and independent leadership.
The charismatic dimension was strongly endorsed across all cultures as contributing to effective leadership.
Team-oriented and participative were also viewed positively by most cultures. humane-oriented showed more variation, with some cultures seeing it as positive (e.g. Southern Asia) and others as neutral (e.g. Nordic Europe). Self-protective and autonomous are seen as negative by some and neutral by others.
3 Another part of the study identified dimensions along which the cultures differed and then looked at how these cultural differences related to differences in how leaders were perceived.
   ▸ Implicit leadership theories are intricately linked with the cultures in which people have grown up.

This study highlights the problem faced by global organisations or individuals who wish to pursue management careers in different countries: how can they ensure leader effectiveness? Simply transplanting leaders who have been effective in one country into another is unlikely to work. Instead, organisations and individuals need to develop cultural flexibility, developing the leader behaviours that are universally perceived as contributing to effectiveness (such as the charismatic dimension) and identifying those attributes specific to the country in question.

Discussion point

If you were taking up a leadership position in a new country, how could you use these findings to help?

For a quiz based on the GLOBE findings, go to http://www.grovewell.com/quiz/.

claim that it is much better suited to the constantly changing world of modern organisations because it is adaptive, helping followers to make sense of the changes and developing appropriate responses to them. There are four distinct components of transformational leadership (Avolio et al., 1999):

1 Idealised influence – followers admire, trust and respect the leader, identifying with him/her. The leader appears to put the followers' needs first, takes a share

in the risks and demonstrates consistency between his/her conduct and principles.
2 Inspirational motivation – leaders give their followers a vision, providing a meaning to their work and a challenge to work towards. They also demonstrate enthusiasm and optimism, convincing their followers that the vision is attainable.
3 Intellectual stimulation – leaders actively solicit new and creative ideas from their followers, questioning assumptions and reframing problems to encourage

innovation. They do not engage in public criticism of followers' mistakes.

4   Individualised consideration – transformational leaders act as coaches or mentors, paying attention to their followers' individual needs and helping them to reach their potential. They encourage personal development and create a supportive climate.

Transformational leadership has been shown to have positive effects on followers' performance (Bass, 1999), and there is good evidence that this effect is cross-cultural (Bass, 1997).

A recent meta-analysis compared transactional and transformational approaches (Judge and Piccolo, 2004). It found that transformational leadership had the largest effect on outcomes (including satisfaction, motivation and performance), closely followed by contingent reward transactional leadership. The other styles of transactional leadership had either no effect or, in the case of laissez-faire, a negative effect. Bass suggests that contingent reward can provide the basis for the building of trust that is necessary for transformational leadership (Bass, 1999).

 Psychological Toolkit Develop your leadership

We have seen how effective transformational leadership is. It certainly appears that some people have an innate ability to be transformational leaders, displaying those leadership behaviours quite naturally. But what about those to whom it does not come naturally? Is it possible to develop your leadership skills?

Barling et al. (1996) undertook a field experiment that indicated the answer is yes. They found that managers trained in transformational leadership were rated more highly by subordinates, created higher organisational commitment in their team and even had improved financial indicators. In the original study, the training involved teaching about leadership behaviours, role-playing and follow-up mentoring sessions. The following exercise is based on that approach, but adapted so that you can work through it on your own.

1   List the characteristics of the best and worst leader you have ever had.
   ▸ Next to each of the characteristics, write down whether you think it relates most to transformational, transactional or laissez-faire leadership.
2   Reread the section on transformational leadership and rate yourself according to how good you think you are at each of the elements, using the following table. (You might like to ask someone who has experience of your leadership to do the

same, and then you can compare their perceptions with your own.)

Element of transformational leadership	My rating (1 – very poor at this → 10 – excellent at this)
Idealised influence	
Inspirational motivation	
Intellectual stimulation	
Individualised consideration	

3   Review the section in Chapter 4 on goal-setting, especially the idea that performance is maximised when we set specific, difficult but attainable goals.
   ▸ Now set yourself a specific but challenging goal for one of the elements of transformational leadership. You might like to choose the element you think you are weakest at or choose to build on the area you believe is strongest.
   ▸ Identify three or four specific situations where you will be able to practise these leader behaviours, and write down how you will know whether you have been successful.
4   After each practice session, either note down your experiences or talk them through with a trusted or experienced colleague. What did you learn? What could you do better next time? What improvements did you notice?

You can repeat this exercise for any of the other elements that you wish to improve on.

Transformational leadership is often also referred to as charismatic leadership, and while some writers like to distinguish between the two (e.g. Bass and colleagues see charismatic leadership as a *part* of transformational), in much of the literature there is little real distinction between how the two concepts are used. Some authors have called for a clarification of the two concepts, pointing out that while charismatic leaders certainly give followers a vision as transformational leaders do, *charisma* itself is a personal quality and should not be subsumed under the general transformational heading (Judge et al., 2006).

Charismatic leaders are seen as exceptionally gifted and particularly emerge as leaders during crises (Trice and Beyer, 1986). Followers personally identify with the leader and his/her mission. Where that identification is primarily with the mission and the values that the leader portrays, it is called socialised charismatic leadership. This type of leader is ethical and oriented towards the group, sensitive to their needs. In contrast, a more personalised style of charismatic leadership occurs when the followers identify directly with the leader rather than the mission or values. Followers tend to idealise and romanticise these leaders and follow them blindly (Rosenthal and Pittinsky, 2006).

Key Research Study Charismatic CEOs

CEO Charisma, Compensation, and Firm Performance

Henry L. Tosi, Vilmos F. Misangyic, Angelo Fanellid, David A. Waldmane, Francis J. Yammarino (2004)

Background: Popular leadership writing promotes charismatic leaders as highly beneficial and critical to organisational success, with many boards of directors appointing CEOs who display charismatic traits. There is also evidence that charismatic CEOs are very highly compensated, with high salaries and bonus packages. However, there is very little evidence that it is CEOs' charisma that promotes success, rather than other leadership attributes such as nurturing talent.

Aim: To find out whether organisations with charismatic CEOs outperform organisations with non-charismatic CEOs and to examine the effect of charisma on the CEOs compensation package.

Method: Senior managers in large US firms completed a questionnaire to assess their CEO's perceived charisma. In addition, data on firm performance and CEO compensation was collected for a ten-year period (or less if the CEO had not been in post that long).

Findings: Using regression analyses, the authors found that there was *no* direct relationship between CEO charisma and firm performance. Interestingly, in uncertain markets, although they did not manage their firms any better, charismatic CEOs boosted stock prices. Charismatic CEOs were paid more than their non-charismatic peers.

Implications: It seems that charismatic CEOs can boost shareholder confidence in uncertain times but that they also cost their firms more, presumably because they are better able to influence decision-makers in compensation discussions. However, CEO charisma is not related to improved organisational performance, which calls into question whether these increased compensation packages are a worthwhile investment.

The concepts of transformational/charismatic leadership are a good way of understanding several of the approaches we have looked at: traits, behaviours, context and attributions (Brodbeck, 2008). They show us that leadership is a process which is partly determined by the leader's traits and partly by behaviours and skills that can be developed. In addition, the model takes account of context by identifying situations where transformational leadership is more or less effective. It also highlights the role of attributions:

charisma is based in leader characteristics but is also an attribution that followers make in response to some of those characteristics.

The transactional/transformational distinction also draws in the ideas of LMX theory: a leader–member relationship that begins with the transactional type of social exchange can develop into the more effective, high LMX relationship that characterises transformational leadership (Graen and Uhl-Bien, 1995). Finally, the transformational approach gives a central place to the role of the followers' emotional responses. In this model, effective leaders encourage and motivate staff, tapping into their emotional energy to influence them rather than using transactional rewards and punishments.

When leadership goes wrong

While early writers on transformational/charismatic leadership pointed out that there were dangers associated with leaders who could evoke such loyalty and commitment from their followers, this 'dark side' has been consistently overlooked in much of the research. However, there has been a strong, if minor, current of research aiming to understand how leadership goes wrong, and this has often focused on narcissism and its relation to charismatic leadership.

Narcissism is a broad personality trait which encompasses arrogance, self-absorption, a sense of entitlement and grandiosity. Unfortunately, several of the things we have identified as important to effective leadership are associated with narcissism, such as personal charisma and having a grand vision. In addition, the narcissist's supreme confidence or dominance encourages people to vote for or choose them as leaders (Rosenthal and Pittinsky, 2006). There is in fact evidence that narcissistic leaders may be effective during times of crisis, being visionary and inspirational. But there is also plenty of evidence of narcissistic leaders leading their countries or organisations into disaster. The problem with studying narcissistic leaders is that we are looking at a very broad array of traits and behaviours, some of which are beneficial to leadership and some of which are not.

In contrast to this broad approach, some researchers have tried to identify more narrow traits that are associated with leader derailment. Hogan and Hogan (2001) take a dramatically different view to understanding leadership from most researchers: instead of looking at what makes an effective leader, they look at how leadership goes wrong. They claim that it is better to study *in*competent rather than competent leadership because:

1   Measures of incompetence (fired or demoted) are easier to find than measures of competence

2 A moral obligation: bad managers make people's lives miserable so we should find out how to identify them

3 The authors also claim that there are so many bad managers in every organisation that it is easy to find people to study.

Previous research on management derailment identified several themes underlying failure, including personality factors such as being insensitive, arrogant or overly ambitious. Hogan and Hogan set out to identify more precisely what personal characteristics impeded leadership effectiveness, with the aim of being able to provide managers with developmental feedback. They developed an inventory which attempted to measure personality dimensions equivalent to recognised personality disorders. Their work resulted in the Hogan Development Survey (HDS), an inventory of 11 scales measuring personality traits associated with leader failure, for example:

- Excitable: moody and hard to please, intense but short-lived enthusiasm
- Bold: unusually self-confident, feelings of entitlement
- Colourful: expressive, dramatic and wanting to be noticed.

Recent work has shown how some of these dimensions are related to transformational leadership. For example, the *colourful* scale is a positive predictor of transformational leadership (Khoo and Burch, 2008). The HDS provides a welcome antidote to the often overly optimistic literature on leadership, pointing out that while these traits are obviously helpful to a certain extent, we need to remember that the very traits associated with positive leadership can also lead to derailment in their extremes. However, despite its popularity, the HDS does suffer from some poor psychometric properties; for example, reliability alphas for some scales are below 0.7 and there are some high intercorrelations between the scales (Hogan and Hogan, 1997), which casts some doubt on its accuracy and usefulness in leadership research.

In a similar vein, Board and Fritzon (2005) explored 'bad' leadership from the point of view of psychiatric disorders. Avoiding the HDS problems, they used an established measure of personality disorders (the MMPI, Minnesota Multiphasic Personality Inventory) to compare the personality profiles of senior business managers with psychiatric and forensic patients (i.e. people with criminal convictions who have been given a psychiatric diagnosis). They found that managers' profiles contained elements that were equivalent to the emotional components of psychopathic personality disorders. Specifically, managers were more histrionic than psychiatric patients; they displayed more superficial charm, were more insincere, egocentric and manipulative. In addition, managers

had similar levels of narcissism and compulsive tendencies (stubbornness, excessive devotion to work, dictatorial tendencies) to the patient group.

The authors suggest that 'successful' people with personality disorder patterns are able to find a way to channel these tendencies in a socially acceptable way. This was supported by their finding that the managers were lower on antisocial and paranoid tendencies. This research highlights an important issue for organisations: characteristics associated with achieving a senior management role are strongly related to personality disorder patterns in psychiatric and forensic populations, hinting that organisations are rewarding and promoting emotionally disordered behaviours which could spell difficulties in the long term. In fact, concern over 'bad' leadership and its consequences has led to the development of contrasting approaches, most notably authentic leadership.

Authentic leadership

Practitioner and researcher interest in authentic leadership has grown dramatically in the last decade, prompted by concerns over the ethical conduct of many of the world's most powerful CEOs (Gardner et al., 2011). Authentic leadership is values-based and involves a high degree of self-awareness on the part of the leader. As well as having various general leader attributes such as confidence and optimism, what sets authentic leaders apart is their high moral character. Walumbwa et al. (2008) describe four components of authentic leadership:

- Self-awareness – understanding our own strengths and weaknesses and being aware of our impact on other people
- Relational transparency – presenting our 'authentic self' to others by freely sharing information, thoughts and feelings
- Balanced processing – objectively analysing all the information to make decisions, including actively seeking out opinions that differ from our own
- Internalised moral perspective – regulating our own behaviours in accordance with our own internal moral standards and values.

Peus et al. (2012) add to this description by identifying two key contributors to authentic leadership: the leader's self-knowledge and self-consistency.

Some authors have proposed that authentic leadership improves performance by encouraging positive organisational behaviour (including follower confidence, optimism, well-being and organisational citizenship behaviours) (Yammarino et al., 2008). However, empirical tests present a rather different picture. In fact, it seems that authentic leadership has both direct and indirect effects on follower outcomes (Peus et al., 2012). It directly improves followers' satisfaction with their leader, their affective commitment and the extra effort they will put into their work. In addition, authentic leadership has an indirect effect on all three outcomes through the leader's increased predictability.

As an antidote to self-centred and unethical leadership, authentic leadership is a welcome addition to our understanding of leadership. And in the context of increased emphasis on ethical management and organisational responsibility, research so far indicates positive outcomes for moral, authentic leaders. However, this concept is still in its infancy, and besides the debate over how authentic leadership is defined and how it can be differentiated from other kinds of leadership, it remains to be seen whether this theory will stand the test of time.

 Fad or Fact? Self-leadership

There is no doubt that leadership is a fashionable topic in the management and psychology literature. But whereas the definition of leadership that we have been working with in this chapter involves influencing a group of people, some researchers have promoted the idea of *self-leadership*. Initially proposed by Manz and Sims (1980) and labelled self-management, it was defined as managing one's own behaviour by setting standards, monitoring and evaluating performance, and giving oneself appropriate incentives. In fact, the authors referred to it as synonymous with self-control, and suggested that good leaders would encourage its development in their followers as it would obviate the need for close supervision.

However, self-management soon developed into the concept of self-leadership. While both are considered self-influence processes, Manz distinguished between them by saying that self-leadership is broader: it includes the self-management processes that address *how* work is to be performed, but also addresses *what* is to be done and *why* (Stewart et al., 2011). Self-leadership has been shown to be related to adaptivity, proficiency and proactivity in both individual and team tasks (Hauschildt and Konradt, 2012). In fact, many positive outcomes have been reported for self-leadership, for example increased productivity, job satisfaction and career success and reduced stress (Stewart et al., 2011). Recently, self-leadership was identified as a process through which transformational (external) leadership results in motivation and, thereby, performance (Andressen et al., 2012). This and other studies have also shown that self-leadership is particularly important for virtual working.

Despite these studies, several authors (e.g. Markham et al., 1998) have argued that self-leadership is not a distinct concept at all but merely a repackaging of old knowledge; for example, personality factors such as conscientiousness or motivational issues such as self-regulation. The response to these criticisms is that self-leadership is a prescriptive model, showing people how things should be done, rather than a descriptive theory (Houghton et al., 2012).

In essence, the attributes that make up self-leadership are certainly important for work performance, and perhaps grouping them together with a catchy title will help people to recognise their relevance. But the essence of leadership is a relationship between the leader and follower(s): you can't have a leader without any followers. This makes self-leadership an oxymoron – an inherently paradoxical term.

▸ Think about the last time you revised for an exam or wrote an assignment for university. This is an example of a task that is ripe for self-leadership: you can decide your own performance-level goals, give yourself incentives if you want to, and organise and plan your own work. According to Manz's definition, did you engage in self-management or self-leadership?

▸ To what extent do you think it is helpful to have a concept of self-leadership?

SUMMARY

In this chapter we have looked at the good, the bad and the ugly side of leadership. Most of our discussion has been around 'good' or effective leadership and we have reviewed several different models that attempt to outline what makes leaders effective. There are three main ways in which leadership has been studied: a focus on the leader's traits or behaviours, a focus on the situation within which leadership occurs, or a focus on the followers' perceptions of and attributions about leaders. The transformational leadership model brings together some of these findings into a cohesive whole, and shows us how leadership can move beyond simply monitoring or rewarding followers into a process that engages followers' emotions and motivation to work towards a greater vision.

We have also considered the bad side of leadership, looking at what happens when leaders derail. Unfortunately, several of the attributes of good leadership can become weaknesses when they are extreme. For example, while we want confident leaders, arrogant ones cause misery for their followers and ultimately can have severe effects on organisational performance.

Finally, we have also reviewed the 'ugly' side of leadership, focusing on how prejudice and discrimination play out in the leadership context. Looking at issues in this area highlights how important our personal leadership 'prototypes' become in our interpretation of a leader's behaviour, and we have seen how these prototypes are related to our cultural values.

TEST YOURSELF

Brief Review Questions

1 How would you define leadership?
2 How are the Big Five traits related to (a) leader emergence and (b) leader effectiveness?
3 Briefly outline the central proposition of LMX theory (leader–member exchange).
4 What are the four leader behaviours in path–goal theory?

Discussion or Essay Questions

1 Compare and contrast transactional and transformational leadership. How are they related to work outcomes?
2 What are the dangers of an overly optimistic approach to leadership theory, and how can they be overcome?
3 Do you think leaders are born or made? Why?
4 Explain the relevance of implicit leadership theory to our understanding of follower perceptions of leadership.

FURTHER READING

- For more information on the GLOBE project, there are several articles available at http://www.grovewell.com/.
- *Authentic Leadership* by Bill George was one of the first popular books written about the concept and helped raise public awareness of the importance of authenticity in leaders: B. George 2003. *Authentic Leadership: Rediscovering the Secrets to Creating Lasting Value*. San Francisco, Jossey Bass, 2003.
- *Leadership in Organizations* by Gary Yukl has further detailed information about all the theories covered in this chapter. G. Yukl, *Leadership in Organizations*, 8th edn. Harlow, Pearson Education, 2013.

References

ANDRESSEN, P., KONRADT, U. & NECK, C. P. 2012. The relation between self-leadership and transformational leadership: competing models and the moderating role of virtuality. *Journal of Leadership & Organizational Studies*, 19, 68–82.

AVOLIO, B. J., BASS, B. M. & JUNG, D. I. 1999. Re-examining the components of transformational and transactional leadership using the Multifactor Leadership Questionnaire. *Journal of Occupational and Organizational Psychology*, 72, 441–62.

BARLING, J., WEBER, T. & KELLOWAY, E. K. 1996. Effects of transformational leadership training on attitudinal and financial outcomes: a field experiment. *Journal of Applied Psychology*, 81, 827.

BASS, B. M. 1985. *Leadership and Performance beyond Expectations*. New York, Free Press.

BASS, B. M. 1997. Does the transactional-transformational leadership paradigm transcend organizational and national boundaries? *American Psychologist*, 52, 130–9.

BASS, B. M. 1999. Two decades of research and development in transformational leadership. *European Journal of Work and Organizational Psychology*, 8, 9–32.

BASS, B. M. & STOGDILL, R. M. 1981. *Stogdill's Handbook of Leadership: A Survey of Theory and Research*. New York, Free Press.

BLAKE, R. & MOUTON, J. 1964. *The Managerial Grid: The Key to Leadership Excellence*. Houston, Gulf.

BOARD, B. J. & FRITZON, K. 2005. Disordered personalities at work. *Psychology, Crime & Law*, 11, 17–32.

BRODBECK, F. 2008. Leadership in Organizations. In Chmiel, N. (ed.) *An Introduction to Work and Organizational Psychology: A European Perspective*, 2nd edn. Malden, Blackwell.

BRODBECK, F. C., FRESE, M., AKERBLOM, S. ET AL. 2000. Cultural variation of leadership prototypes across 22 European countries. *Journal of Occupational and Organizational Psychology*, 73, 1–29.

CHHOKAR, J. S., BRODBECK, F. C. & HOUSE, R. J. 2012. *Culture and Leadership across the World: The GLOBE Book of In-depth Studies of 25 Societies*. Abingdon, Taylor & Francis.

DANSEREAU, F., GRAEN, G. & HAGA, W. J. 1975. A vertical dyad linkage approach to leadership within formal organizations: a longitudinal investigation of the role making process. *Organizational Behavior & Human Performance*, 13, 46–78.

EAGLY, A. H., JOHANNESEN-SCHMIDT, M. C. & VAN ENGEN, M. L. 2003. Transformational, transactional, and laissez-faire leadership styles: a meta-analysis comparing women and men. *Psychological Bulletin*, 129, 569.

EAGLY, A. H. & KARAU, S. J. 2002. Role congruity theory of prejudice toward female leaders. *Psychological Review*, 109, 573.

FIEDLER, F. E. 1967. *A Theory of Leadership Effectiveness.* New York, McGraw-Hill.

GARDNER, W. L., COGLISER, C. C., DAVIS, K. M. & DICKENS, M. P. 2011. Authentic leadership: a review of the literature and research agenda. *The Leadership Quarterly*, 22, 1120–45.

GEIER, J. G. 1967. A trait approach to the study of leadership in small groups. *Journal of Communication*, 17, 316–23.

GERSTNER, C. R. & DAY, D. V. 1997. Meta-analytic review of leader–member exchange theory: correlates and construct issues. *Journal of Applied Psychology*, 82, 827–44.

GRAEN, G. B. & UHL-BIEN, M. 1995. Relationship-based approach to leadership: development of leader-member exchange (LMX) theory of leadership over 25 years: applying a multi-level multi-domain perspective. *The Leadership Quarterly*, 6, 219–47.

HAUSCHILDT, K. & KONRADT, U. 2012. Self-leadership and team members' work role performance. *Journal of Managerial Psychology*, 27, 497–517.

HOGAN, R. & HOGAN, J. 1997. *Hogan Development Survey Manual.* Tulsa, Hogan Assessment Systems.

HOGAN, R. & HOGAN, J. 2001. Assessing leadership: a view from the dark side. *International Journal of Selection and Assessment*, 9, 40–51.

HOUGHTON, J. D., DAWLEY, D. & DILIELLO, T. C. 2012. The abbreviated self-leadership questionnaire (ASLQ): a more concise measure of self-leadership. *Leadership & Entrepreneurship*, 7, 216.

HOUSE, R. J. 1996. Path–goal theory of leadership: lessons, legacy and a reformulated theory. *The Leadership Quarterly*, 7, 323–52.

HOUSE, R. J., HANGES, P. J., JAVIDAN, M., DORFMAN, P. W. & GUPTA, V. 2004. *Culture, Leadership, and Organizations.* Sage.

JUDGE, T. A., BONO, J. E., ILIES, R. & GERHARDT, M. W. 2002. Personality and leadership: a qualitative and quantitative review. *Journal of Applied Psychology*, 87, 765–80.

JUDGE, T. A. & PICCOLO, R. F. 2004. Transformational and transactional leadership: a meta-analytic test of their relative validity. *Journal of Applied Psychology*, 89, 755–68.

JUDGE, T. A., PICCOLO, R. F. & ILIES, R. 2004. The forgotten ones? The validity of consideration and initiating structure in leadership research. *Journal of Applied Psychology*, 89, 36–51.

JUDGE, T. A., WOOLF, E. F., HURST, C. & LIVINGSTON, B. 2006. Charismatic and transformational leadership: a review and an agenda for future research. *Zeitschrift fur Arbeits- und Organisationspsychologie*, 50, 203–14.

KABANOFF, B. 1981. A critique of leader match and its implications for leadership research. *Personnel Psychology*, 34, 749–64.

KHOO, H. S. & BURCH, G. ST J. 2008. The 'dark side' of leadership personality and transformational leadership: an exploratory study. *Personality and Individual Differences*, 44, 86–97.

KOTTER, J. P. 2001. What leaders really do. *Harvard Business Review*, 79, 85–98.

LORD, R. G. & MAHER, K. J. 1991. *Leadership and Information Processing: Linking Perceptions and Performance.* Cambridge, MA, Unwin Hyman.

MCCLELLAND, D. C. & BOYATZIS, R. E. 1982. Leadership motive pattern and long-term success in management. *Journal of Applied Psychology*, 67, 737–43.

MANZ, C. C. & SIMS, H. P. 1980. Self-management as a substitute for leadership: a social learning theory perspective. *Academy of Management Review*, 5, 361–7.

MARKHAM, S. E., MARKHAM, I. S., GUZZO, R. A. & NECK, C. P. 1998. Self-leadership. In *Leadership: The Multiple-level Approaches: Classical and New Wave.* US, Elsevier Science/JAI Press.

NEWPORT, F. 2011. *US Still Prefers Male Bosses, But Many Have No Preference.* Gallup. http://www.gallup.com/poll/149360/Americans-Prefer-Male-Bosses-No-Preference.aspx (accessed 31 July 2013).

OREN, L., TZINER, A., SHARONI, G., AMOR, I. & ALON, P. 2012. Relations between leader–subordinate personality similarity and job attitudes. *Journal of Managerial Psychology*, 27, 479–96.

PEUS, C., WESCHE, J. S., STREICHER, B., BRAUN, S. & FREY, D. 2012. Authentic leadership: an empirical test of its antecedents, consequences, and mediating mechanisms. *Journal of Business Ethics*, 107, 331–48.

ROBBINS, S. P. & JUDGE, T. A. 2007. *Organizational Behavior.* Upper Saddle River, NJ, Pearson/Prentice Hall.

ROSENTHAL, S. A. & PITTINSKY, T. L. 2006. Narcissistic leadership. *The Leadership Quarterly*, 17, 617–33.

ROTHMANN, I. & COOPER, C. 2008. *Organizational and Work Psychology.* London, Hodder Education.

SCHRIESHEIM, C. A., BANNISTER, B. D. & MONEY, W. H. 1979. Psychometric properties of the LPC scale: an extension of rice's review. *Academy of Management Review*, 4, 287–90.

SCHRIESHEIM, C. A., CASTRO, S. L., ZHOU, X. & YAMMARINO, F. J. 2001. The folly of theorizing 'A' but testing 'B': a selective level-of-analysis review of the field and a detailed leader–member exchange illustration. *The Leadership Quarterly*, 12, 515–51.

SCHRIESHEIM, C. A. & NEIDER, L. L. 1996. Path–goal leadership theory: the long and winding road. *The Leadership Quarterly*, 7, 317–21.

STEWART, G. L., COURTRIGHT, S. H. & MANZ, C. C. 2011. Self-leadership: a multilevel review. *Journal of Management*, 37, 185–222.

STOGDILL, R. M. 1948. Personal factors associated with leadership; a survey of the literature. *Journal of Psychology: Interdisciplinary and Applied*, 25, 35–71.

STOGDILL, R. M. 1974. *Handbook of Leadership: A Survey of Theory and Research*. New York, Free Press.

STRUBE, M. J. & GARCIA, J. E. 1981. A meta-analytic investigation of Fiedler's contingency model of leadership effectiveness. *Psychological Bulletin*, 90, 307–21.

TOSI, H. L., MISANGYI, V. F., FANELLI, A., WALDMAN, D. A. & YAMMARINO, F. J. 2004. CEO charisma, compensation, and firm performance. *The Leadership Quarterly*, 15, 405–20.

TRICE, H. M. & BEYER, J. M. 1986. Charisma and its routinization in two social movement organizations. *Research in Organizational Behavior*, 8, 113–64.

WALDMAN, D. A., DE LUQUE, M. S., WASHBURN, N., HOUSE, R. J., ADETOUN, B., BARRASA, A., BOBINA, M., BODUR, M., CHEN, Y.-J. & DEBBARMA, S. 2006. Cultural and leadership predictors of corporate social responsibility values of top management: a GLOBE study of 15 countries. *Journal of International Business Studies*, 37, 823–37.

WALUMBWA, F. O., AVOLIO, B. J., GARDNER, W. L., WERNSING, T. S. & PETERSON, S. J. 2008. Authentic leadership: development and validation of a theory-based measure. *Journal of Management*, 34, 89–126.

YAMMARINO, F. J., DIONNE, S. D., SCHRIESHEIM, C. A. & DANSEREAU, F. 2008. Authentic leadership and positive organizational behavior: a meso, multi-level perspective. *The Leadership Quarterly*, 19, 693–707.

Part 1 Case Study Working for Google: 'Doing cool things that matter'

Google is one of the most well-known brands in the world. Starting with the development of a search engine so effective that 'to Google' became synonymous with searching the web, the organisation has expanded to include a wide range of products and offerings, including the Chrome web browser, Gmail, Google maps and YouTube. To keep the company at the forefront of the industry, Google is looking for employees who are 'great at lots of things, love big challenges and welcome big changes' and will be beneficial to the organisation in the long term. How do they go about finding these people?

© sorendls/istockphoto

The company used to be famous for using brainteaser-type questions at interview, asking candidates to solve puzzles like 'How many golf balls will fit in a bus?' or 'How much would you charge to clean all the windows in Seattle?' The idea was that asking this kind of question would help them to identify people who could think on their feet and come up with creative solutions while also giving the interviewers an insight into the candidate's problem-solving process. But these types of question have become a thing of the past as the recruitment and selection processes at Google have changed over the years.

Managing information and data is an essential component of what Google does, so it is no surprise that the change in selection processes was triggered when they analysed the data they had on people's performance at interview and their subsequent performance in the job. The results came as a shock: the company found that these brainteaser questions were completely unrelated to people's subsequent job performance (Bryant, 2013). As Laszlo Bock (Senior Vice President of People Operations at Google) pointed out, those questions only served to make the interviewer feel smart! He also stated that structured behaviour interviews are the only ones that work; and this is the direction that Google selection processes have moved in more recently.

Besides trying to get a handle on how people approach problems, the other important criterion that Google used to use in selection was a candidate's grade point average from university. But again, their data crunching indicated that this was unrelated to actual job performance (Bryant, 2013), and so this criterion has become less important in the selection processes. In fact, the company now has an increasing proportion of employees who have never been to university, recognising that the skills they are looking for are not necessarily developed in formal education.

Having gone through these changes, the basic selection process at Google currently has three stages (Google, 2014b). First, a potential candidate has a conversation with a recruiter. The majority of these recruiters start on six-month contracts (though may stay longer) and the number can be increased or reduced depending on the organisation's needs (VanderMey, 2012). Their main function is to find people who might be interested in working for Google and a lot of their work involves cold-calling potential candidates and then guiding candidates through the process.

This initial contact is followed up by a phone interview and then on-site interviews with around four or five people. The interviewers could be potential new teammates or supervisors, or they could be people the candidate might never see again. They assess candidates on four main criteria:

‣ leadership
‣ role-related knowledge (looking for variety of knowledge, not just specialist knowledge)
‣ problem-solving skills
‣ 'Googleyness', which includes a candidate's comfort with ambiguity, bias towards action and a collaborative nature.

Interestingly, while Google promotes a 'scientific' approach to evaluating the first three criteria, Sunil Chandra (Vice President of Staffing and Operations) claims that determining this last is more 'art' than science (Halzack, 2013).

The final decision about hiring is made in the light of feedback from all the interviews, by people not involved in the interview. Google considers this to be a more objective approach than leaving it to the interviewers (Halzack, 2013). By having the decision made at some distance from the interview, Google is attempting to remove some of the biases that can occur.

The first attribute that is assessed in Google's selection process is leadership. Yet, somewhat ironically, for most of its history Google had taken a very laissez-faire approach to leadership. The highly skilled and technically competent staff traditionally seemed to think that the best thing a manager could do was to leave them in peace to let them get on with their jobs (Bryant, 2011). In fact, in 2002 Google even conducted a brief experiment and eliminated all the engineering management roles (Garvin, 2013). The experiment only lasted a few months before the company realised that, instead of encouraging ideas and productivity among the staff, removing the managers meant that the founders themselves were continually approached to resolve conflicts and deal with routine, everyday matters. The management positions were reintroduced, although today Google still remains a reasonably flat organisation, with employees given decision-making power and freedom to innovate.

In their continuing quest to identify good leadership within the company, in 2009, Google launched 'Project Oxygen'. This project was a data-mining exercise that reviewed employee surveys, management feedback reports and performance reviews in an effort to find out what characterised a good leader at Google. The project was launched because the company realised that the best managers had the best-performing, happiest teams with the highest retention rates. Project Oxygen's final list of good behaviours, in order of importance, were (Bryant, 2011):

1 Be a good coach
2 Empower your team and don't micromanage
3 Express interest in team members' success and personal well-being
4 Don't be a sissy: be productive and results-oriented
5 Be a good communicator and listen to your team
6 Help your employees with career development
7 Have a clear vision and strategy for the team
8 Have key technical skills so that you can help advise the team.

The interplay between good leadership and effective teamwork is recognised at Google, where collaboration is central to everything they do. The company believes that innovation comes through sharing ideas and working together, and the ability to collaborate to solve problems is an essential ingredient in the 'Googleyness' that they look for in new hires. This extends even to their Googlers-to-Googlers (g2g) education programme, where employees teach each other new skills and knowledge. In fact, this 'Googleyness' is a concept that emerges again and again when employees talk about the company, a shorthand for the culture of the organisation. Laszlo Bock (Bock, 2011) describes this culture as being created and maintained by three important components:

▸ Mission – Google is clear about its mission: to organise the world's information and make it universally accessible and useful. Since this is the driving force behind their efforts, employees get a feeling of meaning to their work and are passionate about their ultimate aim.

▸ Transparency – The senior executives at Google hold weekly meetings where employees can directly ask them questions. Information on the company, including progress reports, project timelines and team goals is all held on the company intranet for all employees to access. The concept is that their employees can be trusted and that open communication is vital.

▸ Voice – There are many ways for Google employees to express their thoughts, opinions and ideas, including surveys, direct emails to the leaders and so on. Feedback is actively sought from every manager's direct reports and used to recognise the best and coach the worst.

In fact, Google has topped *Fortune*'s '100 Best Companies to Work For' list since 2012. Employees say they are proud to work there and 97% say their management is honest and ethical. They also value the company's approach to giving back to the community and supporting charities: for example, Google donates $50 for every five hours of volunteering that an employee does with an approved charity.

One of the reasons people are so keen to work at Google is the legendary list of perks that Googlers get. On their main site, 'Googleplex' in California, employees can enjoy free meals at the cafeterias, snacks and drinks near their offices, free use of the gym, game rooms and on-site medical staff. There are similar facilities available for employees in the London office too, with a games room, music room and a 'coffee lab' to help people to relax and go back to work refreshed without ever leaving the office. There is also travel insurance for employees and their families and reimbursement for training courses. Perhaps the most famous perk is Google's '20 percent time' where employees can work on something unrelated to their official work projects for one day a week.

Why does Google spend so much on these benefits? One reason that the company gives is that they value their employees and want to make their lives better: the benefits are designed to take care of their employees, physically, mentally, emotionally, financially and socially (Google, 2014a). More cynical commentators have suggested that there may be two other reasons. First, by ensuring that employees have everything they need at work, Google can encourage a long hours culture – ten to 12 hours a day is not uncommon. Second, some have suggested that spending money on these perks is actually cheaper than increasing wages.

And there's a darker side to Google's retention efforts too. It has recently come to light that the CEOs of Google and other tech firms like Apple had anti-poaching agreements in place with each other, as well as agreeing on salary levels (Harkinson, 2014). These agreements were so strongly enforced that, in 2007, a Google recruiter who approached an Apple employee was immediately dismissed. These illegal arrangements are currently the subject of a class action lawsuit in the USA which alleges that employees were financially damaged because they simply did not have anywhere else to go that would offer them a better deal.

Despite all these efforts at retention, however, a recent report by PayScale compared retention rates at Fortune 500 companies and revealed that median tenure at Google was just over one year (PayScale Inc., 2013). While this needs to be understood in the context of the typical worker only staying with a Fortune 500 company for 3.6 years overall, Google still had the third lowest job tenure and, significantly, it was also lower than other comparable tech companies such as Yahoo and Microsoft. And this is despite Google employees having the fourth highest median salary. Some have suggested that the reason for this low tenure rate might link back to an inefficient hiring process (Lewis, 2013) that results in too many false positives.

So what is it really like working for Google? As a company with over 42,000 employees in 40 countries, the answer to that question may well be as varied as the people who work there.

Discussion or Essay Questions

1   Google is now using behaviourally based interviews, but many organisations still rely on unstructured interviews. Why do you think that work psychology findings about ways to improve interviews are still not widely understood or applied? What could be done to rectify this?

2   What do you think about Google's approach to decision-making in the selection process? What could be the benefits and drawbacks of having the decisions made by people at some distance from the interview?

3   Compare and contrast the different approaches that Google takes to improve employee retention. To what extent do you think that informal anti-poaching agreements between competitors might be a problem?

4   Google is an instantly recognisable product brand. Do you think that the company has managedto create a recognisable employer brand? Would you like to work for Google? Why or why not?

5   Are the perks that Google employees receive a good way to increase motivation in the organisation? Draw on motivational theories to justify your answer.

6   Does the work psychology literature support Google's belief in the primacy of teamwork and collaboration for effective innovation? What suggestions might you make for helping Google to improve their innovative capabilities even further?

7   Using a leadership theory of your choice, critically analyse the list of leadership behaviours that Google identified. How do they compare with the behaviours that top Google leaders display (you may want to read emerging stories in the news to find out more)? What are the advantages and disadvantages of individual organisations creating their own understandings of good leadership?

References

BOCK, L. 2011. Passion, not perks. *Think Quarterly: The People Issue*. http://www.thinkwithgoogle.com/articles/passion-not-perks.html (accessed 20 February 2014).

BRYANT, A. 2011. Google's quest to build a better boss. *The New York Times*, 12 May.

BRYANT, A. 2013. In head-hunting, big data may not be such a big deal. *The New York Times*. http://www.nytimes.com/2013/06/20/business/in-head-hunting-big-data-may-not-be-such-a-big-deal.html?pagewanted=all (accessed 19 June 2013).

GARVIN, D. A. 2013. How Google sold Its engineers on management. *Harvard Business Review*, 91, December, 74–82. http://hbr.org/2013/12/how-google-sold-its-engineers-on-management/ar/1.

GOOGLE. 2014A. *Benefits – Google Jobs*. http://www.google.co.uk/about/jobs/lifeatgoogle/benefits/ (accessed 20 February 2014).

GOOGLE. 2014B. *How We Hire – Google Jobs*. http://www.google.co.uk/about/jobs/lifeatgoogle/hiringprocess/ (accessed 20 February 2014).

HALZACK, S. 2013. An inside look at Google's data-driven job interview process. *The Washington Post*. http://www.washingtonpost.com/business/capitalbusiness/an-inside-look-at-googles-data-driven-job-interview-process/2013/09/03/648ea8b2-14bd-11e3-880b-7503237cc69d_story.html (accessed 2013-09-05).

HARKINSON, J. 2014. 'I don't want to create a paper trail': Inside the secret Apple-Google pact. *Mother Jones*. http://www.motherjones.com/politics/2014/02/google-apple-class-action-poaching-steve-jobs-wage-theft (accessed 20 February 2014).

LEWIS, A. 2013. Why would anyone quit working for Google? *FoxNews.com*. http://www.foxnews.com/opinion/2013/09/09/here-riddle-for-why-would-anyone-quit-working-at-google/ (accessed 20 February 2014).

PAYSCALE INC. 2013. *Full List of Employee Tenure at Fortune 500 Companies*. http://www.payscale.com/data-packages/employee-loyalty/full-list (accessed 20 February 2014).

VANDERMEY, A. 2012. Inside Google's recruiting machine – Fortune Tech. *Fortune*. http://tech.fortune.cnn.com/2012/02/24/google-recruiting/ (accessed 20 February 2014).

PART 2

SURVIVING AND THRIVING AT WORK

I N PART 1, WE LOOKED AT HOW THE STUDY OF PSYCHOLOGY CAN HELP US TO DEAL with issues of central importance at work: finding the right people for the job, increasing motivation, helping people to work better in teams, developing leadership and so on. In this chapter, we take things a step further and consider aspects of work beyond just 'getting the job done'. Here, we start to explore how we can use psychological knowledge to survive the challenges of the modern workplace and improve our work lives.

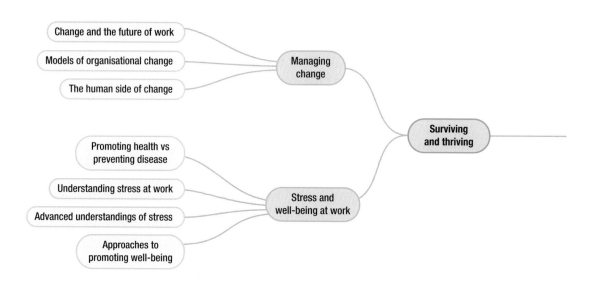

There are three chapters in this section. Chapter 8 discusses the issues around change management, looking at the psychological aspects of change and how we can manage its impact on organisations and individuals. In Chapter 9, we consider different approaches to psychological health at work, contrasting a 'stress' approach with a broad 'well-being' perspective. Finally, Chapter 10 assesses how we can apply the developing field of positive psychology to the workplace, looking at how work can contribute to a greater sense of personal meaning and self-actualisation.

In the extended case study for Part 2, we explore the development of a well-being programme at the BGL Group and how it is used to build employee engagement and enhance organisational performance.

MORE THAN JUST SURVIVAL – MANAGING CHANGE

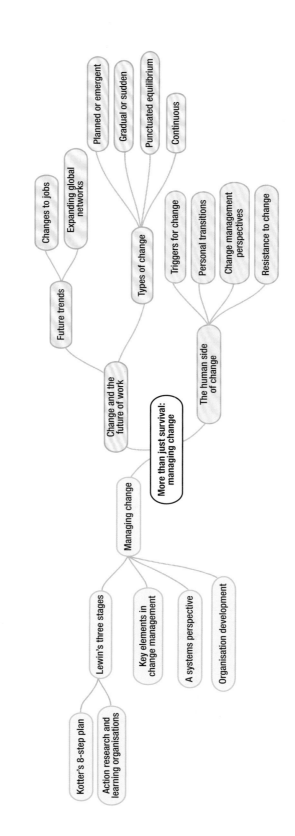

- Change and the future of work
  - Future trends
    - Changes to jobs
    - Expanding global networks
  - Types of change
    - Planned or emergent
    - Gradual or sudden
    - Punctuated equilibrium
    - Continuous

- **More than just survival: managing change**
  - The human side of change
    - Triggers for change
    - Personal transitions
    - Change management perspectives
    - Resistance to change
  - Managing change
    - Lewin's three stages
      - Kotter's 8-step plan
      - Action research and learning organisations
    - Key elements in change management
    - A systems perspective
    - Organisation development

Throughout the first part of this book we have seen how work psychology has implications for both organisations and individuals, and that theme continues in this chapter. We will now look at change from two angles: how we can best manage change to ensure success and organisational efficacy, and how change affects us as individuals. The priority for organisations in managing change is to ensure that there is a smooth transition to the new state. But it is equally important that all of us, as workers in an environment that is constantly changing, are able to develop our own tolerance for change and the skills to deal effectively with a turbulent environment.

We will start by considering the wider environment, looking at some of the drivers for change and attempting to 'predict the future' by exploring how the world of work might change in the next few decades. This will lead us into a comparison of different ways of understanding change, including an assessment of the extent to which change can be managed and whether it is best seen as a gradual process or as a series of revolutionary changes. Based on this understanding of what change is like, we will assess different models for effective change management, from a simple three-step model to more complex approaches which emphasise learning and the development of organisations.

In the final section of the chapter we will discuss how change affects each of us as individuals and how we can effectively manage our own and others' personal transitions. Finally, we will consider the important topic of resistance to change: how people differ in their tolerance of change and why they resist it, as well as the strategies that can be employed to overcome resistance and encourage effective change.

This chapter will help you answer the following questions:

1 Why is change such an important challenge for individuals and organisations in the modern workplace?
2 How does change affect us and what can we do to manage our own responses more effectively?
3 How can change be managed at an organisational level?

CHANGE AND THE FUTURE OF WORK

It is a popular view of organisations that they, like living organisms, need to constantly change and adapt to their environment in order to survive. It is also a popular claim that organisations have to cope with an ever-increasing rate of change (Kotter, 1996). And there is good evidence that these claims are true. For example, a Chartered Institute of Personnel and Development (CIPD)

survey found that HR managers had, on average, experienced seven major reorganisations in the previous three years (CIPD, 2003). However, these changes do not always result in the hoped-for benefits. While claims that 70% of organisational change initiatives fail are more headline-grabbing statements than facts based in research (Hughes, 2011), it is certainly true that change is a complex topic, with often unforeseen consequences for the organisation and the employees; and managing change effectively is essential to organisational success and personal well-being.

Activity Rate of change

Think about what you know of work and business in the last 20 years or so and write two lists: one of the things that have changed (e.g. how people work or the nature of their work), and one list of all the things that have stayed the same.

▸ Do you think it is true that people today are facing increased change at work? Why or why not?

Future trends

What will work look like in the future? Although we cannot say with certainty what will happen, there are some important trends that have been identified that are likely to have a large impact on how we will work in the coming decades. Frese (2008, pp. 399–400), for example, summarised several authors' work to suggest that there were ten major trends that would change how we work in the coming years:

- Dissolution of the unity of work in space and time
- Changing job and career concepts
- Faster rate of innovation
- Increased complexity of work
- Personal initiative vs adaptability to the new workplace
- Global competition
- Both larger and smaller work units will develop
- More teamwork
- Reduced supervision
- Increased cultural diversity.

These trends can be grouped into two general categories: changes to individual jobs and expanding global networks.

Changes to individual jobs

At the individual level, jobs and careers are becoming more nebulous. It is already apparent that the concept of a job for life or a clear career path within one organisation has all but disappeared, and there has been an increase in flexible contracts. This results in employees having to take responsibility for their own career development rather than relying on the organisation, and needing to display personal initiative or adaptability in order to succeed in the new workplace.

In addition, the complexity of work is increasing, so that, particularly in developed countries, many unskilled jobs are becoming scarcer as technology takes over. And for those jobs that remain, the new technology makes higher intellectual demands on those who have to deal with it. Related to this is the rate of innovation, which continues to increase, meaning that individuals need to take control of their own training and organisations will want to encourage curiosity and exploration to ensure they stay ahead of the game.

As we saw in Chapter 6, many organisations are moving towards using teams to structure their work, which means that social skills and teamwork competencies are becoming as critical to success as technical abilities. Self-managed teams and a general reduction in formal supervision will result in responsibilities being delegated and the traditional functions of supervisors being dispersed across the organisation. Again, the implications of this are that individual jobs become more complex and integrated as people take on tasks that have traditionally been designated as either 'worker' or 'management'.

Expanding global networks

With the increase in IT communications and systems, work can increasingly overcome barriers of time and space. People are able to communicate with colleagues across the globe without ever meeting, and the rise in telecommuting means that more and more work is being completed outside the physical organisation. New ways of creating and maintaining networks in this increasingly dispersed workplace will need to be developed. And alongside this change, there is a growing contrast between the increasing size of organisations through mergers and acquisitions, and the success of smaller units in being flexible and innovative. Work in the future will need to find a way to capitalise on these smaller unit advantages by developing cooperative networks that span the globe.

Global competition is becoming the norm, producing a need for international cooperation, imagination and employee initiative in dealing with a turbulent environment. This increased global competition is matched by the increasing cultural diversity of the workforce within nations. Workers will have to learn how to overcome prejudice and bias, as well as dealing with cultural differences and languages.

And finally, globalisation will tend to reduce the power of individual trade unions, meaning that other ways of pursuing justice in organisations will need to be found.

 Activity Future trends

For this activity, choose an organisation you know something about that has 'gone global', for example McDonalds or Unilever. Spend about 20–30 minutes researching the organisation on the internet. Find out what they have been in the news for recently, how they have changed over the last few years and what kind of challenges they face in the future.

▸ Using the list of future trends summarised by Frese (2008), identify three or four that you think will be relevant to this organisation, and suggest ways that the organisation could deal with them effectively.

This list of the potential challenges facing the organisations and employees of the future highlights how important it is for us to understand how we can manage change effectively – both within the organisation and for ourselves as employees. As a starting point, we will look at how change happens.

Types of change

Planned or emergent?

We will be focusing in this chapter on the idea of planned change – that is, how we can attempt to plan for or control change. But there are many people who see change as inherently uncontrollable, unpredictable or chaotic and view the planned approach to change as ineffective and unrealistic. Instead, they promote the idea of 'emergent change' – that is, change which is made up of ongoing adaptations and alterations that ultimately produce fundamental changes that were not planned for or perhaps even expected (Weick, 2000). The emergent approach to change emphasises that change is messy and involves a vast array of different subsystems and contextual factors, so that there is no simple linear cause and effect model that can effectively capture it. In order to have any hope of influencing the course of the change, managers need to be involved in the continuous process all the time.

But if they cannot plan for change, how are managers supposed to be involved? The key is to develop awareness and understanding of the environment. If change is a constant process of mutual interactions between the organisation and the environment, effective management of change is based on the ability to analyse and understand those interactions.

A balanced approach to understanding change recognises that both planned and emergent approaches have their value. Some change in organisations is planned, and there is good evidence that planning well can improve the success of change management. But there is also a lot of emergent change and this approach reminds us of the importance of flexibility and a continuous adaptation to the environment. Burnes (2004a) notes this in a four-year case study of change at a construction firm which used an emergent, open-ended approach to changing culture and a planned approach to changing structure. He points out that one of the essential competencies for successful change management is to understand the organisational context. This means that employees within the organisation may be better placed to promote change than external 'experts' who come in with a model of planned change. While consultants may be able to help the organisation develop a strategy for change or provide models to improve effectiveness, there has to be a heavy reliance on local knowledge and involvement if the change is to succeed.

Gradual or sudden?

Our view of organisational change, how it works and how best to manage it, is shaped by our assumptions about change itself. In line with thinking in the biological sciences, organisational change was, for many years, seen as a gradual, incremental process. As evolution was viewed as gradual change over millions of years, models of change in organisations recognised small changes to products or systems but left out large, sudden changes and even claimed they did not exist. However, as the notion of gradual evolution in biology was challenged by the idea of punctuated equilibrium (sudden large changes interspersed with longer periods of relative stability), so organisational theorists also started to adopt the idea of different models of change. The distinction between gradual change and punctuated equilibrium is illustrated below.

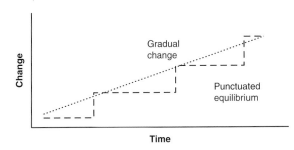

Figure 8.1 An illustration of gradual change and punctuated equilibrium

Activity **Analysing organisational change**

Think of an organisation you know reasonably well (e.g. an employer, your university). Identify some changes that organisation has experienced. For example, it may have redesigned its logo or downsized or reorganised its departments.

▸ Are the changes you have identified examples of continuous/incremental change or revolutionary change?
▸ Were these changes planned and proactive or did they seem reactive?
▸ What kind of pressures for change do you think this organisation will face in the future?

Punctuated equilibrium

Gersick (1991) reviewed models of change from different domains of study, including adult development, the history of science and organisational development, to show how the punctuated equilibrium model is applicable to the study of organisational change. She identified the three main components of this model as *deep structure, equilibrium periods and revolutionary periods*. We will look at each of these in detail.

Deep structure is the durable, underlying structure of the organisation and is very stable. It is essentially the organisation's basic *parts* (how the units of the organisation are configured) and basic *activities* (what the organisation does to maintain its existence). As a simple example, we could view a university's *parts* as being the traditional faculties which focus on specific academic areas of study. Its basic *activities* could be seen as creating and disseminating knowledge.

An organisation's deep structure consists of its culture, strategy, structure, power distribution and control systems (Tushman and Romanelli, 1985). During equilibrium phases, this deep structure persists and limits change. For example, if considerable power resided in the heads of the university faculties, the faculty structure would be likely to persist and any change aimed at dissolving those faculties would be severely limited. Equilibrium periods are not 'static', but they are periods when the organisation carries out its activities and maintains itself in line with its deep structure.

There may well be incremental changes during this time that help the organisation become better and better at what it does (Tushman and Romanelli, 1985), but overall equilibrium is maintained by organisational inertia. This inertia is due to cognitive, motivational and obligation barriers to change. Cognitive barriers include simply not seeing the problem, as well as many of the issues we have considered in previous chapters, such as limits on awareness and attention. Motivational barriers include a fear of failure or dislike of uncertainty, as well as an unwillingness to 'lose' all the work that has been done so far. Finally, there are the feelings of obligation that build up between people and whole networks that work against change. Continuing our university example, cognitive barriers might include not seeing any problem with having a faculty structure or not being aware of changes in the research-funding environment that might impact on how knowledge should be disseminated. Motivational barriers could include lecturers' unwillingness to have to develop new ways of teaching or an administrative fear that a new system would fail and lead to lots of student complaints. Finally, networks of professional identity (such as chartered engineers or management professionals) are often built up around specific subject areas that would act as a barrier to any attempt to dismantle that group.

But these inertial forces are eventually overcome and periods of revolution occur when the whole deep structure is dismantled. The need for revolution can be created either by internal changes that have pulled the basic parts and actions of the organisation out of alignment with each other or by external changes which mean the organisation can no longer access the resources it needs. For example, in universities, the basic activity of 'creating knowledge' is increasingly becoming interdisciplinary, which is at odds with a very rigid faculty structure. If the university is unable to find ways of building interdisciplinary networks, it will become increasingly unable to access research funding and ultimately less able to carry out a basic activity.

Of course, a need for change does not guarantee change, and some organisations may continue to struggle on as they always have in order to avoid change. But to survive and be successful in the long run, the organisation needs to change its deep structure and reassemble itself before embarking on another period of equilibrium.

Continuous change

The punctuated equilibrium model of change in organisations has received considerable empirical support (e.g. Romanelli and Tushman, 1994). This does not mean, however, that all change is brought about with sudden revolutions. Some authors have suggested, in contrast, that continuous and rapid change can underlie some organisations' competitive advantage (Brown and Eisenhardt, 1997). Organisations which successfully engage in continuous change typically rely on the following:

1   Semistructures – the organisation defines and delineates some features of the work, such as responsibilities and project priorities, but leaves other features, such as the design process, flexible. The semistructures allow the organisations to strike a balance between order

Case Study Grocery shopping

For several years, Tesco has been leading the way in creating hypermarkets in the UK: supermarkets over 5,500 m^2 that offer customers everything from fruit and vegetables to TVs and cameras. There are over 200 Tesco stores this size in the UK, with another 130 or so owned by other supermarkets. But shoppers' habits are changing. Where it was once more convenient for shoppers to be able to get everything they needed in one place, the advent of online grocery shopping means that it is now more convenient to simply order everything from home. People are using local shops for 'top-ups' and not bothering to go to the huge supermarkets.

© ImageSource

So Tesco is looking for new ways to use the space and even to recreate itself. Chris Bush, the head of Tesco UK, is suggesting a whole new definition of what Tesco might be. He says he sees the stores becoming places where 'customers can have a meal or coffee with their friends and family, browse for clothes and get their hair done. They can go to yoga classes or attend cookery classes in a space available for the local community to use.'

Based on Butler (2013)

▶ Using the definitions of deep structure put forward by Gersick, identify a supermarket's basic *parts* and *activities*.

▶ As the changes to supermarkets described above come into place, how will they affect the organisation's deep structure? What do you think the supermarkets of the future will look like?

and chaos, giving freedom for change while still maintaining some control and using order to encourage changes.

2 Links in time – successful project managers are able to focus on the current project while at the same having a clear sense of where they are going. These links between current and future projects give the change a direction and help to maintain momentum.

3 Sequenced steps – the organisations themselves are created through a series of sequenced steps in the implementation of change. Managers gain a detailed understanding of the current situation, then determine where they are headed in the future, and then create links between the two. They ensure that parts are developed and stabilised before moving on to the next.

While some organisations are able to achieve this ideal, continuously adaptive state, most do not. The majority of organisations experience the punctuated equilibrium model. They continue as they always have, with perhaps small, incremental changes, until a crisis appears. The organisations that survive are the ones that can undergo the revolutionary change that is needed.

MANAGING CHANGE

One of the reasons it is so important to understand how change happens is that these models can provide a basis for us to try and 'manage' change. In managing change, we are attempting to control either the change itself or its consequences in order to achieve more positive outcomes.

Lewin's three-stage process

One of the earliest models of change management, put forward by Karl Lewin (1951), emphasised how important it was to not only change a situation but also to ensure that the change was maintained. His 'force field' model refers to the current status quo as a 'stable, quasi-stationary equilibrium' which is maintained because the driving forces *for* change are balanced by restraining forces *against* change. So we can bring about change by reducing the resisting forces and/or increasing the driving forces. But how we carry out the change is important: Lewin claimed that if we focus on increasing the driving forces, there is an increase in tension, aggression and emotionality and a reduction in constructive behaviour. A better approach is to reduce the restraining forces, which will still result in change but with a much lower level of tension and a more permanent change.

To do this, Lewin recommended a simple, three-stage process:

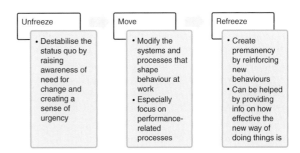

Figure 8.2 Lewin's three-stage change process

As Burnes (2004b) points out, Lewin's approach to change is a group-based, consensual and slow process and was felt by many to be ineffective and inappropriate for turbulent environments. Kanter et al (1992), for example, claimed that organisations are never frozen but are fluid entities. But Lewin's definition of stability as an *equilibrium* recognises this constant change, and when he speaks of 'refreezing' he is talking about reinforcing the new behaviours to stop regression, rather than of a completely static new state.

In fact, one of the most important issues that Lewin addressed in his work was the permanency of the new behaviours. His force field model shows us how, if the new behaviours are not 'refrozen', they will simply revert to the previous state when the driving forces for change are removed. Many organisations today, caught up in the belief that constant change is the only way to survive, are forgetting this final step. They introduce change initiative after change initiative and fail to reap the benefits because their changes do not involve ensuring that the change 'sticks'. We will see later in this chapter how everyone finds change stressful (though our individual ability to cope with change varies dramatically), and any model of change management which does not include some kind of stability or equilibrium runs the risk of exhausting employees.

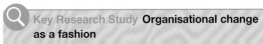
 Key Research Study **Organisational change as a fashion**

What Bandwagons Bring: Effects of Popular Management Techniques on Corporate Performance, Reputation, and CEO Pay

Barry Staw and Lisa Epstein (2000)

Background: Management techniques seem to go in and out of fashion, with managers and academics often jumping on the bandwagon of the latest technique and encouraging everyone to adopt it to improve organisational effectiveness. This is the cause of a lot of change as each new technique (such as total quality management, empowerment or teamwork) is introduced, but is it worth it?

Institutional theory states that organisations do not adopt new ways of doing things simply to be more effective, but because they are also seeking legitimacy and cultural support.

Aims: This study had three main aims. First, to find out whether implementing popular management techniques resulted in increased organisational performance. Second, to establish whether keeping up with the fashions of management improved the organisation's reputation. And finally, to find out whether CEOs who kept up with the fashions were paid more.

Method: The sample consisted of the 100 US companies with the highest sales in 1995. For each of them, measures of corporate reputation, economic performance and CEO compensation were created. In addition, there were three measures of popular management techniques:

1   Exposure: the amount of attention paid to each firm's popular management techniques in news articles.
2   Focus: the proportion of news articles about the firm which were about their management techniques rather than other issues.
3   TQM implementation: whether or not the firm had implemented a specific popular technique.

Findings: None of the three measures of popular management techniques was associated with improved economic performance. But their implementation improved the firm's reputation and increased ratings of their innovativeness and management quality. Performance had little effect on CEO pay, but being associated with popular management techniques did.

Implications: Implementing the latest management fashion is often a costly process and involves varying levels of change within the organisation. This study demonstrates that these popular changes do not necessarily result in the improved performance they claim; but they do result in increased corporate reputation and positive perceptions of the firm. In considering the effects of change, then, we need to look beyond effectiveness measures to consider the social implications too.

Kotter's eight-step plan

Recent work has confirmed the utility of Lewin's model for implementing organisational change. Ford and Greer (2006) demonstrated that change progressed through the unfreezing, moving and refreezing sequence and that more effective changes were brought about by higher levels of change processes at each stage.

Lewin's simple model for managing change has been very influential, and was developed into a more detailed plan by John Kotter. Kotter (1996) looked at what made change interventions fail so frequently and drew up a list of eight steps which expanded on the *unfreezing* and *moving* parts of Lewin's model, giving managers a more detailed guide for avoiding the common pitfalls of change interventions.

Table 8.1 Integration of Lewin's and Kotter's change models

Lewin's stages	Kotter's steps
Unfreeze	1. Establish a sense of urgency – it is important that everyone realises that change *needs* to happen *now*
	2. Create a guiding coalition – gather a group to lead the change who will work well together and have the power to see it through
	3. Develop a change vision – create a vision to guide the change and strategies to implement it
	4. Communicate the vision for buy-in – get as many people on board as possible
Move	5. Empower broad-based action – get as many people actively involved in the change as possible by removing barriers to change and encouraging new ideas
	6. Generate short-term wins – plan for visible achievements and reward those involved
	7. Never let up – consolidate improvements and make continual readjustments to keep change on track
Refreeze	8. Incorporate change into the culture – make it clear how the changes have increased organisational success

Action research and learning organisations

Although Lewin's model has the advantage of simplicity, you may be thinking it is too broad to be of any practical use in managing change. How exactly would we go about 'unfreezing' a situation? How do we 'move' people and change their behaviours? Lewin's model was never meant to stand on its own; instead it should be understood as part of his overall understanding of groups and how they change (Burnes, 2004b). He recommended an approach called *action research* for the actual implementation of change: 'research that will help the practitioner' (Lewin, 1946). Based on a thorough analysis and understanding of the situation ('research'), we then take action to achieve the desired change. In fact, it is simply using the scientific method (see Chapter 1) to guide our management of change.

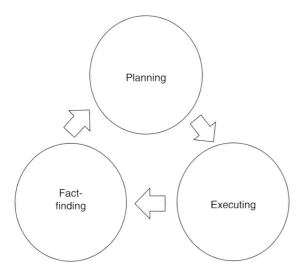

Figure 8.3   The action research cycle

In this cycle we could, of course, start anywhere, but Lewin recommends starting with planning, developing an overall idea of how to reach the objective as well as a clear idea of the first step that needs to be taken. More recent explanations of action research have extended this step by breaking it down further. First comes data gathering for diagnosis of the problem, then feedback of this data to the group, so that discussion and collaborative diagnosis of the problem can take place. Finally, a plan is developed that identifies the possible interventions and chooses the preferred option.

After this, the plan is executed or put into action. This is followed by 'fact-finding', which serves four functions:

1   Evaluation of the action – did it achieve its objectives?
2   Learning – what were the strengths and weaknesses of that action?
3   Basis for next step of planning
4   Basis for modification of the overall plan.

As you can see, the fact-finding step is closely interlinked with and followed by the next planning step, so that action research is an iterative process. This approach is not prescriptive, but emphasises the importance of adapting the change to the specific situation we are in, as well as allowing change management to take account of new or unexpected results of the change.

The action research approach has been developed into the idea of a learning organisation – an organisation that is proactive rather than reactive in its approach to change. A learning organisation encourages and facilitates learning by all its members and engages in continual transformation and development. The learning organisation is one which manages to overcome the fragmentation and competition that is prevalent in most organisations so

that groups can work together, thereby enhancing their ability to produce results that the members care about (Senge, 1990). In a learning organisation, members are constantly engaged in action research to identify areas for improvement or innovation and develop and implement solutions.

Key elements in change management

While there have been several other developments and extensions of Lewin's model, it is perhaps of more use to consider a recent, comprehensive model of the key elements in the change process (Hayes, 2010). It starts by emphasising the importance of an understanding of changes external to the organisation, and the problems and opportunities these changes bring for the organisation. It then goes through five stages in the change process:

- Recognise the need for change and start the process – this involves recognising the external pressures or internal circumstances that mean a change is needed and making decisions about who to involve in the change.
- Diagnosis – identifying a future state that the organisation wishes to move towards needs to be based on an accurate understanding of the current state; the vision of the desired future needs to be attainable.
- Plan and prepare to change – a thorough change plan will need details of how it is going to be implemented and often this list will be very long. But this stage is also about preparing people for change and dealing with potential political aspects of the change, not just planning the technical changes.
- Implement the change – the plan is put into action. However, this is very rarely a straightforward process of just doing what the plan says; it will need to be adapted and refined as the change progresses. Importantly, the implementation needs to be monitored and feedback becomes essential. With change that is more broadly defined and may not have a specific end point, the implementation stage may be more a series of small, incremental steps which are constantly evaluated.
- Sustain the change – this can be done by ensuring that rewards systems reinforce the new behaviours and also by building on the feedback mechanisms to continue to monitor change.

Finally, the model recognises two other key issues. First is the importance of reviewing progress throughout the change. Reviewing should be an ongoing activity which actively seeks out relevant feedback so that the process can be adapted as necessary. And second, woven through all of these stages, of course, must be thorough consideration of the people management issues. Any change at work, no matter how much it seems solely technical, will have an impact on the people who work there, and change agents need to consider issues of motivation, politics, power and so on. We will consider these effects in more detail later in the chapter.

Taking a systems perspective

One way of ensuring that change plans consider all the complex range of results that inevitably occur is by considering how change in one area of the organisation can lead to change in other areas. This is achieved by taking a 'systems perspective', which sees the organisation as a system of interrelated parts that all affect each other. Burke and Litwin (1992) outline a model that does just this.

This model sees the organisation as an open system; that is, it is open to its environment and affected by it. The systems model accounts for both transformational change (in response to the environment and requiring whole new sets of behaviours) and transactional change (brought about by short-term reciprocity between organisational members). It shows how external environmental changes interact with the three transformational organisation factors: mission and strategy, leadership, and culture. These three factors then interact with the transactional factors: organisation structure, systems, management practices and climate. All of these factors combine to influence

employee motivation and individual and organisational performance.

Although complex, this model is important in highlighting how many different factors we need to consider in the management of change. It is not enough simply to develop a good organisational mission and strategy and hope that this will be enough to carry the change through. The impacts of change in any one of these factors will be felt throughout the system, and change in one will lead to change in another, sometimes in unexpected ways. The model also emphasises that changing transformational factors is likely to have much more far-reaching effects than changes in the transactional factors. A final, and particularly important, point of this model is the way it highlights *how* change impacts on organisational performance: it is not a direct effect, but occurs through changes in the employees, and gives particular precedence to the impact on employee motivation.

Organisation development

This emphasis on the 'human' side of organisational change is at the root of organisation development (OD) approaches to change. OD is a very broad area and a subject of study in its own right, but is essentially concerned with organisation-wide interventions to ensure continual organisational survival. Organisational effectiveness is measured not only in terms of production and efficiency but also in terms of the quality of working life and employee well-being. The values underlying this approach are collaborative and democratic, treating people as human beings with needs, rather than just as a 'resource' for the organisation to use. The OD approach seeks to develop work so that people have the chance to develop their full potential and the organisation can achieve all its goals (Margulies and Raia, 1972).

However, later developments in the field seem to have moved away from the focus on individual learning and involvement to emphasise the role of senior managers in decisions about change and to exclude employees who do not fit with the new culture. For example, an OD approach to culture change (Cummings and Huse, 1989) recommends five steps, of which three involve top management (in creating vision, being committed to the change and providing leadership) and one involves modifying structures and systems. The only step to mention other employees recommends selecting those who fit with the new culture and removing those who do not – a far cry from the collaborative approach that OD was based on.

A recent review of OD noted that the field seems to be going through a process of renewal (Burnes and Cooke,

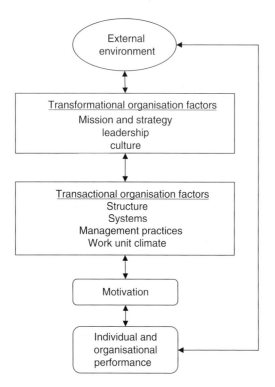

Figure 8.4 A systems model of change
Source: adapted from Burke and Litwin (1992).

2012). The recent business scandals have emphasised the importance of ethics and values in organisations, which fits in well with the original basis of OD, and there is an increased rigour and relevance to OD models. And finally, OD is absorbing theories of emergent change and complexity which were previously seen as challenging the whole approach.

THE HUMAN SIDE OF CHANGE

The first thing to note when we are thinking about how change affects people and how they deal with it is that change is not easy. We are all different in terms of the amount of change we can enjoy and the extent to which change causes us stress, but we all like a certain amount of stability. The second important consideration is that the effects of a particular organisational change will also be different for different people. If we are to manage change and its effects properly, we will need to take account of these different perspectives. The following case study illustrates these two important points in more detail.

Triggers for change

An organisation's attempts to change, whether in adjusting business strategy or restructuring a department, are perceived in different ways by different employees. It is this individual perception of the primary organisational triggers for change that leads to the secondary, personal ones (Stuart, 1995). Stuart's research identified many different triggers for managers, including the following:

Table 8.2 Triggers for change

Positively perceived triggers	Negatively perceived triggers
Freedom	Financial threat
Autonomy	Deviousness
Opportunities for recognition, learning and creativity	Lack of support
	Betrayal
	Insecurity

These triggers set people on a change journey as they come to terms with the changes and try to find a way to deal with them.

Case Study Open-plan office

Padma is an accountant in a large clothing firm. She and four colleagues work together on a range of tasks including preparing financial reports and management statements, liaising with external auditors and so on. They each have their own small office, with a meeting room nearby. One day, her manager announces that the company has decided to move all office staff into open-plan offices in order to improve communication and information sharing. The builders are brought in, the walls are knocked down and the five small offices that Padma and her colleagues worked in are converted to one big open-plan office.

© 06photo/Fotolia

Padma is upset about this change. She feels she needs peace and quiet to do her job properly and to concentrate on all the details she needs to get right. She is also a bit annoyed: this change implies to her that the company does not believe she and her team were communicating properly and have not been doing a very good job. But one of her colleagues, Simon, is quite excited by it. He says he has always found the separate offices quite lonely and he likes having other people around him when he works. He also thinks it will make talking about problems, asking for help and developing new ideas much easier. Padma and Simon do both agree, however, that it seems a bit strange that none of the managers have to 'give up' their own offices, and this makes them suspect that the firm's motives for open-plan offices might not be what they claim.

▶ What potential benefits and drawbacks can you see to this change? If you were Padma's manager, how would you best introduce this change?

▶ How would you feel in this situation? Do you identify most with Padma or Simon? Discuss with the rest of your group, and see if there are individual differences in your responses.

Personal transitions

One of the major contributors to our understanding of how change impacts on people at work is William Bridges, who said 'It isn't the changes that do you in, it's the transitions' (Bridges, 2009, p. 3). He sees change as situational, something that happens at a specific place and time, such as starting a new job or graduating from university. Transition, on the other hand, is the psychological process we go through as we come to terms with that change. Transition psychology is the study of how we adapt to and deal with changes, good or bad.

Psychosocial transition theory (Parkes, 1971) is a useful way of understanding our psychological reactions to change, including the stress we experience and how we deal with crisis and loss. This theory starts by recognising that each of us builds up an 'assumptive world', that is, our assumptions about the world and ourselves (Parkes, 1975). This view of the world and our place in it is based on our experiences in the past and helps to give us meaning and a sense of purpose. In the workplace, this assumptive world could include our beliefs about our career path, how good we are at particular tasks or how much respect and status we gain from our job. Major changes can create a discrepancy between the reality of the world and our assumptions about it. This is a very uncomfortable and difficult experience for us and leads to feelings of insecurity and fear. It is as if the world no longer makes sense and we do not know how we fit in with it any more.

This theory was developed to explain people's reactions to bereavement and loss, and perhaps you are thinking that it is not relevant to change at work because this is surely not as serious as losing a loved one. But work by Holmes and Rahe (1967) looked at how much adjustment people needed to make after different changes in their lives. They asked respondents to rate the extent of social readjustment (i.e. the amount and duration of change in the pattern of their lives) that different life events required. The result was a list of 43 positive and negative life events, ranked in order of how much change they would involve in people's normal lives. *Being sacked from work* or *retiring* were considered to need a similar level of readjustment as *getting married*, while a *change to a different line of work* was seen as being on a par with the *death of a close friend*. Requiring less adaptation than these were a *change in work responsibilities* or *trouble with the boss*, which were similar to *leaving school*. These comparisons are significant because the extent of life changes we experience is highly related to our susceptibility to illness: the higher people's score on this social readjustment scale, the more likely they are to be ill in the next year (Holmes and Masuda, 1973).

Parkes's explanation of psychosocial transitions (PST) points out that we find it very difficult to change our assumptive world in response to life events and challenges, which is why change takes so long and is so often resisted. Anything that makes us feel more insecure, such as threats to our livelihood or fear of what will happen, will delay the transition. In contrast, anything that helps us feel secure or confident will aid us through the transition. And because transition is a process, these interventions can be both before *and after* the change has actually happened. Our response to change is not an instant occurrence, over as soon as the change is; it takes place over weeks, months or even years. Effective transition essentially involves rebuilding our assumptive world to fit more accurately with our new reality.

There are several different models of the transition process. The simplest (Bridges, 1980) sees transition as a three-stage process:

1 Ending – every transition starts with an ending, when we let go of old ways of doing things or an old identity. This is the time where people are dealing with loss.
2 Neutral zone – during this time, the 'old' has gone (e.g. we can no longer do things the way we used to or no longer have our old identity) but the 'new' is not yet fully in place. We recognise that we need to change but we are not sure what will happen.
3 Beginning – it is only towards the end of the transition process that we truly begin the new way of being. We have a new identity or have discovered the new way of doing things.

It is important to note that the transition process occurs for both positive and negative changes. Graduating from university is a great achievement and a positive experience, yet it will still involve a transition: you go from the identity of 'student' to 'graduate'; you have to find a new way of being, with new goals, plans and behaviours.

This model was expanded somewhat by Nicholson and West (1988) to include a stage of *preparation*, which concerns people's psychological readiness for the change. It includes the feelings and motivations people have towards the change, how much warning they have had for it and how well equipped they feel to deal with it. Going into even more detail, Hayes (2010) notes seven distinct phases in the transition process:

1 Shock – at the beginning of a transition, people can be overwhelmed, especially if they had little notice that the change was coming. They feel 'immobilised', unable to take in new information or to plan properly, and the less prepared they were for the change and the more undesirable the change is, the more intense

Case Study **Transitions**

Emma is a financial director who is approaching retirement. She has recently decided to go part-time and work only three days a week, and this change has prompted her to reflect on how people cope with change. Through her career she has been involved in several organisational changes that have meant taking people through the redundancy process, and she has noticed differences in how the changes are handled and the effect they have on those involved in the process.

In a couple of cases, the changes were the result of a merger or acquisition by her company, resulting in a desire to centralise the finance department in one

© Petro Feketa

place and remove duplicated positions. She feels that these changes were handled well. People in the newly acquired company were told straight away what was happening. They were offered new posts if they wished to relocate. If they did not wish to move, they were given a year's notice that the post would be ending, a retention bonus to keep them with the company until the end of that time so that their expertise and knowledge was not immediately lost, as well as time off to seek new work and support in their applications. Emma reflected that people in this situation, after the initial shock, felt that they were being treated fairly and, overall, saw the change in a positive light.

In contrast, she has noticed how her company is handling a current reorganisation. It has made an announcement that several departments are being reorganised and that it is possible that some jobs will be affected. However, it has not announced the details of the changes or who will be affected. Instead, it has started a process of consultation, so it will be several months before people know for sure whether their job is at risk. Emma thinks that the organisation is trying to follow some regulations or procedures, but it has not been explained to anyone and all everyone wants to know is how the change will affect them.

Emma concludes that the most important thing in organisational change is to give people certainty, and knows from experience that while it is tempting to try and give people false hope, in the long run this never works.

▸ How does facing redundancy challenge people's 'assumptive world'?

▸ Emma noticed how important certainty is for people dealing with change. How does this fit in with psychosocial transition theory?

▸ Why do you think giving people false hope is ultimately a bad idea in helping them with personal transition?

this stage will be. In the case of a gradual dawning of awareness of the change, this stage is associated with worrying, with people focusing on how they might lose out.

2 Denial – instead of dealing with the change, people tend to deny it for a while. They focus their attention on other things, perhaps convince themselves that the change is not actually going to happen (or has not happened). People are most resistant to change when in this phase and can get angry if forced to face up to it. This stage is important, though, because refusing to accept the change can sometimes give people the time they need to make the personal transition, rehearsing the implications of the change in their minds (Parkes, 1993).

3 Depression – as denial fades, people begin to face reality and recognise that the change is happening. This

leads to feelings of helplessness, stress and depression and corresponds with Bridges' neutral zone. It can even happen with changes that were initially perceived as positive, if practical problems surface.

4 Letting go – this is the lowest part of the process in terms of mood. For the transition to continue, the individual needs to let go of the old identity or behaviours and accept the new reality.

5 Testing – now that the new reality has 'arrived', people start to engage more actively with it. They test out new ways of being, using a trial-and-error process to see what works in the 'new world'.

6 Consolidation – the behaviours and patterns that are successful in the testing process now become the new norms.

7 Internalisation – the final phase marks the end of the transition. At this point the new behaviours and norms

are fully adopted and the past has been left behind. By reflecting on the process, people can learn from it and use that learning in future changes.

It should be remembered that this represents a successful transition, but, of course, not everyone will make a successful transition through every change they are faced with. Each person can go through these stages at a different speed, or even get stuck and not complete the process.

 Psychological Toolkit Managing transitions

When you complete your university degree, you will go through a transition. This exercise gives you the opportunity to reflect on how you can manage that transition effectively. Work through the activities below to see how you can use the theory and models we have looked at in this chapter to deal with a major change in your life.

The transition process

First, we will start by thinking about a previous change you went through. A good example might be when you started your university course. Whether full- or part-time, starting your course involved taking on, at least partially, the identity of 'student' as well as learning new behaviours and ways of thinking that were probably quite different to your previous way of life. Look back on that time to answer these questions:

▸ When did your *transition* start?
▸ When did it end and how did you know? (Or is it still ongoing? If so, why do you think you have not completed the transition?)

Now think about the extent to which your experience fits with Hayes's seven-phase model. Work through each of these stages and see if you can identify examples of them happening during your transition to becoming a student:

1 Shock
2 Denial
3 Depression
4 Letting go
5 Testing
6 Consolidation
7 Internalisation

The seventh stage, internalisation, includes reflecting on and learning from your experience of transition. You can use this to help prepare for the next transition. So next, we will consider your transition *out* of the student life.

Your current identity and 'assumptive world'

▸ What does it mean to you to *be* a student? How important is this identity to you?

▸ What aspects of this identity do you think you will miss after you graduate? What behaviours do you think you engage in as a student that you will have to leave behind when you graduate?

Facilitating your transition

Parkes (1993) suggests that there are three things we need in order to get through the transition process effectively:

1 Emotional support
2 Protection through the period of helplessness
3 Help in discovering new models appropriate to the changed situation.

Work through the seven transition stages, using Parkes's suggestions to help you write down things you could do to facilitate your transition through each stage after graduation. Draw on what you have learnt about yourself from your transition into university.

Instead of outlining a series of stages, Stuart (1995) suggests that we should think of change as a journey through a number of 'fields' or areas of change. Each individual may take a different path through these fields in their process of dealing with change. It is helpful to be reminded that people deal with change in different ways and that while transition models are useful, they cannot be used in a prescriptive manner that determines how people will react at any one moment.

Change management perspectives

We have reviewed several different approaches to managing organisational change. But they have all been based on the assumption that change *can* be managed, and we need to bear in mind that there are both individual and cultural differences in the extent to which people believe they have control over their world.

Individuals with an internal locus of control believe that they are able to influence their world and are not at the mercy of fate or circumstance. People with an external locus of control believe they are not able to control their world to any great extent and will just have to put up with whatever happens. There are also cultural differences in beliefs about whether we should be in control of, or live in harmony with, our environment, which affect the extent to which people will try to plan and take action for change. So in the discussions which follow, bear in mind that we are starting from the assumption that change *can* be managed. In the International Perspectives section, we explore this assumption in more detail.

International Perspectives Culture and change

Cross-national mergers and acquisitions (M&As) provide a good opportunity to study the effects of cultural differences during times of change. A survey by KPMG (Kelly et al., 1999) found that 83% of the organisations involved in M&As had failed to produce any increase in shareholder value a year after a deal was completed. When they analysed what set the successful companies apart, a focus on resolving cultural issues was one of the keys to success.

The difficulties facing companies engaging in cross-national M&As include differences in working practices, language and general cultural differences. The study found that M&As between countries with a greater cultural similarity were more successful. Deals between the UK and USA were 45% more successful than the global average, those between the UK and Europe were 19% more successful, but those between the USA and Europe were 11% *less* successful. While these success rates for the USA and UK may be at least partially due to greater experience and stricter regulations, the difference between their respective success rates in Europe certainly points to the influence of culture and cultural awareness.

In a study of three multinational companies (MNCs) in the same industry sector, Geppert et al. (2003) looked at how the culture of the headquarter's host country interacted with the culture of the subsidiary in the organisations' management of change. They came to an interesting conclusion: the more globalised the MNC was (i.e. the more homogenous its structures and strategies were across the different national subsidiaries), the more it actually allowed and relied upon national differences to play a key role in its overall portfolio. Similarly, a study of the implementation of a worldwide HR portal in Hewlett-Packard showed that adapting the change process to the national culture (in this case Italy) encouraged a smooth transition and positive acceptance by the employees (Ruta, 2005).

Leadership plays an essential role in change, and particularly in dealing with cultural differences. Gill (2012) compared two mergers between car manufacturers: Renault-Nissan and DaimlerChrysler-Mitsubishi. She concluded that when leadership style fits with the national culture, change can be introduced more successfully. These studies show us that while national cultural differences certainly present a challenge to change management, a culturally sensitive approach can work with and capitalise on these differences to be a source of competitive advantage and success.

Discussion point

Trompenaars and Woolliams (2003) point out that the 'Anglo-Saxon' model of change has dominated thinking in the field of change management. It is born of a task-oriented culture that actively discards tradition, as opposed to the many cultures which respect their traditions and have a more 'being' than 'doing' orientation. To what extent do you think it is possible to manage change successfully in a culture which respects and values traditions? How might change management differ in this kind of country?

Resistance to change

We have seen how change affects us psychologically, so it should come as no surprise that a major issue for change management is dealing with resistance. Even positive change can cause us difficulties in terms of having to readjust to a new way of doing things, and it is rare that a change at work is entirely positive. Most changes involve a complex combination of positive and negative impacts on different people, and each of those people will welcome or resist the change to different extents.

In a seminal article in the *Harvard Business Review*, Kotter and Schlesinger (1979) noted that many managers used a 'one size fits all' approach to managing change, which often led to failure. The authors recommended instead that managers diagnose the sources of resistance to change and use a change management approach suited to the kind of resistance they are likely to encounter. From their experience and analysis of successful and unsuccessful organisational changes, Kotter and Schlesinger proposed four main sources of resistance:

1 Parochial self-interest – that is, people do not want to lose something of value to them and are focused on their own self-interests. Even if a change is obviously good for the organisation or the rest of the team, someone may still resist it if the change is likely to cause him or her extra work or mean a loss of status.

2 Misunderstanding and lack of trust – related to the point above, people may misunderstand the change and believe the costs outweigh the benefits even when this is not the case. This is particularly likely to happen when there is a lack of trust between the change agent and those affected by the change.

3 Different assessments – the change agent may believe that a change will result in many positive effects, such as improved productivity, increased employee motivation and so on. But those affected by the change may see it very differently. This highlights how important it is for change to be transparent so that everyone is aware of all the relevant information.

4 Low tolerance for change – people worry that they may not be able to develop the required new skills and abilities quickly enough or that they simply will not be able to cope with the change. Some people simply find change more difficult than others.

This final point, individual tolerance for change, has been explored in more detail using the Big Five personality traits. People who are more extraverted, agreeable, conscientious and open to experience have more positive attitudes towards organisational change (Vakola et al., 2004). In addition, those who are more able to use their emotions in problem-solving (an aspect of emotional intelligence) are also more positively inclined towards change. But identifying a personality component in our resistance to change does not mean that some people will just never be able to deal with change. Instead, understanding the individual differences can help managers identify those people who may need further support or training in dealing with change.

The resistance to change scale (RTC) is a dispositional measure of how much a person is inclined to resist change (Oreg, 2003) and consists of four factors. The first is the extent to which a person seeks routine in their life rather than seeking out new experiences and unexpected events. The second factor, called emotional reaction, looks at how tense or stressed people get in response to change, regardless of the 'objective facts' of its impact on their life. The third factor evaluates whether a person focuses on the short or long term – the short-term discomfort of change rather than the long-term potential benefits. And the final component of dispositional resistance to change is cognitive rigidity – the extent to which a person is willing to change his or her mind. Cross-cultural studies have shown that this model of dispositional resistance is similar across 17 different countries (Oreg et al., 2008).

The RTC scales are related in the ways we would expect with the Big Five, with neuroticism, for example, positively correlated with the first three scales (Saksvik and Hetland, 2009). But the RTC is helpful in itself in giving a coherent view of a person's reaction to a specific change rather than their overall personality. You can complete the questionnaire for yourself in the following activity.

Activity **Dispositional resistance to change**

You can complete the Resistance to Change questionnaire, specially adapted for students, by going to Shaul Oreg's web page at the Hebrew University of Jerusalem (http://pluto.huji.ac.il/~oreg/) and clicking on the Resistance to Change link. Complete the questionnaire and find out your score for each factor.

▸ According to the results, how much do you tend to resist change? Does this reflect your own understanding of yourself?
▸ What is your lowest scoring factor? Discuss with a colleague how you might be able to improve how you deal with change in this area.

Viewing resistance to change as multifaceted rather than simply a single force that attempts to derail change programmes means that we can find more appropriate ways of managing it. Oreg (2006) presents an integrative model of how our personality and the organisational context of the change both influence the extent to which we will resist change, and the likely outcomes of that resistance.

In this model, our personality affects both our affective and behavioural resistance to change – the extent to which we might feel worried or angry about the change and how likely we are to engage in actions such as complaining about the change or trying to persuade others that it is a bad idea. On the other hand, our perceptions of the outcomes of the change (such as how it may affect our job security or the power we have in the organisation) influence affective and cognitive resistance – how we think and feel about the change. Other context factors related to the change process, such as trust in management, are more strongly related to the behavioural component of resistance to change. And finally, a person's resistance to change has a negative impact on work-related outcomes such as job satisfaction and intention to quit.

Given the effects of resistance to change, not only on the success of the change itself, but also on wider work outcomes, what options are available for its effective management? Kotter and Schlesinger (1979) recommend several different approaches that can be used dependent on the situation, ranging from education to coercion. These are summarised below:

Table 8.3 Managing resistance to change

Education and communication	Helps people to understand the reasons for the change. It can also help to build trust as information is shared rather than change being imposed without explanation.
Participation and involvement	Involve those who are affected by the change in its implementation. This can ensure that potential obstacles are dealt with before they become problems, and encourages feedback on the implications of change.

Facilitation and support	This can happen by providing training in new skills or strategies for dealing with change or simply emotional support for those struggling with the change.
Negotiation and agreement	Offer incentives to those who are likely to resist the change in order to get them on board.
Manipulation and co-optation	Rather than an open, participative approach like some of the previous ones, this involves sharing information selectively or consciously structuring events to ensure the change occurs.
Explicit or implicit coercion	This involves forcing people to change by threatening them. For example, a manager might hint that someone's promotion prospects might be damaged if they resist the change, or even fire them if they do not conform.

This list is helpful in identifying the range of options available to managers as they deal with resistance, which is a natural part of any organisational change. But the effects of these management efforts will, of course, be varied, and given the potentially negative consequences of the later strategies, careful thought needs to be given as to when each is appropriate.

Through all this, however, it is also worth remembering that resistance to change is not in itself a bad thing. It can have positive results, such as slowing the process down so that people have the time they need to adapt or helping to highlight problems with the change that have not been identified before. For this reason, managing change in a participatory way whenever possible is to be preferred, as it ensures that change managers will have access to as much information as possible in guiding the change, and also give the individuals involved some control over the speed of the change and the ability to manage their own responses.

SUMMARY

Change is a fact of life, and change can also be difficult. In this chapter we have reviewed models of change management, from the simple three-step process outlined by Lewin to the more complex systems perspective which encourages us to consider the knock-on effects of any organisational change. In all these discussions, it has become obvious that for any organisational change to succeed, plans need to prioritise a consideration of the human side of change.

We have dealt with these psychological effects of change in detail, looking at how each of us has a different perspective on change and how we can understand and manage transitions so that we can survive the turbulent modern workplace. Understanding the difficulties of personal transitions also helps us to appreciate why people resist change and develop more appropriate strategies for dealing with that resistance.

TEST YOURSELF

Brief Review Questions

1 What is the difference between planned and emergent change?
2 Briefly outline Lewin's three-stage model of change.
3 What is the advantage of a learning organisation in managing change?
4 List some of the positive and negative personal triggers for change and explain why they are important in understanding how organisational change impacts on individuals.
5 What are the four main sources of resistance to change, according to Kotter and Schlesinger?

Discussion or Essay Questions

1 What is the punctuated equilibrium model of change and how is it relevant to our understanding of change management?
2 To what extent can organisational change be managed?
3 How can psychosocial transition theory be used to help manage the effects of organisational change?
4 Is it feasible to remove all resistance to change? What would be the advantages and disadvantages of doing so?

FURTHER READING

- John Hayes's book *The Theory and Practice of Change Management* provides very comprehensive discussions of change topics: J. Hayes, *The Theory and Practice of Change Management*. 3rd edn. Basingstoke, Palgrave Macmillan, 2010.
- The Eos Life-Work resource centre provides a good discussion of the personal transition process, with links to further resources: http://www.eoslifework.co.uk/transprac.htm.

References

BRIDGES, W. 1980. *Transitions: Making Sense of Life's Changes*. Cambridge, MA, Addison-Wesley.

BRIDGES, W. 2009. *Managing Transitions: Making the Most of Change*. Philadelphia, Da Capo Press.

BROWN, S. L. & EISENHARDT, K. M. 1997. The art of continuous change: linking complexity theory and time-paced evolution in relentlessly shifting organizations. *Administrative Science Quarterly*, 42 1–34.

BURKE, W. & LITWIN, G. H. 1992. A causal model of organizational performance and change. *Journal of Management*, 18, 523–45.

BURNES, B. 2004a. Emergent change and planned change – competitors or allies? The case of XYZ construction. *International Journal of Operations & Production Management*, 24, 886–902.

BURNES, B. 2004b. Kurt Lewin and the planned approach to change: a re-appraisal. *Journal of Management Studies*, 41, 977–1002.

BURNES, B. & COOKE, B. 2012. The past, present and future of organization development: taking the long view. *Human Relations*, 65, 1395–429.

BUTLER, S. 2013. Tesco revamp looks to stop giant stores becoming a white elephant. *The Guardian*, 6 August.

CIPD (CHARTERED INSTITUTE OF PERSONNEL AND DEVELOPMENT). 2003. *Reorganising for Success: CEOs' and HR Managers' Perceptions*. London, Chartered Institute of Personnel and Development.

CUMMINGS, T. G. & HUSE, E. F. 1989. *Organization Development and Change*. St Paul, MN, West Publishing.

FORD, M. W. & GREER, B. M. 2006. Profiling change: an empirical study of change process patterns. *Journal of Applied Behavioral Science*, 42, 420–46.

FRESE, M. 2008. The Changing Nature of Work. In Chmiel, N. (ed.) *Introduction to Work and Organizational Psychology: A European Perspective*. Oxford, Blackwell.

GEPPERT, M., MATTEN, D. & WILLIAMS, K. 2003. Change management in MNCs: how global convergence intertwines with national diversities. *Human Relations*, 56, 807–38.

GERSICK, C. J. 1991. Revolutionary change theories: a multilevel exploration of the punctuated equilibrium paradigm. *Academy of Management Review*, 16, 10–36.

GILL, C. 2012. The role of leadership in successful international mergers and acquisitions: why Renault-Nissan succeeded and DaimlerChrysler-Mitsubishi failed. *Human Resource Management*, 51, 433–56.

HAYES, J. 2010. *The Theory and Practice of Change Management*, 3rd edn. Basingstoke, Palgrave Macmillan.

HOLMES, T. H. & MASUDA, M. 1973. Life Change and Illness Susceptibility. In Scott, John P. and Senay, Edward C. (eds.) *Separation and Depression: Clinical and Research Aspects*, vol. 8. Oxford, American Association for the Advancement of Science.

HOLMES, T. & RAHE, R. 1967. The social readjustment rating scale. *Journal of Psychosomatic Research*, 11, 213–18.

HUGHES, M. 2011. Do 70 per cent of all organizational change initiatives really fail? *Journal of Change Management*, 11, 451–64.

KANTER, R. M., STEIN, B. & JICK, T. 1992. *The Challenge of Organizational Change: How Companies Experience it and Leaders Guide it*. New York, Free Press.

KELLY, J., COOK, C. & SPITZER, D. 1999. *Unlocking Shareholder Value: The Keys to Success*. London, KPMG.

KOTTER, J. P. 1996. *Leading Change*. Boston, MA, Harvard Business School Press.

KOTTER, J. P. & SCHLESINGER, L. A. 1979. *Choosing Strategies for Change*. Boston, MA, Harvard Business Review Press.

LEWIN, K. 1946. Action research and minority problems. *Journal of Social Issues*, 2, 34–46.

LEWIN, K. (ED.) 1951. *Field Theory in Social Science: Selected Theoretical Papers*. New York, Harper & Row.

MARGULIES, N. & RAIA, A. P. 1972. *Organizational Development: Values, Processes, and Technology*. New York, McGraw-Hill.

NICHOLSON, N. & WEST, M. A. 1988. *Managerial Job Change: Men and Women in Transition*. New York, Cambridge University Press.

OREG, S. 2003. Resistance to change: developing an individual differences measure. *Journal of Applied Psychology*, 88, 680–93.

OREG, S. 2006. Personality, context, and resistance to organizational change. *European Journal of Work and Organizational Psychology*, 15, 73–101.

OREG, S., BAYAZIT, M., VAKOLA, M., ARCINIEGA, ET AL. 2008. Dispositional resistance to change: measurement equivalence and the link to personal values across 17 nations. *Journal of Applied Psychology*, 93, 935–44.

PARKES, C. 1971. Psycho-social transitions: a field for study. *Social Science & Medicine*, 5, 101–15.

PARKES, C. M. 1975. Determinants of outcome following bereavement. *OMEGA: Journal of Death and Dying*, 6, 303–23.

PARKES, C. M. 1993. Bereavement as a Psychosocial Transition: Processes of Adaptation to Change. In Stroebe, M. S., Stroebe, W. and Hansson, R.O. (eds.) *Handbook of Bereavement: Theory, Research, and Intervention*. Cambridge, Cambridge University Press.

ROMANELLI, E. & TUSHMAN, M. L. 1994. Organizational transformation as punctuated equilibrium: an empirical test. *Academy of Management Journal*, 37, 1141–66.

RUTA, C. D. 2005. The application of change management theory to HR portal implementation in subsidiaries of multinational corporations. *Human Resource Management*, 44, 35–53.

SAKSVIK, I. B. & HETLAND, H. 2009. Exploring dispositional resistance to change. *Journal of Leadership & Organizational Studies*, 16, 175–83.

SENGE, P. M. 1990. *The Fifth Discipline*. London, Century Business.

STAW, B. M. & EPSTEIN, L. D. 2000. What bandwagons bring: effects of popular management techniques on corporate performance, reputation, and CEO pay. *Administrative Science Quarterly*, 45, 523–56.

STUART, R. 1995. Experiencing organizational change: triggers, processes and outcomes of change journeys. *Personnel Review*, 24, 3–88.

TROMPENAARS, F. & WOOLLIAMS, P. 2003. A new framework for managing change across cultures. *Journal of Change Management*, 3, 361–75.

TUSHMAN, M. L. & ROMANELLI, E. 1985. Organizational evolution: a metamorphosis model of convergence and reorientation. *Research in Organizational Behavior*, 7, 171–222.

VAKOLA, M., TSAOUSIS, I. & NIKOLAOU, I. 2004. The role of emotional intelligence and personality variables on attitudes toward organisational change. *Journal of Managerial Psychology*, 19, 88–110.

WEICK, K. E. 2000. Emergent Change as a Universal in Organizations. In Beer, M. & Nohria, N. (eds.) *Breaking the Code of Change*. Boston, MA, Harvard Business School Press.

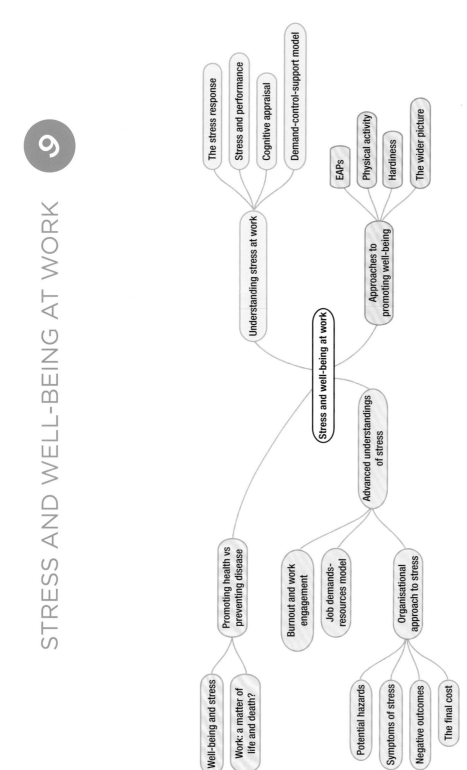

Stress and well-being at work

Understanding stress at work
- The stress response
- Stress and performance
- Cognitive appraisal
- Demand-control-support model

Approaches to promoting well-being
- EAPs
- Physical activity
- Hardiness
- The wider picture

Promoting health vs preventing disease
- Well-being and stress
- Work: a matter of life and death?

Advanced understandings of stress
- Burnout and work engagement
- Job demands-resources model
- Organisational approach to stress
  - Potential hazards
  - Symptoms of stress
  - Negative outcomes
  - The final cost

The central theme of this chapter is how we can develop a workplace which enhances our well-being. We start by contrasting disease prevention with the idea of health promotion as a basic approach to stress and well-being. After defining both these terms, we move on to consider what we know about how stress affects us, both physically and psychologically. The role of individual differences in determining stress outcomes is highlighted through a consideration of the ways we understand and react to potential stressors. We will also be introduced to the idea of 'good' and 'bad' stress as a basis for understanding how it impacts on our lives and how it can be managed.

Building on this, we compare the notions of burnout and engagement, looking at a model of stress and well-being that differentiates between types of stress and incorporates our personal differences. The chapter concludes with an exploration of what organisations and individuals can do to manage well-being at work, acknowledging the central place for social support.

This chapter will help you answer the following questions:

1   Does it make a difference whether we try to prevent stress or promote well-being at work?
2   What happens when we are 'stressed'?
3   How can psychological models help us to understand stress and well-being at work and their impacts on organisational outcomes?
4   How can we promote well-being at work?

PROMOTING HEALTH OR PREVENTING DISEASE?

The traditional medical model of health has focused on preventing and treating disease; and when people think about health at work, prevention and treatment tends to be their primary consideration. 'Health and safety' is often seen as preventing physical harm or, when extended to include mental harm, simply viewed as preventing or reducing the impact of stress. However, there is a growing movement in health care which takes a more holistic approach. Even in the 1970s there were calls for medical models to become more inclusive, with Engel (1977), for example, proposing a model of health and disease which takes account of psychological and social aspects as well as the physical. He noted that an 'objective' diagnosis of illness based on physical symptoms is rarely sufficient, and that the boundaries between 'well' and 'sick' become blurred in real life, subject to cultural, social and psychological influences.

The World Health Organization (WHO, 2005) promotes just such an integrated approach to health, calling on governments, organisations and communities to promote health as a 'positive and inclusive concept' which encompasses not just physical health but mental and spiritual well-being as well. As part of this, it calls on corporations to make health promotion a requirement of good corporate practice, noting that work organisations have a 'responsibility to ensure health and safety in the workplace, and to promote the health and well-being of their employees, their families and communities' (WHO, 2005, p. 5). It is therefore not enough for us to consider health as merely the absence of disease or illness or as limited to physical symptoms. Instead, work psychology needs to take a more positive and proactive view, promoting health and well-being.

Well-being and stress

Stress

Before the current shift in emphasis to employee well-being, and in line with the 'disease prevention' model that was prevalent in health care, most of the research in this area was about stress. When we talk about stress in normal life, we use the word to mean any or all of a combination of three different things, all of which have been studied in stress research (Cooper and Payne, 1988):

- the stimulus or cause: the pressures or demands we experience (e.g. pressure to meet a deadline or an argument with a colleague). These are often called *stressors* in the literature.
- the process: how that pressure is turned into a reaction (e.g. thinking that there is no way we can meet a deadline or seeing an argument as a serious problem).
- the outcome or result: how stress impacts on our lives and work (e.g. feeling anxious or getting a headache). The psychological outcome that we experience is often called *strain* and results in physical and psychological consequences.

In Great Britain, stress accounts for 40% of all work-related illnesses and is defined by the Health and Safety Executive (HSE, 2013) as a 'harmful reaction people have due to undue pressures and demands placed on them at work'. There are two important points to note that are common to this definition and others in the literature. First is that stress is a *reaction* to pressures and second that illness occurs when those pressures are *too high*. There is a strong element of individual difference here. What is too high or 'undue' for one person may be fine for another. To try and explain these individual differences and the complexities of stress-related illness, several models have been proposed. We will consider the foremost of these in this chapter and draw out the key components for a thorough understanding of work stress.

An interesting alternative point of view on the idea of work stress is given by Wainwright and Calnan (2000). They suggest that the emphasis on treating stress as a disease or work injury may make people feel they are passive victims of circumstance rather than active agents, who are often able to withstand the difficult situations they are faced with and can also change their workplaces. We will see how individual resilience and other personal factors are captured by the most recent stress models later in the chapter.

Well-being

We will return to the concept of well-being in Chapter 10, as it is a basic component of the positive psychology movement. Here, it is useful to us to have a working definition of occupational well-being, particularly as it relates to stress. As you might expect from a concept that aims to be holistic and comprehensive, there are a range of meanings, but they generally involve a recognition that occupational well-being is more than just the absence of ill health. In more narrow definitions, it is sometimes

equated with job satisfaction (Sousa-Poza and Sousa-Poza, 2000) but more comprehensive explanations consider it to be a 'summative concept that characterises the quality of working lives' (Schulte and Vainio, 2010, p. 422).

People also use terms such as 'flourishing' and 'thriving' when they talk about well-being, to emphasise the fact that we are not dealing with a neutral concept. Whereas a focus on negative stress helps us to identify the factors that need to be addressed to ensure people are 'OK', a focus on well-being wants to find out what factors create a positive, life-enhancing experience.

Work: a matter of life and death?

For anyone in any doubt that work-related health and well-being is a serious issue, a quick review of the most extreme result of low well-being – suicide – will serve to emphasise its importance. In Japan, work-related deaths have become a serious national issue, and Japanese has words for two types of death related to work: *karoshi* is death from overwork and *karojisatsu* is work-related suicide. *Karoshi* is often due to stroke or heart attack

---

International Perspectives Well-being across the world

Like many psychological concepts, 'well-being' originated in the West and much of the research has been carried out in Europe or the USA. This leads many people to wonder whether well-being means the same thing in different countries or whether there are differences in the kinds of things that influence people's well-being in different cultures.

The understanding that people in the EU have of occupational well-being was evaluated in an EU-wide survey (Buffett et al., 2013). It found that while there was general agreement on a definition that included physical and mental well-being, psychosocial issues and the working environment, there were differences in the emphasis that different countries placed on these elements. For example, while Poland focused almost exclusively on physical well-being, Italy and France did not have any specific activities for this area. The authors conclude that well-being at work in the EU is about the quality of work and the work environment, and includes preventing harm as well as the fulfilment of personal goals.

Going beyond the EU, Gallup conducted a poll of people in 150 countries and found five universal elements of well-being (Rath and Harter, 2010):

▸ Career – liking what you do every day
▸ Social – having strong relationships and love

▸ Financial – overall standard of living and managing personal finances well
▸ Physical – good health and the energy to get through the day
▸ Community – feeling safe and engaging with the area you live in.

Of these five elements, there is some indication that career well-being might be particularly important for men. A longitudinal study in Germany found that, on average, men who went through a period of prolonged unemployment did not recover their levels of life satisfaction even five years after the event (Clark et al., 2008). This was in contrast to men and women's adaptation to other major life events, such as divorce or death of a spouse. So occupational well-being is not just important in terms of a productive workplace, but is a key part of the population's overall health and happiness.

Discussion points

Why do you think there is such good agreement around the world as to what constitutes well-being? Do you think organisations should be involved in promoting well-being? Why or why not?

What might be the reason for the long-term negative effect of unemployment on men's well-being? To what extent do you think this result might generalise to other countries?

brought on by stress and overwork, with Japanese workers feeling under extreme pressure to work very long hours. Increasing rates of *karojisatsu* have forced changes in how Japan views these suicides, with them increasingly being recognised as work-related accidents, and a subsequent pressure on organisations to take some responsibility (Inoue and Matsumoto, 2000). These authors suggest that the high rate of work suicides in Japan is partly because Japan lags behind other developed countries in terms of providing mental health support to employees and in overcoming the stigma associated with accessing that support. Amagasa et al. (2005) identify long working hours, low social support and heavy workloads as contributing factors to the suicide rate.

Further evidence that work is related to suicide comes from a comparison of suicide rates in different occupations. In the late 1970s and early 1980s in the UK, the occupations with the highest rates of suicide were mostly professional, for example veterinarians, pharmacists and doctors. It was thought that this higher rate was due to easier access to a method of suicide, such as drugs (Charlton, 1995). However, the pattern has changed

in the new millennium, with rates for those occupations dropping and rates for manual occupations, such as coal mining and merchant seafaring, increasing (Roberts et al., 2013). These occupations have undergone significant changes, which commentators believe have led to increased stress and difficulties finding re-employment and, ultimately, for some people, suicide. Two other contributing factors in suicide rates are social isolation at work (Berkman et al., 2004) and the self-selection of people at higher risk of suicide to particular occupations, including creative occupations such as musician or artist. However, there is good evidence that suicide prevention schemes can help. Roberts et al. (2013) note that targeting these schemes towards at-risk occupational groups could make a valuable contribution to reducing suicide rates.

These studies demonstrate the value of the WHO's 'health promotion' approach and underscore the importance of work organisations taking a proactive and responsible view of employees' well-being. Suicide is an extreme example of how work-related problems can overwhelm people to the point of not feeling they are able to continue. But occupational stress affects many more people

---

 Case Study **Work-related suicide**

> *I am committing suicide because of my work at France Telecom. That's the only reason.*

This was the note left by a 52-year-old employee who committed suicide in July 2009. Bad enough on its own, it was unfortunately only one of 30 suicides at France Telecom in 2008 and 2009. Another man set himself on fire when he arrived at work and another stabbed himself in a meeting after he'd been told his job would be cut. The media attention surrounding these deaths called for explanations: why were so many employees being driven to such desperate measures?

Unions said it was because employees were under extreme pressure and suffered bullying by management, while also having to deal with the uncertainties of job cuts and restructuring. The HR director, on the other hand, claimed it was too simplistic to assume a relationship between work issues and staff suicides. In fact, the company has argued that the suicide rate of their employees (15.3 per 100,000) is not out of line with the national average (14.7 per 100,000).

The CEO at the time, Didier Lombard, insisted that the organisational restructuring, which involved tens of thousands of job cuts and transfers but no compulsory redundancies, was necessary for the organisation's survival. He rejected claims that his plans were the direct cause of the suicides.

Based on Chrisafis (2009) and Carnegy (2012)

▸ Can France Telecom be held accountable for these deaths or are they an unfortunate statistical artefact that has been latched onto by the media?

▸ Regardless of whether France Telecom is responsible for these deaths, what do you think of the way the issue was handled? Could the directors and CEO have dealt with it better?

than those who reach that point. We will now consider stress in more detail.

UNDERSTANDING STRESS AT WORK

In understanding how stress affects us at work, we need to know some basic things about how our bodies respond to stressors. In this section, we will consider both the physical and psychological responses we have to stress, highlighting the role of our thought processes in determining our response. We will also consider the impact of stress on performance, noting that not all stress is bad. At the end of this section we will bring these strands together by considering a simple model of stress that depicts the roles of work demands and our sense of control over our work.

Foundations of the stress response

The 'fight or flight' response was first described by a physiologist called Cannon (1929), and it is now widely known that when we are faced with a threat, our bodies gear up for action: heart rate and blood supply to the muscles increase, digestion slows down and pupils dilate. Unfortunately for us, this is our built-in response to any kind of threat, and our natural responses do not differentiate between physical, emotional or mental stressors. So while this is a very useful reaction to physical threats to our survival, it is also the reason that continuous stress of the kind we may experience at work can be so harmful. When the 'threats' are continuous, for example if we are continually faced with impossible deadlines or constantly monitored for the smallest mistake in our work, the stress response has no time to dissipate. Instead, our bodies are constantly on high alert, which leads to problems such as high blood pressure, heart disease or exhaustion.

Selye (1956) proposed the general adaptation syndrome (GAS) as a model for this continuous or chronic stress. The GAS has three stages, alarm, resistance and exhaustion, which we go through in an attempt to protect ourselves from harm. The first stage, alarm, is equivalent to the fight or flight response that Cannon outlined, with our bodies mobilising for action and stress hormones being secreted. In the second stage, if the demands or stressors continue, we remain at a higher level of arousal than normal, but try to adapt to (or as Selye said, *resist*) the stressors. Finally, we reach the point where we can no longer cope with the demands or stressors and exhaustion or collapse occurs. The immune response is lowered, and people feel burned out or even suffer heart attacks.

Stress and performance

Based solely on our understanding so far of how stress affects us, we might think that our work performance would be best in conditions where there is no stress at all. But, in fact, Selye also noted that not all stress is bad, and he distinguished between positive *eustress* and negative *distress*. He thought that our response to both types was the same (hence his *general* adaptation syndrome) and that what started out as eustress could become distress if it increased in intensity. This is reflected in a very famous psychological 'law', the Yerkes–Dodson law, which is discussed in more detail in the Fad or Fact section.

 Fad or Fact? **The Yerkes–Dodson law**

A scientific law is a causal relationship that always applies under the same conditions, and it becomes a fundamental principle of the science. Levitt (1967, p. 116) called it 'a statement of a basic relationship in nature', based on findings that are 'verified beyond question'. For example, Boyle's law in chemistry states that the pressure of a gas increases as the volume decreases.

There are very few 'laws' in psychology, partly because it is so difficult to ensure that the conditions in which we conduct experiments are exactly the same each time. However, one finding that has reached the status of law is the Yerkes–Dodson law. Nowadays it is often presented as an inverted U relationship between pressure or arousal on the one hand and performance on the other:

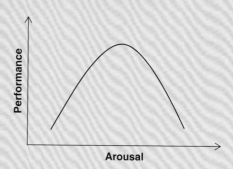

However, the original study (Yerkes and Dodson, 1908) reported something quite different. The experiment involved mice learning that they needed to go into a 'safe' white box rather than a black box which gave them an electric shock. The experimenters, Robert Yerkes and John Dobson, were interested in finding out what effect the strength of the stimulus (electric shock) had on the speed of learning. They found that when the task was easy, a higher shock led to faster learning. But when the task was more difficult (the white and black boxes were made more difficult to discriminate between), learning proceeded most rapidly with medium shocks. In this case, at lower and higher shock levels, the mice did not learn as quickly. This was the basis of the inverted U-curve, essentially a relationship between punishment and learning for more difficult tasks.

However, over time, the Yerkes–Dodson law instead began to be referred to as a relationship between motivation and performance, and then Hebb (1955) introduced an inverted U-curve to describe the relationship between arousal and performance. Although he did not refer to Yerkes–Dodson, authors following him did, and the 'law' came to be used over the next few decades to explain how a huge range of variables interacted. Teigen (1994) provides a summary of some of these:

Table 9.1 Some of the variables included in the Yerkes–Dodson law

Independent variables	Dependent variables
Stimulus strength Degree of punishment Emotionality Level of reward Anxiety Stress	Habit-forming Learning Performance (efficiency or quality) Problem-solving Coping Memory efficiency

Teigen shows how, over time in the psychological literature, almost any of these and other independent variables have been combined with any of the dependent variables and still referred to as the Yerkes–Dodson law. In addition, the majority of them do not include any reference to task difficulty, which is what Yerkes and Dodson were originally investigating.

▸ Given that a scientific law has to be specific about the conditions under which it occurs *and* based on repeated replications, do you think that the Yerkes–Dodson law is real?
▸ Why do you think this law has attained such a level of popularity in the psychological literature?

But recent work indicates that we have differentiated responses to distress and eustress (Nelson and Simmons, 2003). Simmons and Nelson have proposed a holistic stress model which attempts to integrate our understanding of these two types of stress. They suggest that demands or stressors in themselves are neutral and that it is our interpretation or appraisal of those demands that determines our response and the ultimate outcome (Simmons and Nelson, 2007). While a useful conceptualisation of the positive side of stress, the assumption that no stressor or demand can be inherently negative is rather limiting. But the central role given to how we evaluate stressors is important in other modern understandings of stress that we will consider later in this chapter, so we need to look at it in more detail now.

Cognitive appraisal

The centrality of our appraisal of stressors was highlighted by Richard Lazarus and Susan Folkman (1984). They pointed out that cognitive appraisal is a key step in determining how we respond to stressors. If we do not perceive something as a threat, for example, our stress response will simply not be activated. And if we think we have the resources we need to be able to cope with a potential stressor, we will not be as concerned as if we think we cannot meet the challenge. For example, imagine you have a deadline approaching for an essay, but you do not care about your mark on that particular module. You will not perceive that deadline as a stressor. Or let's say you do care about your mark but you have been working steadily on the essay for a couple of weeks and are confident you will actually complete it early. In that case too, your stress response is likely to be minimal. These examples show us that it is not the *deadline* which determines our stress levels, but our *cognitive appraisal* of it.

Cognitive appraisal is the process by which we determine whether a particular encounter or experience is relevant to our well-being (Folkman and Lazarus, 1988). It has two stages:

1 Primary appraisal – we evaluate whether we have anything important at stake, that is, whether there is any potential harm or benefit. This could be direct or indirect, including harm or benefit to our goals or commitments. Our evaluation includes not only ourselves but also others we are close to.
2 Secondary appraisal – assuming we have decided that the event is likely to cause harm or benefit, this stage is where we evaluate our coping options. What can we do to try and reduce the possibility of harm or increase the likelihood of the benefit? Coping options can include changing the situation, accepting it as it is, seeking out new information or changing our behaviour.

Our coping options have two major foci. They are either focused on regulating emotion or on resolving the problem. Research indicates that we are more likely to use problem-focused coping when we believe the situation or problem can be altered and emotion-focused when we see very few options for changing the outcome (Folkman et al., 1986).

 Psychological Toolkit A problem-solving approach to dealing with stress

As much as we might like to avoid it, stress is a normal part of our lives. This exercise will help you to learn better strategies for dealing with stress. Think of something that is causing you stress at the moment (for the purposes of this exercise, it doesn't have to be something big) and work through the following steps recommended by Cartwright and Cooper (1997).

Awareness – the first step is being aware of the problem and admitting it exists. Write down why you think there might be a problem: what signs or symptoms of stress do you have?

‣ This may seem obvious, but very often people prefer not to acknowledge that something is affecting them. Often we do not want to admit there is a problem because we feel it reflects badly on us or is a sign that we're incompetent. Perhaps we would like to believe that we can handle it, or we feel that it shouldn't be affecting us because other people have to deal with much more.

‣ Writing this down can also be useful in helping you recognise signs that you are starting to feel stressed, so that you can notice them earlier in future.

Identify the problem – the second step is being clear about what the problem is. Often when we are under pressure, it can feel as if 'everything' is difficult or that we have a generalised sense of anxiety or irritability. If we are going to address the problem, we need to be precise about what it is.

‣ Write down exactly what the problem is. Spend some time on this to analyse any underlying issues. For example, don't just write 'My boss is stressing me out', but write down exactly why you are having difficulties.

Develop an action plan – think about how you can deal with this stressor. Can you change the situation in any way to remove the stressor or reduce its impact on you? Can you develop some strategies for dealing with it?

‣ Sometimes there is nothing you can do to remove the stressor, and your only option is to develop a way to cope with it. This may involve acceptance, relaxation or meditation techniques, or strategies that help you cope with your response to the stressor.

‣ Write down some specific ideas of things you can do to deal with this problem.

Monitor and review the outcome – after you have carried out your action plan (or during if it is long term), evaluate how well you think it worked. What did you learn from this experience that you can apply to future stressful events? What could you do differently next time?

Demand-control-support model

The role of cognitive appraisal is highlighted in the demand-control-support (DCS) model of workplace stress which emerged from investigations into the link between people's work environment and their risk of cardiovascular disease (Johnson and Hall, 1988). The DCS was built on an earlier model (Karasek, 1979), which suggested that mental strain was the result of an interaction between the psychological demands in a job and 'job decision latitude' – that is, the amount of control a person has over how and when they do their work. The later DCS version added the important component of social support at work, looking at how interactions and breaks with co-workers could influence the strain people felt at work. Social support is an important buffer for psychological strain, with the highest levels of strain found for people in jobs with high demands, low control and low social support (Johnson and Hall, 1988).

The DCS is not without its criticisms, one of the main ones being that it does not take individual differences into account, assuming that the same level of demands, control and support will be ideal for everyone. However, with its basis in studies of large groups of people and its relating of aspects of work to physical outcomes such as cardiovascular disease, it certainly presented a strong basis for future efforts in understanding the impact of work on well-being.

MORE ADVANCED UNDERSTANDINGS OF STRESS AND WELL-BEING

Now that we have established the foundations for understanding stress in the workplace, we are going to consider stress and well-being from a more sophisticated point of view. Work engagement represents a high ideal for both individuals and organisations: people who are fully engaged in their work, gaining personal satisfaction as well as being highly productive. Burnout, on the other hand, is something that individuals and organisations both want to avoid. By exploring these two concepts in more detail, we can build up a model of workplace well-being that has a place for both the positive and negative outcomes of stress.

Burnout and work engagement

Human services professionals are people whose jobs require them to have intense involvement in others' problems and emotions, such as nurses, teachers and social workers. In their work with employees of this kind, Christina Maslach and Susan Jackson identified the phenomenon of burnout, which they described as emotional exhaustion, a cynical attitude towards clients, and dissatisfaction with oneself and one's work efforts (Maslach and Jackson, 1981). Their research showed that burnout was associated with poorer quality of care, higher turnover and absenteeism, and lower morale, as well as personal distress factors, such as insomnia and family problems. The authors suggested that people working in these areas were particularly susceptible to burnout because of the emotionally intense nature of their jobs.

Further research has found that burnout is not unique to those in the human services professions. In fact, this conceptualisation of burnout has been supported in studies across different occupational groups and countries, and includes three factors (Schutte et al., 2000):

- Exhaustion – feelings of being over-extended and drained
- Cynicism – indifference and a distant attitude to work
- Professional Efficacy – how effective the person feels in their job.

Burnout consists of high exhaustion and cynicism combined with low professional efficacy. People suffering from burnout have reached the point of exhaustion and can no longer cope with the demands of their work. Subsequent work in this area has indicated that exhaustion and cynicism represent the 'core' of burnout, while professional efficacy may be more strongly related to work engagement (Schaufeli et al., 2008).

While burnout results from the negative stress that Selye identified, eustress can result in work engagement, defined as a 'positive, fulfilling work-related state of mind' which characterises employees who are active, take initiative and seek out new challenges (Schaufeli et al., 2002). Two of the factors in engagement are polar opposites to the burnout factors. *Vigour* is the opposite of exhaustion, and describes someone with high levels of energy and resilience who invests effort in their work and persists when faced with difficulties. *Dedication* is the opposite of cynicism, and consists of a sense of the significance

of one's work and enthusiasm and pride in it. The final factor, *absorption*, however, is qualitatively different from low professional efficacy. Instead, it is characterised by being fully concentrated on work and happily engrossed in it, finding that time passes quickly and being unable to detach from the job. Overall, engagement is a persistent state of mind; it is not limited to a specific task or time but is overarching and pervasive.

Activity Engagement and fun

The concept of engagement is often equated with the idea of 'having fun' at work. In fact, many definitions of engagement include reference to the idea that engaged employees work hard because they enjoy it or because work is fun. This has led some people to suggest that a way of engaging employees is to introduce 'fun' activities into work.

▸ Have you ever experienced activities of this kind at work? Did you enjoy them? Do you think they helped engage you more?

▸ Do a quick internet search for 'fun workplace engagement activities' and read what some companies have done in their quest to engage their employees. What do you think of the ideas? Are there any you would really like or dislike? Why?

▸ Ask your friends and family and find out what they think. Are there individual differences in the effects these activities might have? Why do you think that is?

You might be thinking that 'engagement' sounds very similar to being a workaholic. In fact, one of the main differences between the two is the relative importance given to non-work life. While workaholics focus all their energies on work to the exclusion of family, friends and the rest of life, engaged employees are engaged in all of life. If we consider the model of well-being as a holistic concept drawing on work, social life, finances, community and physical health (Rath and Harter, 2010), we can see why. In times of stress, workaholics will have much more limited resources to draw on than engaged workers, and they will not be investing any energy in other aspects of their lives that are important in positive well-being.

While workaholism is a different concept from engagement and burnout, they are all related aspects of employee well-being (Schaufeli et al., 2008). Burnout is negatively correlated with engagement but positively with workaholism, while engagement and workaholism are uncorrelated. The following table summarises the relationships between these three concepts and some important work outcomes or characteristics:

Table 9.2 Comparison of burnout, engagement and workaholism

	Burnout	Engagement	Workaholism
Overtime		+	+
Quality of social relations	−	+	−
Health	−	+	−
Job characteristics	+ job demands	+ job resources	+ job demands
Work attitudes	−	+	+ organisation commitment − job satisfaction

Note: + indicates a positive relationship and − indicates a negative relationship

This and other studies indicate that workaholism may be a root cause of burnout, with workaholics using up their resources until they can no longer continue. Job resources seem to be particularly important for engagement (Le Blanc et al., 2008), and we move on to consider this model in more detail now.

Job demands-resources model

A more recent, and very promising, model of stress and well-being at work takes a broader view of demands and control than the DCS and also draws in findings around burnout and engagement. The job demands-resources model (JDR) was first put forward by Evangelina Demerouti and colleagues (2001) and has since gathered substantial research support. It captures both the positive and negative aspects of stress and shows how they are related to job demands (such as workload and pressure) and job resources (such as feedback and participation). Job demands are those things that are challenging to us at work, while resources are those things we can draw on to help deal with challenges. Note that resources can encapsulate both the social support and the job control factors of the DCS model. The model proposes two processes:

- Health impairment – high job demands deplete our energy and lead to burnout
- Motivational – high job resources enhance our motivation and increase engagement.

In addition, the JDR model states that these processes do not simply add together but interact, so that high demands combined with low resources lead to much more exhaustion than we would expect from the main effects. There is also a place for our 'personal resources' in mitigating the negative effects of job demands and enhancing the effects of job resources. Personal resources

include individual differences in our levels of resilience and sense of control we have over our environment. Finally, the model also shows how having plentiful resources can buffer the effects of high job demands. The model is summarised below:

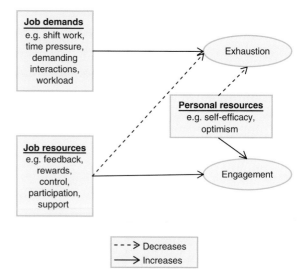

Figure 9.1 The job demands-resources model
Source: adapted from Bakker and Demerouti (2007) and Xanthopoulou et al. (2007).

The JDR model provides a holistic way of viewing stress in organisations. It recognises that demands and resources will vary across different occupations and industries but shows how the specifics of different situations can still be brought together in a coherent explanation of how stress results in personal and organisational outcomes.

 Activity The JDR model

In your work as a student, have you ever felt exhausted or really engaged with your work? According to the JDR model, these experiences are the result of the relative demands and resources you had at the time. Being aware of what they are can help you to build your resources, so that you can avoid exhaustion and even build your engagement in your work.

▶ What kind of demands does your work at university place on you? These demands can be physical, emotional, mental, social or organisational (i.e. demands from the university itself). Write a list of them.

▶ What resources do you draw on in your work? Make sure you take into account the external resources, such as personal tutor support or

feedback on your performance, as well as your own personal resources, such as how resilient you are.
▸ When you compare your two lists, does it help to explain your current feelings of exhaustion or engagement? What can you do to increase the resources available to you?

An organisational approach to stress

So far, we have looked at stress from an individual point of view, answering questions about the things that stress us, how we respond to them and what the work outcomes are. An alternative approach is to view stress as an organisational issue, and this is particularly useful if we are trying to find strategies for reducing employee stress. A model proposed by Palmer et al. (2004) shows how potential stress hazards at work are related to symptoms of stress and negative outcomes. It also calculates the financial costs of stress, which can, unfortunately, sometimes be the only way to get organisations to take this issue seriously. The basic model is shown in Figure 9.2 and a detailed description of its elements follows.

Potential hazards

There are six main hazards with the potential to increase workers' stress, and all of them can be influenced by the organisation's culture.

- Demands – workload, work patterns (e.g. shifts) and work environment
- Control – how much control we have over the way we do our work, and how much involvement we have in key decisions about it
- Support – this includes the resources available to us to do the job, as well as encouragement we might receive from management and co-workers
- Relationships – the extent to which there is conflict, bullying or harassment
- Role – whether there is ambiguity or conflict in the person's role
- Change – how well change is managed.

In a risk assessment for workplace stress, an organisation should address these factors to determine if any or all of them represent significant hazards to the employees.

Symptoms of stress

This model divides stress symptoms into two areas, individual and organisational, and then describes negative outcomes and financial costs for each area. Individual symptoms of stress include raised blood pressure, sleep and gastrointestinal disturbances, increased alcohol, caffeine or nicotine consumption, increased irritability and negative emotions, back pain, tension, palpitations and headaches.

Organisational symptoms occur when the individual impact of stress is combined across the whole group and include increased sickness absence, long hours culture, increased turnover, reduced staff performance, reduced staff morale and loyalty, and increased hostility. Identifying these symptoms can help the organisation decide whether there might be a large-scale problem with stress levels.

Negative outcomes

The negative outcomes for individuals are both physical (coronary heart disease and repetitive strain injury) and psychological (depression and anxiety, burnout). For organisations, the negative outcomes include increased overheads (recruiting and training), reduced profits, increased accidents and increased litigation.

The final cost

For many organisations, it is the 'bottom line' that counts, and this model is particularly valuable in putting figures to the costs of stress. In 1995–6, the individual symptoms and outcomes cost £3.75 billion in the UK and the organisational costs were £370 million (Palmer et al., 2004). More recent figures estimate an overall cost to the UK of £7 billion, including sick pay, lost production and healthcare costs (HSE, 2013), and the European Commission estimated that stress cost the EU €20 billion in 2002 (EU-OSHA, 2013).

The Health and Safety Executive in the UK recommends that while organisations should invest in training employees in how to deal with stress, their main efforts should be directed towards reducing the hazards (HSE, 2004). This is a proactive approach in line with an overall emphasis on well-being rather than a reactive attempt to simply reduce the symptoms of stress.

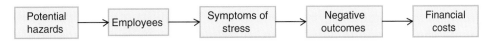

Figure 9.2   An organisational model of stress

APPROACHES TO PROMOTING WELL-BEING

Interventions to manage stress and promote well-being at work can be divided into three broad groups, depending on where in the stress process they aim to take effect (Quick et al., 1997). Primary interventions try to change the *sources of stress*, for example by redesigning jobs or encouraging participative management. Secondary interventions focus on trying to help people *modify their responses* to those stressors which cannot be avoided or reduced, reducing the severity of stress symptoms and hoping to stop their progress into health problems. Tertiary interventions involve *treating the health problem*, and can include providing counselling to employees.

In addition to those three levels of intervention, a more rounded view would also include an *identification* level and give consideration to *rehabilitation* (Le Blanc et al., 2008). Identification focuses on early detection of possible stressors and reactions to stress, while rehabilitation helps those who have had severe health problems due to stress plan their return to work.

Evidence indicates that most organisational interventions are aimed at the secondary level – helping employees to manage their stress and training them in better coping strategies (Giga et al., 2003). A recent meta-analysis of stress intervention studies has demonstrated a medium to large effect size in reducing the negative effects of stress (Richardson and Rothstein, 2008), though again, most of these interventions were aimed at the secondary level. The study used the following five categories for the interventions and investigated their relative effect sizes:

- Cognitive-behavioural – this kind of approach helps employees learn about the role of their thoughts and emotions in appraising stressful events and how to modify their thoughts and feelings in order to cope better. Examples include assertiveness training, hardiness training and collaborative problem-solving approaches, as well as cognitive-behavioural therapy in general.
- Relaxation – this can include meditation or deep breathing exercises and the aim is to help employees to change their physiological state. We saw at the beginning of this chapter what the physical response to stress was, and these kinds of approach increase people's ability to feel relaxed in the face of pressure, rather than allowing the stress response to build up.
- Organisational – these interventions are focused around management techniques or job redesign to reduce the stressors themselves or the impact on employees. Examples include introducing an 'innovation promotion' programme which involved participatory action and goal-setting, or a social support group to enhance coping abilities.
- Multimodal – many 'real life' interventions actually draw on more than one of the categories above. For example, they may combine CBT with relaxation techniques and time management training.
- Alternative or other – this category was for interventions which did not fit into the other groups because they were new or unique. As an example, providing employees with electromyographic biofeedback (feedback on the tension in their muscles or hand temperature) enables them to become more aware of how their bodies are responding to different events.

The meta-analysis found that cognitive-behavioural techniques were most effective out of these five groups, though it should be noted that the number of organisational interventions was very low and the majority of outcome measures were psychological rather than physiological or organisational. We will now consider some examples of organisational and individual interventions in more detail.

Stress and well-being interventions

When it comes to the sort of interventions that organisations generally invest in, those that are focused on the individual are by far the most favoured. Perhaps this is because it is well known that each of us can cope with a different level of stress and reacts in different ways to the same potential stressors. So instead of removing stressors, many organisations have an assumption that the 'problem' in stress and well-being lies in the individual, and when attempts are made to counteract the effects of stress, they are focused on helping employees adapt to the organisational demands (Cartwright and Cooper, 1997). Many employees fall into this trap too, and believe that there is no way the organisation will change so they just have to adapt to fit in. Hopefully, from our discussion of the different models of stress and well-being, you will recognise that this is only one side of the story and that there is much that can be done to reduce the stressors themselves. But even in the most well organisations there will still be potential stressors, and it is important to be aware of what can be done to help people deal with them effectively.

Employee assistance programmes (EAPs)

EAPs began in the USA as a way of dealing with alcoholism among employees, and then expanded to provide assistance to employees dealing with a variety of mental health issues. In 1996, a third of all US companies reported having an EAP (Hartwell et al., 1996) and it is estimated that approximately 8 million UK employees now have access to EAPs, though they are less popular in the rest of Europe (Arthur, 2000).

An EAP can take a variety of forms. Rather than being a specific type of intervention, it is an umbrella term for a whole raft of assistance programmes and well-being initiatives that an organisation can introduce. From an organisational perspective, an EAP is seen as a way of improving productivity and attendance by providing support and assistance to employees on a reasonably individualised basis. Many EAPs are subcontracted to professional companies specialising in providing a range of services, including (EAPA UK, 2013):

- For employees:
  - Short-term psychological services, such as counselling
  - Information and advice, for example money advice and debt management, legal guidance, child and eldercare information, and information on emotional, work life and workplace issues.
- For the organisation itself, EAPs provide:
  - a means for management to refer staff who need support
  - anonymised reports on utilisation – how many staff have accessed different types of support or advice.

An important component of EAPs is that they promise confidentiality. Individualised information about employees is not fed back to the organisation. This means that many people feel more comfortable about contacting an external EAP than they would about discussing an issue affecting their work with their manager or someone within the organisation. EAPs also take a holistic approach to stress, recognising that stressors in our personal life

---

Case Study **EAP**

Heather has been in her job as a digital marketing assistant for three years now. When she first joined the company she loved her job and found the work so engaging that she happily worked many hours of overtime every week. Recently, however, she has started feeling very tired and has trouble concentrating. She finds that at the weekends she has no energy to go out with her friends, and it has been several weeks since she had more than a five-minute phone conversation with her sister, whom she used to talk to regularly.

Heather's manager, John, has noticed a drop in her work quality, and also that in the last couple of months she has taken a few days off sick for the first time since she started at the company. He decides to speak to her about it and arranges a meeting. Heather seems quite upset when he raises the performance issues, and explains that she has been distracted because she was having trouble with her landlord, who is refusing to do some basic repairs to her flat. But she doesn't mention that she is also worried about her father who has been diagnosed with cancer, because she feels uncomfortable talking about that with her boss and is worried she might start to cry. John can tell something else is going on, but feels a bit out of his depth and isn't sure what to do, so he suggests that she contact the company's EAP.

Although reluctant, Heather calls the EAP number she has been given. After an initial conversation in which she describes what is happening, she is reassured that the EAP can help, and is soon called back by a legal expert who provides assistance in how to deal with her landlord, taking her through the process she will need to follow and discussing her options. Second, she is contacted by a counsellor whose practice is convenient for her to get to after work, and they arrange for her to have weekly counselling sessions for six weeks.

As the weeks go by, Heather is able to resolve the problem with the landlord, and finds the counselling helpful in dealing with her concerns and worries about her father. John also notices that her work has started to improve, and is relieved that he does not have to take the performance issues any further.

▸ Have you had any experience of an EAP? How does it compare with this case study?

▸ Is there anything further that John could have done, or should do in the future, as Heather's manager?

▸ Why do you think EAPs have become so popular?

▸ Do you think EAPs represent a good investment for organisations or not? What organisational outcomes do you think they might impact?

often have an impact on our work, and offering support for employee needs to cover all the areas that people might struggle with.

People who use EAP services report a reduction in their symptoms and satisfaction with and appreciation for the service (Arthur, 2000), although there is limited evidence that significant organisational-level improvements are made. This may well be because EAPs provide secondary or tertiary interventions at best, helping employees to deal with stress rather than enhancing their positive well-being.

Physical activity

The general health benefits of exercise are well known, but there is also good evidence that physical activity can promote mental health and help people to deal with stress (e.g. Hamer et al., 2006). The Key Research Study below gives details of one very large-scale study into the effect of exercise on depression and anxiety.

 Key Research Study Physical exercise and well-being

Physical Activity and Common Mental Disorders
Samuel Harvey, Matthew Hotopf, Simon Øverland and Arnstein Mykletun (2010)

Background: It is well established that people who are more physically active have lower levels of common mental disorders such as depression and anxiety. But most of the studies in this area have only considered intense activity, such as organised sports, running or fitness classes. Lighter types of activity or workplace physical activity have shown mixed results.

Aim: This study had three aims. First, to find out whether symptoms of depression and anxiety reduced with an increase in physical activity. Second, whether this relationship was stronger as intensity of exercise increased. Third, whether workplace physical activity showed the same relationship.

Method: As part of a health study in a Norwegian county, over 40,000 people completed the following questionnaires:

▸ Levels and intensity of physical activity, both in leisure time and as part of the job
▸ The Hospital Anxiety and Depression Scale
▸ Level of social support (e.g. how many friends do you have?)
▸ Demographic factors, including education level, smoking habits, physical disability or illness

In addition, physical measurements such as BMI, blood samples, heart rate and blood pressure were taken.

Findings: Those who did more hours of leisure-time exercise a week had lower levels of depression. Intensity of the activity did not make a difference, and workplace activity (such as heavy lifting or walking a lot) was also unrelated to mental health symptoms. There was a small effect of light, regular leisure activity on anxiety but otherwise no relationships were found. The social benefits of exercise seemed to be more important in explaining the relationship than physical benefits.

Implications: Engaging in exercise is a good way to reduce the symptoms of depression, but it is important that this occurs in leisure time, not at work. Light exercise may also help allay anxiety.

Many organisations promote well-being at the individual level by encouraging employees to be more physically active. They may negotiate reduced-cost gym membership for their employees, have company sports teams or even invest in an on-site fitness centre.

Hardiness

In the late 1970s a psychologist called Suzanne Kobasa studied how executives coped with stressful life events. She found that, although their levels of stress were similar, some of the executives suffered significant ill health while others remained healthy. Those who remained healthy were characterised as having higher levels of hardiness (Kobasa, 1979). With her colleague Salvatore Maddi (Maddi and Kobasa, 1984), Kobasa went on to define this concept of hardiness in more detail as consisting of three attitudes or orientations towards the stressful events:

1 Commitment – believing that a meaningful purpose can be found in life and staying involved in events rather than becoming isolated
2 Control – the determination to try and influence events rather than giving up and feeling powerless
3 Challenge – seeing change as a positive challenge rather than a threat and a stressful situation as an opportunity to learn.

There is good evidence that people who are more hardy are less susceptible to the negative outcomes of stress (Beasley et al., 2003). This concept of hardiness shows similarities with several other psychological concepts (such as locus of control) and fits in with the models of stress we have looked at, being particularly useful in clarifying how individuals appraise and deal with stressful events. Hardiness is also closely related to resilience, which is our ability to maintain a stable equilibrium in the face of stressful events (Bonanno et al., 2001). A resilient response to stress is illustrated in Figure 9.3, by comparing it to three other types of responses:

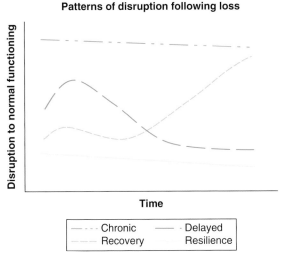

Patterns of disruption following loss

Figure 9.3 Patterns of disruption following loss
Source: adapted from Bonanno (2004). Published by the American Psychological Association, adapted with permission.

Bonanno (2004) suggests that hardiness is one of the 'paths to resilience', or one of the ways that people naturally deal successfully with stressful events. He also points out that resilience is far more common than we might think if we look at the literature around stress and coping, because most studies have focused on when things go wrong. Many employers and consultancies offer resilience training, and the following activity will help you explore your own resilience and how you can develop it.

Activity Resilience

Robertson Cooper is a company founded by two occupational psychologists who specialise in well-being at work (Ivan Robertson and Cary Cooper). On their website (http://www. robertsoncooper.com/iresilience) you can complete a questionnaire and receive a free report on your resilience. Do this, and work through the activities at the end of the questionnaire to find out more about what supports and hinders your resilience to stress.

▸ Normally, occupational psychologists charge for the use of their questionnaires and feedback reports. Why do you think that this questionnaire and its report have been made freely available?
▸ How could you use this resource as a manager?

The wider picture

An important aspect of the studies of hardiness and resilience, as well as the models of stress we have looked at, is the central place they give to social support. We saw at the beginning of this chapter how important social connection was to our sense of well-being, and this has been confirmed in meta-analyses of how people cope with and recover from stress and traumatic events (Ozer et al., 2003). In fact, social connection is one of the five actions that the New Economics Foundation recommends to enhance well-being (Cordon et al., 2008):

Connect	Build relationships with the people around you, at work, home and the community. These relationships will be a source of support for you when you face difficult times.
Be active	Exercise improves mood and helps us to cope with the physical responses to stress.
Take notice	Be aware of the world around you and take time to appreciate beauty and reflect on your experiences.
Keep learning	Learning helps us to feel good about ourselves and our achievements and improves our sense of competency.
Give	We get a sense of reward when we help others, but it also builds reciprocity and trust in the community.

The important thing to remember about well-being is that it is larger than an individual: no one can experience a good life or cope with stress successfully if they are in isolation. Organisational efforts to reduce the impact of stress or enhance well-being will never succeed if they simply try to reduce an individual's negative response to stress.

SUMMARY

Understanding how stress affects us shows us how our natural physical reactions to threats and changes in our environment can be less than adaptive to the modern workplace. Models of stress and well-being tend to focus on the balance between the demands placed on us at work and the resources we feel we have that can help us to meet those demands. Essentially, we feel stressed when the demands outweigh the resources.

We have looked at various interventions and approaches to managing stress and promoting well-being. It is important to recognise that for many people work is an essential part of their overall well-being. The advantage of considering stress as part of a more holistic well-being model is that we can work towards a truly engaging workplace and put employee health at the forefront of our interventions, rather than taking a reactive, symptom-treating approach to managing stress. The benefits for organisations are a more engaged and productive workforce, and for individuals more rewarding work and an integration of work with the other factors that promote well-being. In finding ways to deal with stress and promote our well-being, the evidence indicates that we should concentrate on developing our personal resources (such as resilience), engage in life rather than isolate ourselves and build relationships with those around us.

TEST YOURSELF

Brief Review Questions

1 What is the General Adaptation Syndrome?
2 What is the role of cognitive appraisal in the stress response?
3 What is the difference between burnout and engagement?
4 List six potential hazards at work.
5 What is hardiness and how does it relate to stress management?

Discussion or Essay Questions

1 Compare and contrast the disease prevention and health promotion model for understanding stress at work. Which do you think is most effective?
2 Critically evaluate the job demands-resources model of stress for the management of stress at work.
3 Explain the different approaches organisations can take to help employees manage the stresses of work and enhance their well-being.
4 Why do you think social support and connection are so important for well-being at work?

FURTHER READING

- The *Five Ways to Well-being* report produced by the New Economics Foundation provides an easy-to-read summary of the main evidence behind their recommendations. It is available on their website: www. neweconomics.org.
- More detail on the role of our personal resources (such as self-efficacy) in dealing with stress can be found in a paper by Despoina Xanthopoulou and colleagues: D. Xanthopoulou, A. B. Bakker, E. Demerouti & W. B. Schaufeli. The role of personal resources in the job demands-resources model. *International Journal of Stress Management*, 14 (2007), 121.

References

AMAGASA, T., NAKAYAMA, T. & TAKAHASHI, Y. 2005. Karojisatsu in Japan: characteristics of 22 cases of work-related suicide. *Journal of Occupational Health*, 47, 157–64.

ARTHUR, A. R. 2000. Employee assistance programmes: the emperor's new clothes of stress management? *British Journal of Guidance and Counselling*, 28, 549–59.

BAKKER, A. B. & DEMEROUTI, E. 2007. The job demands-resources model: state of the art. *Journal of Managerial Psychology*, 22, 309–28.

BEASLEY, M., THOMPSON, T. & DAVIDSON, J. 2003. Resilience in response to life stress: the effects of coping style and cognitive hardiness. *Personality and Individual Differences*, 34, 77–95.

BERKMAN, L. F., MELCHIOR, M., CHASTANG, J.-F., NIEDHAMMER, I., LECLERC, A. & GOLDBERG, M. 2004. Social integration and mortality: a prospective study of French employees of electricity of France – gas of France: the GAZEL cohort. *American Journal of Epidemiology*, 159, 167–74.

BONANNO, G. A. 2004. Loss, trauma, and human resilience: have we underestimated the human capacity to thrive after extremely aversive events? *American Psychologist*, 59, 20–8.

BONANNO, G. A., PAPA, A. & O'NEILL, K. 2001. Loss and human resilience. *Applied and Preventive Psychology*, 10, 193–206.

BUFFETT, M.-A., GERVAISE, R., LIDDLE, M. & EEKELAERT, L. 2013. *Well-being at Work: Creating a Positive Work Environment*. Luxembourg, European Agency for Health and Safety at Work.

CANNON, W. B. 1929. *Bodily Changes in Pain, Hunger, Fear and Rage*. London, Appleton.

CARNEGY, H. 2012. France Telecom faces staff suicides probe. *Financial Times*, 6 July.

CARTWRIGHT, S. & COOPER, C. L. 1997. *Managing Workplace Stress*. London, Sage.

CHARLTON, J. 1995. Trends and patterns in suicide in England and Wales. *International Journal of Epidemiology*, 24, S45–52.

CHRISAFIS, A. 2009. Wave of staff suicides at France Telecom. *The Guardian*, 9 September.

CLARK, A. E., DIENER, E., GEORGELLIS, Y. & LUCAS, R. E. 2008. Lags and leads in life satisfaction: a test of the baseline hypothesis. *The Economic Journal*, 118, F222–43.

COOPER, C. L. & PAYNE, R. 1988. *Causes, Coping, and Consequences of Stress at Work*. Chichester, Wiley.

CORDON, C., MARKS, N., AKED, J. & THOMPSON, S. 2008. *Five Ways to Well-being*. London: New Economics Foundation.

DEMEROUTI, E., BAKKER, A. B., NACHREINER, F. & SCHAUFELI, W. B. 2001. The job demands-resources model of burnout. *Journal of Applied Psychology*, 86, 499.

EAPA UK. 2013. *What is an EAP?* Employee Assistance Professionals Association. http://www.eapa.org.uk/page–what-is-an-eap.html (accessed 23 August 2013).

ENGEL, G. L. 1977. The need for a new medical model: a challenge for biomedicine. *Science*, 196, 129–36.

EU-OSHA (EUROPEAN AGENCY FOR SAFETY AND HEALTH AT WORK). 2013. *Stress*. Brussels: European Agency for Safety and Health at Work. https://osha.europa.eu/en/topics/stress/index_html (accessed 26 August 2013).

FOLKMAN, S. & LAZARUS, R. S. 1988. The relationship between coping and emotion: implications for theory and research. *Social Science & Medicine*, 26, 309–17.

FOLKMAN, S., LAZARUS, R. S., DUNKEL-SCHETTER, C., DELONGIS, A. & GRUEN, R. J. 1986. Dynamics of a stressful encounter: cognitive appraisal, coping, and encounter outcomes. *Journal of Personality and Social Psychology*, 50, 992–1003.

GIGA, S. I., COOPER, C. L. & FARAGHER, B. 2003. The development of a framework for a comprehensive approach to stress management interventions at work. *International Journal of Stress Management*, 10, 280–96.

HAMER, M., TAYLOR, A. & STEPTOE, A. 2006. The effect of acute aerobic exercise on stress related blood pressure responses: a systematic review and meta-analysis. *Biological Psychology*, 71, 183–90.

HARTWELL, T. D., STEELE, P., FRENCH, M. T., POTTER, F. J., RODMAN, N. F. & ZARKIN, G. A. 1996. Aiding troubled employees: the prevalence, cost, and characteristics of employee assistance programs in the United States. *American Journal of Public Health*, 86, 804–8.

HARVEY, S. B., HOTOPF, M., ØVERLAND, S. & MYKLETUN, A. 2010. Physical activity and common mental disorders. *The British Journal of Psychiatry*, 197, 357–64.

HEBB, D. O. 1955. Drives and the CNS (conceptual nervous system). *Psychological Review*, 62, 243–54.

HSE (HEALTH AND SAFETY EXECUTIVE). 2004. *Real Solutions, Real People: A Managers' Guide to Tackling Work-related Stress*. Sudbury, Health and Safety Executive.

HSE (HEATLH AND SAFETY EXECUTIVE). 2013. *Stress-related and Psychological Disorders in Great Britain*. http://www.hse.gov.uk/statistics/causdis/stress/ (accessed 24 August 2014).

INOUE, K. & MATSUMOTO, M. 2000. Karo jisatsu (suicide from overwork): a spreading occupational threat. *Occupational and Environmental Medicine*, 57, 284–5.

JOHNSON, J. V. & HALL, E. M. 1988. Job strain, work place social support, and cardiovascular disease: a cross-sectional study of a random sample of the Swedish working population. *American Journal of Public Health*, 78, 1336–42.

KARASEK, R. A. 1979. Job demands, job decision latitude, and mental strain: implications for job redesign. *Administrative Science Quarterly*, 24 (2). 285–308.

KOBASA, S. C. 1979. Stressful life events, personality, and health: an inquiry into hardiness. *Journal of Personality and Social Psychology*, 37, 1–11.

LAZARUS, R. S. & FOLKMAN, S. 1984. *Stress, Appraisal, and Coping*. New York, Springer.

LE BLANC, P., DE JONGE, J. & SCHAUFELI, W. B. 2008. Job Stress and Occupational Health. In Chmiel, N. (ed.) *An Introduction to Work and Organizational Psychology: A European Perspective*. Oxford, Blackwell.

LEVITT, E. E. 1967. *The Psychology of Anxiety*. New York, Bobbs-Merrill.

MADDI, S. R. & KOBASA, S. C. 1984. *The Hardy Executive: Health Under Stress*. Homewood IL, Dow Jones-Irwin.

MASLACH, C. & JACKSON, S. E. 1981. The measurement of experienced burnout. *Journal of Occupational Behaviour*, 2, 99–113.

NELSON, D. L. & SIMMONS, B. L. 2003. Eustress: an elusive construct, an engaging pursuit. *Research in Occupational Stress and Well-being*, 3, 265–322.

OZER, E. J., BEST, S. R., LIPSEY, T. L. & WEISS, D. S. 2003. Predictors of posttraumatic stress disorder and symptoms in adults: a meta-analysis. *Psychological Bulletin*, 129, 52–73.

PALMER, S., COOPER, C. & THOMAS, K. 2004. A model of work stress. *Counselling at Work*, 11, 1–4.

QUICK, J. C., QUICK, J. D., NELSON, D. L. & HURRELL JR, J. J. 1997. *Preventive Stress Management in Organizations*. Washington, DC, American Psychological Association.

RATH, T. & HARTER, J. 2010. *Wellbeing: The Five Essential Elements*. New York, Gallup Press.

RICHARDSON, K. M. & ROTHSTEIN, H. R. 2008. Effects of occupational stress management intervention programs: a meta-analysis. *Journal of Occupational Health Psychology*, 13, 69–93.

ROBERTS, S. E., JAREMIN, B. & LLOYD, K. 2013. High-risk occupations for suicide. *Psychological Medicine*, 43, 1–10.

SCHAUFELI, W. B., SALANOVA, M., GONZÁLEZ-ROMÁ, V. & BAKKER, A. B. 2002. The measurement of engagement and burnout: a two sample confirmatory factor analytic approach. *Journal of Happiness Studies*, 3, 71–92.

SCHAUFELI, W. B., TARIS, T. W. & VAN RHENEN, W. 2008. Workaholism, burnout, and work engagement: three of a kind or three different kinds of employee well-being? *Applied Psychology*, 57, 173–203.

SCHULTE, P. & VAINIO, H. 2010. Well-being at work: overview and perspective. *Scandinavian Journal of Work, Environment & Health*, 36 (5), 422–9.

SCHUTTE, N., TOPPINEN, S., KALIMO, R. & SCHAUFELI, W. 2000. The factorial validity of the Maslach Burnout Inventory-General Survey (MBI-GS) across occupational groups and nations. *Journal of Occupational & Organizational Psychology*, 73, 53–66.

SELYE, H. 1956. *The Stress of Life*. New York, McGraw-Hill.

SIMMONS, B. L. & NELSON, D. L. 2007. Eustress at Work: Extending the Holistic Stress Model. In Nelson, D. L. & Cooper, C. (eds.) *Positive Organizational Behavior*. London, Sage.

SOUSA-POZA, A. & SOUSA-POZA, A. A. 2000. Well-being at work: a cross-national analysis of the levels and determinants of job satisfaction. *Journal of Socio-economics*, 29, 517–38.

TEIGEN, K. H. 1994. Yerkes–Dodson: A law for all seasons. *Theory & Psychology*, 4, 525–47.

WAINWRIGHT, D. & CALNAN, M. 2000. Rethinking the work stress epidemic. *European Journal of Public Health*, 10, 231–2.

WHO (WORLD HEALTH ORGANISATION). 2005. The Bangkok Charter for Health Promotion in a Globalized World. *6th Global Conference on Health Promotion*. Bangkok, Thailand, WHO.

XANTHOPOULOU, D., BAKKER, A. B., DEMEROUTI, E. & SCHAUFELI, W. B. 2007. The role of personal resources in the job demands-resources model. *International Journal of Stress Management*, 14, 121.

YERKES, R. M. & DODSON, J. D. 1908. The relation of strength of stimulus to rapidity of habit-formation. *Journal of Comparative Neurology and Psychology*, 18, 459–82.

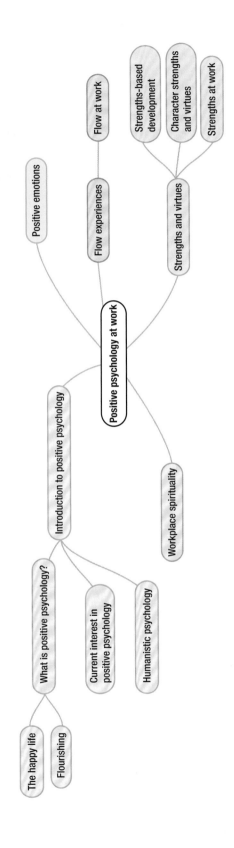

Can work be about more than just 'doing a job'? And what is the place of work in our overall lives? We saw in Chapter 9 that work can have a large impact on our well-being, and in this chapter we are going to explore this topic in more detail by looking at the growth of positive psychology in understanding people at work. We start with a discussion of the positive psychology approach and its focus on developing the best qualities in life rather than trying to 'fix damage'.

We then consider three important parts of positive psychology as applied to work. First, we discuss the role of positive emotions in building our personal resources. Second, we take a detailed look at strength and virtue in the workplace and how this approach is related to development and productivity. This is followed by a discussion of flow experiences at work, defining the experience and exploring the benefits for both workers and the organisation.

Finally, the discussion moves on to workplace spirituality, considering the concepts of inner meaning and purpose, community and social connection, and the extent to which it might be possible or desirable to meet these needs at work.

This chapter will help you answer the following questions:

1 What is positive psychology all about? How does it claim to be different from 'mainstream' psychology?
2 Why are positive emotions important at work?
3 What benefits can be gained from understanding human strength and virtue?
4 Why might flow experiences be valuable in the workplace?
5 Can a workplace provide 'spiritual' meaning?

POSITIVE PSYCHOLOGY: AN INTRODUCTION

In Chapter 9, we looked at the difference between the 'disease' and the 'well-being' model of health in the study of stress at work. We saw that the traditional medical model, which was dominant in psychology for many decades, had its focus on treating or preventing disease. In this approach, psychology seeks ways to treat mental illness or prevent stress and its effects. Positive psychology, on the other hand, takes as its focus the positive qualities of people, how we develop and grow, and how we can live fulfilled lives.

In this section, we will go through the areas that are covered by positive psychology and explore how it is distinguished from other areas of psychology. We will also look at its history and evaluate whether it really is a distinct area of psychology, a 'new science' as some of its proponents claim, or simply an umbrella term for concepts that have been important to psychologists all along.

What is positive psychology?

It may come as a surprise to you that some people define positive psychology as 'simply psychology' (Sheldon and King, 2001). According to this argument, just as other sciences study the typical and normal functioning of their fields, so psychology should take as its subject how the majority of people manage to live their lives perfectly well. Positive psychology has been described as 'the study of ordinary human strengths and virtues' (Sheldon and King, 2001, p. 216) and 'what makes life worth living' (Lyubormirsky, quoted in Jarden, 2012).

The traditional view of psychology was that positive mental health and functioning can be achieved if we understand and take away the 'bad'. In other words, if we understand and take away mental health problems, biases and prejudices, negative emotions and so on, we will help people to live happy and fulfilled lives. Positive psychology points out that there is more to a fulfilled life than merely the absence of the bad. If we are to really help people live and work positively, we need to understand the good – that is, resilience, coping, positive emotions, strengths and virtues.

In their seminal article promoting positive psychology to the American Psychological Assocation, Seligman and Csikszentmihalyi (2000) summarised its main aims as:

- To help normal people become stronger and more productive
- To make high human potential actual.

They also discussed how the field was concerned with the subjective experiences that we value in the past, present and future, illustrated in the following diagram.

| PAST
well-being, contentment
and satisfaction | PRESENT
flow and
happiness | FUTURE
hope and
optimism |

Like work psychology, positive psychology is concerned with both individual- and group-level concepts. At the individual level, traits such as the capacity for love and vocation, courage, interpersonal skill, perseverance, originality, future mindedness, spirituality, high talent and wisdom are important. At the group level, virtues that help individuals develop into better citizens are studied, including responsibility nurturance, altruism, civility, moderation, tolerance and work ethic. This is, of course, not an exhaustive list of what positive psychology covers. In a series of interviews with prominent positive psychologists, Aaron Jarden (2012) asked what they thought were some of the distinctive features of the field. Their answers included a wide range of different topics, such as positive emotions, strengths of character, elements of relationships that help us to flourish, happiness, well-being, meaning in life, authenticity, resilience, personal growth, honesty and optimal functioning.

While there are certain topics that are seen as central to positive psychology, it is really more of a perspective that people take when exploring psychological issues. Instead of the typical 'negative' stance, researchers ask positively oriented questions. For example, instead of asking 'What makes people leave an organisation?' they might ask 'Why do people stay with organisations?' Instead of 'What things cause dissatisfaction with management?' they would ask 'What makes people satisfied with their managers?'

Activity A positive psychology stance

For each of the following possible research questions, write down an equivalent topic that a positive psychologist might be interested in.

Traditional research question	Positive psychology perspective
What effect does increased stress have on sickness absence?	
What are the predictors of turnover?	
How can burnout be prevented?	
What extra costs are involved in having an older workforce?	
What is the impact of bullying at work?	
How does work–life conflict impact on productivity?	

▸ How do you think changing these research questions like this would affect work psychology?

You can probably already see why positive psychology is of interest to work psychologists. In fact, several core areas of research in work psychology have always used a positive approach. For example, the concept of job satisfaction is inherently positive: it looks at how a positive attitude towards our work affects various other outcomes,

such as productivity. Studies of organisational commitment explore how our feelings of commitment towards our employer can bring individual and organisational benefits.

We will now consider some of positive psychology's central tenets and how they can be applied to the world of work.

The happy life

Seligman proposed that positive psychology is all about happiness, and suggested there are three paths to happiness that combine to create 'authentic' happiness (Seligman, 2002). These three paths are:

- Pleasure – also called hedonia, this is about seeking pleasure. For example, we might decide to have a work meeting at a local coffee shop rather than in an office. The relaxed atmosphere, the smells of the coffee and maybe even the background music would make us feel happy.
- Engagement – also called eudaimonia, this is about seeking to use and develop the best in ourselves. We looked at work engagement in the last chapter, and that is a great example of how we can increase the happiness in our life by having work that utilises our talents. For example, if you are great at meeting new people and getting to know them and have a real talent for putting people in touch with others who can help them, you would find a networking event very engaging. Work becomes a pleasure for its own sake.
- Meaning – the final path moves beyond our own pleasures and engagements to considering how belonging to and working towards a higher purpose can enhance our happiness. Feeling that we are part of something important and that we are contributing to the wider community or world is the final piece of the happiness puzzle. For example, you might choose to work for a particular charity organisation because you strongly believe in its mission and gain a sense of meaning from helping to achieve it.

Activity Happiness as a key concept

Go to http://www.isqols.org/, click on 'Oral Histories' and then choose Ed Diener. Watch the video where Diener is talking about happiness and why it is important, and answer these questions:

▸ What contributes to happiness?
▸ Why is happiness important?

All three of these paths are important in happiness and are correlated with subjective well-being, although the relationship of pleasure with well-being is weaker than the other two (Schueller and Seligman, 2010). Hedonia is negatively related to 'objective' measures of well-being such as occupational attainment, while engagement and meaning are positively related. Research has also indicated that while both hedonia and eudaimonia are related to vitality and overall satisfaction with life, they have differential relationships with other psychological aspects (Huta and Ryan, 2010). Hedonia is related to higher positive and lower negative affect. Eudaimonia is related to the feeling of meaning and also deeper experiences, such as those involving awe, inspiration and a sense of connection. In addition, increasing hedonic pursuits leads to short-term increases in well-being, while increasing eudaimonic pursuits leads to longer-term benefits. It seems that if we want to increase overall well-being, we should focus more on finding engagement and meaning in life than pursuing pleasure.

By looking at these three paths to a happy life, we can see immediately why work psychology and positive psychology can contribute so much to each other. We spend a large amount of our lives at work, so any understanding of the 'good life' will necessarily have to include an understanding of work and its interaction with the rest of our lives. In addition, for many people, work is also a way they give meaning and purpose to their lives.

Flourishing

More recently, Seligman has expanded his ideas about happiness to the wider concept of well-being (Seligman, 2011). While his original theory was about happiness and aimed to increase life satisfaction, the updated version is broader and aims to increase *flourishing*. Keyes (2005) defined a flourishing person as someone who has high levels of well-being, with a broad understanding of well-being as encompassing emotional, social and psychological aspects. Seligman proposes that five components contribute towards our well-being: positive emotion, engagement, relationships, meaning/purpose and accomplishment. In essence, he has slightly redefined pleasure as the emotional content, and then added relationships and accomplishment as extra components to this broader concept of well-being.

The centrality of 'flourishing' to the positive psychology effort is well recognised by other authors. Keyes (2005) points out that the mere absence of mental illness is not enough to ensure people are feeling healthy and functioning well. For example, even if you are not currently suffering from a major depressive episode, you are not necessarily happy. Exploring the effects of mental health or flourishing at work should be as important to us as understanding how mental illness affects work.

Case Study Increasing happiness at work

Bill is a sales rep for a large software company and has always felt lucky to have such a great job. He enjoys the work itself as well as many of the surrounding benefits. His job involves quite a lot of travelling in Europe and occasionally further afield. Whenever possible he tries to make sure that he combines his business travel with some time to explore the city he has travelled to. Sometimes, this only involves going out to local restaurants, but on other occasions he is able to arrange his itinerary so that he can take an afternoon or weekend to explore the region. He also enjoys the work: he knows he is very good at talking to people, putting them at their ease even when he has just met them, and finding out exactly what they need and how his products can help them. He has developed good relationships with his customers, which has resulted in repeat business for his company, and he is well regarded.

But recently, Bill has started to feel less happy with life. He's a bit confused by this because he still enjoys his job and the side benefits it gives him. It seems to him that nothing has got worse in his life, but he is somehow less satisfied with it. His organisation has just started to offer its senior staff the opportunity to have sessions with a coach and Bill decides this would be a good issue to discuss with his coach.

▶ If you were Bill's coach, how could you draw on Seligman's theory of authentic happiness to help Bill to explore this issue?

▶ With a partner, discuss how important you think a consideration of happiness is for work psychology. Think about the longer-term outcomes that might result from Bill's drop in happiness.

© Image Source

In his research with a large sample of American adults, Keyes found that while the majority of adults were moderately mentally healthy, only 18% of the population could be categorised as flourishing (having high well-being). Slightly less (16.6%) were what he called 'completely mentally healthy' in that they had high well-being and no mental illness. His findings are particularly interesting to work psychology, because those people who were completely mentally healthy had the lowest work absence rates, low feelings of helplessness, clear goals and were more resilient, outcomes which are important to both organisations and individuals at work.

You may be interested to know that similar results have been found for students: those who were classified as flourishing had higher levels of perseverance and self-control and achieved higher grades (Howell, 2009). Of course, as with all correlational studies, this does not tell us what the causal relationship is, but it does tell us that flourishing, as a key concept of positive psychology, is related to important real-world outcomes.

The current interest in positive psychology

Positive psychology is frequently referred to as a 'new science' or a new area of psychology, with the concurrent belief that it is therefore exciting and dynamic and relevant. In support of this claim, two of the champions of positive psychology, Martin Seligman and Mihaly Csikszentmihalyi, suggest that the field of psychology, while broad before the Second World War, became increasingly narrowly focused afterwards. Before the war, they suggest that psychology had three main aims (Seligman and Csikszentmihalyi, 2000):

1 To cure mental illness
2 To improve the lives of all people by making them more productive and fulfilling
3 To identify and nurture 'high talent' – people with exceptional abilities.

At this time, it was not unusual for psychologists to explore what made life meaningful or what made people effective in their different roles. For example, C. G. Jung dedicated much of his work to exploring our search for meaning in life. However, Seligman and Csikszentmihalyi argue that after the Second World War, the focus of research in psychology narrowed to the treatment of mental illness and pathology. This is perhaps not surprising considering the dreadful impact of the war and how important it was to people to deal with its after-effects. In the authors' view, the emergence of positive psychology at the turn of the century was an important balance to this exclusive focus on the negative side of psychology.

It is interesting to note that Mihaly Csikszentmihalyi traces his own interest in positive psychology to his experience in the war. He wanted to know what made some people keep their integrity and purpose while so many others became helpless and dispirited (Seligman and Csikszentmihalyi, 2000). But when he went to study psychology in the USA he found that the attempt to develop a 'science' of psychology had resulted in scepticism and a study of averages. He was more interested in what made people exceptional, and describes his continuing struggle to reconcile psychology as a study of what *is* and what *could be*.

The other major figure to bring the positive side of psychology back into prominence is Martin Seligman. He was elected president of the American Psychological Association, and in his President's Address (Seligman, 1998) called for a reorientation of psychology as:

> a science that emphasises the understanding and building of the most positive qualities of an individual: optimism, courage, work ethic, future-mindedness, interpersonal skill, the capacity for pleasure and insight, and social responsibility. It's my belief that since the end of World War II, psychology has moved too far away from its original roots, which were to make the lives of all people more fulfilling and productive, and too much toward the important, but not all-important, area of curing mental illness.

Although Seligman and other positive psychologists have since tried to declare positive psychology a completely separate area of study to the rest of psychology (Snyder et al., 2002), this is overstating the case somewhat, and the claim becomes untenable when we understand a bit more about how psychology has developed (Froh, 2004), which we consider in the next section. To attempt to drive a wedge between 'modern' positive psychology and everything that has gone before risks discarding decades of work that emphasised the development of human potential. As Taylor points out (2001), it may mean that positive psychology tries to exclude the very tradition it is trying to represent.

Recently, a leading positive psychologist, Lyubomirsky, has suggested that it may not even be necessary to maintain positive psychology as a separate area because it has become part of everyone's thinking (Jarden, 2012). If this is true, it means that Seligman's call for a reorientation of psychology has been achieved.

In a detailed critique of positive psychology, Held (2004) points out some challenges to the field. She notes that there are some unintended negative side effects of its positive message. For example, the robust finding that optimism and positivity are related to health and longer life could have a depressing effect on those who are already finding life difficult, and implies that all they need to do to 'fix' things is to think positively. Of course, the misinterpretation or misapplication of research findings is not unique to positive psychology, but this caution does remind us to keep positive psychology in balance with the rest of the psychological field.

 International Perspectives Is positive psychology American?

There is no doubt that the current positive psychology movement originated in the USA with Seligman's presidential address to the American Psychological Association. Although many of the subjects studied by positive psychologists have been considered from other perspectives and by researchers around the world, some authors have suggested that the positive psychology banner is based too strongly in American culture to be applicable outside that country.

Barbara Held (2002) notes how a positive attitude has been an essential ingredient of American culture right from the beginning of the nation, promoted and emphasised by its great writers and presidents, and with optimism about human potential seen as inextricable from the ideals of democracy. She also suggests that this emphasis on the positive has become 'tyrannical', creating a demand that Americans should *always* be positive no matter what the cost. While there are reports that positivity is related to better well-being, there is contradictory evidence from studies in other cultures. For example, Japanese people report higher well-being when they are correcting their deficiencies, which are identified within a collectivist context (Kitayama et al., 1997).

The issue of how America's high individualism impacts on positive psychology theory is explored further by Christopher and Hickinbottom (2008). They point out that the 'good life' is primarily seen as involving subjective well-being and measured by individual fulfilment, with questions asking how much a person feels they are meeting their own internal measure of satisfaction with life. In contrast to this, a collectivist-based emotional satisfaction would be concerned more with living in accordance with a wider social context than it would with individual satisfaction. The authors also point out that emotions are valued differently in Western and non-Western cultures, making the measurement of positive emotions culturally contingent.

This unacknowledged bias of equating the good life with individual satisfaction means that positive psychology can miss out on identifying the depth and breadth of human potential and the good life as experienced by the majority of the world's population. Christopher et al. (2008) caution against using the findings of positive psychology, which are rooted in a distinctly American perspective on life, in a prescriptive manner across other cultures.

Discussion points

Do you agree with the argument of Christopher et al. that positive psychology is biased? If so, how would you like to see the field expand?

What is a 'good life' to you? Once you have written down some thoughts, see if you can identify the influence of individualist or collectivist ideologies. You may find this easier if you can talk to some people from a different culture.

In the next section we will consider the contributions of humanistic psychology to the current positive psychology movement, and how it makes more sense to view positive psychology as the continuation of a tradition to bring a welcome balance in the study of psychology. To really understand and help ourselves and others, we need to know how to fix problems and nurture the best in life (Seligman and Csikszentmihalyi, 2000).

Humanistic psychology

Of course, not everyone was focusing on psychological problems and pathology between the Second World War and Seligman's announcement about positive psychology in 1998. In contrast to the prevailing approach of seeing people as essentially passive, responding to stimuli in their environment, the humanistic psychologists promoted the idea that we are *active* participants in life, that we can create our own realities and are motivated to fulfil our potential. This fulfilment of potential is called *self-actualisation*.

You may recognise the term self-actualisation from Abraham Maslow's 'hierarchy of needs', which is often presented to students who are learning about motivation. However, there was much more to Maslow's work than this and he saw psychology as having a key role in helping people to live fulfilled lives, pointing out that this was only possible if psychologists studied healthy, flourishing people.

Maslow also strongly believed that the process of self-actualisation (fulfilling our potential) was a long, difficult process and primarily the task of later life. In fact, he noted that a screening of 3,000 university students revealed only *one* who could be said to be engaged in self-actualisation, which he defined as the 'full use and exploitation of talents, capacities and potentialities' (Maslow, 1954, p. 150). Contrast this with the simplistic way his 'hierarchy of needs' is applied in many business textbooks, where young potential managers are encouraged to think of ways they can help their employees to be 'motivated' by providing them with opportunities for self-actualisation at work.

The real benefit of Maslow's work was not in providing a simple model of motivation at work, but in attempting to explore the high-functioning, self-actualising individual as a pattern for human potential. He identified several characteristics of people engaged in this process, which we can see as one of the first attempts to outline the human potential that is key to positive psychology.

Maslow (1954) described self-actualising people as follows:

- Have a more efficient perception of reality and more comfortable relations with it
- Are more accepting of themselves, others and nature
- Show more spontaneity, simplicity and naturalness
- Are not focused on themselves, but on problems outside themselves. They have a sense of a mission in life
- Like some solitude and demonstrate a certain level of detachment; that is, they have a sense of the wider world that puts the specific situation into context
- Are independent, with a strong sense of autonomy
- Have 'peak experiences' more often. These experiences involve a loss of the self in an activity or transcendence
- Have a feeling of identification with the rest of humanity and a deep desire to help them
- Have deeper and more profound interpersonal relationships
- Are strongly ethical
- Have a generally creative approach to life.

As we go through the rest of this chapter and consider the other contributions that positive psychology can make to our understanding of human behaviour, you may find it useful to refer back to this list and compare current developments with this original outline.

Carl Rogers was influenced by Maslow's work and is another of the most well-known humanistic psychologists. His work was the basis for the person-centred approach to counselling and therapy which is still going strong today. This is a non-directive approach which allows individuals to develop their own sense of self and develop towards their true potential (Rogers, 1951).

Rogers suggested that we have a basic striving towards actualising and enhancing the self. His emphasis was on psychology that helped people towards the 'good life', where we are continually striving to fulfil our potential by being 'fully functioning' people (Rogers, 1961). Rogers claimed that when we are fully functioning, we will be more open to experience and live each moment fully. We will trust ourselves and our choices, as well as our sense of right and wrong, and will act constructively, being more creative in our approach to life. But Rogers did note that this is not an 'easy' path, and it is worth remembering as we continue our discussion of positive psychology that Rogers's 'good life' is about experiencing all of life fully, both the good and the bad, and does not focus exclusively on the positive side of life.

Based on Bugental's (1964) discussion of humanistic psychology as a 'third force' in psychology alongside behaviourism and psychoanalysis, Greening (2006) outlined the five basic postulates of the approach. These postulates, as applied to our study of work psychology, are:

1   **We are more than the sum of our parts.** If we are trying to understand how and why people behave at work, it is no good trying to just add together individual measures such as 'extraversion plus intelligence' to predict people's behaviour at work. We need to understand people as a whole.
2   **We exist in a human context.** Although extracting the person from the situation can help us to understand some of their behaviour, context is an essential part of our experience. For example, while high intelligence tends to predict success in many jobs, an organisational culture that promotes conformity and unthinking following of the status quo is unlikely to reap the benefits of an intelligent workforce.
3   **We are conscious.** We are aware of ourselves and those around us and can consciously choose to adapt or behave in particular ways at work. For example, we would probably all consciously adapt our communication style when talking to the CEO who is visiting our department for the day.
4   **We have choice.** While we may not be able to choose everything in life, we certainly have control over substantial parts of it. And with that choice comes responsibility for our choices. At a very simple level, we have the choice whether to go to work or not, and are aware that with that choice comes consequences that we need to take responsibility for.
5   **We are intentional and seek meaning in our lives.** For many people, this search for meaning includes their jobs. We want work that is meaningful and we will put a lot of effort into trying to attain it.

Humanistic psychology has been criticised for not being scientifically rigorous enough and positive psychologists, in their attempt to launch this new field, wanted to distance themselves from those criticisms (Seligman and Csikszentmihalyi, 2000). In fact, as we saw in the very first chapter of this book, it is difficult to decide how the scientific process can be applied to the complex, subjective world of the mind. Certainly, many of the humanistic psychologists valued and promoted a scientific approach to studying psychology, but had a different interpretation of what that approach should involve. For them, our felt experience and the meaning we attach to events cannot be separated from more 'objective' or observable data if we are to really understand psychology. For example, if we are attempting to understand the importance of work in people's lives, it would not be enough to simply count the number of hours people spend on their work and conclude that the longer they spend at work the more important it is to them. We would also want to know why people work, what they are aiming for, how important work feels to them in comparison to other things and so on.

In summary, there are two important things that humanistic psychology reminds us of. First, that we live in a subjective world which we essentially create for ourselves. That is, we interpret events around us and build up our own sense of their meaning, which may well be far removed from any 'objective' reality. And second, we are active agents in our own lives; we do not simply respond passively to everything that happens.

Having considered the origins and scope of positive psychology, we will now move on to discuss three key areas in more details: positive emotions, strengths and virtues, and flow experiences.

POSITIVE EMOTIONS

There are two main ways in which positive emotions are studied in positive psychology. The first is simply to see them as *markers* of well-being or flourishing, while the second is to explore their role in *producing* flourishing (Fredrickson, 2001). Essentially, this is answering the question of whether we feel happy or joyful or interested because we are flourishing, or whether those positive emotions actually contribute to making our lives better.

Negative emotions can be seen as serving the function of providing a 'specific action tendency'. That is, they narrow our thoughts and behaviours to a specific set of options. The evolutionary advantage of this is obvious: if we are afraid of a predator, we don't spend time wondering what to do, we just fight or flee. But what benefit do positive emotions provide? They are certainly not associated with a limited range of options; instead they seem to have quite vague effects on our actions. Fredrickson (1998) has suggested that positive emotions *broaden and build* rather than narrow and focus. When we experience positive emotions such as love, joy or pride, our thought-action repertoires broaden and we build our personal

resources. These personal resources include resiliency, social relationships, new ideas and so on. A detailed example will help us to see how this can be applied in the workplace.

Imagine that you have just achieved something you've been working hard towards. You will naturally feel a sense of pride in your accomplishment. This positive emotion will probably encourage you to share your success with others as well as to plan for future goals and achievements. These actions and thoughts will, in all likelihood, result in you achieving more in future, and have the long-term effect of increasing your well-being. In addition, if you are faced with a difficult task in the future, you will be able to draw on both your feeling of accomplishment from the past as well as the plans you have made to overcome the obstacle more effectively.

One important 'resource' for work is our coping mechanisms. If positive emotions can help improve our ability to cope with stress, we will be able to maintain higher levels of well-being when faced with difficult circumstances. Research with a student sample indicates that positive emotions really do result in better coping in the longer term (Fredrickson and Joiner, 2002). Another personal resource is hope, the belief that we can meet our work-related goals and the motivation to persist with them. There is evidence that positive emotions at the end of one work day predict how hopeful people feel the next day, and subsequently their vigour (levels of energy), dedication and absorption at work (Ouweneel et al., 2012), demonstrating how positive emotions influence work engagement.

Fredrickson's research shows that, as a consequence of their broaden-and-build effect, positive emotions initiate 'upward spirals' that contribute to our well-being (Fredrickson and Joiner, 2002) – that is, as we experience more positive emotions, we broaden our behavioural repertoire and build our personal resources, which in turn help to improve our well-being and therefore have a long-term effect on our lives. By attempting to increase the positive emotions that employees experience at work, an organisation could thereby reap longer-term benefits in terms of increased creativity, commitment and engagement.

STRENGTHS AND VIRTUES
Strengths-based development

Continuous professional development is widely recognised as an important part of modern careers. It helps us to keep on top of current knowledge, up to date with current issues and technologies, and ensures we are able to do our jobs well. If you have ever had experience of it, you will know that it is very often based on a 'gap' idea: you identify the gap between what you know or can do and what you need to know or do, and then find a way to attain the required skill or knowledge level. Much of the development rhetoric in organisations is based around the idea that we need to identify our weaknesses and build up our skills in those areas.

A survey of managers across the world found that the majority (between 60% and 75% depending on country) believed the best way to improve was by knowing their weaknesses rather than their strengths (Hodges and Clifton, 2004). In contrast to this widely held view, the study actually found that the best managers are those who can manage the unique talents and abilities of their team (their strengths) rather than those who concentrate on trying to help everyone become 'well rounded' by building up their weaker areas. The following table illustrates the difference between the two approaches to development:

Weakness-based development	Strengths-based development
Identify your weaknesses	Identify your strengths
Try to find ways to develop skills in that area i.e. change yourself ('you are not good enough')	Find ways to use them more in your work i.e. change your environment ('you are good enough, you need to find a way to shine')

Strengths-based development improves employee engagement (Hodges and Clifton, 2004), which we saw in Chapter 9 is linked to important organisational outcomes such as profitability, customer satisfaction and turnover (Harter et al., 2002). This is exactly the approach that the positive psychology study of strengths and virtues promotes. By focusing on our strengths rather than our weaknesses, we can live a fuller, more flourishing life.

 Psychological Toolkit Strengths-based development

This developmental activity is rooted in the principles of positive psychology. The first task is based on an intervention which was shown to improve happiness over a six-month period (Seligman et al., 2005). The second two tasks help you to apply the exercise specifically to your work life.

Using a strengths-based approach is not to say that we should just ignore weaknesses or simply stick to what we know; but it is about finding a way to use your strengths more effectively and frequently. Most people would agree they would far rather spend their working day doing something they are good at and

uses their talents than something they struggle with. So you can use this approach for several purposes:

▸ To frame your search for a career
▸ To guide career decisions at key moments
▸ To identify developmental opportunities you will enjoy
▸ To find ways to reshape how you do your current work to take more effective advantage of your strengths.

Go to http://www.authentichappiness.sas.upenn.edu and take the VIA survey of character strengths. You will need to register and will get a report on your strengths, identifying your top five or 'signature strengths'.

Read through your signature strengths and undertake the following tasks:

1 For each strength, think of one new and different way you could use it in the next week.
2 At the end of the week, look back at how things went and consider the following questions.
   ▸ What did it feel like to consciously use each strength?
   ▸ What did you learn through the experience?
   ▸ How was this exercise different from weakness-based developmental activities you may have undertaken in the past?
3 Now that you have seen how you can use your strengths on a day-to-day basis, take some time to think about your current work (if you are employed) or future career goals. For each of your signature strengths, develop a plan for how you might be able to use that strength in your work.

Character strengths and virtues

The *Diagnostic and Statistical Manual of Mental Disorders* (DSM) is a handbook published by the American Psychiatric Association which summarises current understandings of what can go wrong in human psychology, enabling psychiatrists and psychologists to identify symptoms of mental disorders. The character strengths and virtues (CSV) has been developed as an attempt to summarise what can go *well* in human psychology (Peterson and Seligman, 2004). It 'describes and classifies strengths and virtues that enable human thriving' (Seligman et al., 2005, p. 411), and was drawn up in the belief that good character can be developed but that we need to know how to do so.

The CSV consists of six overarching 'virtues' which are further subdivided into 24 'strengths' and are used in different spheres of life. The table below outlines this categorisation.

Table 10.1   Character strengths and virtues

Virtue	Sphere	Strengths
Wisdom and knowledge	Cognitive: how we attain and use knowledge	Creativity Curiosity Open-mindedness Love of learning Perspective
Courage	Emotional: using our will to overcome obstacles	Authenticity Bravery Persistence Zest
Humanity	Interpersonal: nurturing and befriending others	Kindness Love Social intelligence
Justice	Civic: strengths that build community life	Fairness Leadership Teamwork
Temperance	Self-restraint: strengths that protect from excess	Forgiveness Modesty Prudence Self-regulation
Transcendence	Meaning: creating connections to the larger world and universe	Appreciation of beauty and excellence Gratitude Hope Humour Religiousness

Source: Seligman et al. (2005). Published by the American Psychological Association, adapted with permission.

Several researchers have suggested that this initial structure of six virtues needs refining. Summarising several studies and adding their own data, Shryack et al. (2010) noted that there was more support for a model of five virtues, and suggest from their own data that there may be three overarching virtues: Temperance, Intellectual and Interpersonal. A recent large-scale study of 450,000 US adults revealed five main virtues rather than the original six (McGrath, 2014).

Strengths at work

While this is a relatively new area of research, investigation into the role of virtues and strengths in the workplace has already begun. For example, it has been found that of all the strengths, hope and zest are most strongly associated with life satisfaction (Park et al., 2004). There is some evidence that strengths are related to work satisfaction too. Those who see their work as a calling (related to the strength of *zest*, according to Peterson and Park) reported fewer days of absence from work and higher work satisfaction (Wrzesniewski et al., 1997). In addition, the *humanity* virtue is related to work satisfaction in jobs which directly involve other people, such as sales or teaching (Peterson and Park, 2006).

Strengths influence work behaviour in other ways as well. For example, *hope* is particularly important in sustaining the efforts of people working in uncertain environments (Luthans and Jensen, 2002). The sense of work as a calling is more likely to occur if we are using four or more of our 'signature' strengths at work (our top five strengths), and in this case we are also more likely to have positive work experiences, such as higher job satisfaction, engagement and meaning (Harzer and Ruch, 2012).

 Key Research Study   Virtue and leadership

The value of Virtue in the Upper Echelons: A Multisource Examination of Executive Character Strengths and Performance

John J. Sosik, William A. Gentry and Jae Uk Chun (2012)

Background: The benefits of character strengths include helping to build an ethical climate in the organisation and improving performance. Yet much of the leadership literature focuses on character flaws and how they result in derailment and problems with ethical judgement, rather than how strengths might improve performance and lead to desired outcomes.

Aim: To identify how four executive character strengths (integrity, bravery, perspective and social intelligence) influence performance. Second, to compare strengths with traditional competencies (sound judgement, strategic planning, results orientation and global awareness) in predicting performance.

Method: A total of 191 executives (CEO, CFO or similar) were rated by at least two direct reports on the four character strengths, and by at least one boss or board member on performance. Relative weight analysis was used to identify the contributions of strengths and competencies to performance.

Findings: Integrity, bravery and social intelligence accounted for a sizeable amount of variance in executive performance, though perspective did not contribute significantly to performance. Traditional competencies were slightly better than strengths in predicting performance (accounting for 47% of variance compared with 37%).

Implications: While it has already been established that executives' character flaws can have negative impacts on the organisation, this study shows the benefit of specific strengths on performance. Because strengths can be developed, this information can help in executive development programmes as well as contribute towards better selection decisions.

A more specifically work-focused approach to strengths has been developed by Luthans and colleagues, referred to as psychological capital (PsyCap). Like the CSV, PsyCap emphasises that the individual can develop and grow, but is slightly different from the CSV approach in that it strives to capture specifically organisationally related concepts describing a person's stage of positive psychological development (Luthans et al., 2007). Four main constructs make up our psychological capital: self-efficacy, optimism, hope and resilience. These constructs are considered to be 'capital' in the sense that they add value to our lives by bringing rewards in the present and benefits in the future. Research indicates that PsyCap is related to both higher performance and higher satisfaction for people in a range of jobs and industries (Luthans et al., 2007).

FLOW EXPERIENCES

Have you ever been so absorbed in an activity that you lost track of time and even forgot to eat or sleep? Csikszentmihalyi (2000) came across this phenomenon when he was studying the creative process and trying to understand autotelic activity – that is, activities that we engage in because they are intrinsically rewarding and enjoyable. He found that people engaged in autotelic activities reported very similar experiences across a wide range of activities, including playing chess, rock climbing and dancing. He called this experience *flow*, because people said it felt as if they were being carried along in the water. Flow is essentially a state of complete absorption in what we are doing so that we lose awareness of other things, and is characterised by (Nakamura and Csikszentmihalyi, 2009):

* An intense and focused concentration on the moment
* A merging of action and awareness
* Loss of reflective self-consciousness
* The sense that you can deal with the situation because you know how to act next (feeling of control)
* Distortion of temporal experience (time speeding up or slowing down)
* The activity is rewarding in itself: sometimes the end result is just an excuse to undertake the process.

These characteristics have been summarised into three key dimensions of a flow experience: complete absorption in the activity, enjoyment and intrinsic motivation (Bakker, 2008). Some claim that two dimensions (absorption and enjoyment) explain the findings better (Llorens et al., 2013), and that intrinsic motivation or interest in the activity is more a 'prerequisite' of a flow experience,

but recognise that further research is needed to refine our understanding.

Flow is described as a 'dynamic equilibrium' (Nakamura and Csikszentmihalyi, 2009). It is a case of balancing opportunities for action with our capacities for action, or in other words balancing the challenge with our skills (Csikszentmihalyi, 2000). If the challenge becomes too great for our skills we can become anxious, and if our skills exceed the challenge we get bored. Research shows that employees who have the balance of high skills and high challenge experience flow more often (e.g. Llorens et al., 2013; Csikszentmihalyi and LeFevre, 1989). It is important to remember that it is a person's *subjective* perception of his or her own skills or the level of challenge that is important in determining whether a flow experience happens, rather than any external assessment.

Flow at work

Some of the earliest research on flow experiences demonstrated an important finding for work psychology: people experience flow far more often at work than in leisure pursuits (Csikszentmihalyi and LeFevre, 1989), and this is true for people at all levels of work, from management to blue collar workers. This echoes findings we discussed in the previous chapter about work being a key component of well-being (Rath and Harter, 2010). Flow experience is of importance in work psychology for other reasons too, not least because people who are in flow are operating at full capacity. The intrinsic motivation dimension of flow is related to higher extra-role performance (employees doing more than is formally expected of them), while work enjoyment is most strongly related to in-role performance (Bakker, 2008). In fact, you could see flow as providing the ultimate benefit to both the individual and the organisation. For the individual, the activity is rewarding and engaging, and the organisation benefits from the full application of the individual's abilities and talents.

Flow experiences are related to increased positive affect (Clarke and Haworth, 1994) and personal development (Csikszentmihalyi, 1997). This latter is because flow happens when we are stretching ourselves, a challenge and use of skills that is above our own personal average. However, not all the outcomes of flow are positive. There is some indication that flow can be addictive and that it is related to risky behaviour (Schüler, 2012).

Bakker (2008) developed a questionnaire to measure how frequently people experience flow at work and looked at how flow relates to job demands and performance. He found a complex pattern of relationships between job demands and the three dimensions of flow.

Case Study Flow experiences

You're right in the work, you lose your sense of time, you're completely enraptured, you're completely caught up in what you're doing . . . there's no future or past, it's just an extended present in which you're making meaning.

Mark Strand, poet

▸ Have you ever experienced 'flow'? Write your own description of what it was like.

The following extracts illustrate how people describe the different aspects of the flow experience Csikszentmihalyi, 2006). Identify which of the six aspects of the flow experience (Nakamura and Csikszentmihalyi, 2009) they illustrate:

> Concentration is like breathing: you never think of it. The roof could fall in and, if it missed you, you would be unaware of it.
>
> Chess player

> You're so involved in what you're doing, you aren't thinking about yourself as separate from the immediate activity. You're no longer a participant observer, only a participant. You're moving in harmony with something else you're part of.
>
> Rock climber

> You feel like . . . there's nothing that will be able to stop you or get in your way. And you're ready to tackle anything, and you don't fear any possibility happening, and it's just exhilarating.
>
> Cyclist

> You are not aware of the body except your hands . . . not aware of self or personal problems . . . . If involved, you are not aware of aching feet, not aware of self.
>
> Surgeon

> Two things happen . . . After it's passed, [time] seems to have passed really fast. I see that it's one o'clock in the morning and I say, 'Ah-ha, just a few minutes ago it was eight o'clock.' But then while I'm dancing . . . it seems like it's been much longer than it really was.
>
> Social dancer

Work pressure had a positive relationship with absorption but not with enjoyment or intrinsic motivation. Emotional demands showed a positive relationship with absorption but negative with enjoyment, while social support from colleagues improved work enjoyment. Opportunities for growth at work and autonomy in choosing how and when to work were both positively related to all three flow dimensions. This suggests that the best way to increase the likelihood of flow experiences for employees is to grant them more autonomy and provide more opportunities for growth.

We mentioned the idea of an 'upward spiral' in our discussion of positive emotions, looking at how they can build our personal resources, which in turn increase our positive emotions. Research indicates that a similar upward spiral can operate with flow experiences. For example, higher self-efficacy beliefs (a personal resource that we can draw on to deal with challenges) facilitates work-related flow. In addition, work-related flow positively influences self-efficacy (Salanova et al., 2006). But it is not only personal resources which can be involved in an upward spiral, organisational resources can be as well. Social support, innovation and clear work goals increase the frequency of flow experiences, which in turn increase the organisational resources themselves. This implies that even small efforts to increase the flow-related resources available to employees can result in an increasing spiral of benefits for both the individual and the organisation.

Although it seems to be possible for everyone to experience flow, some people experience it far more often than others. Csikszentmihalyi suggests that some people have *autotelic* personalities – that is, they do things for their own sake rather than to achieve some external reward (Csikszentmihalyi, 1997). These people enter flow more easily and have meta-skills such as curiosity, low self-centredness, interest in life and persistence, which help them to stay in flow. If they find themselves in a situation which seems beyond their current skills and makes them anxious, they are motivated to learn new skills in order to deal with it. On the other hand, if they are taking part in an activity that is not much of a challenge, experiencing boredom will motivate them to find a way to make the activity more challenging or find a different, more challenging task (Moneta, 2004).

 Activity Can you 'create' a flow experience?

Flow experiences can't be 'forced', but there are things that we can do to increase the likelihood of them happening. The three main prerequisites for flow experiences are (Csikszentmihalyi et al., 2005):

1   Clear performance goals (you know what you want or need to do)
2   Good and frequent feedback (you know how well you are doing)
3   A match between the task challenge and your skill level (the task stretches you).

Think about your own work (either as a student or in employment) and identify the extent to which you think each of these prerequisites are met in your work.

On your own, or in discussion with a colleague, develop some practical ideas for how you might be able to increase the likelihood of experiencing flow in your work.

Like other areas of positive psychology, flow theory is related to and builds on work in several different psychological traditions. You may recognise similarities with the self-actualisation that humanistic psychologists were interested in, as well as with the concept of intrinsic motivation. It also provides a demonstration of how hedonic and eudaimonic pursuits can be combined: people in flow experience pleasure and are engaged in their work. Flow captures important information about optimal performance and self-development.

WORKPLACE SPIRITUALITY

Would it surprise you to know that the CSV model of virtues we looked at above was originally developed from an analysis of the recommendations that different cultures and religions help you live a good and moral life?

Many of the questions that positive psychology addresses were previously the preserve of religion and philosophy. They gave guidance on how to live a good and moral life, gave examples of outstanding paragons of virtue to emulate, provided paths towards fulfilment and pointed towards the meaning in life. A great deal of knowledge about human potential and development can be found in these traditions and it would be unwise for us to ignore or dismiss it. Positive psychology can provide us with the scientific approach to evaluate and apply some of these insights. The CSV, for example, drew on the writings of Confucianism, Taoism, Buddhism, Hinduism, Athenian philosophy, Judaism, Christianity and Islam to develop a ubiquitous model of our human strengths (Dahlsgaard et al., 2005).

In discussing spirituality at work, we need to be careful to delineate it from religion. In the past, spirituality was not separated from religion, but in our increasingly secular society it has become important to more clearly define what we mean by both these terms. A religion is an organised belief system about how humanity relates to the supernatural, whatever that is defined as being. Spirituality, on the other hand, is about the individual search for meaning, purpose and belonging. While this search often takes place within organised religion, it is not limited to it. In fact, the growing body of research on spirituality at work recognises that this search, for many people, takes place at least partly within their work.

So when we talk about spirituality at work, we are not talking about building a workplace around particular religious values or requiring that employees profess a specific religion or undertake certain religious practices. On the contrary, it is about a personal, unique search for meaning in life, in which work can play an essential part. Spirituality is closely linked to the third 'path to happiness' outlined by Seligman (2002): meaningfulness. Recognising the importance of spirituality at work necessitates a recognition that people want to be involved in work that will give some meaning to their lives (Ashmos and Duchon, 2000). Based on their research, Ashmos and Duchon suggest the following definition of spirituality at work: 'recognition of an inner life that nourishes and is nourished by meaningful work that takes place in the context of community' (p. 139).

Workplace spirituality can be understood at the level of the individual, group and whole organisation (Milliman et al., 2003). At the individual level, the idea of meaningful work goes beyond the normal concerns of work psychology in helping to make work interesting or challenging. It is about the sense of contributing to something bigger. At the group level, spirituality is concerned with establishing a community, a group of people who will support us and to which we contribute. And finally, at the organisational level, spirituality is about finding a sense of connection with a larger purpose, having an organisation whose goals we identify with. As at the group level, this is a two-way process: individuals identify with and contribute to the organisation's mission, and the organisation respects and cares for the individuals.

Milliman et al. (2003) found that spirituality at each of these levels was related to positive organisational outcomes, including organisational commitment, intrinsic work satisfaction, job involvement, organisation-based self-esteem and reduced intention to quit. Individual and group aspects of spirituality seem to be more important in these relationships than the organisational aspect.

A recent review of the work spirituality literature (Karakas, 2010) noted that the benefits of spirituality for individual and organisational performance were proposed to work through three pathways, by:

* Enhancing employee well-being
* Providing employees with a sense of meaning at work
* Providing a sense of community.

The review shows that there is good evidence for spirituality having positive effects on a wide range of individual and organisational outcomes, including increased morale, commitment, well-being and productivity, as well as creativity and fulfilment. Workplace programmes that are recommended for bringing about these results include optional yoga sessions, multi-faith prayer rooms or having industrial chaplains.

So far, our discussion of spirituality has been entirely positive. But several people have raised concerns about the idea of spirituality at work. Reva Brown, for example, claims that the whole concept is too ill-defined to be of any use and is essentially a synonym for concepts such as organisational culture (Brown, 2003). She goes on to list several negative applications of the concept which are closely tied to criticisms of organisational culture interventions, namely using it to control the workforce, to manipulate meaning and to avoid conflict.

Another major caveat with spirituality at work is that for the majority of people spirituality and religion are still closely intertwined. There is a danger, which is widely recognised in the literature, that work spirituality interventions can become divisive if they are hijacked by exclusive religious groups (Karakas, 2010).

We also need to consider the important issue of the inherent paradox between spiritual and material: for the majority of organisations, it is material success that counts. But introducing a more spiritual frame of reference could result in outcomes that are unrelated to material success, or even turn our definition of success itself on its head. The following exercise helps you to explore this in more detail.

 Activity A spiritual workplace?

What would a spiritual workplace look like to you? Write down your ideas and then get together with several other colleagues and see what kind of similarities or differences you have. (If your group is primarily people of all the same age, it would be a useful exercise to ask some people from different age groups for their opinion too.)

▸ Draw up a list of companies you know about that seem to have a more spiritual approach to doing business. What is it that they do that you recognise as 'spiritual'?

▸ Now draw up a list of companies you think are incompatible with the idea of a spiritual workplace. Why is this? Do you think there is any way they could be changed to take account of the spiritual?

While bearing these issues in mind, the field of spirituality at work is an important one, not least because, like positive psychology in general, it helps us to focus on human potential and to recognise employees as whole people.

SUMMARY

This chapter has explored the idea that work can be about more than 'doing a job', using the positive psychology approach to discuss how work can provide a sense of meaning in people's lives. We saw that the tradition of humanistic psychology, giving a central place to the search for meaning and self-development, is taken up in the current interest in positive psychology, with its focus on the happy or flourishing life.

By reviewing three areas of positive psychology research and theory, we gained an insight into how these topics could be applied to work, from the use of positive emotions to build personal resources, to identifying and using strengths in our work, to the beneficial effects of flow experiences.

Finally, we rounded off the chapter by considering the idea of spirituality at work, with its emphasis on helping people find meaning in their lives and its relevance at the individual, group and organisational level.

TEST YOURSELF

Brief Review Questions

1 What are the valued subjective experiences that positive psychology attempts to investigate?

2 How does Seligman define the three paths to happiness?

3 Outline the broaden-and-build theory of positive emotions.

4 Contrast weakness-based with strengths-based development.

5 Define a 'flow' experience.

6 How is spirituality different from religion?

Discussion or Essay Questions

1 Compare and contrast Maslow's description of a 'self-actualising person' with a positive psychology description of the components of a flourishing life.

2 Is positive psychology too positive?

3 Why do people experience flow more often at work than in their leisure time? What are the implications of this for individuals and organisations?

4 To what extent should organisations try to meet employees' spiritual needs?

FURTHER READING

- For a summary of research findings using the Values in Action (VIA) survey of character strengths, go to http://www.viacharacter.org/www/en-us/research/summaries.
- *The Oxford Handbook of Positive Psychology and Work* explores how positive psychology can be applied to change, leadership, work environments, work life and organisations: P. A. Linley, S. Harrington, & N. Garcea. *Oxford Handbook of Positive Psychology and Work*. Oxford: Oxford University Press, 2010.

References

ASHMOS, D. & DUCHON, D. 2000. Spirituality at work. *Journal of Management Inquiry*, 9, 134–45.

BAKKER, A. B. 2008. The work-related flow inventory: construction and initial validation of the WOLF. *Journal of Vocational Behavior*, 72, 400–14.

BROWN, R. B. 2003. Organizational spirituality: the sceptic's version. *Organization*, 10, 393–400.

BUGENTAL, J. F. 1964. The third force in psychology. *Journal of Humanistic Psychology*, 4, 19–26.

CHRISTOPHER, J. C. & HICKINBOTTOM, S. 2008. Positive psychology, ethnocentrism, and the disguised ideology of individualism. *Theory & Psychology*, 18, 563–89.

CHRISTOPHER, J. C., RICHARDSON, F. C. & SLIFE, B. D. 2008. Thinking through positive psychology. *Theory & Psychology*, 18, 555–61.

CLARKE, S. G. & HAWORTH, J. T. 1994. 'Flow' experience in the daily lives of sixth-form college students. *British Journal of Psychology*, 85, 511–23.

CSIKSZENTMIHALYI, M. 1997. *Finding Flow: The Psychology of Engagement with Everyday Life*. New York, Basic Books.

CSIKSZENTMIHALYI, M. 2000. *Beyond Boredom and Anxiety*. San Francisco, Jossey-Bass.

CSIKSZENTMIHALYI, M. 2006. *Flow and Education*. Philadelphia: University of Pennsylvania, Positive Psychology Center. http://www.ppc.sas.upenn.edu/csikszentmihalyipowerpoint.pdf (accessed 23 September 2013).

CSIKSZENTMIHALYI, M., ABUHAMDEH, S. & NAKAMURA, J. 2005. Flow. In Elliot, A. J. & Dweck, C. S. (eds.) *Handbook of Competence and Motivation*. New York, Guilford Press.

CSIKSZENTMIHALYI, M. & LEFEVRE, J. 1989. Optimal experience in work and leisure. *Journal of Personality and Social Psychology*, 56, 815–22.

DAHLSGAARD, K., PETERSON, C. & SELIGMAN, M. E. 2005. Shared virtue: the convergence of valued human strengths across culture and history. *Review of General Psychology*, 9, 203–13.

FREDRICKSON, B. L. 1998. What good are positive emotions? *Review of General Psychology*, 2, 300–19.

FREDRICKSON, B. L. 2001. The role of positive emotions in positive psychology: the broaden-and-build theory of positive emotions. *American Psychologist*, 56, 218.

FREDRICKSON, B. L. & JOINER, T. 2002. Positive emotions trigger upward spirals toward emotional well-being. *Psychological Science*, 13, 172–5.

FROH, J. J. 2004. The history of positive psychology: truth be told. *NYS Psychologist*, 16, 18–20.

GREENING, T. 2006. Five basic postulates of humanistic psychology. *Journal of Humanistic Psychology*, 46, 239.

HARTER, J. K., SCHMIDT, F. L. & HAYES, T. L. 2002. Business-unit-level relationship between employee satisfaction, employee engagement, and business outcomes: a meta-analysis. *Journal of Applied Psychology*, 87, 268–79.

HARZER, C. & RUCH, W. 2012. When the job is a calling: the role of applying one's signature strengths at work. *The Journal of Positive Psychology*, 7, 362–71.

HELD, B. S. 2002. The tyranny of the positive attitude in America: observation and speculation. *Journal of Clinical Psychology*, 58, 965–92.

HELD, B. S. 2004. The negative side of positive psychology. *Journal of Humanistic Psychology*, 44, 9–46.

HODGES, T. D. & CLIFTON, D. O. 2004. Strengths-based Development in Practice. In Linley, P. A. & Joseph, S. (eds.) *International Handbook of Positive Psychology in Practice: From Research to Application*. New Jersey, Wiley and Sons.

HOWELL, A. J. 2009. Flourishing: achievement-related correlates of students' well-being. *The Journal of Positive Psychology*, 4, 1–13.

HUTA, V. & RYAN, R. M. 2010. Pursuing pleasure or virtue: the differential and overlapping well-being benefits of hedonic and eudaimonic motives. *Journal of Happiness Studies*, 11, 735–62.

JARDEN, A. 2012. Positive psychologists on positive psychology. *International Journal of Wellbeing*, 2 (2), 70–149.

KARAKAS, F. 2010. Spirituality and performance in organizations: a literature review. *Journal of Business Ethics*, 94, 89–106.

KEYES, C. L. 2005. Mental illness and/or mental health? Investigating axioms of the complete state model of health. *Journal of Consulting and Clinical Psychology*, 73, 539–48.

KITAYAMA, S., MARKUS, H. R., MATSUMOTO, H. & NORASAKKUNKIT, V. 1997. Individual and collective processes in the construction of the self: self-enhancement in the United States and self-criticism in Japan. *Journal of Personality and Social Psychology*, 72, 1245–67.

LINLEY, P. A., HARRINGTON, S. & GARCEA, N. 2010. *Oxford Handbook of Positive Psychology and Work*. Oxford, Oxford University Press.

LLORENS, S., SALANOVA, M. & RODRÍGUEZ, A. M. 2013. How is flow experienced and by whom? Testing flow among occupations. *Stress and Health*, 29, 125–37.

LUTHANS, F., AVOLIO, B. J., AVEY, J. B. & NORMAN, S. M. 2007. Positive psychological capital: measurement and relationship with performance and satisfaction. *Personnel Psychology*, 60, 541–72.

LUTHANS, F. & JENSEN, S. M. 2002. Hope: a new positive strength for human resource development. *Human Resource Development Review*, 1, 304–22.

MCGRATH, R. E. 2014. Scale- and item-level factor analyses of the via inventory of strengths. *Assessment*, 21, 4–14.

MASLOW, A. H. 1954. *Motivation and Personality*. New York, Harper & Row.

MILLIMAN, J., CZAPLEWSKI, A. J. & FERGUSON, J. 2003. Workplace spirituality and employee work attitudes: an exploratory empirical assessment. *Journal of Organizational Change Management*, 16, 426–47.

MONETA, G. 2004. The flow experience across cultures. *Journal of Happiness Studies*, 5, 115–21.

NAKAMURA, J. & CSIKSZENTMIHALYI, M. 2009. Flow Theory and Research. In Lopez, S. J. & Snyder, C. R. (eds.) *Oxford Handbook of Positive Psychology*. Oxford, Oxford University Press.

OUWENEEL, E., LE BLANC, P. M., SCHAUFELI, W. B. & VAN WIJHE, C. I. 2012. Good morning, good day: a diary study on positive emotions, hope, and work engagement. *Human Relations*, 65, 1129–54.

PARK, N., PETERSON, C. & SELIGMAN, M. E. 2004. Strengths of character and well-being. *Journal of Social and Clinical Psychology*, 23, 603–19.

PETERSON, C. & PARK, N. 2006. Character strengths in organizations. *Journal of Organizational Behavior*, 27, 1149–54.

PETERSON, C. & SELIGMAN, M. E. 2004. *Character Strengths and Virtues: A Handbook and Classification*. Oxford, Oxford University Press.

RATH, T. & HARTER, J. 2010. *Wellbeing: The Five Essential Elements*. New York, Gallup Press.

ROGERS, C. R. 1951. *Client-Centered Therapy – Its Current Practice, Implications, and Theory*. Boston, MA, Houghton Mifflin Company.

ROGERS, C. R. 1961. *On Becoming a Person*. Oxford, Houghton Mifflin.

SALANOVA, M., BAKKER, A. B. & LLORENS, S. 2006. Flow at work: evidence for an upward spiral of personal and organizational resources. *Journal of Happiness Studies*, 7, 1–22.

SCHUELLER, S. M. & SELIGMAN, M. E. 2010. Pursuit of pleasure, engagement, and meaning: relationships to subjective and objective measures of well-being. *The Journal of Positive Psychology*, 5, 253–63.

SCHÜLER, J. 2012. The Dark Side of the Moon. In Engeser, S. (ed.) *Advances in Flow Research*. New York, Springer.

SELIGMAN, E. P. 2011. *Flourish: A Visionary New Understanding of Happiness and Well-being*. New York, Free Press.

SELIGMAN, M. 1998. The President's Address. In *APA Annual Report*. Washington, American Psychological Association.

SELIGMAN, M. E. 2002. *Authentic Happiness: Using the New Positive Psychology to Realize your Potential for Lasting Fulfillment*. New York, Free Press.

SELIGMAN, M. E. & CSIKSZENTMIHALYI, M. 2000. Positive psychology: an introduction. *American Psychologist*, 55, 5.

SELIGMAN, M. E., STEEN, T. A., PARK, N. & PETERSON, C. 2005. Positive psychology progress: empirical validation of interventions. *American Psychologist*, 60, 410–21.

SHELDON, K. M. & KING, L. 2001. Why positive psychology is necessary. *American Psychologist*, 56, 216.

SHRYACK, J., STEGER, M. F., KRUEGER, R. F. & KALLIE, C. S. 2010. The structure of virtue: an empirical investigation of the dimensionality of the virtues in action inventory of strengths. *Personality and Individual Differences*, 48, 714–19.

SNYDER, C., LOPEZ, S. J., ASPINWALL, L., FREDRICKSON, B. L. ET AL. 2002. The Future of Positive Psychology: A Declaration of Independence. In Snyder, C. R. & Lopez, S. J. (eds.) *Handbook of Positive Psychology*. New York, Oxford University Press.

SOSIK, J. J., GENTRY, W. A. & CHUN, J. U. 2012. The value of virtue in the upper echelons: a multisource examination of executive character strengths and performance. *The Leadership Quarterly*, 23, 367–82.

TAYLOR, E. 2001. Positive psychology and humanistic psychology: a reply to Seligman. *Journal of Humanistic Psychology*, 41, 13–29.

WRZESNIEWSKI, A., MCCAULEY, C., ROZIN, P. & SCHWARTZ, B. 1997. Jobs, careers, and callings: people's relations to their work. *Journal of Research in Personality*, 31, 21–33.

From its beginnings as an insurance underwriter
20 years ago, the BGL Group has developed
and expanded to become a major financial
services company. It now employs more than 3,000
people in several different areas of the business,
including legal services, insurance brands and
the price comparison site comparethemarket.com.
Interestingly, although BGL is successful
and consistently reports increased profits, its plans
for the future are not solely profit-based. Instead,
the BGL strategy explicitly states that increasing
employee engagement and meeting CSR (corporate
social responsibility) targets such as charitable
giving, are just as important to the business as
profits and customer satisfaction.

© BANANASTOCK

The well-being programme at BGL is of central importance to this strategy. As Steve Dewar, Senior Manager for
Wellbeing, says: 'BGL sets ambitious targets but has a habit of meeting them too! And we recognise that if we
want to continue to drive the business forward, we need people who are healthy, fully engaged and have fun
working here.'

There are two main reasons that well-being is seen as so important at BGL. Firstly, it is a natural expression of the
BGL culture, which genuinely puts employees at the centre of the organisation. BGL not only recognises that it
has a duty of care towards its people, but there is also a sense that treating employees well and providing
well-being support is the 'right thing to do'. Secondly, BGL believes that well-being initiatives provide a good
return on investment: they can help to sustain high performance, reduce absenteeism and contribute to attracting
and retaining talented people.

The original well-being programme

The well-being programme was originally introduced in 2010 following an internal employee opinion survey which
asked employees whether they thought BGL took their well-being seriously. Results showed that 69% of
employees agreed, a finding that provided the stimulus to improve what was becoming a key driver of
engagement.

The 'My Wellbeing' programme was born, consisting of four main pillars:

1 My Health – which included subsidised private health care, eyecare vouchers and access to an employee
   assistance programme (EAP).
2 My Fitness – including discounted rates to local gyms, sports massage and a lunchtime walking club.
3 My Happiness – support on dealing with money issues and personal legal matters.
4 My Relaxation and Energy – subsidised osteopathy, at-desk massage and sleep workshops.

Just two years after its launch, the 2012 survey showed that the well-being programme was already having a
positive effect on the employees, with 85% agreeing that BGL took their well-being seriously: a 16% increase in
18 months. Mark, who joined the company recently, emphasises how different it is to work at BGL compared with
his previous employer. 'The company genuinely seems to care about us and I'm really enjoying my work. We have
inter-team competitions with prizes, I use the on-site gym several times a week and the annual Fun Day is a great
day out with my family. It makes me proud to work here!'

For the first couple of years, although different proposals, initiatives and offerings were added to the programme,
there was little measurement of what kind of impact they were having or whether the employees were finding
them useful. Now, however, efforts are being made to review and refine the offering and to take a more proactive,
planned approach to developing the programme. One of the drivers for this is the rapid growth that BGL is
undergoing, and which is set to continue over the next few years. The management at BGL recognised that
growth at this speed and the increasingly diverse workforce would bring challenges that a coherent and
well-resourced well-being programme could help to meet.

The development of the programme

As a first step in refining the programme, an internal employee survey was conducted, specifically looking at awareness, usage and the usefulness of the various services and benefits. The survey also asked employees to rate their overall health in a number of categories including fitness, sleep, emotional well-being and energy. Results showed that there was high awareness among the staff of the general well-being programme and that they really appreciated its provision. However, there were varying levels of awareness of the different elements of the programme. Some initiatives, such as providing free fruit to all employees, were well known, while others, such as access to the EAP, were not. In addition, the survey identified that some elements of the programme, for example, access to doctors for second opinions, were rarely used, while other elements, such as the on-site gym, were very popular.

The survey also asked employees for suggestions for future well-being offerings, with the aim that the company will invest in in the most popular suggestions. For example, many employees said they would like to see fitness classes and yoga provided on site, and so BGL is now talking to potential service providers and has begun a pilot of aerobic classes in the on-site gym. Another suggestion was help with quitting smoking – but as this was less popular, rather than providing the service directly, BGL is going to provide links and point employees in the right direction so that they can access support themselves.

Alongside the internal research, BGL also engaged a consultancy to conduct external research: case studies of other companies with well-being programmes that could provide a benchmark and a review of the academic literature on the elements of a successful well-being programme. This research identified several elements that BGL was already doing, including using well-being to drive retention and engagement, having an employee-led offering which provides the services that employees themselves say they need, and being committed to an ongoing programme. The research also identified a few things that BGL could work on to make the programme more effective. These included having clear return on investment measures, including well-being in their CSR reporting and looking at how a positive and more formal approach to flexible working could help develop the business. This last point is a particularly important challenge for BGL because it has traditionally encouraged a culture of face-to-face engagement and regular networking based on conventional working hours.

Overall, the research demonstrated that while the well-being offering did not need to undergo radical change, it would benefit from continuing evolution and development. Based on the internal and external research, and in consultation with BGL's Executive Board, the well-being programme is being simplified and rebranded into two main areas: My Workplace and My Health.

My Workplace focuses on creating an environment which will stimulate, inspire and refresh. Some of the initiatives being considered here include providing outdoor meeting pods, changing the look and feel of building exteriors and increasing the natural light in offices. BGL is also discussing the introduction of a cycle-to-work scheme, and so consideration needs to be given to the extra facilities that will be needed to support this, such as secure bicycle parking and additional showers/changing rooms. The My Workplace aspect of the well-being programme also includes traditional health and safety issues: Steve Dewar was formerly Health and Safety Manager and explains that the H&S policy will ultimately be transformed into a broader and more engaging well-being statement: 'We're moving away from old fashioned compliance statements to demonstrating a commitment from the top that we want to create an environment that supports our long term physical and emotional well-being.'

The second area, My Health, is underpinned by nutritional education and line manager training, and includes both physical and emotional/mental health. Some aspects of the original well-being programme are being retained and improved, such as more access to sports massage and osteopathy, and healthy eating options at the on-site restaurants. But there are also bigger developments afoot, for example building well-being suites at all sites, considering on-site gyms at other locations and introducing organised team sports. In addition, training for line managers will include resilience training: how to improve their own resilience but also how to develop it in their teams and support people as and when they need it.

Current challenges and benefits of the programme

In rolling out this revamped well-being programme, BGL is facing several challenges. One of them is striking a balance between 'push' and 'pull'. This is the challenge of respecting employees' private lives and not trying to interfere in their out-of-work activities and lifestyle, while still recognising that non-work life is intricately connected with work performance. For example, it is well known that good nutrition and exercise are important to our general health and vitality and subsequently our ability to perform well at work. But how can an organisation really influence the food and exercise choices that employees make? BGL's approach to dealing with this is to offer healthy eating options in the work restaurants and free fruit in the offices, provide on-site gyms or reduced local gym membership, and allow employees to take advantage of these offers if they wish to. By making the well-being packages as attractive as possible, BGL is aiming to encourage employees to make informed decisions about health and nutrition that will ultimately have a positive impact on their work.

A second major challenge is to find ways of aligning the well-being programme with HR systems, policies and processes. Having joined-up systems will ensure that the programme is easier to administer. For example, a cycle-to-work scheme has tax advantages for participating employees and may even involve salary sacrifice. This would clearly be much easier to administer if it was linked directly with payroll. Alignment of the well-being programme with absence reporting and turnover statistics will also make the return on investment (ROI) easier to calculate.

Calculating this ROI is the third challenge for the organisation. It is not easy to directly measure what impact a well-being programme is having on employees, but BGL is focusing on three key performance indicators: absenteeism, attraction and retention, and employee engagement. Being able to measure these and demonstrate improvements is an important part of justifying the expenditure on well-being as the Group expands.

The company's commitment to employees' well-being is emphasised in the BGL Group's values, which include 'Just . . . be happy'. BGL believes that well-being can contribute in specific other areas too. To take an example, another of its values is 'Just . . . be creative' and many activities contribute to encouraging innovation and creativity among employees. From idea labs and forums where employees can post their improvement ideas for development, to break out rooms where they can go for informal meetings or a break from their normal work, to fun competitions, there are many things that help to improve well-being and also encourage collaboration and creativity at work.

As this book went to press, BGL Group's 2014 employee opinion survey results had just been revealed and the number of employees who believe BGL takes their well-being seriously has risen to 93%; an increase of 8% on the 2012 result. Overall, the investment that BGL makes in its well-being offering is substantial and wide ranging. While it might originally spring from a culture which sees it as the organisation's responsibility to care for employees, it is certainly bearing fruit elsewhere. As a recent candidate told the executive recruitment team, 'It's your well-being programme that really sets the company apart and makes me want to work here.'

(With thanks to the BGL Group and Steve Dewar, Senior Manager for Wellbeing, for their involvement)

Discussion or Essay Questions

1 Why do you think BGL choose to take such a positive, proactive approach to employee well-being? How does this compare with other organisations you know about?

2 How do the models of well-being that BGL has used compare with academic models? What are the advantages of using an employee-led definition of well-being as opposed to a model from the literature? Are there any aspects of well-being that are being missed in this programme?

3 What are the implications of health and safety policies becoming part of a wider well-being programme?

Consider both the potential advantages and disadvantages of this approach.

4 With lots of creativity and fast expansion of a business comes a fast pace of change for the employees who work there. To what extent do you think a well-being programme might be able to help an organisation manage change effectively?

5 One of the challenges BGL faces, in common with many other organisations, is striking a balance between respecting employees' privacy and trying to encourage healthy lifestyles. To what extent do you think an organisation has a right to influence an employee's non-work life?

PART 3

CUTTING-EDGE PSYCHOLOGY

PART 1 OUTLINED THE DAILY CHALLENGES OF WORK AND HOW WE CAN USE psychology to craft a better workplace. In Part 2, we built on this by looking at how it can be used to help us to thrive in difficult circumstances and to create more fulfilling work lives. In Part 3, we are going even further, to explore the edges of current thinking in work psychology and to gain an insight into exciting new developments.

In Chapter 11, we find out how psychology is being applied to different areas of business, including consumer, coaching and economic psychology as well as new developments into understanding how we interact with computers. In this chapter we consider in detail the

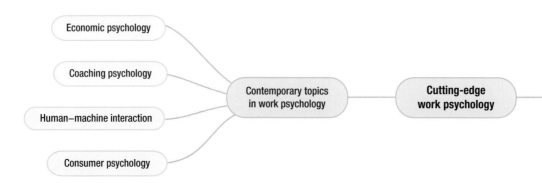

interrelationships between technology and psychology: how technology is changing the way we work and also how it opens up new applications of psychology. And finally we draw this part and the book to a close in Chapter 12 by taking a detailed look at how psychological research is conducted. This is your springboard to a lifetime of psychological expertise: learning how to identify well-conducted research so that you can stay up to date with psychological applications in your future career, whatever that might be.

The case study in Part 3 illustrates these issues by describing an occupational psychology consultancy project, from the initial meeting with the client organisation through to the final delivery and implementation of the findings.

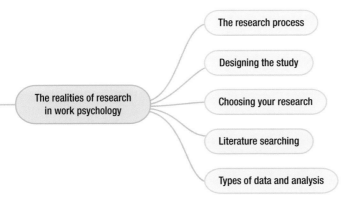

CONTEMPORARY TOPICS IN WORK PSYCHOLOGY

11

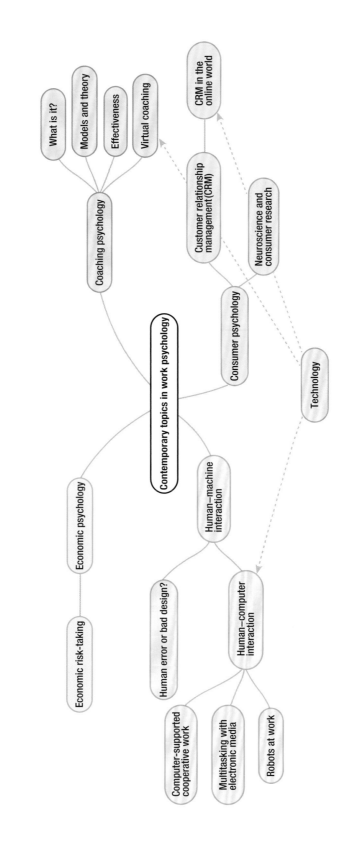

Contemporary topics in work psychology

Coaching psychology
- What is it?
- Models and theory
- Effectiveness
- Virtual coaching

Customer relationship management (CRM)
- CRM in the online world

Neuroscience and consumer research

Consumer psychology

Technology

Economic psychology
- Economic risk-taking

Human–machine interaction
- Human error or bad design?

Human–computer interaction
- Computer-supported cooperative work
- Multitasking with electronic media
- Robots at work

This chapter explores recent developments in work psychology, highlighting a few interesting growth areas and with a particular emphasis on the impact and use of new technologies. First we discuss human–machine interaction, tracing its development from time and motion studies to modern concerns with how we interact with technology, its effect on our work lives and how computer systems are designed.

Next, we look at economic and consumer psychology, reviewing the insights that psychology can give into how we make financial decisions and what products we choose. In this section we will find out more about the impact of social media on the management of customer relationships. Finally, we turn to look at coaching psychology, discussing how an application of psychological techniques can help clients to reach personal and professional success. We round off the chapter by considering the use of technology in enabling virtual coaching.

This chapter will help you answer the following questions:

1 How does psychology help us to design 'human-friendly' machines?
2 What are the important individual factors we need to take into account when dealing with economics?
3 How can psychological insights help us to understand people as consumers?
4 In what ways can psychology be used to help people reach their work goals?

The International Perspectives section in this chapter is a self-contained topic exploring how psychology can help us to understand expatriate assignments and how we can use psychology to improve the success of these costly investments for the organisations involved.

International Perspectives **Expatriation**

Expatriate assignments are an increasingly important part of the global workplace, yet they can be among the most challenging assignments an employee can take on. Not only does the expatriate have to adjust to a new workplace, but also a new culture and often a new language. In addition, workers on international assignments will experience differing levels of strain in their families: either their families will move with them and have to adjust to the new country as well, or the expatriate has to adjust to living apart from his or her loved ones.

Expatriate assignments are costly to the organisation, and selecting people who are more likely to succeed in expatriate assignments is important. Research has shown that specific personality factors (higher extraversion, openness, emotional stability and agreeableness) and competencies (task and people orientations and non-ethnocentric attitudes) are associated with greater expatriate success (Shaffer et al., 2006, Tsai-Jung et al., 2005).

The extent to which an expatriate feels comfortable in the new situation is referred to as 'adjustment' and underlies relevant work-related outcomes such as performance, turnover intent and job satisfaction (Hechanova et al., 2003). Adjustment is typically viewed as having three elements: degree of comfort with the general environment, the work environment and interaction with host nationals. Hechanova et al.'s meta-analytic study found the following antecedents influenced all three elements of expatriate adjustment:

▸ the expatriate's self-efficacy
▸ how frequently the expatriate interacted with host nationals
▸ how supportive the expatriate's family was.

To understand expatriate success you also have to take into account how an individual's career interacts with the three stages of pre-expatriation, expatriation and repatriation (Pargneux and Cerdin, 2009). For expatriates themselves, one of the most valued aspects of international assignments is the extent to which they allow opportunities for learning and new work experiences. However, the resultant high expectations that expatriates have about their careers can cause dissatisfaction upon returning home (Bonache, 2005), and this highlights how important it is to ensure that the assignment fits with the individual's career characteristics.

Discussion points

Given that international assignments are so costly to the organisation and have such a large potential for failure, why do you think they are still so widespread?

If you were given the task of selecting employees for a two-year expatriate assignment, what factors would you want to assess? Would it make any difference what country you were sending them to?

HUMAN–MACHINE INTERACTION

From its beginnings, a strong theme in work psychology has been how people interact with machines. We cannot just assume that people will use a machine in exactly the way it has been designed. Instead, good design takes account of human psychology: how we behave, our perceptions and our decision-making processes.

Human error or bad design?

Frederick Taylor's influence on work psychology was in using time-and-motion studies to make manual work practices more efficient, with the emphasis on how to train employees to use tools most effectively. During and after the Second World War, work psychologists broadened their approach to consider how machines could be designed to take account of the way humans naturally behave (Grudin, 2011). For example, during the war, a common error made by aeroplane pilots was that they retracted the wheels instead of the flaps after landing (Roscoe, 1997). This was seen as a pilot error until a psychologist, Alphonse Chapanis, was brought in to investigate why this error only seemed to happen with certain aircraft. He immediately noticed that the switches for the flaps and wheels in these aircraft were nearly identical and right next to each other, meaning that pilots could easily get them mixed up. Chapanis pointed out that this 'pilot' error was really a design error, and suggested the simple solution of fixing a small rubber wheel to the wheels switch and a wedge-shape on the flaps control. This solved the problem: there were no more 'pilot errors' and the design was standardised worldwide.

Employees can, of course, be given training in how to act safely and to abide by safety rules. However, recognising that people do not always use machines the way they are 'supposed' to is an important part of ensuring a safe working environment. Unfortunately, workers are often put under pressure to maximise productivity, even at the expense of their own safety. As an example, consider the following scenario. During the trial stages of a new product, a machine which produces wet wipes seems to get clogged up regularly. The correct procedure for dealing with this is to use the safety cut-out to stop the entire machine, clear the blockage and then start it up again. But this results in a lot of waste and downtime. The machine operators, under pressure to increase productivity, find that if they are careful they can simply reach into the running machine and clear the blockage without switching it off. No matter how hard the designers of a machine work on trying to make it safe, the people who operate the machine on a daily basis are bound to find ways round the safety procedures, sometimes with disastrous consequences. Understanding the wider culture of the organisation and the pressures and expectations on the workers is essential to ensuring a really safe workplace. The case study below explores this in more detail.

 Case Study A 'safe' machine

Lynda Trebilock had been a cleaner at DeliCo Ltd, a meat processing plant, for only two months when she was killed in a work accident. She crouched down to check the cleanliness of one of the machines when a heavy metal flap suddenly closed on her head. She died from the injuries.

How did this happen? The machine itself had a safety 'proximity' switch that prevented the flap being opened unless there was a metal container in place to collect the product, so it simply should not have been possible for Mrs Trebilock to get into that dangerous position.

The problem arose because the factory sometimes used a plastic container to collect the product. But a plastic container could not activate the proximity switch, so the people operating the machine had come up with a work-around. They put a metal clipboard over the switch, effectively 'tricking' the system into thinking there was a

© Thinkstock

metal container in place and raising the heavy metal flap. When Mrs Trebilock crouched down to inspect the machine, it seems the clipboard was dislodged and the flap dropped on her.

(Daily Mail reporter, 2009)

▶ This machine was designed with what would have seemed a sensible safety precaution, yet it did not stop someone being fatally injured. If you were to redesign this machine to improve safety, what would you need to take into account?

▶ DeliCo was found guilty of breaching health and safety laws, yet the machine itself had safety cut-outs. What else should DeliCo have done to ensure workers' safety?

▶ Is there such a thing as a 'safe' machine?

Moving beyond the idea of simply providing employees with training about the correct or safest ways to use machines, more recent understandings of safety at work consider the role of overall organisational culture. This was brought to prominence after the Chernobyl disaster, when the report of the International Nuclear Safety Advisory Group (INSAG, 1988) first used the phrase 'safety culture', a culture in which safety is the number one priority for the organisation. If safety is given priority over everything else the organisation does, which some authors have argued should always be the case in high-risk industries (Cooper, 2000), then the likelihood of workers bypassing safety systems is much reduced.

Human–computer interaction

The most prominent machine in our everyday work lives must be the computer. It is hard to imagine a workplace today without computers, yet less than 40 years ago only 50,000 computers were sold worldwide per year (Gartner, 2013). The current figure is above 355 million a year, and we use computers for work and leisure, for everything from communication to ordering groceries. The study of human–computer interaction (HCI) has undergone a similar boom in interest.

HCI research is undertaken in two main areas (Olson and Olson, 2003):

- Design of computer systems – attempting to develop useful and useable, as well as aesthetically pleasing, software and hardware
- Evaluation of systems in use – finding out what effect computing systems have on the individual, group, organisation and wider society.

We will look at research in both these areas, first by considering the role of design in computer-supported cooperative work and second by looking at how mobile media influence our attention and concentration.

Fad or Fact? Technology makes us more productive

In 1993, Erik Brynjolfsson wrote an article called 'The productivity paradox of Information Technology', noting that productivity in the USA had not kept pace with advances in computing power. This was especially true for the service sector. The research seemed to indicate that, despite an expectation that computers would make organisations more productive, all the investment in IT was not paying off at a national level. Brynjolfsson suggested four main reasons for this gap between our expectations and the reality of IT:

- Mismanagement – it is difficult to manage IT and information, so the potential gains are never realised. This is the explanation people usually latch on to but may not be the most important contributing factor.
- Redistribution – while some organisations may benefit, this gain comes at the expense of other companies, leaving little overall net gain when measured at a national level.
- Time lags – the beneficial effects of IT investment may take a long time to show.
- Mismeasurement – the gains may well be real, but current measures do not capture them.

Brynjolfsson also suggests that the contribution of IT is more likely to be around helping us to do new things in new ways, rather than simply producing more of the same. Landauer (1995) picks up on this theme when he discusses the difference between phase one and phase two computer applications. Phase one applications do the same task as a human but much more efficiently, for example calculations or mechanical operations. Phase two applications are designed to help people think and are much more difficult to develop. Examples include decision-making, persuading, creating, pattern recognition and even filling in missing information. One reason that computers may not have had the impact on the service sector that was expected is because they cannot duplicate these human thought processes. The other important factor here is how useable the system is. Even if the application could help us with complex thought processes, if we cannot use it easily it will lead to errors or simply be ignored.

In fact, as usability and utility of computer systems has increased, there is evidence of a good improvement in productivity (Brynjolfsson and Hitt, 2003), especially when measured over the longer term.

- Why do you think new advances in IT have a time lag before we see improvements in productivity?
- Do you think computers have made us more productive? Why or why not?

Computer-supported cooperative work

Computers have the potential to enhance cooperative work (work which involves people communicating with each other) and to produce an output that relies on their integrated efforts. 'Collaboration technologies' are programmes or features that support group work, including email, instant messaging, shared calendars, document markup, desktop conferencing and so on (Palen and Grudin, 2003).

When we are trying to understand how technology is adopted and used at work, it is important to bear the wider context in mind. For example, a study of group calendars in the 1980s showed that the majority of managers and secretaries in organisations did not use them, despite their being available and theoretically able to save people time by managing changes and cancellations. The reasons for this were given as (Grudin, 1988):

- paper diaries were more easily accessible (could be carried into meetings, for example)
- group calendars required the contributions of lots of individuals, but only benefited a few
- although most employees had computer access, the computers were not networked well enough for the software to work effectively.

However, the picture had changed dramatically by the 1990s, when a follow-up study indicated much more widespread use of group calendars (Palen and Grudin, 2003). This was seen to be because technology had addressed some of the issues which had prevented its adoption. The applications had become easier to use and provided individual users with benefits such as meeting reminders, rather than benefiting only a few. There had also been a change in infrastructure so that computers were much more widespread and better networked.

While many software applications may have the potential to improve our work life and efficacy, this potential can only be realised if they are designed in a way that will encourage adoption. We also need to be aware of some of the unintended drawbacks of new technologies. For example, while email has widened communication and given us the ability to share work objects such as documents quickly and easily with a group, it has had the consequence that many people suffer information overload (Olson and Olson, 2003), receiving more emails than they actually need to do their jobs properly.

A human-centred approach to designing technology starts from an understanding of how people naturally behave in order to design interfaces that are more intuitive, easier to learn and have fewer errors (Oviatt, 2006). Instead of assuming that we will simply adapt to any new technology, human-centred design takes our cognitive and perceptual limits as a starting point and points out that designs which reduce our cognitive load will allow us to perform better.

We have limited attention and working memory, which act as bottlenecks in our information processing, while cognitive load refers to the resources we have available for completing a task and the demands placed upon them.

Cognitive load is an important aspect of the usability of any technology or computer system. For example, we tend to lose interest in web pages if they are too demanding, if they contain too much text or we have to click too many links to get to the information we want (Share-Bernia, 2005).

Oviatt (2006) presents several principles for interface design which can enhance performance, suggesting that interfaces should:

- Build on or adapt to our current experience, behavioural patterns and work practices rather than trying to change them
- Support our natural multimodal communication (i.e. do not just rely on one mode of communication, such as text)
- Minimise cognitive load at both the input stage (by making the input needed as simple as possible) as well as the output stage (by removing unnecessary, distracting features)
- Minimise interruptions by the system, as these disrupt our ability to engage in higher-level thinking.

 Activity Redesigning an interface

For this exercise, go to your university's library web page. From here, navigate to a relevant research database, such as PsychInfo, and carry out a search on a relevant topic. For example, you might want to search for more information about human-centred interface design.

▸ Now consider the process you went through for this activity and the different interfaces you used. Using Oviatt's principles of design, what improvements could you suggest to either the designers of your university web pages or the database search?

Multitasking with electronic media

The second major area of human–computer interaction research is in understanding the impact of computers on us. One of the most interesting changes brought about by recent technology changes has been the increase in 'multitasking'. Friedman (2006), a columnist with the *New York Times*, suggested that multitasking in the Information Age has led to an 'Age of Interruption', where attention spans shorten and we are incapable of taking the uninterrupted time we need to develop higher thought processes.

Linda Stone, a top executive with both Apple and Microsoft before she retired, differentiated between multitasking and 'continuous partial attention'. The former is an attempt to get as many things done as possible in order to free up time for ourselves and be more productive, while the latter is motivated by the desire to be connected and not miss anything (Stone, 2013). By making this distinction, Stone is emphasising the difference between what we are doing (the tasks) and how we are doing it (partial attention), as well as the ubiquitous nature of modern communicative technologies. However, in practical terms, a distinction between the two is less helpful: any multitasking involves a split in attention, and it is that partial attention to something which causes us problems.

What we commonly think of as multitasking is more accurately referred to as *task-switching*. We are capable of true multitasking only when the tasks are fully automated – that is, when they do not require conscious attention. But real multitasking on tasks that require simultaneous cognitive processing is impossible for us. If you're not convinced, try reading something at the same time as you work out a simple calculation. Or telling someone about your day while you write down what you had for lunch yesterday. You can even see it in action if you try walking down a busy street while talking to your friend. You will be able to do both things at once as long as there are no obstacles to avoid or other people to walk around. But as soon as you have to think about where you are walking next, in other words bring it to conscious attention, you will find your conversation falters or you trip or bump into something. Instead of being able to process two tasks simultaneously, we have to keep switching our attention back and forth between the tasks. This leads to a loss in performance compared with keeping our attention focused on a single task.

The detrimental effect of task-switching on performance has been demonstrated in academic settings. For example, students who spent more time using electronic media (social networking, gaming, texting, etc.) had lower grades, and two-thirds of students in this study reported using electronic media during lectures or while studying, indicating that attempts to multitask negatively impacted on grades (Jacobsen and Forste, 2011). In addition, people who spent more time instant messaging were more highly distractable from academic tasks (Levine et al., 2007). In an experimental study, students who were allowed to text during a lecture scored significantly worse on an exam covering the lecture content than those who were not allowed to text (Ellis et al., 2010). Similar findings emerged for students in both the USA and Europe: those who used social networking sites more had a lower grade average (Karpinski et al., 2013). The authors of this study point out that the problem is the 'disruptive' use of social networking, when people attempt to multitask rather than concentrate on the task in hand.

 Activity Multitasking

Conduct an experiment on yourself. Find a chapter in a textbook that you have not yet read. Sit somewhere quiet where you will not be interrupted, well away from your computer, and switch your phone off (not just to silent). Set a timer for 15 minutes and read the text, keeping focused on just this task. At the end of the time, put the book down and write down everything you can remember.

Now, repeat the exercise with a different (new) chapter. This time, do whatever you like as well as reading. You can text friends, check any networking sites you want, look things up on the internet. Again, at the end of 15 minutes, write down everything you can remember from the textbook.

▶ Did you notice any difference between your 'multitasking' exercise and the one where you removed interruptions?

▶ Why do you think most people think they are good at multitasking when all the evidence indicates we can't actually do it?

The same problems with task-switching occur in the workplace. For example, a study of clinicians in emergency rooms identified that multitasking (or task-switching) led to gaps in the flow of information about patients (Laxmisan et al., 2007). The increased cognitive load brought about by task-switching leaves us susceptible to errors and decreases our overall performance.

Robots at work

Imagine your boss was a robot. That day might not be as far off as you think. We are now used to the way technologies can help us communicate with people over long distances, using both video and audio. But recent developments around 'telepresence' have the potential to expand this even further.

Telepresence is the sense of being in an environment in which you are not physically present. To a certain extent, you can get this through videoconferencing: you are able to see and hear the person you are communicating with. But mobile robotic telepresence or mobile remote presence systems (MRPs) combine videoconferencing with mobile robots which can move around in and interact with the environment. The aim of these MRPs is to facilitate social interaction between humans (Kristoffersson et al., 2013). The simplest MRPs look just like a computer monitor on wheels but they can be more complex than this, including robotic arms or hands that the pilot of the system can use to interact with the distant environment.

Attempts have already been made to use MRPs to encourage communication between co-workers who are separated by distance. A major advantage of MRPs is that they can be used in informal communication: the pilot of the MRP can use it to wander the hallways just as if he or she were really there and strike up a conversation with people encountered along the way (Lee and Takayama, 2011). MRPs also allow their pilots to demonstrate commitment by being present in the organisation and to capture and maintain people's attention in a way that would not be possible using other technologies such as email. Importantly, pilots could build social connections with co-workers, and the MRPs helped colleagues who had never met feel that they had got to know each other. On the downside, MRPs were still considered difficult to drive, and pilots had trouble splitting their attention between using the system and the conversation they were trying to have. Another issue with MRPs is how social norms develop around treating them as machines or people. For example, sometimes the MRP was viewed as an extension of the pilot, with people naturally making space for it during conversations or local workers asking for permission from the pilot before moving it; sometimes, the MRP was treated as a machine, with a local worker adjusting the system's volume without checking with the pilot or the pilot simply logging off and leaving at the end of a conversation, abandoning the MRP in the room.

The research so far indicates that MRPs certainly have the potential to increase social interaction between geographically distributed workers. The use of MRPs in hospitals is also on the rise, and evidence so far indicates that patients respond positively to them: there are gains in efficiency, reduced waiting times and improved outcomes (Kristoffersson et al., 2013).

Studies of 'real' robots in workplaces, robots which are controlled by computers rather than a human pilot, indicate that people generally accept them (Leite et al., 2013). (Note that this review only discussed social robots, designed to interact with people, not industrial robots used in manufacture.) But they also point out that the more human the robot looks, the more people expect it to be able to behave in complex, human ways, for example by using emotion and engaging in interactive conversation.

In this section, we have seen how HCI research highlights the importance of human psychology in the design of machine and computer systems if they are to deliver the potential benefits that we expect from them. The impact of new technology on our social and attentional world is also important because new technology can have unexpected side effects. We now turn to consider another important area of modern business: economics.

ECONOMIC PSYCHOLOGY

Economics is the discipline that attempts to understand how we allocate resources, as individuals (microeconomics) and as organisations or markets (macroeconomics). Traditionally, economists used models which assumed people were rational, because they could be more easily captured in mathematical equations and could make reasonably accurate predictions (Camerer, 1999). The assumption was that non-rational behaviour was not important in understanding these kinds of decisions and that the human element could be viewed as 'disturbances' in the operation of rational economic laws (van Raaij, 1981). Over the last few decades, however, economics and psychology have become more unified, with models now taking account of psychological findings about our cognitive processes. This merging field is referred to as economic psychology or behavioural economics, and the traditional 'rational' models have been replaced with more realistic 'behavioural principles'. Economic psychology is the study of the causes and consequences of economic behaviour, viewing economic behaviour as 'the function of human motives, perceptions, attitudes expectations and bounded by the economic conditions' (van Raaij, 1981, p. 6).

In their discussion of how psychology can contribute to our understanding of financial crisis, Gärling et al. (2009) note that economic models which assume we act in rational or sensible ways will always fail. In highly complex situations such as the stock market, our capacity to make rational decisions is simply overtaxed, and cognitive biases have a greater impact. So rather than seeing economic psychology as the study of the 'irrational' part of economics, we should instead see it as finding the *regularities* in our perceptions and decisions that account for our economic behaviour (Gärling et al., 2009). These regularities may not appear rational, but they reflect more accurately how our minds work.

The first issue of the *Journal of Economic Psychology* highlighted its relevance to organisational studies by discussing how managers and executives made economic decisions. Van Raaij (1981) also noted that many of the decisions we make at work, for example concerning overtime or workload, are essentially 'economic', and that economic and organisational psychology can contribute to each other in many different ways. Economic psychology has become even more important since the credit crisis of 2008, because it offers a more realistic understanding of how individual decision-makers behave when faced with uncertainty than the traditional macroeconomics approach does (Ormerod, 2010).

While the field of economic psychology is extensive, we will focus here on the important topic of economic risk-taking.

Economic risk-taking

Like much of economic psychology, this area draws on cognitive psychology to understand and predict people's risk-taking behaviour. In order to understand people's risk-taking, we need to know about their risk perception and risk propensity or attitude.

Risk perception considers how we view a situation. Rather than acting upon objective 'facts' about how much risk is involved, the key determinant of whether we will take a risk is how we perceive it. Different people can view the same risk in different ways. Our perception of risk is an assessment of the uncertainty involved and how much we believe we can control it, as well as how serious we believe the consequences might be.

Risk propensity is our tendency to take or avoid risk, and is closely related to our attitude towards risk. Some people prefer to avoid all risk (referred to as risk-averse), viewing risks as being threats of loss, while others are risk-takers, viewing risks as potential gains. Meta-analysis has shown that generally women are more risk-averse than men, although this difference depends on the situation and also changes over the lifespan (Byrnes et al., 1999).

The influence of the situation in determining risk behaviour deserves further exploration. Someone who takes risks in the social world may well be quite conservative with financial investments, and to understand their behaviour better we need to know more about their motives for taking risks. Zaleskiewicz (2001) distinguished between two types of economic risk-taking based on people's motives: instrumental or stimulating. The table below illustrates the difference in more detail.

Both types of risk-takers tend to be more impulsive and disinhibited than non-risk-takers, but there are also clear differences between the two types. Stimulating risk-taking is associated with thrill and adventure-seeking, while instrumental risk-taking is associated with orientation towards the future and rational thinking. People who seek out risk because of its stimulating effect are more likely to engage in gambling, and they are also more likely to take recreational, ethical and health risks. On the other hand, they are less likely to take business risks because they do not get the same sense of excitement from it. Those who were instrumental risk-takers were more likely to take business risks (e.g. investment) because their aim was to achieve an end goal rather than to feel stimulated.

This distinction adds to the growing evidence that risk-taking is not a stable trait across all situations, and is explored further in the Key Research Study.

 Key Research Study Situational risk-taking

Domain Specificity in Experimental Measures and Participant Recruitment: An Application to Risk-Taking Behavior

Yaniv Hanoch, Joseph G. Johnson, and Andreas Wilke (2006)

Background: An unfortunate aspect of psychological research is that so many studies are based on limited populations and attempt to generalise to the whole population, leading to the suggestion that risk-taking is a stable trait. However, there is growing evidence that risk-taking is 'domain-specific', that people who are risk-takers in one situation may be risk-avoidant in another.

Aim: To find out whether people who took risks in one domain (e.g. recreational) would also take risks in another domain (e.g. financial).

Method: Participants were recruited from four different domains: recreational (e.g. sky divers, scuba divers, bungee jumpers), gambling (casino gamblers), investment (stock-trading clubs) and health. In this final domain, both risk-takers (smokers) and health-seekers (gym members) took part.

Participants completed the domain-specific risk-taking scale (DOSPERT), which assesses how likely people are to take risks in the four domains, how risky they think those activities are and how much benefit they expect to gain.

Findings: As expected, within each domain, people from the relevant sample scored higher on risk-taking and on expected benefits. For example, people from the Recreational risk-taking group scored higher on recreational risk-taking than people from the other groups. Regression analyses showed that the perceived benefits were a better predictor of risk-taking behaviour than was perception of risk.

Table 11.1 Comparison of instrumental and stimulating risk-taking

Instrumental risk-taking	Stimulating risk-taking
Take the risk with the aim of achieving a future benefit (goal orientation)	Take the risk because it feels exciting (excitement orientation)
E.g. investment for pension	E.g. gambling
Associated with more cognitive processes, deliberation and consideration of possible consequences	Associated with emotional processes, focus on present rather than future, impulsive, concentrate on possible gains
Considerable weight given to possible losses	Potential losses unimportant

Implications: When deciding whether to take a risk, the expected benefits are more important to us than the perceived risk. Furthermore, people who take risks in one domain of their life are not necessarily going to take risks in others. That means that measures of risk-taking behaviour need to be domain-specific in order to be useful.

Having looked at one influence on our financial decision-making, we now turn to consider the area of consumerism in more detail by exploring the field of consumer psychology.

CONSUMER PSYCHOLOGY

Consumer psychology is a specific sub-section of psychology that concentrates on understanding our thoughts, feelings and behaviours in relation to products or services that we buy. In this section we are going to consider two interesting applications of psychology in this area: using neuroscience to extend our understanding of our behaviour as consumers and looking at how to manage the customer relationship.

Neuroscience and consumer research

Recent advances in neuroscience have made it possible to study some aspects of our brain's responses more directly than ever before. Instead of relying on eye-tracking or heart rate, researchers can use functional magnetic resonance imagery (fMRI) to see what parts of the brain are activated in response to different stimuli. This has proved particularly interesting to people working in marketing and consumer behaviour because of the potential these approaches have for avoiding problems with self-report measures.

In their review of the emerging consumer neuroscience literature, Solnais et al. (2013) suggest neuroscience can contribute to understanding consumer behaviour by giving us insight into the areas of the brain involved in making consumer decisions and how we perceive the value of different products, the influence of rewards on purchase behaviour, and how emotions, motivations and attention impact on consumption. There are four main areas in which neuroscience can help to develop consumer psychology:

- Decision-making
  - How are consumer preferences formed?
  - Could they be predicted from neural activity?
- Rewards
  - How might attractive marketing stimuli activate the brain's reward system?
  - How do they influence perceived value?
- Memory
  - How is product and advertising memory formed?
  - How does it influence consumer behaviour?
- Emotions
  - How are marketing stimuli processed on a motivational and emotional basis?

Case Study The neuroscience of direct mailing

Virtual advertising, whether by email or integrated adverts in web browsing, is generally a cheaper alternative than direct mail of physical adverts or catalogues. Virtual advertising has certainly shown incredible growth over the last few years, to the detriment of direct mailings. But a recent study indicates that virtual adverts may not be as effective. Using fMRI, it was found that people's brains responded differently to adverts displayed on a screen than they did to physical cards. The physical adverts activated a wider range of brain systems and involved more emotional processing than the virtual ads.

Adapted from Milward Brown (2009)

© SUPER STOCK

▸ Why would it be important to businesses to engage people's emotions in advertising?

▸ If you were planning an advertising campaign and trying to decide whether to use direct or virtual adverts, how would this case study inform your decision?

▸ This research was conducted on behalf of Royal Mail. What implications does this have for our interpretation of the results? What further information would you like to have about the study?

As an example of how neuroscientific research is helping to advance our understanding of consumer psychology, and building on our discussions of risk-taking above, we will discuss one of these areas in more detail: consumer preferences and decision-making. Several studies have demonstrated that when people are making decisions about products, they are integrating 'intangible' information such as the brand image into their evaluation of a product (Solnais et al., 2013) – that is, we use emotional processing rather than purely rational decision-making when choosing products. While this is probably no surprise, we have seen throughout this book how it is always important in psychology to check our 'common sense' understandings of how we function.

Perhaps a more unexpected finding concerns the common approach in marketing of thinking of 'brands' as 'personalities'. Many marketers have claimed that we anthropomorphise products, ascribing human traits to objects, and have even developed scales for assessing brand personalities (e.g. Aaker, 1997). Neuroimaging research can help to explore this issue, because different areas of the brain are activated when we are thinking about people compared with when we are thinking about objects. In fact, an fMRI study found that when people were describing brands, it was the object-processing part of the brain that was activated, not the people-processing part (Yoon et al., 2006). While self-report measures have made it appear that we describe brands in similar ways to people (e.g. reliable or exciting), it seems that this is not how our brain actually processes the information at all.

Some useful general findings are emerging in this area, such as how marketing stimuli can engage the brain's reward system, but there is also a need to be cautious in using neuroscientific research in consumer psychology (Solnais et al., 2013). First, the many different approaches used in this research create a challenge in generalising the results to the consumer domain. Second, the sheer complexity of the brain makes identifying the individual cause and effect of different variables very difficult. And finally, there is a problem with *reverse inference* in neuroimaging data: we reason 'backwards from the presence of brain activation to the engagement of a particular cognitive function' (Poldrack, 2006, p. 59) – that is, when a particular brain area is activated, we infer that this is because a specific cognitive process is active. For example, if the amygdala is active (a part of the brain associated with emotions), we infer that some kind of emotional processing is taking place. However, the neuroimage itself does not show us these cognitive processes, and other factors could be creating this brain activation.

At almost the opposite end of psychology from the detailed world of neuroscience, we now turn to consider a more social aspect of consumer psychology: relationship management.

Customer relationship management

Managing the customer relationship is seen as an essential part of modern business, as it recognises the long-term value of attracting and retaining customers (Bolton and Tarasi, 2007). Historically, it was based on the idea of market segmentation: identifying groups of customers based on their value to the organisation and then developing appropriate strategies for managing those relationships. For example, Reinartz and Kumar (Reinartz and Kumar, 2002) differentiated between high- and low-profit and short- and long-term customers and suggested that companies use different strategies for dealing with them, including knowing when 'losing' a customer would actually be beneficial.

A psychological approach to customer relationship management (CRM) focuses on applying what we know about how social relationships are created and maintained to the field of business. While a lot of the research is specific to different kinds of relationship, such as marital or friendship, some of the findings are general enough to be useful here. Hennessey and Vincent (2005) suggest that we draw on social psychology findings in designing business practices for forming and maintaining relationships between employees and customers:

- Match employees to customers based on values and interests rather than based on location or size of account
- Recognise that because 'liking' is so important in relationships, that it may be appropriate to pass the customer on to a colleague if that initial contact is not working.

Based on exchange theory, customer relationships can be maintained by ensuring that the benefits to the customer exceed the costs (including the cost of changing company). Vandermerwe (2000) distinguishes between 'lock-in' and 'lock-on' in defining customer relationships. Product lock-in occurs when the customer has no choice but to stay with the organisation, either because that company has a monopoly or because the customer has made a large investment and would lose too much by leaving. Lock in is based on making the switching costs too great for the customer. Lock-on is when the customer freely chooses loyalty to the organisation, and is based on maximising the perceived benefits to the customer.

Activity Lock-in or lock-on?

Mobile phones provide a good example of the lock-in vs lock-on approach to customer relationship management. Lock-in happens when you sign a contract, typically for 18 months or more.
In exchange for this you often get a handset at a greatly reduced price and a service package of minutes, texts and data, but cannot leave the contract early. Lock-on is more common with pay as you go services, in which case you pay for a certain level of service but have to buy a handset at a higher retail price.

▸ Which approach do you prefer? Why? What costs and benefits does this approach have for you personally?

▸ What kind of offers or rewards are you aware of that mobile phone companies are using to try and maintain customer loyalty? Could they be classified as lock-in or lock-on? Which are most effective with you?

Adding value for the customer is one way in which businesses can build and maintain lock-on relationships, and this can be done at three levels (Hennessey and Vincent, 2005):

1 Value for money – meeting the customer's expectations for the basic product or service
2 Added value – exceeding expectations, for example by delivering ahead of time or including extra features
3 Created value – the business suggests new or innovative ways that the customer can benefit. This stage is only possible if there is a good relationship between the customer and the business.

An understanding of individual psychology can help organisations to identify the extra value that different customers will appreciate, such as friendship, aesthetics or fitting in with ethical values, and thereby develop better customer relationships.

CRM in the online world

If managing customer relationships is challenging, managing them in a virtual world can be even more so. Hemp (2006) pointed out that CRM in the virtual world becomes a relationship between the business and the customer's avatar (their online visual representation). He notes that advertising 'has always targeted a powerful consumer alter ego: that hip, attractive, incredibly popular person just waiting to emerge (with the help of the advertised product) from an all-too-normal self' (p. 54), and that one of the advantages of the online world is that marketers can find out about these hidden dreams more directly because people often display them in their

avatars. Tracking people's web-browsing is another very information-rich approach to understanding consumer behaviour. However, there are many drawbacks that go along with these approaches, not least of which is people's concern for privacy.

The greatest problem that businesses face with online customers is converting their website visits into purchases. But using avatars can help businesses with this. Instead of simply presenting information to potential customers, it has been shown that adding an avatar increases their satisfaction, attitude towards the product and intention to buy (Holzwarth et al., 2006). A more attractive avatar was perceived as more likeable, and a more expert avatar was seen as more credible, both of which influenced the avatar's persuasiveness. Having some kind of relationship with a person, whether that person is real or virtual, increases the likelihood that consumers will buy a product.

So far we have considered CRM as mostly a one-way relationship: the business does all it can to manage the customer relationship, offering what the customer wants in order to increase future purchasing. However, Faase et al. (2011) point out that the advent of Web 2.0 technologies (or social media) allows a greater two-way interaction between the business and the customer, and suggest the term *social CRM* as a strategy which encourages customer engagement and involvement with the business, using the framework below:

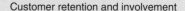

Customer retention and involvement

⇧

Customer engagement (two-way interaction, user-generated content, harnessing the power of the crowd)

⇧

Customer management (building relationships and retaining customers based on that knowledge)

Figure 11.1 A framework for social CRM

Faase et al.'s research indicates that social media add value across all the domains of CRM (including customer behaviour, lifetime value and so on) but has the largest effect in the marketing domain. Out of the different technologies available, social networks, blogs and multimedia sharing added the most value and should be considered first by companies wanting to improve their online CRM.

Psychology has a wide range of applications for modern business concerns, from working out the most effective ways to advertise, to giving guidance on how to manage customer relationships and making best use of new technology. In the final section of this chapter, we look at how psychology is used in coaching at work.

COACHING PSYCHOLOGY

We often associate coaching with sports. Coaches are there to help athletes perform to the best of their ability, and Howl (2005, p. 227) suggests that a comparison can be drawn between professional athletes and CEOs because both have 'relatively short, financially lucrative careers that continue only as long as they perform at exceptional levels'. Executive coaches are hired for a range of reasons, including a desire to increase personal performance and creativity, enhance relationships, become more responsive to change and to improve communication and leadership skills (Howl, 2005).

The burgeoning interest in coaching psychology can be seen in the increasing number of research articles published on the subject over the years. Between 1927 and 2005, fewer than 20 articles about coaching psychology were published (Grant, 2011), but just five years later over 130 articles were published in a single year. Specialist coaching psychology groups have also been set up in the psychological societies of countries across the world, aiming to share research and practice in the professional use of psychology in coaching. The interest in coaching is even more obvious when we see that it has become a mainstream developmental activity (Grant et al., 2010) rather than something offered to just a few key executives.

In this section we will explore the field in detail, looking at recent developments and particularly the use of technology for virtual coaching.

What is coaching psychology?

Several authors have tried to define coaching in order to delineate it from other related areas, such as mentoring, counselling and appraisals. Drawing these lines of demarcation, however, is not easy because there is significant overlap (Peterson et al., 2013). Whitmore's (1992, p. 10) simple definition of coaching is that it unlocks 'people's potential to maximise their own performance'. A more complex definition is provided by Passmore and Fillery-Travis (2011), which emphasises how the coach uses various interventions which are aimed at encouraging clients to develop their own self-awareness and personal responsibility. Common to all these definitions is the idea that coaching is not about telling the client what to do, but encouraging clients to develop their own solutions and paths.

Coaching *psychology* specifically uses psychological approaches and models to enhance client's well-being and performance at work and home (Passmore et al., 2013). However, the authors of this definition do point out that the similarities between coaches' and coaching psychologists' practice far outweigh the differences, and coaching psychology might be better thought of as the *scientific study* of coaching rather than a specific approach to the practice of coaching. In addition, because coaching psychologists are regulated by psychologists' professional bodies in various countries, there can be some assurance of qualification, experience and expertise which non-psychologist coaches are not subject to.

Coaching models and theory

Although there are a variety of different coaching models, a review by Dingman (2006) identified six generic components in the process:

Formal contracting	• Agreement made between the coach and client (and the organisation if necessary)
Relationship-building	• Sessions are used to develop trust and respect between the coach and client
Assessment	• Coach evaluates the client's strengths, weaknesses and development needs
Getting feedback and reflecting	• Results of assessment are used as basis for goal-setting
Goal-setting	• Goals or outcomes for the coaching relationship are decided • Action plan is developed
Supportive implementation and evaluation	• The action plan is evaluated at set times • This component includes the beginning and the termination of the coaching sessions

Coaching can be for skills, performance or development (Grant et al., 2010). The first type of coaching focuses on helping the client to attain specific skills, for example presentation or negotiation skills. The second tends to be based on a performance appraisal and helps a client to solve a specific workplace problem, usually by setting goals and dealing with the challenges that arise along the way. The third type of coaching is more future-focused, helping clients to reflect on and understand themselves in order to develop personally and professionally. While the skills and knowledge that a coach needs in order to address these three types of coaching differ somewhat, there are a few general skills that are essential to coaching success (Bono et al., 2009):

1 Diagnostic and planning capabilities – including accurate assessment, questioning and listening skills
2 Intervention and problem-solving capabilities – including the ability to build relationships, give feedback, motivate and keep clients accountable

3   Knowledge – of both business and psychology
4   Personal qualities – such as authenticity, integrity, experience and professionalism.

One of the key benefits of coaching is that it can be flexible and responsive, with the coach able to help the coachee in an ongoing process of development. Yet this is also one of the main challenges for coaching psychology as it tries to be evidence-based (Cavanagh and Palmer, 2011). An evidence base takes time to establish and test but coaching psychology is a very new field. So does this mean that coaches do not yet have an adequate evidence base to use and should simply make their best guess? Not at all. As in other applied areas of psychology, coaching can draw on the broad, established evidence base of psychology.

Because the business application of coaching psychology developed out of the use of psychology in sports coaching, Gould and Wright (2012) suggest that coaching psychology can effectively draw on research from this field. The emphasis in sports coaching is on helping individuals and teams to achieve their best performance. Coaching psychology aims to enhance people's well-being and work performance by helping individuals in their personal and professional growth and development (Grant, 2011). Specific areas of knowledge for coaching psychologists include theories of goals and change, an understanding of group processes, and practical knowledge of specific skills such as cognitive behavioural techniques.

The effectiveness of coaching

Worldwide, billions are spent each year on corporate coaching, but it is difficult to evaluate coaching effectiveness because there are such a wide range of applications (Grant, 2013). The majority of published studies are case studies aimed at helping practitioners to improve their practice, giving narrative descriptions of the kinds of interventions or approaches that worked in specific coaching relationships. While helpful to individual practitioners, these kinds of studies are less useful in providing evidence for the utility of coaching and justifying the billions that are spent on it. However, there are a growing number of studies which have demonstrated that coaching provides a financial return on investment (ROI) as well as other benefits to the participants and the organisation (Feggetter, 2007).

One of the issues facing coaching psychologists is in defining the outcomes that we expect to be improved as a result of coaching. Because coaching is used so broadly, there are a wide range of outcomes, and studies have been conducted that demonstrate coaching has an impact on outcomes such as leadership style, waste reduction, well-being, absence rates and safety behaviour (Grant, 2013). While the evidence base for coaching is growing, there

is still a need for further research using standardised measures, so that we can establish greater consistency in the studies. This is a challenge for coaching psychology because one of the basic components and, indeed, strengths of the field is that the goals or outcomes are developed individually with each client.

A promising approach to dealing with this diversity in coaching outcomes is to use goal attainment scaling (GAS) (Spence, 2007). GAS involves the coach and the client jointly identifying goals and developing a scale to measure progress towards them. The scale mid-point on a five-point scale is defined as a behaviour which is deemed to be realistic but stretching for the client, called the *expected outcome*. Above this midpoint, the client and coach agree accomplishments which represent *more than expected* and *best expected outcome*, as well as two lower levels of *less than expected* and *worst expected*. This goal chart can then be used to evaluate progress after set interventions. Perhaps most usefully for coaching psychology research, GAS can be used to compare progress across many different individually set goals. Additionally, GAS takes account of the individual's abilities and perception of challenge, but because the scale is agreed jointly with the coach, it also provides a greater level of objectivity.

 Psychological Toolkit Goal Attainment Scaling

Goal attainment scaling is based on a method developed to evaluate treatments for mental health interventions (Kiresuk and Sherman, 1968), which, just like coaching interventions, are extremely varied and tailored to the individual. GAS provides a great way to evaluate your own goal attainment in different areas of your life. Spence (2007) gives an example of a GAS chart for the goal of becoming more social, and below is an example for the goal of becoming more organised:

Higher order goal: become more organised		
Lower order goal: follow a realistic task list ('to do' list) each day		
+ 2	Best expected outcome	Complete > 4 items from the task list
+ 1	More than expected outcome	Complete 3–4 items from the task list
0	Expected outcome	Complete 1–2 items from the task list
− 1	Less than expected outcome	Complete 1 item from the task list
− 2	Worst expected outcome	Do not complete any items from the task list

You can complete this exercise on your own, but it will be more valuable if you can work with another person, taking turns being the 'coach' and 'client'. This will give you some practice in developing your own coaching skills as well.

With your coach, discuss some areas in which you would like to develop and decide on two or three goals. (You may want to refer back to the Psychological Toolbox exercise in Chapter 4, where you were developing career goals – coaching is often used to help people develop their careers.) Then work through the following steps together:

1   Start by thinking of higher order goals, quite general aims that you would like to achieve. Then define that aim more closely as a specific lower order goal that you can measure, as in the example above.

2   The next step is for you and the coach to identify a specific behaviour that would show you have improved in this area. For example, if your goal is to 'exercise more', this could be a set number of completed gym sessions.

3   Now agree with your coach the level of attainment that is realistic but stretching. This is your expected outcome.

4   Complete a GAS chart as above, using your expected outcome as the midpoint and providing four other levels of attainment that you can measure.

5   Identify what your current level of attainment is on your chart and make a note of it. This will allow you to see your progress as you develop.

6   Your last step is to agree an action plan with your coach that you think will help you to achieve your goal. You can then meet again at set time points to evaluate your progress.

The GAS will allow you to see your relative progress across different goals in a standardised way. You can even compare progress with other people using this five-point scale and use it to encourage or challenge yourself to even greater achievements. The advantage of this approach is that it takes into account how challenging the goals are to you personally, rather than conducting a simple comparison across people that takes no account of individual talents and difficulties.

Based on a review of psychotherapy outcomes, McKenna and Davis (2009) suggested there were four 'active' ingredients in coaching success. The most important factor, contributing about 40% of the variance in coaching success, is *client and environmental factors*. These include those things the client brings to the first session which are outside the control of the coach, such as the client's readiness for coaching, relationships with other people and support networks. This highlights how important the client is in the coaching process: coaching will simply not succeed if the client is not invested.

Closely related to this is the next most important factor: the *quality of the coaching relationship*. This relationship, sometimes referred to as a 'working alliance', is an interpersonal process, and it is the relationship itself that is the essential ingredient, rather than specific interventions or approaches that are used (Lambert and Barley, 2001). De Haan's (2008) research with experienced coaches shows that positive development occurs for the client when the coach–client relationship is defined yet flexible, when the client trusts the coach and the coach is able to reflect his or her observations to the client in a way that will be heard.

It should not be forgotten that a major contributing factor is simply *hope and expectancy*. Also referred to as a placebo effect, the mere fact that a client believes a coach may be able to help can itself lead to an improvement in outcomes. This is also a reminder that building a client's hope and beliefs that he or she can achieve goals is a key part of coaching.

Finally, *the specific techniques* the coach uses are also responsible for a significant amount of variance in the outcomes. The models that coaches use need to be relevant to the individual client and help to strengthen the other three active ingredients (McKenna and Davis, 2009). That is why it is important for coaches to keep up to date with theoretical developments and practical research in the field rather than just relying on their own trial-and-error efforts.

Virtual coaching

A significant number of coaching sessions are conducted without the coach and client ever meeting face to face, and the majority of coaches will use some form of technology to communicate with clients over a distance (Ghods and Boyce, 2013). Reviews of therapies other than coaching have indicated that one of the advantages of using technology is to expand the provision of therapy to people who would not otherwise be able to access it (Mallen et al., 2005). It can also be a lot more cost-effective, allowing both coach and client to save on travel time and expenses. However, difficulties arise because, as we've seen, the coaching relationship is central to successful outcomes, and managing these interpersonal issues over a distance presents a unique challenge.

Studies in counselling and psychiatric contexts indicate that effective therapeutic relationships can indeed be developed through various audio or video media (Day

Case Study Virtual coaching

Mary is an experienced and well-regarded coach. She has personal experience of management and leadership positions in the manufacturing industry and, starting from informal mentoring within her organisation, gradually developed herself as a freelance executive coach. She has recently become interested in expanding how she can offer coaching sessions and has identified several technologies that she believes may be of value:

- Online strengths, values and personality assessments
- Online videoconferencing technologies such as Skype or Facetime
- File-sharing applications.

▸ What advantages do you think each of these technologies could potentially offer Mary in expanding her business?

▸ From your own experience of using similar applications, what could be some potential difficulties Mary might face? How would you suggest she overcomes these problems? It is worth thinking here particularly of how the technologies might impact on the coaching relationship.

© PhotoDisc/Getty Images

and Schneider, 2002). Research in virtual coaching is still at an early stage, but does seem promising. The few studies published have focused on telephone coaching and have highlighted how the coach and client have to invest more effort into building a trusting and effective relationship in the absence of visual cues (Ghods and Boyce, 2013). How recent advances in online video conferencing may impact on the coaching relationship is yet to be established.

SUMMARY

In this chapter, we have looked at the ways psychology can be applied and used in specific business areas. From how we interact with machines to how we make financial decisions, an understanding of psychology is essential to any attempt to scientifically predict and control the business environment. We have seen how individual differences such as our approach to risk-taking has an impact on economics, as well as how our natural ways of thinking and behaving, needs to be taken into account in the design of machines. From the basic building blocks of cognition in neuroscience studies, to understanding how customer relationships can be built and maintained, to coaching people to reach their potential at work, psychology is a valuable resource for anyone

seeking to make their business more productive and effective.

The second theme of this chapter was looking at our relationship with technology. We saw how computer systems need to be designed around human perception and cognition if they are to reach their potential in helping us work. But we also explored how technology is changing us, thinking about the impact it has on our attention spans and thought processes, and our work, by expanding our flexibility in how and when we work, and even opening up new areas for psychological application, such as virtual coaching.

Because business is inherently about people, the applications of psychology to work are as varied as our work. In this chapter, we have explored some of these exciting new developments, but there will continue to be more as our work constantly changes.

TEST YOURSELF

Brief Review Questions

1 What are the two main areas of human-computer interaction research?

2 List the four principles for interface design suggested by Oviatt.

3 Briefly outline the advantages and disadvantages of mobile remote presence (MRP) systems in the workplace.

4 Contrast instrumental and stimulating risk-taking.

5 What is social customer relationship management?

6 What are the six components of the coaching process?

Discussion or Essay Questions

1 With an understanding of psychology as it relates to machine or computer design, is it possible to argue that all errors are 'design flaws' and there is no such thing as 'human error'?

2 Why is an understanding of risk-taking important to economic psychology?

3 Neuroscience is becoming increasingly popular in the business press. Why do you think this is? What advantages and risks does it bring?

4 Is coaching a good investment for a business?

FURTHER READING

- An interesting, detailed study on people's reactions to mobile robotic presence systems in the workplace is given in the paper Now I have a body: Uses and social norms for mobile remote presence in the workplace. *Proceedings of the SIGCHI Conference on Human Factors in Computing Systems*, 2011. ACM, 33–42. Includes qualitative discussion of how people reacted to the MRPs, both as pilots and colleagues.

- For a discussion of how psychology can help to understand the recent financial crisis, read T. Gärling, E. Kirchler, A. Lewis & F. Van Raaij, Psychology, financial decision making, and financial crises. *Psychological Science in the Public Interest*, 10 (2009), 1–47.

- Chapters 23, 24 and 25 in *Business Psychology in Practice* by P. Grant (ed.) *Business Psychology in Practice*. London, Whurr Publishing) discuss some interesting case studies of coaching in different contexts.

References

AAKER, J. L. 1997. Dimensions of brand personality. *Journal of Marketing Research*, 34 (3), 347–56.

BOLTON, R. N. & TARASI, C. O. 2007. Managing customer relationships. *Review of Marketing Research*, 3, 3–38.

BONACHE, J. 2005. Job satisfaction among expatriates, repatriates and domestic employees: the perceived impact of international assignments on work-related variables. *Personnel Review*, 34, 110–24.

BONO, J. E., PURVANOVA, R. K., TOWLER, A. J. & PETERSON, D. B. 2009. A survey of executive coaching practices. *Personnel Psychology*, 62, 361–404.

BRYNJOLFSSON, E. & HITT, L. M. 2003. Computing productivity: firm-level evidence. *Review of Economics and Statistics*, 85, 793–808.

BYRNES, J. P., MILLER, D. C. & SCHAFER, W. D. 1999. Gender differences in risk taking: a meta-analysis. *Psychological Bulletin*, 125, 367–83.

CAMERER, C. 1999. Behavioral economics: reunifying psychology and economics. *Proceedings of the National Academy of Sciences*, 96, 10575–7.

CAVANAGH, M. & PALMER, S. 2011. Educating coaching psychologists: responses from the field: conclusions from Cavanagh & Palmer. *International Coaching Psychology Review*, 6, 124–5.

COOPER, M. D. 2000. Towards a model of safety culture. *Safety Science*, 36, 111–36.

DAILY MAIL REPORTER. 2009. Cleaner has head cut off in giant meat blending machine. *Daily Mail*, 16 July.

DAY, S. X. & SCHNEIDER, P. L. 2002. Psychotherapy using distance technology: a comparison of face-to-face, video, and audio treatment. *Journal of Counseling Psychology*, 49, 499–503.

DE HAAN, E. 2008. I struggle and emerge: critical moments of experienced coaches. *Consulting Psychology Journal: Practice and Research*, 60, 106.

DINGMAN, M. E. 2006. Executive coaching: what's the big deal? *International Journal of Leadership Studies*, 1, 2–5.

ELLIS, Y., DANIELS, B. & JAUREGUI, A. 2010. The effect of multitasking on the grade performance of business students. *Research in Higher Education Journal*, 8, 1–10.

FAASE, R., HELMS, R. & SPRUIT, M. 2011. Web 2.0 in the CRM domain: defining social CRM. *International Journal of Electronic Customer Relationship Management*, 5, 1–22.

FEGGETTER, A. J. 2007. A preliminary evaluation of executive coaching: does executive coaching work for candidates on a high potential development scheme? *International Coaching Psychology Review*, 2, 129–42.

FRIEDMAN, T. 2006. The age of interruption. *The New York Times*, 5 July.

GÄRLING, T., KIRCHLER, E., LEWIS, A. & VAN RAAIJ, F. 2009. Psychology, financial decision making, and financial crises. *Psychological Science in the Public Interest*, 10, 1–47.

GARTNER. 2013. *Computer Sales Statistics*. International Data Corporation. http://www.statisticbrain.com/computer-sales-statistics/ (accessed 7 October 2013).

GHODS, N. & BOYCE, C. 2013. Virtual Coaching and Mentoring. In Peterson, D. B., Freire, T. & Passmore, J. (eds.) *The Wiley-Blackwell Handbook of the Psychology of Coaching and Mentoring*. Oxford, Wiley-Blackwell.

GOULD, D. & WRIGHT, E. M. 2012. The Psychology of Coaching. In Murphy, S. M. (ed.) *The Oxford Handbook of Sport and Performance Psychology*. Oxford, Oxford University Press.

GRANT, A. 2013. The Efficacy of Coaching. In Peterson, D. B., Freire, T. & Passmore, J. (eds.) *The Wiley-Blackwell Handbook of the Psychology of Coaching and Mentoring*. Oxford, Wiley-Blackwell.

GRANT, A. M. 2011. Developing an agenda for teaching coaching psychology. *International Coaching Psychology Review*, 6, 84–99.

GRANT, A. M., PASSMORE, J., CAVANAGH, M. J. & PARKER, H. M. 2010. The State of Play in Coaching Today: A Comprehensive Review of the Field. In Hodgkinson, G. P. & Ford, J. K. (eds.) *International Review of Industrial and Organizational Psychology 2010*, vol. 25. New York, Wiley-Blackwell.

GRUDIN, J. 1988. Why CSCW applications fail: problems in the design and evaluation of organizational interfaces. *Proceedings of the 1988 ACM Conference on Computer-supported Cooperative Work.*

GRUDIN, J. 2011. Human–computer interaction. *Annual Review of Information Science and Technology*, 45, 367–430.

HANOCH, Y., JOHNSON, J. G. & WILKE, A. 2006. Domain specificity in experimental measures and participant recruitment an application to risk-taking behavior. *Psychological Science*, 17, 300–4.

HECHANOVA, R., BEEHR, T. A. & CHRISTIANSEN, N. D. 2003. Antecedents and consequences of employees' adjustment to overseas assignment: a meta-analytic review. *Applied Psychology*, 52, 213–36.

HEMP, P. 2006. Avatar-based marketing. *Harvard Business Review*, 84, 48–57.

HENNESSEY, J. & VINCENT, R. 2005. The Psychology of Customer Relationship Management. In Grant, P. (ed.) *Business Psychology in Practice*. London, Whurr Publishers.

HOLZWARTH, M., JANISZEWSKI, C. & NEUMANN, M. M. 2006. The influence of avatars on online consumer shopping behavior. *Journal of Marketing*, 70 (4), 19–36.

HOWL, J. 2005. Why Chief Executives Hire Coaches. In Grant, P. (ed.) *Business Psychology in Practice*. London, Whurr Publishers.

INSAG. 1988. Basic Safety Principles for Nuclear Power Plants 75-INSAG-3 Rev 1. Vienna, International Atomic Energy Agency.

JACOBSEN, W. C. & FORSTE, R. 2011. The wired generation: academic and social outcomes of electronic media use among university students. *Cyberpsychology, Behavior, and Social Networking*, 14, 275–80.

KARPINSKI, A. C., KIRSCHNER, P. A., OZER, I., MELLOTT, J. A. & OCHWO, P. 2013. An exploration of social networking site use, multitasking, and academic performance among United States and European university students. *Computers in Human Behavior*, 29, 1182–92.

KIRESUK, T. J. & SHERMAN, M. R. E. 1968. Goal attainment scaling: a general method for evaluating comprehensive community mental health programs. *Community Mental Health Journal*, 4, 443–53.

KRISTOFFERSSON, A., CORADESCHI, S. & LOUTFI, A. 2013. A review of mobile robotic telepresence. *Advances in Human Computer Interaction* 2013, 1–17.

LAMBERT, M. J. & BARLEY, D. E. 2001. Research summary on the therapeutic relationship and psychotherapy outcome. *Psychotherapy: Theory, Research, Practice, Training*, 38, 357.

LANDAUER, T. K. 1995. *The Trouble with Computers: Usefulness, Usability, and Productivity*, Cambridge, MA, Taylor & Francis.

LAXMISAN, A., HAKIMZADA, F., SAYAN, O. R., GREEN, R. A., ZHANG, J. & PATEL, V. L. 2007. The multitasking clinician: decision-making and cognitive demand during and after team handoffs in emergency care. *International Journal of Medical Informatics*, 76, 801–11.

LEE, M. K. & TAKAYAMA, L. 2011. Now, I have a body: Uses and social norms for mobile remote presence in the workplace. *Proceedings of the SIGCHI Conference on Human Factors in Computing Systems.*

LEITE, I., MARTINHO, C. & PAIVA, A. 2013. Social robots for long-term interaction: a survey. *International Journal of Social Robotics*, 5, 291–308.

LEVINE, L. E., WAITE, B. M. & BOWMAN, L. L. 2007. Electronic media use, reading, and academic distractibility in college youth. *CyberPsychology & Behavior*, 10, 560–6.

MCKENNA, D. D. & DAVIS, S. L. 2009. Hidden in plain sight: the active ingredients of executive coaching. *Industrial and Organizational Psychology*, 2, 244–60.

MALLEN, M. J., VOGEL, D. L., ROCHLEN, A. B. & DAY, S. X. 2005. Online counseling reviewing the literature from a counseling psychology framework. *The Counseling Psychologist*, 33, 819–71.

MILWARD BROWN. 2009. *Using Neuroscience to Understand the Role of Direct Mail*. Milward Brown. https://www.millwardbrown.com/Insights/ CaseStudies/NeuroscienceDirectMail.aspx (accessed 11 October 2013).

OLSON, G. M. & OLSON, J. S. 2003. Human–computer interaction: psychological aspects of the human use of computing. *Annual Review of Psychology*, 54, 491–516.

ORMEROD, P. 2010. When Rationality Fails: Lessons from the Credit Crisis. Keynote speech at *Economic Psychology: New Methods and Findings*. Bolton, University of Bolton, 26 March.

OVIATT, S. 2006. Human-centered design meets cognitive load theory: designing interfaces that help people think. *Proceedings of the 14th Annual ACM International Conference on Multimedia.*

PALEN, L. & GRUDIN, J. 2003. Discretionary adoption of group support software: lessons from calendar applications. *Implementing Collaboration Technologies in Industry.* New York, Springer.

PARGNEUX, M. & CERDIN, J.-L. 2009. Career and international assignment fit: toward an integrative model of success. *Human Resource Management*, 48, 5–25.

PASSMORE, J. & FILLERY-TRAVIS, A. 2011. A critical review of executive coaching research: a decade of progress and what's to come. *Coaching: An International Journal of Theory, Research and Practice*, 4, 70–88.

PASSMORE, J., PETERSON, D. B. & FREIRE, T. 2013. The Psychology of Coaching and Mentoring. In Peterson, D. B., Freire, T. & Passmore, J. (eds.) *The Wiley-Blackwell Handbook of the Psychology of Coaching and Mentoring.* Oxford, Wiley-Blackwell.

PETERSON, D. B., FREIRE, T. & PASSMORE, J. 2013. *The Wiley-Blackwell Handbook of the Psychology of Coaching and Mentoring.* Oxford, Wiley-Blackwell.

POLDRACK, R. A. 2006. Can cognitive processes be inferred from neuroimaging data? *Trends in Cognitive Sciences*, 10, 59–63.

REINARTZ, W. & KUMAR, V. 2002. The mismanagement of customer loyalty. *Harvard Business Review*, 80, 86–95.

ROSCOE, S. N. 1997. *The Adolescence of Engineering Psychology.* Santa Monica, CA, Human Factors and Ergonomics Society.

SHAFFER, M. A., HARRISON, D. A., GREGERSEN, H., BLACK, J. S. & FERZANDI, L. A. 2006. You can take it with you: individual differences and expatriate effectiveness. *Journal of Applied Psychology*, 91, 109–25.

SHARE-BERNIA, J. 2005. Psychological Principles and the Online Evaluation Environment. In Grant, P. (ed.) *Business Psychology in Practice.* London, Whurr Publishing.

SOLNAIS, C., ANDREU-PEREZ, J., SANCHEZ-FERNANDEZ, J. & ANDREU-ABELA, J. 2013. The contribution of neuroscience to consumer research: a conceptual framework and empirical review. *Journal of Economic Psychology*, 36, 68–81.

SPENCE, G. B. 2007. GAS powered coaching: goal attainment scaling and its use in coaching research and practice. *International Coaching Psychology Review*, 2, 155–67.

STONE, L. 2013. *Continuous Partial Attention.* http://lindastone.net/qa/continuous-partial-attention/ (accessed 7 October 2013).

TSAI-JUNG, H., SHU-CHENG, C. & JOHN, S. L. 2005. The relationship between expatriates' personality traits and their adjustment to international assignments. *International Journal of Human Resource Management*, 16, 1656–70.

VANDERMERWE, S. 2000. How increasing value to customers improves business results. *Sloan Management Review*, 42, 27–38.

VAN RAAIJ, W. F. 1981. Economic psychology. *Journal of Economic Psychology*, 1, 1–24.

WHITMORE, J. 1992. *Coaching for Performance.* London, Nicholas Brealey.

YOON, C., GUTCHESS, A. H., FEINBERG, F. & POLK, T. A. 2006. A functional magnetic resonance imaging study of neural dissociations between brand and person judgments. *Journal of Consumer Research*, 33, 31–40.

ZALESKIEWICZ, T. 2001. Beyond risk seeking and risk aversion: personality and the dual nature of economic risk taking. *European Journal of Personality*, 15, 105–22.

THE REALITIES OF RESEARCH
IN WORK PSYCHOLOGY

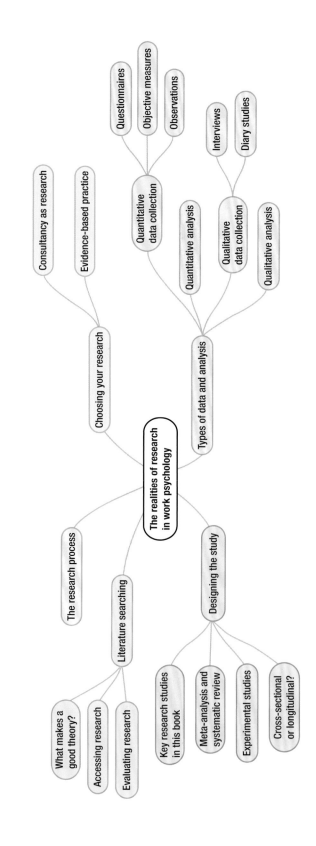

In Chapter 1, we established that psychology is the science of the mind, and we explored what it meant to use the scientific method to understand the world. Central to the scientific method is the concept of conducting research: gathering observations (data), then analysing and interpreting them. How we do this research is important. If we are not rigorous at each point of our research, the conclusions we come to will not be worth anything. In this chapter, we will go through the stages of research in work psychology, evaluating different approaches and methods, so that you can build your understanding of how research is conducted and begin to identify what makes a good study.

The aim of this chapter is not to turn you into a fully fledged researcher, but to develop your ability to critically assess published research so that you can use it as a basis for your own practice. So we won't be going through the details of how to conduct statistical tests or analyse interview transcripts. If you want to know about these things, look at the Further Reading section at the end of the chapter. Instead, we will be taking a higher-level critical view of work psychology research so that you know what to look for when assessing a study and are aware of both the strengths and limitations of the scientific approach.

This chapter will help you answer the following questions:

1 Why is good research important and how should it be carried out?
2 What role does research play in linking theory and practice in work psychology?
3 How can we ensure we have a good foundation for our research study?
4 What different ways can research studies be designed?
5 How is data analysed and interpreted?

THE RESEARCH PROCESS

No matter what approach a researcher uses in his or her work, there are five main steps that need to be covered:

1 Identify the research area and construct a research question. Many people start this by identifying something they want to know the answer to. For example, 'What makes some people such inspiring leaders?' or 'How can we improve the productivity of our workers?'
2 Review the literature. This stage involves finding out what researchers already know about this topic. We may find the answer to our question in a previously published study. Or we may find that our initial ideas on the subject have already been researched and either supported or found to be incorrect. Only if we know what has already been found can we start to

design a useful research study to explore our topic in more detail. Reviewing the literature means finding out about current, relevant theory that can help guide our own research.
3 Design the study. This step is about clarifying the variables, the kind of data that will be collected and how we will go about it, the sample of respondents or participants we will access and the timescales involved. There is a wide range of options here, and the decisions that researchers make determine the quality and applicability of their eventual findings. If the study is quantitative, it is likely to be guided by specific hypotheses: expectations for the results that are based in the preceding literature review. If the study is exploratory it may not have hypotheses but instead more general research questions.
4 Collect the data. Many people assume that the data collection part is the 'actual' research, but you can see that it only comes after we have done a great deal of work. Anyone who goes out to collect data without having spent considerable effort on the first three stages will end up with unusable or misleading data that will be of no help in adding to our understanding of psychology or answering the question they were interested in.
5 Analyse and interpret the data. The more complex our data and research questions, the more sophisticated our analytical tools need to be. It is important to recognise that any scientific study, however 'objective' it may appear to be, involves some level of interpretation by the researcher. Whether this is interpreting the meaning of statistics or considering the implications of the findings for practical application, this step is essential for turning the raw data of our study into something that can be used by other researchers or practitioners.

An essential consideration in the design, implementation, analysis and application of research is the ethical framework within which the study takes place. We explore this important aspect of research in more detail in the Psychological Toolkit section – remember to bear it in mind as we discuss the stages of research in more detail throughout this chapter.

 Psychological Toolkit Ethics in research

Ethics are an essential part of research for two reasons. First, because work psychology research deals with humans, we need to ensure that no one is harmed by taking part in our studies. Second, because the conclusions and findings of work psychology research are used as the basis for determining policy, developing organisational strategy and otherwise impacting on our everyday life, we need to ensure that they will be used in an ethical way.

In designing research, ethical considerations centre around a few important points:

▸ Informed consent – people should be given enough information about the study at the start to make an informed decision about whether they want to take part.
▸ Confidentiality – all participant data should be kept confidential and any identifying information removed from the results. It needs to be made clear to the participants if there are any limits to confidentiality.
▸ Withdrawal – it should be remembered that participation is voluntary at all times and that anyone can stop taking part in the study at any time.
▸ Debrief – participants should be told at the end of the study what it was all about.

There is also debate about the use of deception in psychological research. Sometimes, deception as to the true reasons for a study may be seen as essential because we do not want the participants to change how they respond by second-guessing the research aims. But there is an argument that any deception is unethical, and it can lead to distrust of psychologists as well as conflicting with the principle of informed consent. If deception is used, it should be kept to a minimum and participants told about the real nature of the study at the earliest opportunity.

And finally, we need to ensure as far as possible that the findings of research are used ethically as well. Part of this involves making sure that we do not make extravagant claims for our research by being open about its limitations. The other side of it is to ensure that findings are used for beneficial purposes only and not as an excuse to marginalise, harm or discriminate against certain people.

▸ Imagine you have been given the task of designing a research study to investigate employee satisfaction at your workplace. Work through each of the principles above to decide how you would ensure you were conducting ethical research. What might be some particular challenges you could face as an employee within the organisation?
▸ What potential harm could come from your study? Think through the issues of guaranteeing confidentiality and how the findings might be used by the organisation.
▸ To what extent do you think researchers are responsible for how the results of their studies are used?

CHOOSING YOUR RESEARCH

The first step in carrying out research is to decide what we want to know more about. This question can be approached from different angles. Either we want to conduct research in order to develop, test or refine a theory or we can approach it from a more practical angle, with the desire to find the solution to a particular question or problem we are facing in the workplace. Ideally, of course, both of these approaches would result in theoretically sound and eminently practical conclusions. As Kurt Lewin (1951) said, 'There is nothing so practical as a good theory.' So in this section we consider the interplay between practice and research by exploring consultancy and evidence-based practice.

Consultancy as research

The consultancy cycle, illustrated below, can be seen as a form of research in itself. It starts by agreeing the contract between the consultant and the client. This is important in setting expectations for both sides and in determining the direction of the consultancy process. It is common at this stage for the problem to be discussed, but it is in the next stage that the problem is clarified. By gathering information, the consultant can determine whether the 'presenting problem' might have underlying causes and help to refine what he or she needs to do.

Based on the data gathered in that stage, the consultant then develops a range of potential solutions to the problem. Ideally, these solutions will be based on good evidence rather than a 'hunch' or the latest management fad, and the best solution for the specific situation will be chosen. This decision is often made in consultation with the client to ensure that it takes account of any important organisational issues. The chosen solution is then implemented, but you will notice that the cycle does not stop here. An essential part of good consultancy is to evaluate the solution. This not only helps to ensure that any problems are dealt with as they arise, but also develops the consultants' knowledge base and experience so that future solutions can be made even more effective.

After evaluation, the consultant may re-contract with the client or, if there is no further need for their services, disengage.

There are advantages for researchers who are also actively engaged in management practice (Saunders et al., 2009). They will have easier access to the data they need, whether research participants or organisational metrics. They also know the organisation better than an outsider, which can help give them insights into the topic they are studying. But they also face particular challenges, such as having to overcome their own assumptions about a

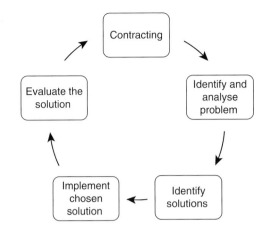

Figure 12.1 The consultancy cycle

situation they are familiar with and negotiating the dual role of 'researcher' and 'management practitioner'.

Evidence-based practice

It would be a rare management consultant who did not attempt to claim that there was good evidence for his or her interventions and suggestions. And yet, what kind of evidence is actually good enough? As Briner and Rousseau (2011) point out, what sets the professional practitioner apart from the layperson or the con artist is the *quality* of the evidence they base their claims on. Yet a survey of members of the US-based Society for Industrial and Organizational Psychology (SIOP) (Silzer et al., 2008) showed that the majority of practitioners and researchers in the field of work psychology believed there was a gap between research and practice. Research was seen as sometimes out of touch with the realities of occupational psychology practice, while practitioners seemed unaware of some of the relevant research that they could use. Clearly, a major challenge for evidence-based practice in work psychology is finding that link between the research and practice.

In evidence-based practice we can differentiate two different types of scientific inquiry (Briner and Rousseau, 2011). First there is 'basic science': the exploration of new ideas and approaches in the field. In medicine, for example, this would be the testing of a new drug for a particular disease. In work psychology, this could be testing a new intervention to reduce stress at work.

The second type of inquiry is concerned with researching effective practice. This is done by finding the best interventions for particular groups of people (taking the complexities of their context into account) and by conducting systematic reviews. We discuss systematic reviews in more detail later in the chapter.

The evidence-based practitioner is not someone who simply follows suggestions made in the research literature without thinking through their implications. Being evidence-based is about actively considering and integrating four sources of information in making decisions (Briner et al., 2009):

- *The practitioner's own expertise and judgement.* This involves thinking about similar situations that we may have experienced in the past, what happened and what we learned from them, as well as how relevant and applicable our experience is to this particular case.
- *Evidence from the local context.* Gathering evidence from the specific organisation or context that will help to refine the problem and gain insight into it. This includes gathering information about what the people involved think about the situation, conducting internal surveys, seeking out relevant objective facts such as the current interventions or strategies that are in place, evaluating the costs and benefits of any intervention, and a consideration of the wider environmental context.
- *Critical evaluation of the best research evidence.* Finding relevant systematic reviews about potential causes of the problem and evaluations of different interventions, as well as industry-level comparison data against which the specific situation can be judged.
- *Perspectives of those who may be affected.* Finally, the practitioner needs to consider how employees and managers feel about the suggested interventions, or whether they have alternative suggestions.

An evidence-based intervention, then, would draw on personal experience and up-to-date knowledge of theory and interventions to produce a context-specific solution that has the highest possible chance of success.

 Activity Evidence-based practice

Your manager, knowing that you have studied work psychology, has asked you for your input into a problem she has regarding high levels of absence in the production department. She has noticed that absence levels have increased over the last year and wants to know what can be done to fix the problem.

▸ Using the four sources of information available to evidence-based practitioners, how would you go about helping your manager decide what to do?

Briner and Rousseau (2011) presented seven characteristics of evidence-based practice in fields such as medicine:

1   The term 'evidence-based' is used or well known

2   The latest research findings and summaries are accessible

3   Articles reporting primary research and traditional literature reviews are accessible to practitioners

4   'Cutting-edge' practices, panaceas and fashionable new ideas are treated with healthy scepticism

5   There is a demand for evidence-based practice from clients and customers

6   Practice decisions are integrative and draw on the four sources of information and evidence described above

7   Initial training and continuing professional development (CPD) adopt evidence-based approaches.

The authors suggested that although occupational psychology is not as strongly evidence-based as some other fields, as a profession it is in a very good position to be able to adopt these characteristics. One of the challenges for occupational psychologists attempting to promote evidence-based practice is that they are often not the key decision-makers. Instead, they often act in a consultative capacity, presenting evidence to the managers who make the final decision. In that case, an important responsibility is to present the information in a way that will encourage the best, evidence-based decision.

Evidence-based practice is undoubtedly important in work psychology, but we need to remain critical about the *nature* of that evidence. Cassell (2011) points out that the construction of evidence is not an objective, technical task but instead laden with politics, personal values and interests. What each researcher considers 'high-quality evidence' will vary, and even the peer reviews that are the hallmark of high-quality journals are subject to these individual understandings.

 Case Study 'Good' evidence

Steve and Maria both work for a small management consultancy. They have just had an initial meeting with a new client, a large magazine publisher which is about to acquire an independent, online-only publishing company and wants to ensure that the acquisition goes as smoothly as possible. Specifically, the publisher is concerned that talented employees from the smaller publisher might leave once the acquisition is announced.

Maria's background is very scientific. Her undergraduate degree was in maths and it was only later that she retrained as a psychologist. She values quantitative research and is a bit suspicious of studies that are based on

© MACMILLAN/PAUL BRICKNELL/DEAN RYAN

interviews or qualitative analysis, believing them to be too context-specific to be of use in practical application. Maria has found a review article in a high-quality work psychology journal that identifies the top five ways to retain talented people, and wants to use that as a basis for their recommendations to the client.

Steve, on the other hand, has two decades of experience in management consultancy and tends to think that trying to put a number on something as complicated as human behaviour is misleading. He believes that experience is a much better guide to what will work and what won't. He remembers that ten years ago he was involved in a similar acquisition, and that one of the most important things that seemed to keep people onside during the changes was keeping them informed at all times of what was happening and how it might affect them.

Together, Maria and Steve need to develop a suggested plan of action for their client which outlines the steps the client can take to try to retain the talented employees from the new company.

▸ What kind of 'evidence' do you think Maria and Steve would want to present to their client? What conflicts might arise as they try to put together a unified recommendation?

▸ How would you suggest that Maria and Steve try to work together in this situation? Is there a way for them both to use what they view as 'good' evidence or do you think they are mutually exclusive?

▸ What is your own opinion about what makes high-quality evidence?

LITERATURE SEARCHING

What makes a good theory?

The sheer number of different theories and models in psychology can be overwhelming. As Kagan (1998) points out, psychology is a young science and has very few fundamental principles: almost anything can be hypothesised, and very rarely disproved. So how can we navigate and assess the vast array of theories available in the literature?

There are three important criteria which stand out when evaluating psychological theories: scientific rigour, usefulness and comprehensiveness (Sutton, 2007). First, as a social science, psychology attempts to describe the world according to scientific principles. A scientific theory binds facts together so that they can be understood all at once and makes testable predictions of future states (Kelly, 1955). A good scientific theory, according to Kelly, should also meet further criteria:

- It should inspire the production of new ideas, which in science would mean the formulation of testable hypotheses. Although hypotheses should be stated in concrete, testable ways, the theory itself should be abstract enough that it can be traced through many different phenomena. A higher level of abstraction is not the same as over-generalisation. The latter takes the concrete results from one situation and imposes them upon another, while the former suggests underlying causes that could account for both the observed results and others.
- A theory needs validity. Support for a good theory can be built up by finding support for the hypotheses generated from it. In its search for scientific validity, psychology has tended to create very specific, concrete mini-theories which have then been over-generalised to other situations (Kagan, 1998).
- Although a theory is abstract, it should allow the clear operational definition of variables. Operational definition is a statement of how the chosen variable links the antecedent to the consequence.
- A theory should concern itself with properties rather than categories. It is not simply a description of different groups of people or behaviours, but an explanation of the properties of the people or behaviours that *result* in those groupings.

Second, while scientists might ideally like to discover the universal truth underlying their chosen field of study, we can generally only edge towards a closer approximation of it. In fact, the usefulness of a theory in everyday applications can be another test of its accuracy. Particularly in an applied area such as work psychology, the usefulness of a theory when taken out into the world at large is a good indication of how 'good' that theory is. McClelland (1996) makes the suggestion that our study of psychological phenomena should perhaps start by asking what would be useful rather than reliable and statistically accurate. He gives the example of competencies, which were developed as something to be useful in the workplace and have excellent prediction of job performance, yet were not derived from any current psychological theory.

Finally, there is the criterion of comprehensiveness. A comprehensive theory would be able to predict a wide range of human behaviour across a range of different contexts. As you may have realised by reading this book, psychology is very far from having a grand unified theory. And while this can be frustrating when people want straightforward answers to their questions, it also means it is an exciting field in which to work, with lots of new ideas to be explored. When we are evaluating a theory, then, one that predicts outcomes across a range of situations will be better than one which is only accurate within a limited set of parameters. A good example of a more comprehensive theory is goal-setting, which has been found to predict performance in many different workplaces and for many different jobs (see Chapter 4 for further details).

Accessing research

There are many publications that can be accessed when conducting a literature review, for example trade magazines, professional body publications, newspaper articles and even blogs. The following activity helps explore the differences between the kind of publications that can be accessed on the web and those accessed through dedicated databases.

 Activity **Comparing search engines**

In today's internet-focused world, you may be tempted just to use a general internet search like Google to conduct your literature review. But a word of caution: even though a lot of information is freely available on the web, many of the higher-quality studies are still only accessible via special databases. Try this activity to find out what difference it makes to use the different databases and search engines.

▸ In your browser, open up four tabs and conduct a search using the keyword 'presenteeism' in each of the following searches. Write down the sorts of things that you find on the first page of results for each search.

Search engine/database	Type of results	What is it best used for?
Google		
Google Scholar		
EBSCO		
PsychInfo		

Traditionally, research has been published in specialist peer-reviewed journals and access provided to individuals or institutions who pay for subscriptions. 'Peer review' means that the article has been evaluated and reviewed by other experts in the field (usually two or more anonymous reviewers). The aim of these reviews is to ensure that the theory, method, analysis and conclusions of the study meet basic scientific requirements. The advantage of a peer-reviewed article is that it has gone through one stage of verification and checking before you read it, so you can have more confidence in the reliability of the findings.

Increasingly, these journals are offering the option for authors to make their articles 'open access', which means they are freely available on the web. There are three main types of open access journals (Pringle, 2004). First, there are traditional, long-established journals that have moved towards an open access model so that their articles are available freely to anyone who wants to read them. The second type are those which are new and are using open access as a way of increasing their profile, and the third type are local journals which are aiming to garner an international audience.

Going even further than open access, the *British Medical Journal* is also leading the way in promoting 'open data': from 2013, the journal no longer publishes any paper which does not make its (anonymised) data available on request. By making the data available, the *BMJ* is attempting to ensure that important trials are not lost, inadvertently repeated or even mis-reported, leading to bad treatment decisions. For more information on this campaign, go to www.alltrials.net. Psychological journals may well follow this move, and it could lead to much greater transparency in research and increased trust in research reports when the original data can be checked.

In the International Perspectives section, we consider the implications of open access for researchers and practitioners across the world.

International Perspectives Open access

For a long time, access to cutting-edge research and developments in the field of psychology, just as with other sciences, has been restricted to those people who can afford to pay the subscription fees of the journals. These fees can be very high. Take, for example, two of the top work psychology journals:

▸ An international print subscription to the *Journal of Occupational and Organisational Psychology*, published by the British Psychological Society, costs around $96 for an individual and around $500 for an institution.
▸ An international print subscription to the *Journal of Applied Psychology*, published by the American Psychological Association, costs around $500 for an individual and over $1,000 for an institution.

Although there are also packages available for several journals at once, the costs for accessing the range of literature needed to develop timely and well-informed research quickly add up. This means that poorer institutions, particularly in developing countries, simply cannot afford to access the publications they need in order to stay up to date with the field. This problem prompted UNESCO to issue guidelines for the development and promotion of open access (Swan, 2012). It suggested that encouraging open access provides three benefits. First, it enhances the research process by speeding up the literature review stage of research, encouraging interdisciplinary approaches and making best use of computational search tools. Second, it makes research output more visible and therefore easier to use. And finally, it increases the impact of the research as it reaches a wider academic and non-academic audience.

However, there remains the thorny issue of who is expected to pay for the costs of publication. With an open access model, readers can no longer be charged for these costs, and several different business models have emerged to deal with this change (Swan, 2012):

1 Article-processing charge – the authors of the paper pay the publication fee (usually from a research or institution grant)
2 Community publishing – editing, peer review and so on is done on a voluntary basis by people in the academic community so that there are no publishing costs
3 Institutional membership – the university or research institute pays a flat rate for all publications by their authors that year, or is invoiced at regular intervals
4 Advertising or sponsorship – revenue raised from adverts is used for the publication costs, or a government body may sponsor the journal
5 Institutional subsidy – this can be direct, by providing hosting for the online publications, or indirect, through their employment of researchers

who devote some of their time to reviewing articles

6   Hard copy sales – online access is free but readers have to pay for a hard copy.

Discussion points

To what extent do you think that open access can help researchers and practitioners in developing countries? Can you identify any potential drawbacks?

Which of the business models outlined above do you think is fairest to researchers and practitioners in both developed and developing countries?

Evaluating research: integrity and reliability

One of the important questions we need to ask when conducting a literature review is: *how reliable is this evidence?* It can be tempting to think that anything published in an academic journal is true and the authors' conclusions can be taken at face value. Unfortunately, this is not always the case. A recent study of academics in top AACSB-accredited (Association to Advance Collegiate Schools of Business) US business schools found that the majority of them knew of members of the faculty who

had engaged in research misconduct within the last year (Bedeian et al., 2010). Two types of misconduct were investigated:

1   Fabrication, falsification and plagiarism
    including: selecting or withholding data to strengthen the findings, using another person's ideas without giving credit, making up results
2   Questionable research practices
    including: publishing same data in more than one article, making up hypotheses after data is known, developing relationships with editors to help publication, circumventing ethical requirements

The second category of misconduct was more widespread than the first, but it is still disturbing that the majority of academic staff know of people in their faculty who had engaged in most of these behaviours. The case study below explores this issue in greater detail.

Does this mean we should dismiss academic research as just as unreliable as any other claim you might find in a trade magazine or a blog? Not at all. What it does mean is that we have to develop our own critical awareness of both the strengths and the limitations of published research. We can't just ignore evidence because it 'might' be unreliable or incomplete; instead we need to use it in a 'conscientious, explicit and judicious way' (Briner,

 Case Study Research fraud

In early September 2011, a psychology professor at Tilburg University in the Netherlands was accused of research fraud over a period of several years. Diederik Stapel was a charismatic and dedicated professor who published a huge number of research papers, and these allegations sent shock waves through the scientific community.

The investigation into this fraud was conducted at three universities where Stapel had worked, and eventually found evidence of fraud in 55 of Stapel's publications. They concluded that Stapel routinely fabricated or altered datasets. The impact of this fraud is extensive. Not only does it destroy the trust that people have in scientific research but it has damaged the publishers and the bodies which awarded the research grants to Stapel, as well as causing extensive waste of time and money as other researchers attempted to replicate Stapel's findings. In addition, it has adversely affected the lives and careers of people who worked with Stapel and were unaware that he had given them fabricated data to work on.

© mindweb2/Fotolia

The Levelt Noort and Drenth Committees (2012) and Verfaellie and McGwin (2011)

▸ The investigation into these allegations of fraud was made as transparent and publicly available as possible. Why do you think this decision was made?

▸ Unfortunately, this case of fraud is not an isolated instance. What can universities, journal publishers and individual academics and practitioners do to try and ensure scientific integrity?

2013, p. 14). Some useful things to bear in mind when considering published research are (Briner, 2013):

- The strength of relationships is likely to be exaggerated because there is a bias towards publishing positive results and the practice of HARKing (Hypothesising After Results are Known) is widespread.
- Because journals want to publish new and exciting studies, straightforward replications are less likely to be published, so it's hard to know whether the results can be generalised.
- Statistical significance does not tell us the *practical* importance of a result.

Evidence-based practitioners will make their own informed decisions based on the evidence collected from several sources and their judgements about its quality and reliability. It is only by knowing how research is conducted that we can make those informed decisions, which is why we now move on to consider research design.

DESIGNING THE STUDY

Key Research Studies in this book

In each chapter of this book, we have seen a Key Research Study outlined. These were chosen not only to highlight some important content of that chapter, but also to illustrate the range of different methods that are used in work psychology research. This table summarises the topics and the main methodologies, and the rest of this section uses these studies to illustrate the different approaches that we can take in designing research.

Chapter and research topic	Main methodology
1. Application and benefits of occupational psychology	Web-based quantitative and qualitative survey
2. Validity and utility of selection methods	Meta-analysis
3. Training effectiveness	Meta-analysis
4. Personality and motivation	Meta-analysis
5. Detecting lies	Experimental with matched samples
6. Groupthink	Qualitative case study: comparison of good and bad decision-making
7. Charismatic CEOs	Quantitative survey and use of secondary data
8. Popular management techniques	Secondary data analysis, textual analysis
9. Exercise and well-being	Large-scale quantitative survey and physical measurements
10. Executive character strengths	Quantitative survey: other report
11. Risk-taking	Quantitative survey with specific sub-groups

Meta-analysis and systematic reviews

In Chapters 2, 3 and 4, the key research studies were all meta-analyses. These are a type of systematic review that focuses solely on quantitative analysis of a research question that has been addressed by many researchers before. The aim is to find a definitive answer to a specific question. Meta-analysis is an increasingly important part of research because it enables researchers and practitioners alike to gain an overview of the findings of the previous years, or even decades. This helps us not to repeat ourselves and to 'rediscover' things that are already well known. It also helps to bring some clarity to a literature which is often full of slightly contradictory findings. By comparing results across different replications, we can identify which theories or models are most appropriate to explaining our world and continue to refine them.

Meta-analyses are particularly helpful to practitioners because they help guide the most up-to-date practices and methods in the workplace. For example, imagine we want to know what dispositional variables are most important in predicting performance. A meta-analysis will give us an overall measure of the strength of these relationships: self-efficacy has a correlation of .26 with performance (Judge and Bono, 2001) while conscientiousness has a correlation of .23 (Barrick and Mount, 1991).

But they do, of course, have their disadvantages. Within work psychology particularly, the complexities of the context in which the research was done can get lost during meta-analysis. So while we may have a clearer idea of one main finding, many other variables that may have influenced the outcome in specific studies are disregarded.

Systematic reviews adopt a broader approach, drawing together a wide range of evidence to address a practice-based question. Rather than relying solely on statistical synthesis, they take account of contextual factors and qualitative information relevant to the question as well. There are seven stages to a high-quality systematic review (Petticrew and Roberts, 2006):

1 Define the question. To be of use to evidence-based practice, this should be done in consultation with practitioners. Find out what it is that the potential users of the review actually want to know.

2 Decide what type of studies you will need to review in order to answer the question. This involves identifying criteria you will use to include or exclude certain studies. For example, if you want to know whether one thing causes another, you will need to exclude correlational studies and include longitudinal studies.

3 Conduct a comprehensive literature search. Now that you know what you are looking for, you can collect

a list of all the relevant studies. This relies on the judicious use of key words and relevant databases.

4 Screen the results. Any comprehensive search will identify many more studies than meet your strict inclusion criteria. Use the criteria from step 2 to filter out any studies that do not address your question properly.

5 Critically evaluate the studies. This involves assessing each study individually for the level of quality of its evidence.

6 Synthesise the findings. This may be done quantitatively, for example in calculating effect sizes for a particular relationship, or qualitatively by providing a narrative description of the findings. When discussing findings, it is important to relate them to the quality of information you gathered in the previous step. An important point here is to evaluate potential publication bias: studies finding non-significant effects will be less likely to be published than those which do find significant effects, and this could therefore skew our understanding.

7 Disseminate the findings. Here, it is worth considering who will make use of the review. A combination of extensive reports, academic journals and practitioner articles will ensure that the findings are made available to the widest audience.

Experimental studies

'Experiment' might be one of the most misused words that has made the transition from scientific language to everyday speech. The popular media often presents things as experiments that really aren't, helping to bolster some conclusions or recommendations by giving them the veneer of scientific reliability. However, a real experiment has to meet the following criteria:

- Clearly defined, measurable variables
- Experimental control.

An experiment aims to find out the effect of one variable upon another, helping us to establish cause and effect. The hypothesised 'cause' is known as the independent variable, and the 'effect' or outcome is known as the dependent variable. In work psychology, the most common dependent variable is worker performance, which can be operationalised in many different ways; for example, perceived leader effectiveness, output on a production line, customer satisfaction and so on. But we might also be interested in other dependent variables, such as changes in people's well-being, stress levels, job satisfaction or organisational commitment. The independent variables (the things we think will *cause* the change in the dependent variable) are also very varied, and can range from physical conditions (lighting or heating levels) to experiences or training (a specific health and safety seminar or a team-building exercise).

Control is the second essential ingredient of an experiment. If we want to be sure that any change in our dependent variable is really due to the change in our independent variable, we need to control any other variables that might affect our outcome. The case study below explores this further.

True experimental studies are particularly difficult to do in applied research for several reasons. First, they involve randomly assigning people to different groups and treatments. For example, imagine you wanted to find out whether a pay increase would boost motivation. In a true

Case Study **Call centre experiment**

Ben is the manager of a team of 20 call centre staff. His department seems to have a higher number of customer complaints than others in the same organisation and he has been given the task of improving customer satisfaction. From talking to the staff, he knows that they find their chairs very uncomfortable and are quite annoyed that other teams have had completely new equipment refits within the last six months. Ben thinks this must be the cause of the problem, so at the next budget meeting he insists that his team are given new desk chairs. The next month, he finds customer complaints have dropped. Ben is pleased and tells his colleagues how his experiment worked, recommending that if they have similar trouble, the solution is as easy as replacing the chairs.

▸ What were Ben's dependent and independent variables?

▸ What other factors might have influenced the drop in customer complaints that Ben was so pleased with?

▸ What should Ben have done to conduct a real controlled experiment? How feasible do you think this would be?

© ImageSource

experiment you would need a control condition; that is, a group which experiences no change but is otherwise the same as your experimental group. Even if you could manage to convince the management of an organisation that they should increase the wages of a randomly chosen sample of the workforce while the rest of the workforce stayed the same, all sorts of problems would arise with this perceived injustice that would impact on your findings.

Second, in applied research it is impossible to control for every possible confounding variable. This problem was highlighted in a series of experiments at the Hawthorne plant of the Western Electrical Company in the late 1920s and is discussed in detail in the Key Research Study. Now known as the Hawthorne effect, it is a reminder that we change our behaviour in response to a lot of different stimuli, and that knowing we are part of a study will in itself have an effect on our behaviour.

Key Research Study   The Hawthorne effect

The Hawthorne Experiment: Western Electric Company

Elton Mayo (1933)

(There are further details about this and other similar studies in F. J. Roethlisberger & W. J. Dickson (1939) *Management and the Worker*. Cambridge, MA, Harvard University Press.)

Background: This chapter reports on the series of famous experiments that took place at the Hawthorne plant. For many years, psychologists and managers had been attempting to conduct experiments to find out how to increase the productivity of assembly line workers. Based in Taylor's scientific management approach, the guiding premise was that optimum physical conditions (light or heat, for example) would result in optimal worker productivity. They became aware, however, that attempts to design controlled experiments were continually defeated by 'human factors'.

The original study

Aim: To determine the effect of lighting levels on worker productivity.

Method: Workers were separated into two rooms. In one room (the experimental group) the lighting levels were gradually reduced, while in the other room (the control group) lighting levels remained constant. The output of the two rooms was compared.

Findings: There was no difference between the two groups: they *both* showed an increase in productivity.

Implications: Something other than the physical conditions must be affecting productivity. As Mayo puts it: 'One may organise, and apparently scientifically, a carefully contrived inquiry into a human industrial problem and yet fail completely to elucidate the problem in any particular' (p. 55).

The follow-up studies

Aim: To determine the effect of various conditions (individual and group pay changes, rest breaks, lighting) on productivity.

Method: Several different studies were carried out over several years. Methods included having control groups or not, separation of groups in different rooms or keeping them together, measuring output or observation of the workers.

Findings: No matter what changes were made or methods were used, there was an increase in productivity by both individuals and groups. This even happened when conditions were returned to their pre-experiment levels.

Implications: The variables that the experimenters thought they were manipulating were *not* the cause of the increased productivity. Instead, Mayo suggested it was the feeling of being studied that created the effect, and noted that 'where human beings are concerned, one cannot change one condition without inadvertently changing others' (p. 56). The 'Hawthorne effect' is now used as a shorthand to refer to the human factors that influence a study and are difficult to control for: the mere fact we know we are being observed changes our behaviour.

True experimental studies are mostly limited to a laboratory setting, where we can have greater control over confounding variables, but they still require careful design and interpretation. In applied research, quasi-experimental studies are more realistic because they do not rely on true random assignment to the experimental or control group. Good examples of quasi-experimental designs in this book include the study on detecting lies in Chapter 5 and the risk-taking study in Chapter 11: they used 'matched' groups who differed on specific variables of interest and made comparisons between them.

This approach enables us to conduct scientific research while still taking account of the realities of organisations and work. However, it does mean that we need to be very careful in interpreting our findings that we have taken good account of the context and any unanticipated external factors that might have caused the change in our dependent variable.

Cross-sectional or longitudinal?

When we conduct research can have implications for the kind of conclusions we can draw as well. Imagine we wanted to know whether employee motivation was related to performance levels. We decide that we will get employees to complete a questionnaire measuring their motivation levels at the same time as we gather information about their performance. The simplest way of doing this is using a cross-sectional design: collecting all the data at a single point in time. If we do this, we can see whether the two variables are related. But we can't tell if one causes the other. Does motivation change performance or does performance change motivation? The only way we can answer that question is by conducting longitudinal research. In this design, we collect our data at several different time points. This enables us to track how levels of motivation and performance change over time as well as using statistical techniques to determine whether one influences the other.

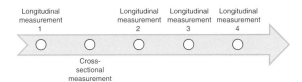

It is probably already obvious to you that longitudinal studies are much stronger designs for answering research questions. The problem is that they are also much more resource-intensive. They require more commitment from both researchers and the organisations and the participants involved in the study, as well as more money and time to conduct properly. There is also the added issue that results are not available immediately, which in a pressured organisational or research environment can mean the value of the study is not recognised. You will find as you read more of the work psychology literature that most of the studies are cross-sectional, simply because fewer resources are required for this design than for longitudinal research. However, when you come across a good longitudinal study it is worth taking careful note of its results, as it can often answer questions that cross-sectional research cannot.

TYPES OF DATA AND ANALYSIS

It is easy to distinguish between quantitative and qualitative data. Quantitative data is anything that can be expressed in numbers while qualitative data uses text or speech, or sometimes even images and more abstract data such as movement or interaction. Both are useful in different ways when we want to find out more about an aspect of work psychology. If, for example, we are interested in finding out how leadership style affects the motivation of the followers, we can use both approaches:

- A quantitative approach could measure leadership style and motivation by asking participants to complete questionnaires where they rate the frequency of certain behaviours or the strength of certain feelings on a scale. We could then compare whether a 'better' leadership rating resulted in higher motivation.
- A qualitative approach could conduct interviews with the leader and the followers and ask them for their own understandings and experiences of leadership styles and motivation. We could then draw out themes from the interviews to make suggestions for how the two concepts are related.

In this section, we will consider the different types of data we can collect for each approach and how we can analyse the data. We will not go into the details of analysis; instead the emphasis is on helping you to understand what different types of data can and can't tell us. For information about the details of how to make particular analyses, refer to the Further Reading section at the end of this chapter.

Quantitative data collection

Questionnaires

A lot of psychological studies use self-report questionnaires to gather data. These questionnaires have the advantage that they are a relatively simple way to collect a range of data on variables of interest to us. Of course, designing a questionnaire is not simply a case of writing a few questions that we think will work: a good questionnaire is both reliable and valid, issues that we explore in detail in Chapter 2.

Despite their widespread use, we do need to bear in mind that self-report measures are not perfect. People responding to questionnaires may try to use them to achieve their own ends rather than simply answering the questions the researcher is hoping to collect data on. For example, if employees are asked to indicate whether they are actively seeking other employment, they may use the question to indicate either commitment to the organisation (saying no even if they are) or dissatisfaction (saying yes even if they are not). In addition, any questionnaire asking us about our internal states or traits relies on us having accurate knowledge of those variables. We can't tell the researcher more than we actually know about ourselves, and self-knowledge varies from person to person.

An alternative approach to self-reports is to use other-reports, where people fill in a questionnaire about someone they know or work with. This was the approach used in the study in Chapter 10 which looked at executive character strengths. Other-reports allow researchers to address questions about how the person comes across to others and how their actions are perceived by people within the organisation, as well as avoiding some self-serving bias. This is not to say that other-reports are free from bias, of course. Anyone completing a questionnaire about their boss is going to be acutely aware of the political ramifications of their ratings and comments, and this could well affect how they respond. Despite this, other-reports provide a valuable addition to our toolkit in exploring work psychology.

Objective measures

You will also notice that in applied psychological studies, including those we have looked at in this book, frequent use is made of 'objective' measures such as company performance, turnover rates or sickness absence. When we are researching well-being, for example, these objective measures can include data about physical health, such as was collected in the study in Chapter 9. This kind of data is particularly helpful in relating latent psychological variables to tangible, real-world outcomes, and is very useful in demonstrating the value of research to people in business.

Observations

We have seen how difficult it is to design a controlled experiment in an applied field such as work psychology, and for many researchers it is more important to observe actual behaviour in a natural setting. This kind of data collection is closer to the reality of working life because researchers can see the behaviour they are interested in right in front of them, rather than asking people to report on their own and others' behaviour and possibly running into problems with memory effects and self-presentation bias. Findings based on this kind of observation are much easier to apply because they are based in the real-life setting we are trying to understand.

A good observational study will still need to be clear about exactly what variables are being measured (observed). For example, if we want to know whether friendliness increases tips for waiting staff, we need to define exactly what we mean by 'friendliness'. This involves breaking down the behaviour we want to observe into smaller, distinct acts that we can count easily. In our example, this could include the number of times the server smiles, how long they engage the restaurant customers in conversation and how often they help customers make decisions by recommending certain food. Adding up the

results would give a 'friendliness score' for each of the staff members, and this could be related to the value of the tips they receive.

The drawbacks of observational studies centre on the fact that we have little or no control over potential confounding variables, and that it can be surprisingly difficult to decide how to measure the behaviour we want to observe.

 Activity Observation

You have been contracted to conduct a research study on a chain of coffee houses. They want to find out whether positive customer service practices are associated with higher sales. You have decided that the best way to address this question is to undertake an observational study.

▸ What observable behaviours do you think would constitute 'positive customer service practices'?
▸ What kind of ethical issues do you think you might need to consider in conducting this study?

Quantitative data analysis

In analysing quantitative data, we are interested in establishing a *difference* or a *relationship*. For example, we might want to know whether there is a difference between the job satisfaction of doctors and nurses, or whether a safety initiative had the desired impact by comparing accident rates before and after training. If we are more interested in evaluating a relationship between two variables, we might want to know whether workers' job satisfaction is related to their accident rates. All the different statistical tests you come across are basically attempting to answer these two questions: *is there a difference?* or *is there a relationship?*

The way we answer these questions is to use statistics. We do not just look at our results and say 'Ah, doctors scored 5.9 out 10 on job satisfaction and nurses scored 6.5, so nurses are more satisfied with their jobs.' Instead, we need to know whether that difference is *significant*; that is, is it likely to be a real finding or merely a chance occurrence? The reason we use statistics so much in social science research is that we are dealing with a very complex world, and sometimes the relationship we are looking for could just happen by chance. For example, it may be that in the particular hospital and on the specific day you carry out your research, doctors are less satisfied than nurses, but at another time or with a different group of participants, this difference would not show up. The significance level tells us whether the difference between the groups (or the relationship between the variables) that we found in our study is larger than we would expect purely as a result of chance.

But what cut-off can we use to say that we have got 'real' findings and not just random fluctuations? In psychology, we typically use p<0.05, which means that the *probability* of this finding being due to chance is *less than five in a hundred* (or 5%). The lower the probability value, the more confident we can be in the findings. If we have a probability value of p<0.01, for example, we can be 99% confident, and with a p<0.001, we can be 99.9% confident in our findings.

A note on samples

There are a couple of important things to bear in mind when considering the sample of participants in a research study: representativeness and size.

If you want to be able to generalise your findings to other situations, you will need to ensure that you have participants who are representative of the wider population. This can be particularly important in work psychology. Many psychological studies are carried out with university students, and then attempts are made to generalise the findings to the working population. But a sample of university students is likely to differ in very important and relevant ways from a sample of employees: they tend to be younger, they are not being paid and they have very little experience of work. In the same way, we should exercise caution in generalising from full- to part-time employees or managerial to non-managerial staff, or even from one organisation to another. The more representative your sample, the more applicable your results are to different situations.

Second, the bigger your sample, the less chance there is that your findings will be swayed by one or two unusual results. This means that you are more likely to be able to identify clear relationships or differences. In statistical terms, larger samples result in more significant findings (lower p values) because there is a lower probability that your findings are due to chance.

In qualitative research, it is simply not possible to collect and analyse data from a large sample. Just think of the time it would take to collect and analyse 100 five-minute questionnaires compared to the time to collect and analyse 100 hour-long interviews. So the priority in qualitative research is to try and build a representative sample by ensuring that we collect data from a range of people who represent different perspectives on or sides of an issue.

For example, if you wanted to explore people's perceptions of strike action, you might choose an interviewee from each of several categories to ensure you get a good understanding of the range of perspectives: those actively involved in a trade union, employees who are not involved in the union, those in management directly involved in negotiations, those in management who are not involved in the dispute, and perhaps even customers or people outside the organisation as well. This brings us on to considering qualitative data in more detail.

Qualitative data collection

Can a number really capture anything important about our minds or behaviour? Many people would say no, and that to really understand psychology at work we need to use detailed, in-depth data that cannot be reduced to a number. Qualitative research focuses on our *socially constructed* reality, meaning that when we are dealing with human psychology 'reality' is not some objective thing out there in the world that we can measure accurately, but is made up of our perceptions and interpretations. For example, it is not so much the fact that someone has lost their job that is important, but how they make sense of that change. Qualitative research takes the individual's point of view seriously (Alvesson and Deetz, 2000) rather than trying to average out responses and find general laws of behaviour that fit everyone.

Qualitative research methods are very diverse, but we will focus here on perhaps the two most widespread methods: interviews and diary studies.

Interviews

You may have experienced an interview for yourself, for example when applying for a job. But if not we have all seen them on TV, whether a political interview or a chat show talk with a celebrity. Interviews are a common means of finding out information, and Burgess (1984, p. 102) described them simply as 'conversations with a purpose'.

Interviews can be more or less structured depending on what the researcher wants to find out:

- A structured interview has a very strict set of questions and prompts that the researcher will work through in a specified order. The advantage of this is that each participant is asked the same questions in the same way and it attempts to reduce some of the inter-individual variation in data collection. However, the downside is that this can feel very stilted to the participant and will mean the researcher does not have the flexibility to explore different areas in more detail.
- An unstructured interview is one where the researcher does not have a schedule of questions and only a general idea of the topic they wish to explore. The conversation is allowed to unfold naturally around the topic. While this can be less formal and intimidating to participants, it does mean that the researcher may miss out important concepts or sub-topics and that interviews with different participants may not cover any similar ground, making analysis more difficult.

- A semi-structured interview attempts to capture the advantages of both the other types of interview. The researcher starts with a clear schedule of possible questions and a suggested order for them, but also makes changes where needed during the course of the interview itself. For example, if the researcher finds that a participant is particularly knowledgeable on a certain topic or has a useful example to illustrate a point, time can be given to explore this rich information, rather than rigidly adhering to a schedule. Overall, similar data can be gathered from each participant but without losing the individuality that makes qualitative data so useful.

Interview questions need to be constructed in a way that will not 'lead' the participants into answering in a way the researcher wants them to, just as good questionnaire items will be as well balanced as possible. To ensure that as much of the interview data is captured as possible, most researchers record their interviews and make notes as well.

Focus groups can be thought of as a group interview, and group size tends to range from six to 12 people, with an average of nine (Millward, 2006). The larger the group, the more difficult it can become for the researcher to facilitate it properly. Besides enabling the researcher to gather information from several people at once, focus groups have the added layer of complexity of group dynamics and social interaction (Millward, 2006). Analysing these elements can help the researcher to understand how concepts and phenomena are constructed by groups.

Diary studies

While interviews are useful for cross-sectional data and can sometimes be used over a period of time to collect longitudinal data, diary studies are more commonly used when we want to find out about a phenomenon over a length of time. They are particularly useful for examining change. In a diary study, participants will be asked to complete a written diary at specific points over a period of time. Just as with interview questions, the questions in the diary study need to be open ended so that participants are free to respond as extensively as they wish.

A more recent approach to diary studies is to use audio diaries. The advantage of an audio diary approach is that it captures the immediacy of people's thoughts and feelings, rather than the more processed results of a written diary (Crozier, forthcoming). In addition, an audio diary study can provide a participant-led approach to data collection, with the participant free to respond naturally to the minimal guidance of the researcher. Equally importantly, because audio responses tend to be easier and quicker to make than written accounts, audio diary studies may

avoid some of the attrition problems that longitudinal studies often run into.

Qualitative data analysis

Qualitative data analysis is about trying to interpret the meaning and symbolism in the data we have collected so that we can better understand the people or situations we are studying. It is not just about taking people's answers to questions at face value, but understanding why they may have given that answer, what other meanings are associated with it, what they may be trying to express and even what they may be trying to hide. Most forms of qualitative analysis focus on identifying *themes* in the data. This is done by going through the data, identifying meaningful chunks and applying a label to them (or *coding*).

Activity Themes

Here is an extract from a three month diary study about authenticity at work. The participants were asked 'What does it mean to "be yourself" at work? Is it just about how you behave or is there more to it?'

> *I believe that being yourself at work is about how you behave, interact with people and present yourself at work (both physically and by communicating). I think how you behave is a big factor, especially in relation to how to approach your role. There appears to be more of a pressure to have a 'professional approach' to your work and job, 'putting in the hours' and striving to maintain standards with a lower workforce, less resources, yet a higher workload. This I think has an adverse impact on how you are at work, and therefore you don't behave like yourself – that's my opinion anyway and the way I feel at the moment in my current employment. In summary I think that the pressure and influences from work determine very much how you behave, which then impacts on whether you act like 'yourself'.*

▸ Go through the extract and identify 'themes'. You can do this by highlighting or circling parts of the text and writing brief keywords or explanations.
▸ Imagine you had ten more extracts in answer to this question. How could you use your initial list of themes for the subsequent analyses?

The involvement of the researcher in both data collection and the analysis processes is one of the aspects of qualitative research that is most controversial. Some argue that the more involved we are in the research, the less objective it may be. However, many qualitative researchers would respond that so-called 'objective' psychological research is simply a myth: we are always involved in our research, and to imagine that we have no effect on the people or situations we are studying is naive.

We have all had experience of the 'observer effect' in our own lives: just think how your own behaviour changes when you know you are on your own and when you feel you are being watched. The observer effect is well known in other branches of science as well: it is simply not possible to observe something without changing it in some way. The instruments a scientist uses to collect the data often change the system being observed, and the more sensitive the system the more we affect it. So we need to consider the observer as *part* of the system. Qualitative research recognises this, and has a strong tradition of including observer reflections as part of the analysis rather than claiming that the researcher is an outside observer reporting objectively on what has happened. As Cassell and Symon (2011, p. 647) put it when summarising their study of work psychologists' understandings of qualitative research, 'it is important that we draw attention to our own interests and practices as part of a reflexive process'.

Given that qualitative research comes from such a different place to quantitative research, how can we assess its quality? A recent interview study with work psychologists concluded that they were generally sceptical of the value of qualitative research for three reasons (Cassell and Symon, 2011):

1 Qualitative research cannot meet the criteria of quantitative research so is seen as 'second best' or only of use for exploratory work
2 Many psychologists don't know how to evaluate qualitative research or see it as having less rigorous quality criteria
3 There is not much good qualitative research being done and its worth is not being demonstrated well enough.

While quantitative research focuses on reliability, validity and generalisability as key criteria for assessing the quality of the work, there is much more debate about how to evaluate qualitative research. Part of this debate lies in the fact that qualitative methods and analyses are so diverse that it is difficult to come up with a definitive list of criteria that every study could be evaluated against (Symon and Cassell, 2012). However, from a practical point of view and especially when we are learning about research, it is very helpful to have a recommended list of important qualities of 'good' qualitative research.

Sarah Tracy (2010) provides just such a list of key markers of quality, ranging from the choice of topic to how a researcher approaches the analysis. As a first step, she suggests that the topic of the research should be relevant and timely, something that will be of use to both theorists and practitioners. In this choice of topic, there are two other important markers of quality: resonance (the research should have some impact on the audience) and significant contribution (the research extends our knowledge base). In terms of data and concepts, it is important that the research does not oversimplify. Here, the researcher has to strike a balance between using rich enough data to represent the real complexities of the issue and ensuring that the study is methodologically rigorous. The study itself should be conducted ethically, but the researcher should also give consideration to ethicality in how the findings will be applied.

Another important issue that is highlighted in qualitative research is self-reflexivity – the researcher should be able to explain how he or she has approached the topic and how this may have influenced the findings. This is in contrast to the 'objective' approach valued by many quantitative researchers, where the researcher aims to be completely separate from the research. Credibility is another key marker or quality research: the research should be explained in such a way that readers can understand it and come to their own conclusions. Finally, the research should be coherent, integrating its own findings with the literature and using appropriate methods to address its goals.

Interestingly, these key criteria could just as well be applied to quantitative research and would give a much more detailed understanding of its real quality than the narrow focus on methods that is common in that arena. Perhaps the most useful thing to come out of this debate is an awareness of what determines the quality of psychology research in general. Many people believe that the best research uses a combination of qualitative and quantitative methods, enabling us to develop theory from the rich, lived experiences of people as well as testing hypotheses in a rigorous manner.

SUMMARY

We have referred to a lot of research in this book, both quantitative and qualitative, and as you read more you will discover a wide range of different approaches and methods in work psychology research. In this chapter, the aim has been to help build your understanding of how and why research in work psychology is done so that you can refine your ability to tell good from bad research, or helpful from not-so-helpful. This is perhaps the most important skill you can develop at university, because it will mean you will never be left behind and can always keep up to date with the latest developments in your chosen field.

TEST YOURSELF

Brief Review Questions

1 Briefly outline the five steps in the research process.
2 What is a systematic review and why can it be helpful to practitioners?
3 Define an experimental study.
4 What is the Hawthorne effect?
5 Why is sample size important in research?

Discussion or Essay Questions

1 We would expect doctors to be using the most up-to-date research in making medical decisions, yet we do not seem to have the same expectations of managers or consultants. Why is this? Does it need to change?
2 How can we identify a good theory in psychology?
3 Critically compare and contrast the contributions that quantitative and qualitative research can make to our understanding of work psychology.
4 How can we evaluate the quality of psychological research?

FURTHER READING

* The Social Science Research Methods Knowledge Base (http://www.socialresearchmethods.net/kb/index. php) is an online textbook that gives lots of detail about research methods relevant to work psychology (and social sciences in general).
* For detail and further reading on several different psychological effects on scientific research, including the Hawthorne effect and placebo effect, see http://www. psy.gla.ac.uk/~steve/hawth.html.
* For detailed help on statistics, try Julie Pallant's book, *The SPSS Survival Manual* 4th edn. McGraw-Hill Education, Maidenhead, 2010.
* *Online Qualitative Data Analysis* is a website with learning materials to help you understand and use different qualitative techniques: http://onlineqda.hud.ac.uk/ index.php.

References

ALVESSON, M. & DEETZ, S. 2000. *Doing Critical Management Research*. London, Sage.

BARRICK, M. R. & MOUNT, M. K. 1991. The big five personality dimensions and job performance: a meta-analysis. *Personnel Psychology*, 44, 1–26.

BEDEIAN, A. G., TAYLOR, S. G. & MILLER, A. N. 2010. Management science on the credibility bubble: cardinal sins and various misdemeanors. *Academy of Management Learning & Education*, 9, 715–25.

BRINER, R. B. 2013. Unreliable evidence? Understanding and working with the limitations of the academic literature. *OP Matters*, 19, 11–15.

BRINER, R. B., DENYER, D. & ROUSSEAU, D. M. 2009. Evidence-based management: concept cleanup time? *The Academy of Management Perspectives*, 23, 19–32.

BRINER, R. B. & ROUSSEAU, D. M. 2011. Evidence-based I–O psychology: not there yet. *Industrial and Organizational Psychology*, 4, 3–22.

BURGESS, R. G. 1984. *In the Field: An Introduction to Field Research*. London, Allen & Unwin.

CASSELL, C. 2011. Evidence-based I–O psychology: what do we lose on the way? *Industrial and Organizational Psychology*, 4, 23–6.

CASSELL, C. & SYMON, G. 2011. Assessing 'good' qualitative research in the work psychology field: a narrative analysis. *Journal of Occupational and Organizational Psychology*, 84, 633–50.

CROZIER, S. FORTHCOMING. *Methodological Considerations for the Use of Longitudinal Audio Diaries in Work Psychology: Adding to the Qualitative Toolkit.*

JUDGE, T. A. & BONO, J. E. 2001. Relationship of core self-evaluations traits – self-esteem, generalized self-efficacy, locus of control, and emotional stability – with job satisfaction and job performance: a meta-analysis. *Journal of Applied Psychology*, 86, 80.

KAGAN, J. 1998. *Three Seductive Ideas*. London, Harvard University Press.

KELLY, G. A. 1955. *The Psychology of Personal Constructs*. New York, W. W. Norton.

THE LEVELT NOORT AND DRENTH COMMITTEES. 2012. *Flawed Science: The Fraudulent Research Practices of Social Psychologist Diederik Stapel*. Netherlands, Commissie Levelt.

LEWIN, K. (ED.) 1951. *Field Theory in Social Science: Selected Theoretical Papers*. New York, Harper & Row.

MCCLELLAND, D. C. 1996. Does the field of personality have a future? *Journal of Research in Personality*, 30, 429–34.

MAYO, E. 1933. The Hawthorne Experiment: Western Electrical Company. In *The Human Problems of an Industrial Civilization*. New York, Macmillan.

MILLWARD, L. J. 2006. Focus Groups. In Breakwell, G. M., Hammond, S., Fife-Schaw, C. & Smith, J. A. (eds.) *Research Methods in Psychology*. London, Sage.

PALLANT, J. 2010. *SPSS Survival Manual: A Step by Step Guide to Data Analysis Using SPSS*. Maidenhead, Open University Press.

PETTICREW, M. & ROBERTS, H. 2006. *Systematic Reviews in the Social Sciences: A Practical Guide*. Oxford, Blackwell.

PRINGLE, J. 2004. *Access to the Literature: The Debate Continues*. Nature Publishing Group. http://www.nature.com/nature/focus/accessdebate/19.html (accessed 20 October 2013).

SAUNDERS, M., LEWIS, P. & THORNHILL, A. 2009. *Research Methods for Business Students*. Harlow, Financial Times/Prentice Hall.

SILZER, R., COBER, R., ERICKSON, A. & ROBINSON, G. 2008. *Practitioner Needs Survey: Final Survey Report*. Bowling Green, OH, Society for Industrial–Organizational Psychology.

SUTTON, A. 2007. Implicit and Explicit Personality in Work Settings: An Application of Enneagram Theory. PhD, University of Leeds.

SWAN, A. 2012. *Policy Guidelines for the Development and Promotion of Open Access*. Paris, UNESCO.

SYMON, G. & CASSELL, C. 2012. Assessing Qualitative Research. In Symon, G. & Cassell, C. (eds.) *Qualitative Organizational Research: Core Methods and Current Challenges*. London, Sage.

TRACY, S. J. 2010. Qualitative quality: eight 'big-tent' criteria for excellent qualitative research. *Qualitative Inquiry*, 16, 837–51.

VERFAELLIE, M. & MCGWIN, J. 2011. *The Case of Diederik Stapel*. Psychological Science Agenda. https://www.apa.org/science/about/psa/2011/12/diederik-stapel.aspx (accessed 20 October 2013).

© Aldo Murillo/istockphoto

Part 3 Case Study **Research in practice: the challenges of psychology consultancy**

Gateway is a small organisation development consultancy specialising in the areas of employee engagement and culture change. It directly employs about four or five chartered psychologists and several research assistants, as well as having several freelance consultants who are brought in for specific projects. Jessica is one of them, an Occupational Psychologist who has worked with Gateway on a number of previous projects, providing psychological and statistical expertise in support of their work.

Most recently, Gateway won a competitive bidding process for an employee engagement survey at AllStar. Over the years, Gateway has developed a good relationship with AllStar, providing expertise in research and development projects, and delivering practical results and clear recommendations that the organisation can use to improve its business.

AllStar has been conducting employee engagement surveys on the core staff for a number of years because it recognises that engagement provides many benefits to the organisation, including voluntary effort, higher performance and commitment and lower staff turnover. But AllStar is a large organisation and is heavily reliant on its associate, or non-core, staff. Associates at AllStar have a major role in supporting the ongoing efforts of the organisation. They tend to have a long-standing relationship with AllStar and contribute at a high level, developing products and providing strategic influence, and are important ambassadors for the AllStar brand. Because of the critical role that these associates play, AllStar decided to expand the employee engagement survey to these roles.

This extension of the survey was not a straightforward issue, however. Recent changes at AllStar have meant that the company has had to refocus on its commercial viability: there have been significant reductions in budgets, changes to working patterns and significantly, a reduction in face-to-face meetings with many of the associate staff. With rumours abounding that the associates feel an increasing distance from the company, AllStar is concerned about the impact these changes might have on engagement levels. The head of the HR department wants to conduct a benchmarking study with the aim of identifying the drivers of engagement for senior associates. Associate staff tend to have a different experience of working for the organisation and it is important to capture this experience in order to understand how engagement can be improved.

This was the context in which Gateway won the bid to provide research expertise in designing the survey, analysing the findings and presenting recommendations to the board. The study took place over four months and used a mixed methodology of a questionnaire survey and telephone interviews. The objectives of the study were as follows:

1 To design a survey that can be used in subsequent years to provide the basis for continual improvement.
2 To establish the links between specific drivers of engagement and their outputs, so that resources can be targeted appropriately.

As a first step, Jessica conducted a review of the employee engagement literature. She used a simple model of engagement that linked important drivers, such as communication and trust, with organisationally relevant outputs, such as dedication, effort and advocacy. The review also took account of demographic factors that could influence engagement, such as age and length of service.

Once she had an outline model, Jessica then met with AllStar's steering group to discuss the elements they wanted to include in the survey. One of the challenges Jessica often faces in her consultancy work is balancing the findings from her research with the wishes and aims of the clients. In this case, there were some things that Jessica knew from her literature review were important to engagement, such as the employee's induction experience, but AllStar was reluctant to include in the survey. The reason was that the steering group knew there was nothing they could do at that stage to change this and so did not want to give the survey respondents the feeling that they could influence it by responding in certain ways. In other cases, the content of the survey questions was acceptable but the steering group wanted to use wording that Jessica felt would bias or guide responses in a certain direction. Deciding on the final content of the survey took a lot of negotiation and compromise, with Jessica working to create a survey that would ultimately be rigorous and reliable enough to provide solid results but also something that AllStar would be willing to send out to its employees.

Once the survey was finalised, a large sample of associates responded to it. Jessica, and the Gateway consultancy, were careful to assure the respondents of the anonymity and confidentiality of the results. For this, they kept to market research principles of anonymity: at the start of the survey they explained that they would not report findings from any group with fewer than ten respondents unless each person in that group gave their express permission.

The survey was followed up with some telephone interviews which explored themes around engagement, identifying particular issues or challenges as well as examples of best practice. A further ethical issue arose here as Jessica occasionally had to deal with employees who were experiencing psychological distress. In these cases, she needed to deal sensitively with the issue and be able to recommend further sources of support to the employee. She also had to find a way, when reporting on the results, to pass on the individual's views without compromising their anonymity in any way.

Overall, the survey and the interviews found that engagement levels in the associate employees, although still positive, were worryingly low. Gateway identified that while engagement had traditionally been strong for these employees, the recent organisational changes threatened to destabilise or erode it and that action needed to be taken to ensure that the risk to the business was minimised. This was a difficult and challenging set of findings to feed back to AllStar, but Gateway focused on using the results to identify specific, practical actions that the steering group could take to address the engagement issue, such as improving communication and increasing involvement in decisions.

In analysing and presenting the findings of the survey, Jessica faced another challenge. She knew how important it was, when interpreting any statistical test, to be aware of the limitations and to have a good understanding of what the test could actually say. But her contact at Gateway emphasised to her that the client would not be interested in the details of the statistics and even told her to take all reference to the details of the tests out of her report. This meant that any findings would not be provided with the requisite information about significance levels and Jessica had to be very careful about how she worded everything to ensure that the readers of the report would be aware of the extent to which the findings could be used as a basis for action. This was a particularly tricky challenge to deal with, and Jessica eventually decided on an approach which provided the steering group with the headline findings and made practical, prioritised recommendations that were based on her detailed statistical analyses.

Jessica was aware that, as a chartered psychologist, she had an ethical responsibility to ensure that her work did not harm others. The way she kept to this ethical principle was by presenting the results in their entirety (i.e. not picking and choosing the 'best' or 'most palatable' results to present) and providing the findings in a balanced way to the client. In her presentations to the steering group and later the board of AllStar, Jessica focused on explaining clearly both what had been found *and* the limitations of the study.

Another issue that Jessica and the other consultants at Gateway faced in feeding back the results of the study to AllStar were that psychological terminology was seen as too challenging and off-putting for the senior board members, even if the consultants were there in person to explain it. The terminology had to be changed to be more operationally focused. Jessica is aware that this ability to 'translate' psychological knowledge into business-oriented language is one of the key skills that psychology consultants need. Without it, psychologists can be dismissed as 'irrelevant' or 'too academic' and the real insights they can offer are simply not understood.

Adapting the findings to different audiences was a further challenge. Jessica identified three distinct audiences for the study results: the respondents themselves, the steering group at AllStar, and the AllStar executive board. Each of these groups had different interests in the results and wanted different things out of it. Part of Jessica's job here was to identify what those groups wanted and to provide it in a way that stayed true to the actual findings of the study.

▶ For the respondents, she focused on demonstrating that their views had been captured accurately, providing plenty of detail and exhibiting empathy in how she reported back. She knew they would be less interested in the business case and more interested in ensuring that their views were being accurately represented.

▸ In presenting to the steering group, Jessica went through an iterative process, ensuring that the wording she was using in presenting the results was acceptable to them. Although she had some challenging findings to report, she needed to find a way to express them that the steering group would accept and be able to act on.

▸ And finally, in her presentation to the board, Jessica focused on the strategic issues and the practical recommendations for improvements. She was also careful to point out examples of best practice within the organisation as well, providing a balance of achievements and challenges for the board to reflect and act on.

Overall, Gateway, with Jessica's help, was able to deliver on their project. They identified areas of good practice within the organisation and also areas where improvements could be made. They set up a survey that AllStar can continue to use in future years to measure employee engagement and to evaluate the impact of any interventions. What happens next is up to AllStar. As Jessica says, 'Once you've completed the project, you hand over control to the client.'

Note: all names and organisational details have been changed to protect anonymity.

QUESTIONS FOR DISCUSSION

1   Jessica's literature review identified areas that were important to engagement but that the client organisation did not want to include. This balancing of the client's desires and a robust theoretical model is difficult. How would you approach it? What would be the implications of your approach for future work with the client?

2   Consultancies are often contracted for only a small part of an implementation process – for example, only the initial research study, as in this case. How can they maintain their ethical standards when they know the findings of their research will soon pass out of their control?

3   Adapting the findings of a research project to different audiences is an important skill for researchers and consultants. What important issues do they need to be aware of when doing this?

4   What tensions can you identify in the case study between the 'ideal' of research and the 'reality' of practice? How did Jessica resolve them? What would you do?

5   One of the important skills in consultancy is relationship management. What relationships did Jessica have to manage in this case study? What are the implications of how she did this for her future employment prospects with both Gateway and AllStar? To what extent did this case follow the general consultancy model outlined in Chapter 12?

GLOSSARY

Term	Definition
360° appraisal	A way of measuring an employee's performance which draws on the evaluations of superiors, peers, subordinates and sometimes even customers or clients (also known as multisource appraisal).
Abnormal psychology	The study of deviations from the 'norm' of human psychology. (Note that there is debate over what constitutes normal psychology.)
Action research	Research based on a thorough analysis and understanding of the situation ('research') and which takes action to achieve the desired change.
Adverse impact	Sometimes, groups of people score differently on a selection measure. If this difference means that one group is less successful in gaining the job, then the measure has an *adverse impact* on that group.
Affect	A general term for our emotional responses.
Applied psychology	Takes the theories and models from theoretical psychology and applies them to understanding and solving real-life problems.
Assessment centre	A combination of several selection methods to distinguish between job candidates, usually based on a competency framework.
Assumptive world	Our set of assumptions about the world and our place in it. This can be challenged when we experience change.
Attitude	An evaluative judgement of an object.
Attributions	The processes we use to make sense of other people's behaviour, the reason we think they did something.
Authentic leadership	Leadership that is based in the leader's personal values and involves a high degree of self-awareness. Authentic leaders are set apart from other leaders by their high moral character.
Autotelic personality	People with an autotelic personality engage in activities because they find them inherently rewarding rather than to achieve some external reward.
Behaviour modelling training (BMT)	A type of training based on social learning theory that defines the behaviours to be learnt, provides clear models of those behaviours and gives feedback as people practise them.
Behaviour Observation Scale (BOS)	A performance-rating scale that is used to measure how frequently an employee engages in specific job-related behaviours.
Behavioural theory of leadership	Attempts to identify the behaviours that leaders exhibit rather than their personal traits. These behaviours are often categorised as people-focused or task-focused.
Behaviourally Anchored Rating Scales (BARS)	Used to measure employee performance, these are numerical scales that are 'anchored' by specific behaviours. Less effective behaviours are given a low score while more effective behaviours are given a higher score.
Bias	In selection procedures, bias occurs when a measure systematically over- or under-estimates the performance of people from different groups.
Big Five	A comprehensive, universal model of personality that recognises five broad traits: Extraversion – outgoing and confident vs reserved and quiet Agreeableness – friendly and considerate vs forthright and argumentative Emotional stability – calm and unemotional vs sensitive and easily upset Conscientiousness – organised and dependable vs flexible and disorganised Openness to experience – creative and imaginative vs down-to-earth and conventional

Term	Definition
Biodata	A collection of information about a person's life and work experience, such as qualifications or job history.
Biological determinism	The belief that our behaviour is primarily determined biological factors such as genes and brain structures.
Biological psychology	The study of how our physical makeup explains or affects our minds.
Broaden and build theory of positive emotions (Frederickson)	A model of the evolutionary value of positive emotions which postulates that when we experience positive emotions such as love, joy or pride, our thought-action repertoires *broaden* and we *build* our personal resources. These personal resources include resiliency, social relationships, new ideas and so on.
Burnout	The end result of prolonged stress at work: emotional exhaustion, cynical attitude towards clients, and dissatisfaction with oneself and one's work efforts.
Character Strengths and Values (CSV)	An attempt to provide a universal model of human strengths and values, developed as an attempt to summarise what can go well in human psychology.
Classical conditioning	Simple associative learning: we learn to associate a new stimulus with a certain response.
Coaching psychology	Psychological approaches and models which are used to enhance a client's well-being and performance at work and home.
Cognitive appraisal	Cognitive appraisal is the process by which we determine whether a particular encounter or experience is relevant to our well-being.
Cognitive bias	Shortcuts that our minds make to try to save us time when dealing with a complex world can become the source of biases in decision-making, for example when making decisions in interviewing (see Chapter 2 for details of these biases).
Cognitive dissonance theory (Festinger and Carlsmith)	This theory posits a mismatch between our privately held attitudes and publicly displayed behaviour (or between two different attitudes); it suggest this is uncomfortable and that we will want to change either the attitude or the behaviour to match.
Cognitive evaluation theory (Deci and Ryan)	The suggestion that it is not a particular reward itself that affects our motivation but our interpretation of that reward as either an indication of our competence or a sign of control over our behaviour.
Cognitive load	The demands which a task places on the mental resources we have available (such as memory).
Cognitive psychology	The study of our mental processes, such as perception, memory, attention and thinking.
Cohesion	The strength of the interpersonal bond between group members.
Collaboration technologies	Programmes or features that support group work, including email, instant messaging, shared calendars and document markup.
Competency	Meaningful workplace behaviours or outcomes that are associated with effective performance in a job. Often used as the basis for selection decisions.
Competency framework	A detailed description of all of the competencies required for a particular job, which can be used as a basis for selection, development and performance appraisal. An organisation-wide competency framework outlines the competencies required by workers across the whole organisation.
Construct validity	The extent to which a test accurately measures the construct that it claims to.
Consumer psychology	The study of our thoughts, feelings and behaviours in relation to products or services that we buy.
Content validity	The extent to which a measure is representative of the *whole* of the ability or attribute that it claims to measure
Contingency theory	Recognises there is no 'one best way' but that the best course of action is dependent (contingent) on the situation. Contingency theories attempt to define the characteristics of a situation that determine which approach will work best.
Contingency theory of leadership (Fiedler)	Defines aspects of the situation that interact with leader styles to determine effectiveness.
Corporate social responsibility (CSR)	A strategic approach to setting out the ethical principles which guide the organisation's actions, including taking responsibility for the effect of those actions on all potential stakeholders.

Term	Definition
Criterion validity	How well a measure predicts something important in the real world of work. This link can be established *concurrently* or *predictively*: Concurrent criterion validity is where the test and criterion measure are taken at the same time – indicating whether the test predicts current employees' performance. Predictive criterion validity is where there is a time gap between the two – indicating whether the test predicts future performance.
Declarative knowledge	Knowledge that you can express, for example in a written test.
Demand-Control-Support model of stress	A model which explains how the mental strain we experience is the result of the balance between the demands of our job, the control we have over the job and the social support we can access.
Demands-Resources model of stress	A model which captures both the positive and negative aspects of stress and shows how they are related to job demands (such as workload and pressure) and job resources (such as feedback and participation).
Developmental psychology	The study of the human lifespan, looking at how we change and develop from birth to old age.
Economic psychology	The study of the causes and consequences of economic behaviour.
Emergent change	Change which is made up of ongoing adaptations and alterations that ultimately produce fundamental changes that were not planned for or perhaps even expected.
Employee assistance programme (EAP)	Umbrella term for a collection of assistance programmes and well-being initiatives that an organisation can introduce to help employees deal with potential stressors.
Employer branding	The idea that an organisation can build up a brand (or reputation) for itself as an employer: a good employer brand can help the organisation to attract and retain the best calibre and best suited employees.
Engagement	Feeling positive towards work and being actively involved in it.
Equity theory	Suggests that we want fairness and are motivated by how equitable we think our efforts and rewards are in comparison with other people's.
ERG theory (Alderfer)	A theory that suggests we are motivated by the needs for existence, relatedness and growth.
Eudaimonia	In positive psychology, this term is used to indicate happiness from seeking to use and develop the best in ourselves.
Expectancy theory (Vroom)	This theory states that our level of motivation for a particular action is based on our expectations about the outcome or end result of our efforts. The more likely we feel it is that our efforts will result in a desirable outcome, the more motivated we will be.
Experiment	A research design characterised by clearly defined, measurable variables and strict control over the experimental conditions.
Face validity	A measure with face validity appears to the observer to assess what it claims to.
Flow experience	A state of complete absorption in what we are doing so that we lose awareness of other things.
Functional magnetic resonance imagery (fMRI)	A method of imaging the brain to see what parts are activated in response to different stimuli.
Fundamental attribution error	A cognitive error that commonly occurs when we are attempting to explain people's behaviour: we tend to overestimate the effect of personality or internal qualities and underestimate the effect of the situation.
General Adaptation Syndrome (GAS)	A model of our reactions to continuous or chronic stress. The GAS has three stages: alarm, resistance and exhaustion, which we go through in an attempt to protect ourselves from harm.
General mental ability (GMA)	The psychometric term for intelligence, a measure of how accurately and quickly you can process complex information.
Goal attainment scaling (GAS)	A way of measuring progress towards goals which involves a coach and a client jointly identifying goals and developing a scale to measure progress towards them.
Goal-setting theory (Locke and Latham)	A theory of motivation and performance that emphasises how conscious goals can affect performance.
Groupthink (Janis)	The tendency some groups have towards seeking agreement, to the exclusion of a realistic appraisal of the situation or consideration of alternative courses of action.

Term	Definition
Habituation	A simple kind of learning where we become accustomed to a stimulus and begin to ignore it.
HARKing	Hypothesising After Results are Known – a widespread but very poor research practice. Instead of developing hypotheses and then testing them, this practice involves conducting the analysis and then developing hypotheses that fit in with any statistically significant findings.
Hedonia	In positive psychology, this term is used to indicate happiness from seeking pleasure.
Hubris syndrome	A personality disorder defined by a narcissistic attitude and excessive self-belief.
Implicit leadership theory	Suggests that a leader's effectiveness is to a large part determined by the followers' perceptions, and that the followers have an unconscious set of expectations about what a leader will be like. Those leaders who conform better to the expectations are seen as more effective.
Implicit needs (McClelland)	This theory holds that motivation is based on our individual levels of three main (unconscious) needs: Affiliation – desire to build friendly, cooperative relationships Achievement – drive to do well, to succeed Power – desire to have influence over others.
Individual differences	The study of how and why we differ from each other, particularly in terms of personality and intelligence.
Input-mediator-output model of teams	A model for understanding the complex interactions of different variables on the teamwork process which identifies the inputs to the teamwork and the variables that mediate those inputs into relevant outputs.
Instrumental risk-taking	Taking risks in order to achieve a particular outcome.
Inter rater reliability	A measure of how well two or more different raters (e.g. interviewers) agree in the ratings they give to an individual.
Internal consistency (internal reliability)	This is used to check that different parts of the test are measuring the same thing. For example, if we have a questionnaire that measures cognitive ability, are a person's scores on one half of the questionnaire similar to their scores on the other?
Intrinsic rewards	The inherent rewards (for example, a feeling of enjoyment) we experience simply from undertaking an activity.
Jargon	Vocabulary or terminology used in a particular organisation or group that is unfamiliar to people outside that group.
Job analysis	A process of identifying the knowledge, skills and behaviours associated with job performance.
Job characteristics model (Hackman and Oldham)	A theory that emphasises how particular job characteristics (such as skill or task variety) influence our internal motivation.
Job satisfaction	A job attitude which is an evaluation of how happy or content we are with our jobs.
Karojisatsu	Japanese term for work-related suicide.
Karoshi	Japanese term for death from overwork.
Kinesics	The movements we make when we communicate, such as gesturing with our hands, nodding our heads or making eye contact.
KSAs	Knowledge, skills and abilities required to perform effectively in a particular job.
Leader	Someone who is able to influence others to work towards a goal.
Leader–member exchange theory (LMX)	Recognises that leaders have different relationships with different followers: high quality of exchange with an 'in-group' and low quality of exchange with an 'out-group'.
Learning organisation	An organisation that is proactive in its approach to change, encouraging and facilitating learning by all of its members and engaging in continual transformation and development.
Learning style	The suggestion that different people learn things in different ways, that each of us has a 'style' that suits us best and we should try to find learning opportunities that match our style. Evidence indicates this is not the case.
Linguistic communication channel	Written or spoken language, including intonation, rhythm and paralanguage.
Management by objectives	A form of performance management where goals are agreed between the employee and the manager and later performance appraisals are based on the extent to which these goals are achieved.

Term	Definition
Mobile robotic telepresence or mobile remote presence systems (MRPs)	A system which combines videoconferencing with mobile robots which can move around in and interact with the environment.
Motivating potential score	A way of scoring different jobs for how potentially motivating they are, based on an evaluation of their job characteristics.
Motivation theory	An explanation of the intensity, direction and persistence of the effort we put into work.
Multitasking	The common term for the perceived ability to do more than one thing at a time. Multitasking is only possible for activities which require no conscious processing. In reality, when we think we are multitasking we are actually switching our attention from one task to another repeatedly.
Non-linguistic communication channels	Non-verbal communication, including body movements, the intonations or emphasis we give to words, facial expressions, and physical distance.
Open access	Journal articles that are freely available to read on the internet.
Operant conditioning	Explanation of how the *consequences* of a response or action influence our learning.
Organisation development (OD)	An approach to organisational change that emphasises organisation-wide interventions to ensure continual organisational survival.
Organisational commitment	A person's psychological bond to an organisation: how attached they feel and how much effort they will put into supporting it.
Paralanguage	Any noises we make that are not speech itself but still serve to communicate a message.
Parallel forms reliability	If we have more than one version of a test, a person's scores must be similar on both versions in order to be reliable.
Path–goal theory of leadership (House)	This theory states that leadership is essentially *motivational*: that is, an effective leader motivates followers by clarifying the path they need to take in order to achieve goal.
Personal transitions	The psychological processes we go through when dealing with change.
Procedural knowledge	Knowledge of how to do things, also known as skills.
Projective test	A measure of aspects of the unconscious mind. The idea behind these tests is that when there ambiguities in how something can be perceived, we *project* our own internal thoughts and feelings onto the picture. The psychologist can then interpret these projections as indications of our unconscious mind.
Proxemics	The study of the role of interpersonal space and touch in communication.
Psychometrics	Literally a 'measure of the mind', these are systematic ways of trying to measure psychological phenomena, such as intelligence or personality traits.
Psychopathology	*See* abnormal psychology.
Punctuated equilibrium model of change	This model proposes that sudden large changes are interspersed with longer periods of relative stability.
Reference	Information given by a previous employer about a job candidate's performance, commonly used as part of the selection process.
Reliability	A measure of the extent to which a psychometric test gives consistent results.
Risk perception	Our perception of the risks associated with particular actions, including an assessment of the uncertainty involved and how much we believe we can control it, as well as how serious we believe the consequences might be.
Risk propensity	Our tendency to take or avoid risk, closely related to our attitude towards risk.
Scientific management	An attempt to use the scientific method to study management techniques; it aims to find the most efficient ways of doing a job in order to improve productivity.
Scientific method	Five-stage process for explaining why things are the way they are: Observe patterns or regularities in the world Develop a possible explanation (theory) From that explanation, develop a specific prediction Test the prediction Evaluate the explanation and refine it if necessary.
Self-actualisation	Striving towards fulfilling our full potential. A centrally important theme in humanistic psychology.

Term	Definition
Social learning theory	Suggests we learn complex behaviours by copying other people.
Social psychology	The study of how we interact with other people and behave in groups.
Statistical significance	A measure of how likely our research findings are to have occurred by chance. The commonly used cut-off point is $p < 0.05$.
Stimulating risk-taking	Taking risks because it makes us feel excited.
Strengths-based development	An approach to personal and professional development which builds on our strengths and finds new ways of applying them, rather than focusing on weaknesses.
Stress	A general term for the sense that we are under pressure, usually used to mean negative pressure or levels that we can not comfortably cope with. Eustress – positive stress Distress – negative stress
Systematic review	A type of research study which systematically draws together and evaluates a wide range of evidence to address a practice-based question.
Talent management	Attracting, developing and retaining the people the business needs to meet its current and future goals.
Test–retest reliability	A measure of the consistency of a test when given to the same people on different occasions.
Thematic Apperception Test (TAT)	A type of projective test used to measure a person's implicit needs: the person is shown an ambiguous picture and writes a brief story in response to it. The psychologist then analyses the story to identify the unconscious needs or motives that it demonstrates.
Trait theory of leadership	Centres around identifying the personality traits associated with leadership.
Transactional leadership	Leadership based on a transaction between the leader and the follower in which good performance is rewarded and poor performance is punished.
Transfer of learning	An area of study which tries to determine how best to help people transfer or apply their learning from one context to another, because the content of what we learn is often reliant on the context in which we learn it.
Transformational leadership	Leadership based on engaging followers' emotions and inspiring them to achieve certain goals.
Two factor theory (Herzberg)	A motivation theory which suggests that hygiene factors (such as a good working environment) are important for removing worker dissatisfaction but that only motivational factors (such as recognition or responsibility) can bring about satisfaction.
Validity	The extent to which a psychometric test is actually measuring what it claims to.
Well-being	General term for psychological, social and physical health and contentment.
Work sample	An exercise that is designed to be as close as possible to the work done in a particular job. A work sample provides evidence of how a job applicant performs in a realistic job situation.
Work–life balance	A balance between the time and resources we invest in work and home or leisure activities. Sometimes also referred to as work-non-work balance to emphasise that work is a part of our lives.

INDEX